T0314098

TRADE IN THE ANCIENT
MEDITERRANEAN

THE PRINCETON ECONOMIC HISTORY
OF THE WESTERN WORLD

Joel Mokyr, Series Editor

A list of titles in this series appears at the back of the book.

Trade in the Ancient Mediterranean

PRIVATE ORDER AND PUBLIC INSTITUTIONS

TACO TERPSTRA

PRINCETON UNIVERSITY PRESS

PRINCETON & OXFORD

Published by Princeton University Press
41 William Street, Princeton, New Jersey 08540
6 Oxford Street, Woodstock, Oxfordshire OX20 1TR

press.princeton.edu

LCCN 2018957367
ISBN 9780691172088

British Library Cataloging-in-Publication Data is available

Editorial: Rob Tempio and Matt Rohal
Production Editorial: Natalie Baan
Jacket Design: Carmina Alvarez
Production: Jacquie Poirier
Publicity: Julia Hall, Jodi Price, and Alyssa Sanford

Jacket image courtesy of Shutterstock

This book has been composed in Arno Pro

Printed on acid-free paper. ∞

Printed in the United States of America

10 9 8 7 6 5 4 3 2 1

CONTENTS

ACKNOWLEDGMENTS

SEVERAL ORGANIZATIONS HAVE PROVIDED me with financial support, allowing me time away from teaching to dedicate myself entirely to research and writing. I extend my sincerest gratitude to the Loeb Classical Library Foundation at Harvard University, the Alice Kaplan Institute for the Humanities at Northwestern University and the Balzan Foundation. Without their generous support, it would have taken me many years longer to finish this book. I further thank Northwestern's Center for Economic History for the funds to draw the maps and acquire reproduction rights for the images displayed herein.

I also express my gratitude to the University of Ghent for inviting me as a visiting fellow for the spring term of 2016. The beautiful scenery of a medieval "producer city," the excellent research facilities and, most of all, the intellectual environment of the History Department have been greatly stimulating to my work. In particular Wim Broekaert, Koen Verboven and Arjan Zuiderhoek have been wonderful colleagues and willing sounding boards. I greatly enjoyed our conversations over Trappist beer and frites about Roman economic history, medieval economic history, Belgian politics and much else besides. I am also grateful for the feedback I received from the participants of the "Sinews of Empire" conference at the Norwegian Institute at Athens in December 2015, and thank the organizer, Eivind Seland, for inviting me.

A special word of appreciation should go to Alain Bresson and Dennis Kehoe for discussing the manuscript with me in May 2017. Our day-long conversation has greatly helped me in improving the book, and the end result is much the better for it. I am also profoundly grateful to Arjan Zuiderhoek for his willingness to read a large part of the manuscript and give me extensive feedback. I owe a similar debt of gratitude to Roger Bagnall, Tim Earle and Vincent Gabrielsen, all of whom have read and commented on individual chapters. A word of thanks should also go to Alain Bresson, Christelle Fischer-Bovet, Hannah Friedman, Joe Manning and Andrew Wilson for allowing me access to some of their (at the time still) unpublished work.

My Northwestern Classics Department colleagues have been a constant source of support and encouragement. I am grateful to them all for offering me their thoughts, and thank in particular Bob Wallace and John Wynne. Mira Balberg deserves a mention for discussing late-antique religion with me, giving me advice on Biblical texts and providing me with useful reading suggestions. Further, I most warmly thank Joel Mokyr in the Economics Department for having been an effective and motivating editor. I also thank him for having put me in touch with Rob Tempio at Princeton University Press. It has been a pleasure working with Rob throughout the production process of this book. I also wish to express my gratitude to the three anonymous Princeton UP readers, whose comments have been extremely helpful in improving the manuscript.

On a more personal note, I thank Karel, Sanne and Frits for their support when I much needed it. Finally, I am grateful to my parents for their warmth and love. Once again, this book is for them.

TRADE IN THE ANCIENT MEDITERRANEAN

FRONTISPIECE. The *macellum* (marketplace) of Puteoli, Italy, ca. 200 CE.
Photo courtesy of Barbara Caffi.

1

Introduction

Globalization and the Nation State

When the fruits of the Industrial Revolution began to be reaped in the course of the nineteenth century, a period of rapid economic expansion followed. Steamships and trains improved transportation, machines allowed for the mass production of goods, and the telegraph and telephone sped up communication. Global markets for commodities and manufactured goods alike became increasingly interconnected. This growing connectivity benefited from the fact that the world's nations were cosmopolitan in a way unthinkable now, operating almost entirely without ID requirements, visas or other cross-border restrictions. In addition, this was a time of economic development largely unchecked by labor laws, unions or social safety nets. Finally, it was the height of European imperialism, with about half the planet's populated surface governed by some form of imperial or colonial rule. The result of this potent technological, economic and political mix would be the so-called first global economy, already established by the 1870s.[1] In a famous passage in *The Economic Consequences of the Peace*, John Maynard Keynes lauded this "extraordinary episode in the economic progress of man":

> The inhabitant of London could order by telephone, sipping his morning tea in bed, the various products of the whole earth, in such quantity as he might see fit, and reasonably expect their early delivery upon his doorstep.... He could secure forthwith, if he wished it, cheap and comfortable means of transit to any country or climate without passport or other formality... and could then proceed abroad to foreign quarters, without knowledge of their religion, language, or customs, bearing coined wealth upon his person, and would consider himself greatly aggrieved and much surprised at the least interference. But, most important of all, he regarded this state of affairs as normal, certain, and permanent.[2]

1. Jones 2007: 143–47.
2. Keynes 1920: 9–10.

The outbreak of war on July 28, 1914, revealed that the first global economy had been none of those things. "The projects and politics of militarism and imperialism, of racial and cultural rivalries, of monopolies, restrictions, and exclusion" were to play "the serpent to this paradise," Keynes wrote. The Wall Street Crash of 1929 and the Great Depression of the 1930s finished off what was left of the first global economy. How paradisiacal it had all been much depended on whom you asked, I suppose. But in any case, an "extraordinary episode" it undeniably was.

After the Great Depression, World War II prevented economic globalization from reemerging. The process only began shifting gears again in the early 1950s, speeding up significantly after the 1970s following market deregulation and liberalization. The collapse of the Soviet Union reopened Russia and Eastern Europe to foreign investment, and by the turn of the century large emerging economies had firmly joined the global capitalist mainstream, most notably China. With these developments the world had entered a new phase of ever deepening and accelerating interconnectedness, the "second global economy."[3]

But now a backlash against this seemingly unstoppable process is underway, almost exactly a century after World War I brought the first global economy to a violent halt. Among electorates in many Western democracies there is a growing sense that the payoffs of globalization have been too disappointing for too many, the burdens too unevenly distributed, the benefits too unequally shared. In the political and public discourse the question is increasingly being asked if globalization "works for everyone," indeed if it is even capable of working for everyone. The merits of heightened trade barriers, curbed migration and strengthened borders or, in the case of the European Union, restored borders are discussed in a way that they have not been in decades. Nation-states have always exerted a strong influence over people's sense of collective identity and economic self-determination. But that influence is growing again after a long period in which supranational organizations enjoyed broad and almost unquestioned support.

The sour mood gripping many societies at the moment seems largely to be expressed in a nihilistic desire to demolish the status quo, seen by large numbers of citizens as rigged against them. In *Age of Anger*, Pankaj Mishra has attempted to capture what is driving the current destructive temper. He notes that in the recent past, the shocks of modernity were "absorbed by inherited social structures of family and community, and the state's welfare cushions," whereas now "individuals are directly exposed to them in an age of accelerating competition on uneven playing fields, where it is easy to feel that there is no such thing as either society or state, and that there is only a war of all

3. Jones 2007: 150–52.

against all." The results are not pretty: "An existential resentment of other people's being, caused by an intense mix of envy and sense of humiliation and powerlessness . . . is presently making for a global turn to authoritarianism and toxic forms of chauvinism."[4]

If nativist sentiments and zero-sum thinking are on the rise, industrial-scale, interstate warfare of the kind that marred the twentieth century still seems only a remote possibility. All the same, the period of political turbulence we live in might see the end of the second global economy. Some of its pillars are being chipped away while others are being openly questioned, a slow erosion with an uncertain outcome. Developments are too young for predictions yet, and they are likely to remain so for some time to come. But one way or the other, changes are afoot in how the world economy is governed. The coming years will teach us to what degree national governments, under pressure from electorates demanding a retreat from globalization, will dismantle the inter-connected economic world order constructed after World War II.

I note these things here because this book will be devoted to the role of states in the economic development of the ancient Mediterranean. State ideology, economic migration, commercial connectivity and social trust will be recurring themes, and just as I was writing about these matters the intensity of the current political discourse was reaching new heights. Of course as I deal with the ancient world, the states to be discussed were not nation-states with flags, passports and national anthems. Moreover, the ancient world was pre-modern in nature and did not have the benefits of mechanized transportation and lightning-fast communication that the Industrial Revolution would bring. The primary sector always remained the bedrock of the economy and overall output always remained low by modern standards.

Yet if the rise of the Greco-Roman world was not comparable to the first, let alone the second global economy, an "extraordinary episode in the economic progress of man" it was also. How much so is visible in long-term data suggesting that economic activity reached levels not seen again until the high Middle Ages or the start of the Early-Modern Period. The data also suggest that ancient economies in the aggregate followed a trend of growth and decline, an observation that is central to the discussion in this book.

The Mediterranean Economy in the Long Run

In the bar chart below (fig. 1.1), we see the number of known Mediterranean shipwrecks dated 1500 BCE–1500 CE, broken down by half century.[5] Not every ship type is equally visible. Wooden hulls have mostly disintegrated,

4. Mishra 2017: 13–14.
5. Wilson 2011: fig. 2.5, building on the fundamental work by Parker 1992.

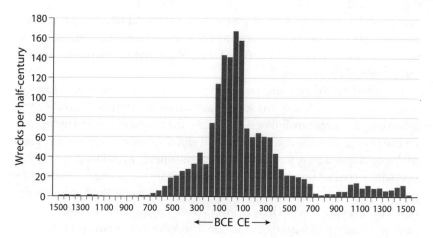

FIG. 1.1. Mediterranean shipwrecks by half-century. Image courtesy of Andrew Wilson.

leaving behind only nonperishable material such as tiles, bricks, blocks of stone and marble, but most of all ceramic containers. We are therefore seeing predominantly transport vessels, not warships.[6]

This chart is not as straightforward to read as it might appear, as both Andrew Wilson and Michael McCormick have emphasized.[7] For one thing, ships that carried perishable cargoes such as grain, timber and textiles have all but vanished from the seafloor. Secondly, in Roman times wooden barrels began to be used alongside the traditional ceramic amphorae, making a larger percentage of shipwrecks invisible archaeologically. Wilson argues that this change in large part accounts for the remarkable drop in the bars from the first to the second century CE. But incomplete data may also explain that effect, perhaps more so than a shift from amphorae to barrels. Recent work by McCormick on new shipwreck discoveries shows that the decline from the second to the eighth century CE was much more gradual than figure 1.1 would suggest.[8]

What matters for my purposes is the trend line ca. 700 BCE–ca. 700 CE, the shape of which is increasingly being confirmed by new data. Much scholarly work has focused on the Roman-era high point. In earlier representations of the dataset it appeared in the late-republican period, but it has now shifted to the time of the early empire with Wilson's incorporation of new finds and his more sophisticated data-processing methodology. To explain the imperial-era peak, Philip Kay in *Rome's Economic Revolution* concentrated on the phase

6. Iron cannon increase the visibility of Early-Modern warships, though: Wilson 2011: 37.

7. Wilson 2011: 33–39; 2014: 150–54; McCormick 2012: 89–97.

8. McCormick 2012: 84, fig. 3.12.

just preceding it. He notes that the late second and early first centuries BCE show a significant rise, a phenomenon he attributes to the development of finance during the later Roman republic.[9] But he largely limits his discussion to that timeframe. He acknowledges that "Rome acquired control over developed trade and communication networks throughout the Mediterranean" and that "some of the economic developments which we see in the second century represent the continuation of processes that had begun earlier, under the influence of contact with the Hellenistic world."[10] But he does not assign those older processes any particular significance in his explanatory model. Instead, he points to Roman-era monetary flows as the main driver of economic change:

> During the second century [BCE], increased inflows of bullion combined with the contemporaneous expansion of the availability of credit to produce a large increase in monetary liquidity. This in turn resulted in a major upward inflection in Roman economic activity and the creation both of a more complex system of production and distribution and of an enormous material culture that was to reach its height under the Principate.[11]

These multiplier effects could occur because large sections of the Mediterranean economy were still operating without coinage when the Roman increase in monetary liquidity began. In Kay's estimate, Italy's monetization level rose from 39 to 68 percent between 150 and 50 BCE, and levels are likely to have risen also elsewhere. Rather than produce inflation, as standard economic theory would predict, the expansion of the money supply therefore fueled economic activity. It increased the size and degree of commercialization of the nonagrarian sector and stimulated overseas trade.[12] Kay's observations and explanations coincide with those of David Hollander. Several years earlier in *Money in the Late Roman Republic*, Hollander had already concluded that the "expansion of Roman banking and the creation of business networks throughout the Mediterranean in the late Republic were the two primary developments allowing for the growth of trade."[13]

Kay's and Hollander's analyses seem compelling to me. However, they do not explain what in my view is the most remarkable aspect of the shipwreck graph, namely the steady climb starting around 700 BCE, to which Rome initially contributed nothing. The Romans were not a maritime people in the

9. Kay 2014: 143–44.

10. Kay 2014: 1, 327.

11. Kay 2014: 327.

12. Kay 2014: 314–18, 329. Kay notes that there probably was some inflationary pressure, but that it seems to have remained mild.

13. Hollander 2007: 104–11. Quotation on p. 111.

Iron Age, and when for military reasons they finally began plying the seas late in the fourth century BCE, this was only a limited phenomenon. In the subsequent century they were still entirely absorbed by warfare on the Italian peninsula and Sicily.[14] Roman long-distance trade supported by advanced financial institutions would become a significant factor in the Mediterranean from the mid-second century BCE onward. But the smooth climb of the trend line centuries beforehand suggests that what was happening then continued a process initiated earlier.

The shipwreck graph is not the only image telling us to extend our gaze backward beyond the time of the Roman republic. Another image doing so is presented by figure 1.2. It shows the data on levels of Pb (lead) pollution obtained by coring the Greenland ice sheet.[15] The mining of the metal itself released substantial amounts into the atmosphere, but the Pb pollution we see in figure 1.2 was caused mainly by the extraction of silver. Airborne particles were carried to Greenland by a strong south-to-north atmospheric transport, were captured by snowfall and then trapped in the compacted strata of ice. Research on the stable isotope signatures of the lead in the ice cores has shown a heavy contribution from silver mines in the Spanish Rio Tinto region.[16] Future analyses promise to give us a much more detailed picture of the geographical source distribution, especially as the study of anthropogenic lead pollution in lake sediments and peat bogs in Spain, Sweden, Britain and Switzerland is also intensifying.[17]

The data on atmospheric Pb pollution have a clear significance for ancient economic history, especially in their relation to silver mining. From early on in Mediterranean history, silver was extracted to manufacture decorative ornaments and to produce bullion. Moreover, from the mid-sixth century BCE onward it was used to mint coins.[18] Pollution levels can thus be taken as a proxy variable for economic activity.[19] However, as is the case with the shipwreck graph, the picture presented by the Pb pollution data is not free of interpretation problems, as Hannah Friedman cautions.[20] A shift from silver to gold in minting new coins might, for instance, have produced a drop in the

14. Hopkins 1978; Harris 1979; 2017; Kay 2014: 21–42.

15. Hong, Candelone, Patterson and Boutron 1994.

16. Some 70 percent for the period 366 BCE to 36 CE: Rosman, Chisholm, Hong, Candelone and Boutron 1997: 3416.

17. Renberg, Bindler and Brännvall 2001; Hillman et al. 2017; McConnell et al. 2018; Friedman forthcoming.

18. Introduction of coinage: Von Reden 2010: 20–25.

19. McCormick 2001: 53, 703; Wilson 2002; De Callataÿ 2005; Jongman 2007a: 188–89; Kehoe 2007: 547–48; McConnell et al. 2018.

20. Friedman forthcoming.

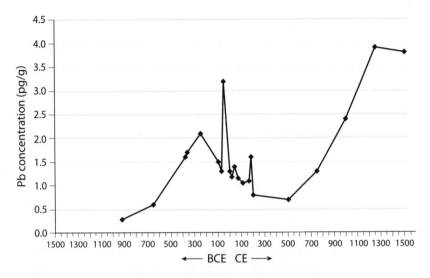

FIG. 1.2. Atmospheric lead pollution in the Greenland ice sheet.
Image courtesy of François de Callataÿ.

trend line not necessarily indicative of a decline in economic activity. Friedman also notes that because of the prevailing winds in the troposphere, the sample of Pb pollution in the Greenland ice sheet may not be representative of all silver mining occurring in the ancient world. Some production areas such as the Rio Tinto may be overrepresented, while others such as the Kosmaj (Serbia) may be underrepresented. But problems of sample collection and interpretation notwithstanding, the value of the data as a general gauge of long-term economic development is not in doubt.

Figure 1.2 shows some notable differences from figure 1.1. The Pb diagram follows a jagged trajectory, the result mainly of a paucity of data points.[21] But most conspicuous is the sustained rise after the late-antique or early-medieval low point, a rise not seen in the shipwreck graph. The latter effect should be attributed to the decreased visibility of wrecks due to a shift from amphorae to wooden barrels, which was all but complete in the Middle Ages.[22] But despite these differences, two entirely different datasets display comparable trend lines and seem to tell a broadly similar story ca. 700 BCE–ca. 700 CE. If the data reflect general, long-term economic developments, as they seem to, then the question of what those might have been is highly pertinent.

21. Wilson 2014: 157. See McConnell et al. 2018 for more fine-grained data. I thank Andrew Wilson for allowing me a preview of this article, which unfortunately appeared too late for me to take full advantage of it.

22. Wilson 2011: 37.

One long-term process largely agreeing with the image in both graphs is demographic growth and decline. The end of the Bronze Age saw a massive population contraction in Greece, but from the late second millennium BCE onward there was steady, aggregate demographic growth around the Mediterranean. From the available data, Walter Scheidel concluded that with all due caution,

> we may assume that between the twelfth century BC and the second century AD, the population of the part of Europe that was eventually taken over by the Roman empire approximately quadrupled in size, at a long-term average annual growth rate of around 0.1 percent.... After the depression of population numbers following the disintegration of the western and much of the eastern Roman empire in the fifth and sixth centuries, the formerly Roman part of Europe (with the exception of Greece) generally re-attained peak Roman population levels by the twelfth or thirteenth centuries, and after another slump caused by the Black Death consistently exceeded them from the mid-fifteenth century onwards.[23]

An increase in population size generated rising levels of consumption and production and thus at least aggregate economic growth. Whether certain areas and periods also experienced per capita growth is an open question, although a large and growing number of scholars, including Scheidel, argue that the answer should be yes.[24] But one way or the other, demography only partially explains long-term economic trends. As Willem Jongman has pointed out, shipping and metal extraction "had obviously increased by much more than could be expected from just population growth. Similarly, decline was much steeper than could be expected from just demographic contraction."[25]

State Formation and the Mediterranean Economy

Another phenomenon was also occurring: the trend lines in both graphs broadly track the formation, growth and disintegration of Mediterranean states. The period between ca. 700 BCE and ca. 50 CE witnessed a process of pronounced state consolidation. After the collapse of the Aegean Bronze-Age societies around 1200 BCE, city-states formed during the Iron Age in the eastern and central Mediterranean.[26] During the late sixth and early fifth centuries

23. Scheidel 2007: 42–43.

24. Hopkins 2002; Saller 2002; Morris 2004: 259–60; Scheidel 2007: 43–44; Jongman 2006; 2007a; 2007b; 2014; Ober 2015: 81–84; Erdkamp 2016; Harper 2017: 29–38. See also chapter 6.

25. Jongman 2007a: 191.

26. Osborne 2009; Terrenato and Haggis 2011; Hansen 2013.

BCE, the Achaemenid empire reached its maximum extent, tying together the East Mediterranean from Egypt to Thrace.[27] Its retreat and conquest by Alexander in the second half of the fourth century BCE resulted in the emergence of three large kingdoms. Those would in turn all fall to Rome, which had meanwhile steadily been consolidating its hold on the Italian peninsula.[28] In the west as well, a city-state, Carthage, was on the rise. Between the sixth and third centuries BCE it would bring Sardinia, Sicily, Corsica and large parts of North Africa and Spain under its control, in effect building an overseas empire.[29] Just as the Hellenistic kingdoms, it would ultimately be defeated and taken over by Rome.

This process of ongoing territorial unification in the west, center and east would culminate in the emergence of the largest state the ancient Mediterranean would ever know: the Roman empire. After its disintegration, state formation occurred again in the early Middle Ages, a process that would grow stronger especially after ca. 1000 CE, and that continued into the Early-Modern Period with the birth of the European nation-state.[30]

A knotty problem needs to be addressed at this point in the discussion. There are "as many definitions of the state as there are social theorists."[31] The Roman empire and the Hellenistic kingdoms may be clear-cut cases, but especially for earlier societies the question of what counts as a state is not an easy one to answer. Chris Wickham was confronted with the same problem in his study of the early Middle Ages ca. 400 CE to ca. 800 CE with its many emerging states and statelets. As a solution he offered a set of five parameters to conceptualize an "ideal type" of the state:

> the centralization of legitimate enforceable authority (justice and the army); the specialization of governmental roles, with an official hierarchy which outlasted the people who held official position at any one time; the concept of a public power, that is, of a ruling system ideologically separable from the ruled population and from the individual rulers themselves; independent and stable resources for rulers; and a class-based system of surplus extraction and stratification.[32]

No definition of the state will satisfy everyone, and Wickham's as well has its drawbacks. For one thing, it does not include control over a specific territory, an aspect all but universally associated with states. Problematic for my

---

27. Wiesehöfer 2013: 199–202.

28. Hellenistic kingdoms: Ma 2013. Roman Republic: Harris 1979; Mouritsen 2013.

29. Ameling 2013; Pilkington 2013.

30. Tilly 1990; Wickham 2005.

31. Wickham 2005: 57 n. 2.

32. Wickham 2005: 57 with 303–06.

purposes is that one can question if cities such as Tyre, Sidon and Byblos ca. 900 BCE fall under the definition, as at that time their monarchies may still have been more personalized and less institutionalized than Wickham's ideal type would call for. It is also debatable how well his definition covers Greek city-states, especially if they had a democratic form of government such as classical Athens. Of course that is a broader problem, as the statehood of Greek city-states under any definition is a topic of debate.[33]

However, Wickham's "ideal type" does not represent a checklist of prerequisites. Even if in a particular society one or more of the five parameters were present to only a lesser degree, it might still qualify as a state. Admittedly, some purity is sacrificed in adopting such a flexible approach. But for my purposes, ignoring definitional imperfections for the sake of argument brings major benefits. Being able to put the Roman empire, classical Athens and eighth-century BCE Tyre on the same plane allows me to analyze how their establishment of public authority affected economic conditions. Obviously those three societies varied widely in their governmental structure. But by calling them all states, I do not mean to argue that they were comparable that way. What I argue instead is that their emergence as public entities influenced the economic landscape beyond the capabilities of private individuals or groups of private individuals.

None of this is to say that private individuals could not profoundly alter the economic landscape. They could and did, as can be seen clearly in their role in the early Iron Age, when long-distance cultural and mercantile links were reestablished following the collapse of Mediterranean Bronze Age societies. That process of civilizational renewal was initially driven by individual traders unconnected to any emerging public institutions. As Tamar Hodos noted, it "is particularly evidence for trade, in its most general sense, that characterizes the beginning of a new impetus in the Mediterranean in the early first millennium, initially conducted by individuals working in an independent rather than state capacity."[34]

But figures 1.1 and 1.2 suggest that from ca. 700 BCE onward, state formation began to have a positive influence on the economic activities of those pioneering individuals. A practical reason why that might have been the case readily comes to mind: states provided a transportation infrastructure, aiding traders in their mercantile endeavors. The construction of maritime harbors formed an important part of that process, which is relevant especially for understanding figure 1.1. Harbors started to appear in the Aegean in the eighth

33. See Zuiderhoek 2017: 149–59 for a discussion with references. For Athens as a "natural state," see also chapter 2.

34. Hodos 2006: 3–4. Bronze Age and Iron Age trade, see also Meyer 2006.

century BCE; witness for instance the 100-meter-long mole dated to that time on the island of Delos. Literary evidence tells us that seaports began to be built on the initiative of powerful Greek monarchs such as Polycrates of Samos (Hdt. 3.60).[35] In the context of developments in Archaic Greece, the evidence shown in figure 2.2 is relevant as well. The sixth-century BCE introduction into the Greek world of coinage on an official weight standard stimulated the building process by making it easier to finance major public works.[36] In later periods as well, rulers decided on the creation of Mediterranean harbors, including some of the largest and most famous ones, such as Alexandria's.[37] In the Roman empire, funding harbor construction remained "something like an imperial—or at least public—privilege," falling to either emperors or cities.[38]

Port infrastructure was complicated to build, requiring specialized engineering skills that had to accumulate over time. The process of learning by doing that started in the Iron Age continued until, in the words of Lionel Casson, "the essential elements of a harbor had been worked out by the fifth century B.C. The successive centuries saw chiefly elaboration of facilities and increase in size." But he adds that later developments still included some major advances:

> The Hellenistic Age brought to harbor construction the vastness of size and the layout according to an integrated plan that characterized the architecture of the times. In addition, it contributed a feature of the highest practical importance, the lighthouse. . . . The Romans introduced a significant innovation, the use of concrete that would set under water. This powerful and flexible material enabled them to strike out boldly and plant harbors where nature had nothing at all to offer.[39]

Apart from facilitating overseas shipping, the construction of harbors had a stimulating economic effect by integrating public and private monetary flows. Especially if public works went hand in hand with rising levels of monetization, multiplier effects of the kind identified by Kay will have followed. Such effects likely were at work well before the time of the later Roman republic. They are almost certain to have been felt, for instance, in Ptolemaic Egypt,

35. Casson 1971: 362; Blackman 1982a: 93.

36. See Von Reden 2010: 35–41 for Greek monetization and the financing of public works and services.

37. See chapter 5 for details on Alexandria's harbor. See also chapter 2, Appendix, for the harbors of Carthage.

38. Arnaud 2014: 172. Roman harbors, see also Blackman 1982a; 1982b.

39. Casson 1971: 365–67.

where taxation levels were high and where in the course of the third century BCE the economy went from being largely unmonetized to largely monetized.[40]

Because of its geographical size the Roman empire is especially significant for the effect of tax spending on economic integration. The impact of one on the other has been studied by Keith Hopkins in what is now a classic article.[41] Hopkins' fundamental assumption in his "taxes and trade" model was that a number of rich areas—including Spain, southern Gaul, North Africa, Asia Minor, Syria and Egypt—were revenue exporters, paying more in imperial taxes than they received in public spending. The central government partly invested the collected money at its source, but sent most of it out it to pay for the legions on the frontiers in provinces that were tax importers. The amount of revenue going to the defensive armies was considerable. As the largest item in the state budget, the military probably accounted for over 50 percent of public spending.[42] But for this process of monetary redirection to continue, the net-contributing provinces had to find a way to fill their deficits. Without a counterbalancing revenue stream, they would not have had the money to pay their fiscal dues the following year. Engaging in trade was the answer, according to Hopkins. By producing and exporting agricultural surplus and manufactured goods, tax-exporting provinces earned back cash, thereby balancing out their losses.

In a follow-up paper Hopkins incorporated rent-taking by Roman aristocratic landowners into his model. Members of the Roman senatorial elite possessed large tracts of provincial land, from which collectively they received rent income on a par with the state's annual revenue net of army costs. This rent sustained the elite's ostentatious lifestyle, and like the tax revenue received by the state, it was spent at some distance from its place of origin, chiefly in Rome but also in local and regional capitals around the empire. Just like taxes, rent contributions were predominantly paid in money, not in kind. To allow provincial laborers to pay their dues in subsequent years, these monetary flows therefore needed reverse ones, and here as well the solution was to engage in surplus production and exports to earn back cash.

Taxation and rent payments counterbalanced by trade thus produced what Hopkins proposed was a "mildly developmental" economic effect, creating a "thin veneer of monetary and economic integration" over an essentially agrarian economy.[43] This model has not been universally accepted but, as Scheidel observed, "the debate is primarily concerned with the question of whether the

40. Von Reden 2011. See also chapter 3.
41. Hopkins 1980.
42. Hopkins 2002: 199–200.
43. Hopkins 2002: 219, 224.

central state and its associated élites played an absolutely crucial or merely a very significant rôle in commercial development: the overall importance of state formation is not in doubt."[44]

Enforcement and the State

The topic of the economic role of states brings me to the main theme of this book. Mention of Douglass North, the father of New Institutional Economics, is inescapable here. North's work has had a profound impact on the field of ancient economic history, and I think it is fair to say that Neo-Institutionalism has now established itself as the default paradigm in both Greek and Roman scholarship.[45] Examples abound. Elio Lo Cascio argued that "the theoretical framework proposed by North can allow a better insight into the performance of the Roman Empire as a unified political organization."[46] Joseph Manning, in a monograph on the Ptolemaic economy, wrote: "understanding how local economies were linked to the central state requires a model of the state. I adopt in this book North's neo-classical theory of the state."[47] In a recent work on classical Greek history, Josiah Ober specified that Neo-Institutionalism's "insistence that institutions . . . and organizations (including, but not only, states), along with markets and networks, are fundamental determinants of economic change, grounds the arguments of this book."[48]

But difficulties arise with this wholesale adoption of Neo-Institutionalism in ancient economic history, specifically with regard to its concept of the state. In *Structure and Change in Economic History*, North defined a state as "an organization with a comparative advantage in violence, extending over a geographic area whose boundaries are determined by its power to tax constituents," continuing that "an organization which has a comparative advantage in violence is in the position to specify and enforce property rights."[49] The latter part of that definition is problematic when applied to Greco-Roman history, and not just there.[50] First of all, in nonstate-level societies, including chiefdoms and tribes and arguably even bands, basic property rights were also specified.[51] Their complexity could increase along with growing sociopolitical

44. Scheidel 2011: 22.

45. To the point where some have begun to question its usefulness: Verboven 2015.

46. Lo Cascio 2006: 221.

47. Manning 2003: 10.

48. Ober 2015: 5.

49. North 1981: 21.

50. E.g., Boix 2015: 119–21 for the period of earliest state formation in Mesopotamia and the Near East.

51. Earle 1991: 71–74.

complexity, but the state was not a *conditio sine qua non* for their creation. More importantly, if states could in theory enforce private property rights, they did not necessarily do so in practice.

In the abstract, the idea of casting the state in the role of third-party enforcer is an attractive one. Already in 1651 Thomas Hobbes explained the logic of that notion in the *Leviathan*:

> If a covenant be made, wherein neither of the parties perform presently, but trust one another; in the condition of mere nature . . . upon any reasonable suspicion, it is void: but if there be a common power set over them both, with right and force sufficient to compel performance, it is not void. For he that performeth first, has no assurance the other will perform after; because the bonds of words are too weak to bridle men's ambition, avarice, anger, and other passions, without the fear of some coercive power. (14.18)

But this line of reasoning has a serious deficiency, as Peter Leeson points out in a deliberately provocative book, *Anarchy Unbound*: "Hobbes overlooked the possibility of *self*-governance: privately created social rules and institutions of their enforcement."[52] Leeson offers theoretically grounded historical case studies showing that transactions with delayed performance under "anarchy," loosely defined as the absence of formal government, are perfectly possible. Moreover, he posits that if a state is sufficiently rapacious, its dissolution and replacement by private order can be positive for economic performance. In support of that claim he cites the case of Somalia, arguing that the complete disappearance of government there in 1991 had by the early 2000s produced a marked improvement in the country's economy.[53] These studies lead him flatly to declare that Hobbes had it all wrong.

In so doing he is giving the intellectual achievement of the *Leviathan* too short shrift, but he is correct in treating its disregard of nonlegal enforcement as a significant gap. Even in well-functioning states governed by the rule of law, much economic interaction still depends on private order, including bargaining "in the shadow of the law."[54] That socioeconomic reality should come as no surprise. As Eric Posner has argued, courts have trouble determining contractual obligations and understanding business relationships because in both repeat and one-shot deals the number of unpredictable contingencies is large. Courts, therefore, "are not good at deterring opportunistic behavior in contractual relationships, but parties are. This is why so much contractual behavior depends on reputation, ethnic and family connections, and other elements

---

52. Leeson 2014: 1, italics in original.
53. Leeson 2014: 15–31, 170–96.
54. Cooter, Marks and Mnookin 1982. See also Posner 2000: 153–61.

of nonlegal regulation, and not on detailed and carefully written contracts enforced by disinterested courts."[55]

Still, the basic notion, as formulated by Hobbes, that a central task of the state is to act as society's ultimate enforcer is appealing. The idea was introduced into modern economic thinking well before North. An expression of it can be found in the work of Keynes, who wrote in *A Treatise on Money* that

> it is a peculiar characteristic of money contracts that it is the State or Community not only which enforces delivery, but also which decides what it is that must be delivered as a lawful or customary discharge of a contract. . . . The State, therefore, comes in first of all as the authority of law which enforces the payment of the thing which corresponds to the name or description in the contract.[56]

It should be noted here that Keynes makes a critical distinction between third-party *enforcement* and third-party *adjudication*. But contrary to what he seems to imply, states do not need to involve themselves in both tasks. They can assume some variation of adjudication without necessarily assuming enforcement, operating along a continuum from least forceful to most forceful. That continuum is cogently captured in a framework of "dispute settlement mechanisms" developed by Beth Yarbrough and Robert Yarbrough.[57] Though designed to study modern international trade relations, the framework serves my present purposes equally well. It consists of four main categories, conceptualized as fluid rather than fixed and exclusionary:

1. Third-party information gathering on alleged violations, and dissemination of that information, followed by group retaliation, potentially ending in ostracism.
2. Nonbinding third-party adjudication resulting in a recommended remedy, potentially followed by multilateral retaliation; no third-party enforcement.
3. Binding third-party adjudication without third-party enforcement; retaliation by the aggrieved party, permitted only if a violation has been confirmed.
4. Binding third-party adjudication and enforcement; no private retaliation allowed.

The potential benefits of the state assuming the task of both arbiter and enforcer in a reliable, unbiased way are obvious. Yet public adjudication

55. Posner 2000: 153.
56. Keynes 1930: vol. 1, 4.
57. Yarbrough and Yarbrough 1997: 139–48.

without public enforcement can still be beneficial to economic performance, depending on the state's level of impartiality, the quality of its arbitration and the sophistication of its legal framework. Conversely, if the state's legal institutions are poor, adjudication with full enforcement can be harmful to economic development. A wide range of possible outcomes is imaginable, and historical ones depend on the specific circumstances of individual societies. But in all cases, what matters is that for a proper understanding of the state as an authority of law, distinguishing between adjudication and enforcement is imperative.

Getting the two concepts confused is all too easy. It is tempting to take evidence for disputants submitting to the jurisdiction of official courts of law as confirmation of the existence of third-party enforcement. That assumption seems to have informed the work of, for instance, Sheilagh Ogilvie. In *Institutions and European Trade*, she sets out to portray medieval merchant guilds as nothing but rent-seeking monopolists interested only in creating barriers to entry and bending the rules of trade to their advantage. The argument that such associations might have been critical for contract enforcement is incorrect, she contends. Traders could turn to the state to perform that task, an option they often preferred over internal dispute settlement within their own organizations. In a typical expression of that view, she asserts that "Wherever European merchants traded during the medieval Commercial Revolution . . . state enforcement was available and long-distance merchants voluntarily used it to enforce contracts."[58]

However, what she is referring to in making such claims is not state enforcement but state adjudication. To explain medieval traders' preferences, she repeatedly emphasizes the quality and impartiality of official courts of law. But no matter how informative such alleged legal superiority may be about public institutions of adjudication, it tells us little about enforcement. A verdict by a medieval judge still had to be effectuated. The private-order mechanisms necessary to do so operated within and between medieval trading organizations, which by implication seem to have had the central role in contract enforcement that Ogilvie categorically denies they had.

Avner Greif, by contrast, does take the view that medieval trading coalitions were key to private-order enforcement, providing an essential service to the functioning of markets.[59] Much in his analysis is specific to medieval Europe, but his observation that Ogilvie wrongly equates courts with third-party enforcement has general validity: "The premise here is that all historical courts were the same and similar to a modern, effective court. . . . The issue is not

58. Ogilvie 2011: 302–03.

59. Greif 1989; 2006. For the debate between Ogilvie and Greif, see Edwards and Ogilvie 2012; Greif 2012.

whether . . . courts existed . . . , but whether they differed substantially from each other and from their modern equivalents."[60] In other words, if we see public institutions of adjudication operating in any given historical society, we still need to establish what mechanisms of enforcement underpinned them.

In the study of Roman law, a position close to Ogilvie's is taken by what David Ratzan has called the "legal centralists." Ratzan rightly dismisses their denial of the importance of nonlegal sanctions as "historically incorrect and theoretically confused." But he equally thinks that their counterparts, whom he labels "legal skeptics," are at a loss to explain, for instance, official petitions to Roman state authorities: "If the government did not care, why bother complaining to it? . . . At the very least, we must imagine . . . Roman subjects as buying *something* of value in their contracts, petitions, and trials. What was it?"[61] That question might *mutatis mutandis* be asked of Ptolemaic subjects, classical Athenian subjects, or for that matter the subjects of all ancient states.

But is the problem as intractable as Ratzan presents it as being? I suggest that the solution is in fact quite simple, hiding as it were in plain sight. What a plaintiff bought, or hoped to buy, with an investment in legal action was an official recognition of his position. Such an imprimatur by an authoritative public body enhanced the chances that collective action would be taken against his adversary. The latter's reputation would be diminished, as would his social room to maneuver, especially in the long run if he became the object of repeated official censure. Scholars of ancient law tend not to think in such terms, and when they do they tend to see reputational mechanisms and collective action as alternatives to official legal procedures. But private order and public institutions were not working in opposition as competitors in a "market for enforcement." On the contrary, they worked together. The more seamlessly they did so, the more effective enforcement would be.

The outcome of public institutions reinforcing private order does not equate to third-party enforcement in the sense of North, Keynes or Yarbrough and Yarbrough. North fully acknowledged that such enforcement has historically been rare. It became more widespread only after the Industrial Revolution and even then remained limited to a small number of societies. That historical argument is elaborated in his *Violence and Social Orders*, written with John Wallis and Barry Weingast.

The authors distinguish between two social orders based on how societies limit and control violence: open-access and closed-access societies. In the first, physical force is consolidated into official military and police organizations that are subordinate to the political system. Citizen identity in the open-access order is defined as a set of impersonal characteristics and rights

60. Greif 2012: 448.
61. Ratzan 2015: 215–16, italics in original.

possessed by all citizens. This shared set of impersonal rights at the heart of civil society prevents the executive from abusing its power. All open-access societies conform to Max Weber's definition of a state as "a human community that (successfully) claims *the monopoly of the legitimate use of physical force within a given territory.*"[62] Only a handful of states in history have come close to the Weberian ideal type. Today only about twenty-five countries containing about 15 percent of the world's population fall into that category.[63]

By contrast, the much more prevalent second type of social order, the closed-access society or "natural state,"

> reduces the problem of endemic violence through the formation of a dominant coalition whose members possess special privileges. The logic of the natural state follows from how it solves the problem of violence. Elites—members of the dominant coalition—agree to respect each other's privileges, including property rights and access to resources and activities. By limiting access to these privileges to members of the dominant coalition, elites create credible incentives to cooperate rather than fight among themselves.[64]

Natural states were the only ones in existence before the early nineteenth century and still form the majority today. They do not achieve a monopoly on violence, nor do they need to for their survival. Their assertion of physical force is a continuous rather than a discrete variable. The more force they manage to appropriate, the more effective they will be as governing organizations. Relationships within and between the elite coalitions that rule them are strongly personal, and status and hierarchy tend to be defined by individuals' social personas. Yet public institutions can grow in complexity, allowing them to become more impersonal and less dependent on the individuals controlling them at any given moment. Through that process an enhanced stability and durability of the state and its ruling coalition can be achieved. But even if increasingly stable and durable social arrangements are to the advantage of governing elites, nothing about the push toward complexity is teleological in nature. Natural states are as capable of regression as progression in this regard, depending on ever-changing external circumstances and internal power struggles.

Those ideas are thought-provoking and contain much of interest to the social theory–minded historian. Nevertheless, squeezing all recorded human history into a binary framework of open- versus closed-access societies is re-

62. Weber 1965: 2, italics in original (including the original German).
63. North, Wallis and Weingast 2009: xii, 21–22, 73, 110.
64. North, Wallis and Weingast 2009: 2–6, 18. Quotation on p. 18.

ductive in the extreme. The dichotomy inevitably creates friction when applied to some historical societies. In addition, the framework's simplicity limits its usefulness for a student of the premodern world, who is left with only the concept of the natural state. North, Wallis and Weingast acknowledge that natural states differ widely, a problem they address by distinguishing between "fragile," "basic" and "mature" ones. However, those three manifestations differ primarily in "the sophistication of the organizations they can support."[65] Such sophistication is a sliding scale, and the classificatory distinctions are more idiomatic than substantive analytical tools. But the shortcomings of *Violence and Social Orders* notwithstanding, it offers useful insights into premodern states' use of force, interference in trade and stability of governance. I will be referring to it repeatedly in this book, and will engage with it more fully in chapter 2.

From early on in North's work, his thinking about what makes states successful was predicated on the economic development of medieval Europe and the subsequent rise of the Western world.[66] The period of change culminating in the Industrial Revolution and the "Great Enrichment," to use Deirdre McCloskey's evocative phrase, has been extensively studied by economic historians.[67] But identifying the "rule of law" as a critical factor in that change may be erroneous. Seeing the economic expansion of industrializing Britain as the result of well-defined property rights enforced by the state is in any case a "gross oversimplification."[68] Though at the epicenter of the Industrial Revolution, British society in the 1700s and early 1800s still relied on private-order institutions, including reputation mechanisms and social ostracism of serial cheaters. Rather than economic development resulting from third-party enforcement, it would seem that causation worked the other way around. British society was transformed by the Industrial Revolution. As its economy became more urbanized and anonymous, reputation mechanisms became untenable and enforcement was consequently transferred to the public sector.

Janet Landa has proposed an abstract microeconomic theory that is much in line with these historical events. She enumerates the options open to middlemen to cope with "contract uncertainty," the term she employs for a lack of third-party enforcement. All options bear costs, which middlemen seek to reduce by moving from individual to collective action. As trade increases in volume and middlemen increase in number, unanimous collective action becomes ever harder to achieve and ever less cost effective. Landa posits that

65. North, Wallis and Weingast 2009: 41–49. Quotation on p. 41.

66. North and Thomas 1973. On the evolution of North's thinking, see also Wallis 2014.

67. McCloskey 2016.

68. Mokyr 2009: 368–88. Quotation on p. 378.

traders' cost-optimizing calculus thus leads to the emergence of the "protective state," a phrase borrowed from the work of James Buchanan and meaning "that part of government which acts as the enforcing institution of society."[69] She concludes that the resulting social order ensures a more Pareto-efficient equilibrium.

> The existence of social order (1) reduces unnecessary transaction costs arising from a trader's breach of contract . . . ; (2) facilitates the impersonal process of exchange by encouraging the trader to trade with outsiders, thus ensuring all opportunities for trading are exhausted; and (3) gives the trader the opportunity to shift some of the resources tied up in the protection of contracts into trade or capital accumulation.[70]

Landa does not invoke historical examples, but does not seem to see this shift toward a Pareto-superior social order as contingent on industrialization. Instead she presents her ideas as a general theory on the emergence of an "exchange economy with legally binding contract." Yet if the emergence of the "protective state" is such a natural outcome of economic actors' cost-optimizing behavior as she makes it seem, the question might well be asked why it has materialized so rarely.

To return to the ancient states that will be the subject of this book, they were non-Weberian in nature, not claiming a monopoly on violence. As powerful organizations they did have a "comparative advantage in violence," but they did not employ it to "enforce agreements such that the offending party always had to compensate the injured party to a degree that made it costly to violate the contract." Of course, expecting them to do so would be setting the bar too high. As already noted, North admitted that the conditions for such state behavior "are seldom, if ever, met in the real world," including the postindustrial one.[71] We should, thus, not measure the states of the ancient world against modern nation-states with fully developed institutions of public enforcement. But effective enforcement is indispensable for commercial exchange, and the question of how and to what extent it involved the state is relevant for our understanding of ancient economic history. An exhaustive treatment of all ancient societies is a near impossibility, and even a partial discussion would require a separate book. But a brief survey of some selected examples will suffice to show the limits of state enforcement.

In Greek city-states some degree of public physical force in defense of justice was available through city representatives, and such force was well under-

69. Buchanan 1975: 95.
70. Landa 1994: 62.
71. North 1990: 58.

stood to be necessary. Aristotle, in the *Politics* (6.1321b40–22a7), showed awareness that law enforcement occasionally required publicly administered violence. But in the small, face-to-face societies of Greek cities, laws were respected out of civic obedience and concern for social order as much as out of fear of sanctions, as Mogens Hansen has pointed out.[72]

Greek city-states did not maintain a body of bailiffs or civil enforcement officers, even if Athens had a public-order apparatus of market overseers, jailors and Scythian archers.[73] The effect of that lack of public support on commercial disputes becomes visible especially when we scale up the canvas. What of enforcement between rather than within communities? To resolve intercommunity disputes over business affairs, Greek city-states maintained a system of seizure of goods by private individuals. A citizen of one city could request court approval to seize goods from any of the community members of his adversary to satisfy his claim. City-states could choose to supersede this principle of collective responsibility by agreeing on rules laid down in interstate treaties. But ultimately, this system was a form of private justice, albeit subject to customary law and court oversight.[74] Such a system was not unique to Greek city-states or for that matter antiquity. Greif has shown that a similar "community responsibility system" governed relations between medieval trading centers in Italy, Germany and England.[75]

With the formation of the Hellenistic kingdoms in the third century BCE, large states commanding impressive powers of physical force entered the scene. In the relatively well documented Ptolemaic kingdom, a new legal order was established that combined central state control with the autonomy of local communities. Papyrological evidence shows that legal proceedings could be consequential in land disputes, as we learn from the records of a second-century BCE family conflict over the inheritance of an estate. Manning, in his analysis of the case, concludes that the "authority of the Egyptian court had enormous influence upon the local community. . . . The complaints addressed in petitions to local and regional Ptolemaic officials were resolved, in theory, through the authority of a local Egyptian court."[76] Nevertheless, whatever respect the word of the court may have enjoyed in the adjudication of community disputes over real estate, for a full assessment of the Ptolemaic legal system we need to consider how the state employed its coercion machinery.

72. Hansen 2002: 30–32.

73. Herman 2006: 216–38; Bresson 2016: 239–50.

74. Bravo 1980; Bresson 2007: 45; 2016: 318.

75. Greif 2006.

76. Manning forthcoming. On this dispute, see also Manning 2004: 763; 2018: 212–15.

In *Law and Enforcement in Ptolemaic Egypt*, John Bauschatz has recently argued that the Ptolemaic kingdom had an extensive organization of police officials charged with maintaining public order at the village level.[77] According to his study, this coercion apparatus targeted not only crime but also debt. Yet the debt for which one could land in prison was predominantly public in nature, in particular tax arrears. Bauschatz argues that detention for private debt also occurred, but the evidence he cites is extremely meager and ambiguous.[78] Even if it did occur occasionally, there was nothing systematic or institutionalized about it. Ptolemaic creditors could not count on public officials to enforce their claims.

Under the formulary procedure of Roman law, considered to be Rome's classical legal system, the execution of court verdicts was a form of state-sanctioned self-help. In the republican era and well into the empire, a successful plaintiff had the right to seize the person of the debtor and take him into custody, forcing him to work off his debt.[79] In later times he was also allowed to confiscate and auction off his debtor's entire property in a process resembling bankruptcy proceedings. The rules were relaxed in the course of the imperial period to allow for the seizure of individual assets, making for a more efficient way to satisfy debts.[80] But state-provided force did not form part of the system. "Judgment given, the duty of the judge was over. If the convicted party did not obey the judgment it was up to the plaintiff to take further steps. He was not given physical help by the authorities."[81]

In the course of the imperial period, various innovations of civil procedure were introduced, eventually to result in a comprehensive new system in the mid-fourth century CE.[82] It is clear that this development accompanied a pronounced hierarchization of the Roman legal process, characterized by a strict division between an upper and lower social class.[83] Some measure of public enforcement also emerged as part of the reform. A handful of legal texts mention bailiffs charged by special fiat with the execution of certain verdicts.[84] Much about these men remains unknown, including how numerous they were and what verdicts they might have been commissioned to enforce. But we do

---

77. Bauschatz 2013.

78. Bauschatz 2007: 7–9.

79. In a law promulgated by Zeno (486 CE) and another by Justinian (529 CE) we still hear of private prisons, which the emperors attempted to abolish: *Cod. Just.* 9.5.1–2.

80. Kaser and Hackl 1996: 382–407; Du Plessis 2015: 70–71, 77–78; Rüfner 2016: 265.

81. Crook 1967: 82.

82. Rüfner 2016.

83. Garnsey 1970; Kaser and Hackl 1996: 519–21.

84. *Exsecutores dati*: Litewski 1974: 227–29, 242–43; Von der Fecht 1999: 56; Díaz-Bautista Cremades 2013: 87–88.

know that, as other court functionaries, they charged fees for their services, a practice inviting corruption.[85] A mandate of Justinian (*Nov. 96 pr.*, 539 CE) aimed to stop them from colluding with plaintiffs in initiating spurious lawsuits and splitting the gains, apparently a widespread practice.

What all this amounts to is that ancient states fell somewhere in category 2 or 3 in the adjudication and enforcement framework of Yarbrough and Yarbrough, cited above.[86] Arguably, the Roman empire late in its history took some steps in the direction of category 4. But those steps were imperfect and incomplete and in part even counterproductive. None of this is to say that legal institutions did not matter for the economic performance of the ancient world. A large part of this book will in fact be devoted to arguing that they did matter. But I reiterate that in evaluating their impact, we should be careful to distinguish between public adjudication and public enforcement.

The Argument of This Book

The two central tenets of this book have now been made clear. First, state formation and consolidation had an aggregate positive effect on the economy of the ancient Mediterranean, starting in the Late Iron Age and peaking sometime in the Roman imperial period. Second, we should not ascribe that effect to ancient states acting as third-party enforcers of private property rights. Two questions follow. First, what did states' positive influence consist of? Second, what was the state's role subsequently, when economic decline set in?

The idea that state behavior can have both positive and negative effects on economic performance is at the heart of North's historical analysis. In *The Rise of the Western World*, he juxtaposed successful states such as the Dutch Republic and England in the 1500s and 1600s with less successful ones such as contemporary France and Spain. The latter, he proposed, "failed to create a set of property rights that promoted economic efficiency."[87] For the reasons discussed above, I will not follow North's ideas about the role of states in defining and enforcing property rights. However, that states' actions can be both helpful and harmful is a key issue to address.

As for harmful action, one might suppose warfare to have been the predominant type, because of its destructive potential and because Greco-Roman history had no shortage of it. Yet armed conflict seems not to have been the

85. Corruption: MacMullen 1988: 137–70. Legal fees: Di Segni, Patrich and Holum 2003; Haensch 2015.

86. See Ratzan 2015: 215–18 for a good discussion of the Roman empire as a category 3 state (not a term Ratzan uses) based on Egyptian papyri.

87. North and Thomas 1973: 120. The point is repeated in North 1990: 113–17.

disruptive force one might have expected.[88] Figures 1.1 and 1.2 suggest that the ancient Mediterranean experienced at least aggregate growth during a time when interstate warfare was frequent. Of course, not all military action is detrimental to economic performance. But even if things turned severely negative sum, as doubtless happened in several major conflicts, it seems that in the long run the effect was offset and more by positive factors. That observation brings me to one of the main arguments of this book: ancient states were beneficial to growth because they created institutions conducive to economic development, even if that was not necessarily the intention.

The last point deserves emphasis. In this book I am nowhere arguing for a "public economic policy" designed and executed by designated state representatives. By now it is a truism that no such policy existed in antiquity, an argument made already by Moses Finley.[89] But if the basic idea remains generally accepted, modifications to it have begun to emerge in the scholarly literature. Darel Engen, for instance, in a book on Athenian commerce, suggested that in "granting honors and privileges for trade-related services, Athens adapted and manipulated traditional institutions to formulate a practice that was flexible enough to acknowledge and exploit the dual desires for honor and profit that existed in the Greek economy, thereby fulfilling its trade policy."[90] Those are interesting new ideas worth exploring (see chapter 2).

By accounting for a desire for honors, Engen goes a long way toward incorporating ideology into his analysis. I propose that a much greater emphasis on the force of ideology is warranted for our understanding of ancient economic development. Rulers had to legitimize their power, an essential dynamic of natural states that North, Wallis and Weingast acknowledge but spend little time discussing.[91] Carles Boix has recently argued (contra Weber) that in what he calls "monarchical regimes," any ideological beliefs about the ruler's legitimacy cannot be disentangled from subjects' fear of the ruler's coercive capabilities and their instrumental calculations about the benefits of social order.[92] But regardless of whether one sees rule-legitimizing ideology as an independent or an ancillary source of support for monarchical regimes, its political reality had economic effects. In the Hellenistic kingdoms it led state representatives and the social classes wishing to emulate them to engage in behavior with expansionary effects, such as conspicuous consumption. The same held true for the Roman empire, even if unlike the Hellenistic kingdoms

88. But cf. McConnell et al. 2018: wars produced temporary setbacks in silver mining.
89. Finley 1999: 150–76. For a recent discussion of the topic, see Gabrielsen 2011.
90. Engen 2010: 5–6.
91. North, Wallis and Weingast 2009: 53–54, 57.
92. Boix 2015: 69–70.

it was not in direct competition with peer polities, which might have reduced the need for rule-legitimizing consumptive patterns.

Ideology had not just macroeconomic but also microeconomic effects, and to study those we can build on North's extensive work on social norms. North has repeatedly emphasized the significance of normative rules that structure society by providing informal constraints on individual behavior. Collectively those constraints can be considered a public good because they create social order and reduce economic uncertainty. Concretely, norms, beliefs and ideologies are ways of solving collective-action problems such as freeriding.[93] To those ideas I add that the social impact of ideologies related to or promoted by states increased if states were larger and wielded greater power. That effect is particularly relevant for the case of the Roman empire as the largest and most powerful state in the ancient Mediterranean.

Nevertheless, I do not mean to imply here that a bigger state size was always preferable. City-states especially had many advantages, and their economic success in premodern European history, from classical Athens to medieval Venice, suggests that the efficiencies they produced could be considerable. To date, no comprehensive theory exists to explain why this might have been the case. But it is not difficult to see how city-states may have hit something of a "sweet spot" in their geographical extent and population size. A variegated literature has pointed to the benefits of their limited dimensions for public finance, information exchange, technological innovation and intracommunity cooperation.

John Hicks, in A Theory of Economic History, was attracted to city-states because of their historical prevalence, success and persistence. He posited that their small scale was "favourable to the growth of a diversified trade." However, the structure of his argument required him to introduce legal institutions: "It is here that the city-state form of organization shows its superiority. The possibility of having recourse to regular legal institutions within the individual city state makes it easier for new kinds of trade to be carried on securely."[94] But he inserts this element into his theory without any explanation of how such institutions might have emerged. As the discussion above has shown, his assumption also requires qualification in light of current Neo-Institutional work. Although Hicks sees the absence of formal legal institutions as an "insuperable obstacle" to intergroup commercial diversification, Leeson in his already-cited Anarchy Unbound makes a good case for the possibility of trade between heterogeneous groups based on private order.[95]

93. North 1981: 36–45; 2005: 103–08. On Roman civic ideology and social norms, see Verboven, 2015: 55–56.

94. Hicks 1969: 42–59. Quotations on p. 46.

95. Leeson 2014.

Just as Hicks, Joel Mokyr presents city-states as "optimally sized" units of organization, but for a different reason. Although he, too, suggests that they might have had an advantage in contract enforcement, he proposes that they were well equipped predominantly for "the information-processing needed for trade," adding that they "played, from the later Middle Ages on, an increasingly pivotal role in the generation of new useful knowledge and innovations."[96] The role of any single medieval or Early-Modern city-state as an engine of creativity and innovation was usually just short lived. But as David Stasavage has pointed out, "While city-states were innovators for only a relatively brief span of time, all the evidence suggests that they retained their advantage with regard to public credit."[97] City-states' superior ability to borrow compared to territorial states was a product mainly of their political structure. The greater representativeness of their public bodies allowed them to make more credible repayment commitments to lenders, giving them easier access to long-term credit.

We are far less informed about the fiscal regimes of ancient city-states, but we do know that public borrowing was common in Greek cities, which may well have enjoyed a credible-commitment advantage similar to the one described by Stasavage.[98] Their small scale and political structure also spurred information exchange and institutional innovation, elements adduced by Ober to explain their "efflorescence," defined mostly in economic terms. In addition, their nature as a collection of small, autonomous states allowed them to be agile in their collective-action response to outside pressure: "The endemic risk posed to Greek communities by would-be predatory states, Greek and non-Greek alike, fostered decentralized cooperation by rewarding the high levels of mobilization that were facilitated by federalism and democracy."[99]

But whatever advantages Greek and other ancient city-states may have drawn from their limited scale, in the long run they could not compete with bigger polities because of their restricted access to resources. In the ancient Mediterranean they ended up either being incorporated into larger states, as happened with Tyre and Athens, or growing into dominant empires themselves, as happened with Carthage and Rome. The incorporation of city-states into larger empires did not necessarily mean that they lost all the advantages of their small size. Much of the political and civic culture and decision-making process of Greek cities, for instance, remained the same under Hellenistic

96. Mokyr 2002: 280–81.

97. Stasavage 2011: 43–46. Quotation on p. 44.

98. Migeotte 1984; Mackil 2015: 481–84.

99. Ober 2015: 70. On Greek institutional innovation, see Ober 2015: 117–20.

rule.[100] But obviously with the arrival of kings and, later, emperors as powerful hegemons, cities' self-governance diminished and their political ecology changed, both individually and collectively.[101] Nonetheless, in the aggregate their integration into larger state units seems to have been beneficial for economic development, as suggested by the upward economic trends in the proxy data presented in figures 1.1 and 1.2.

The downward trends past the Roman-era inflection point are equally significant.[102] Those trends have recently been studied from a Neo-Institutional perspective by Daron Acemoglu and James Robinson, but unfortunately their analysis fails to convince on all counts. In the second, more subsidiary part they assert that Roman emperors feared Schumpeter-style creative destruction and sought to suppress technological progress. In support of that claim, they cite two infamous stories: one of a man who was beheaded after showing his invention of unbreakable glass to Tiberius (Pliny *NH* 36.195; Petr. *Sat.* 51; Dio 57.21.7), the second of a man who was dismissed after showing Vespasian an efficient way of moving heavy columns (Suet. *Vesp.* 18).[103] But to take these two almost certainly fictional tales as proof of a multi-reign, empire-wide policy aimed at stamping out innovation is patently absurd. (For my own thoughts on the matter of Roman innovational development, see chapter 7.)

The first and more institutional-analytical part of the discussion concerns state predation. Acemoglu and Robinson argue that the seed for the fall of Rome had been planted when the republic turned into the empire. At that time, growth ground to a halt because Rome's "extractive institutions" had reached their limit. Citing the shipwreck and lead pollution graphs as evidence, they conclude that the "experience of economic growth during the Roman Republic was impressive, as were other examples of growth under extractive institutions, such as the Soviet Union."[104] The regrettable comparison to the USSR aside, one reason why this line of thinking is fallacious has already been indicated. Both the shipwreck and the lead pollution graph show a steady rise centuries before Roman influence began. Acemoglu and Robinson's argument would imply that all Mediterranean states from the Iron Age onward were characterized by "extractive institutions," in which case there would be nothing exceptional about the Roman republic. That argument would be interesting, but it is not the one offered.

100. See Strootman 2011 for a good discussion.

101. Ober 2015: 293–315.

102. Acemoglu and Robinson 2012: 158–75.

103. Infamous since Finley 1965. For a different evaluation of the same stories, see Greene 2000: 46–50; Wilson 2002: 4.

104. Acemoglu and Robinson 2012: 170. Cf. Hopkins 1978 for a widely accepted model of socioeconomic change from republic to empire.

More fundamentally, it is generally agreed that fiscal pressure went down after the republic collapsed because Rome's institutions became less, not more extractive (see the introduction and concluding remarks to chapter 3 for some details). In addition, the work by Hopkins discussed above shows that imperial levels of taxation were generally low. In his estimate, total state spending required no more than 10 percent of minimum Roman GDP, meaning that actual taxation levels were lower than that, perhaps between 5 and 7 percent.[105]

Finally, Acemoglu and Robinson make no attempt to differentiate between either the early and later empire or between east and west, presenting things as on a universally downward trajectory after the end of the republic. This will not do. Much current work by Roman economic historians has focused on per capita growth, which seems to have begun under the republic and continued well into the empire. Both Jongman and Paul Erdkamp, for instance, have recently argued that real incomes continued to rise into the second or perhaps even the third century CE.[106] After that point we need to be careful to distinguish between the western part of the empire, where universal decline set in, and the eastern part, where some areas continued to do well, as Bryan Ward-Perkins has shown (see further, chapter 6).[107]

Where Acemoglu and Robinson fail, Ward-Perkins makes the correct assessment: "A prerequisite for understanding the decline of the Roman economy is . . . the acceptance that it was a closely interlocked structure in which commerce and regional specialization, as well as the redistributive power of the state, all had an important role to play."[108] The economy of the empire was sustained by a complex but delicate equilibrium that was eventually tipped off balance, in part by stochastic events.[109] It was robust enough to withstand one or more manageable shocks such as the severe but brief period of civil war during the "year of the four emperors," 69 CE. But ultimately the imperial economy could not withstand several prolonged and simultaneous shocks, as happened in late antiquity. "Rome's empire was always poised uncertainly between fragility and resilience, and in the end the forces of dissolution prevailed."[110] For my purposes there is no need to discuss all the endogenous and exogenous factors that have been proposed to explain the decline and ultimate demise of the Roman world. Staying with my main theme, I will limit

105. Hopkins 2002: 201. For Roman taxation, see also Hopkins 1980; Potter 2014: 51–61; Scheidel 2015; Tan 2015.

106. Jongman 2006; 2007a; 2007b; Erdkamp 2016.

107. Ward-Perkins 2000b; 2005.

108. Ward-Perkins 2000b: 382.

109. Verboven 2015: 56–57; Harper 2017.

110. Harper 2017: 286.

myself to a study of one aspect of state behavior in late antiquity that I propose produced an institutional shock, adversely affecting the Roman system of intercommunity trade.

In the chapters to follow I will make these ideas concrete, focusing as much as I can not on what "the state" did but on what people did: people in their capacity as Greek city councilors, Ptolemaic officials or Roman magistrates; people in their capacity as long-distance traders, financiers or consumers of goods. This approach is intended to avoid speaking in abstractions where possible and to keep the discussion grounded in the sources. As for the book's structure, it does not attempt a narrative history from the birth of ancient states to the ultimate collapse of the Roman empire. Instead, the separate chapters present targeted studies, organized loosely chronologically, into the ways in which ancient states influenced economic performance. Each study discusses a selected set of sources, but all aim to elucidate the broader economic developments occurring around the Mediterranean at the time.

In chapter 2 I will discuss the trade diaspora, an institution that was all but obligatory for regular, long-distance trade in the absence of third-party enforcement. Traders could do business in a foreign community because people from their homeland had moved there permanently and could vouch for them. If a promise to pay or deliver according to agreement was not fulfilled, foreign settlers could be held accountable for any debt of their fellow citizens. All members of a diaspora network, itinerant and stationary alike, ultimately faced expulsion if they behaved opportunistically. To reduce the vast amount of source material to a workable level, I will take the Phoenicians as a leading thread. Because of their centuries-long Mediterranean mercantile tradition, we can trace their interaction with public institutions through much of Greco-Roman history.

In studying that interaction, I will engage with the social-order theory proposed by North, Wallis and Weingast, specifically their postulate that natural states control trade, which is useful if applied flexibly.[111] I will approach the topic from two mirrored angles to argue that states' role in trade had a beneficial effect on Mediterranean economic development: the public authority that Phoenician civic bodies claimed over their native diasporas, and the public authority asserted by host societies over those diasporas. As for the first angle, Phoenician ruling elites promoted trade from early on. The political institutions of some Phoenician cities still did so in the Hellenistic and Roman periods, involving themselves in the operation of their native trading associations overseas. As for the second angle, I will show how the institutions of Greek "public friendship" (*proxenia*) and subsequently Roman imperial

111. North, Wallis and Weingast 2009: 38.

ideology supported private order by facilitating the coordination of collective action.

The chapter is diachronic, treating a longer time span than chapters 3 to 5. It thereby sets the stage for the subsequent treatment of the Mediterranean economy, addressing long-term institutional developments connected to state formation, and touching on topics to be discussed later. An appendix will examine developments at Carthage, a city-state that grew into an empire at approximately the same time as the Hellenistic states, including the Ptolemaic kingdom on which chapter 3 centers. The trade diaspora will be a theme again in chapter 5, while Roman state ideology will recur there and in chapter 4.

In chapter 3 I will shift the discussion to mid-third-century BCE Syria-Palestine, an area ruled by the Ptolemies at the time. As in all Hellenistic states the power structure of the Ptolemaic kingdom was strongly personalized. A small number of state actors surrounding the king were allowed access to agricultural surplus, making them influential men politically and economically. The process by which the ruling elite negotiated power through conspicuous consumption, diplomatic tokens and gift-giving drove the wheels of an expanding economy of long-distance trade in both luxury goods and agricultural staples.

To investigate these matters, I will study the activities of a certain Zenon, who was an agent of the Ptolemaic finance minister Apollonios. We know of both men through a large collection of papyri containing correspondence between Zenon and his principal, and between members of a larger network of agents. By tracing the activities of these men we can analyze how as a public official Apollonios managed the Ptolemaic overseas territory of Syria-Palestine, at the same time allowing us to see how as a businessman he managed his private affairs there. Following Mancur Olson's ideas about how state actors provide public goods if doing so allows them to reap the benefits, I will argue that the activities of Apollonios and his agents fit the model of the "stationary bandit."[112] Apollonios was incentivized to keep Syria-Palestine socially stable and economically productive and thus to prevent its overexploitation. As we will also see, the Ptolemaic state that Apollonios served provided public goods, including a banking system and a public-order apparatus.

Contract enforcement and transaction costs under the Roman empire will be the topic of chapter 4. The unification of the Mediterranean Basin by a single state ameliorated economic conditions in practical ways: monetary and metrological systems were standardized, removing costly barriers to trade. Legal rules were standardized as well, which held the potential for an even greater transaction-cost-reducing effect. However, without third-party en-

112. Olson 1991; 2000.

forcement, private means still had to be employed to enforce contracts. It is therefore not immediately clear why transacting parties would adopt the Roman legal system.

I will argue that contracts drawn up in accordance with imperial law and in the presence of witnesses were "publicly embedded," which increased their enforceability and reduced enforcement costs. Witnesses were listed following a status hierarchy largely determined by the civic order created by the state. Political officeholding conferred the highest social standing, while priesthoods of the imperial cult and the possession of freeborn citizenship also provided status. Acting as a witness to formal contracts gave members of Roman society an opportunity publicly to reaffirm their personal status and to endorse the civic order from which it derived. By allowing their social standing to be tied to contracts, witnesses provided transacting parties with incentives either to meet their contractual obligations or, should it come to that, cooperate in official litigation. I will argue that this enforcement-enhancing effect was an "emergent property," the result of legal, social and ideological factors interacting in an undesigned and unintended fashion.[113] Legal documents recorded on wax tablets from Pompeii and Transylvania will provide the source material for the discussion. They give insight into contracting practices in two different socioeconomic settings, having been found respectively in the old imperial heartland and a young province.

Chapter 5 will discuss the changing world of the fourth century CE, a time of social ferment heightened by the Roman emperors' adoption of Christianity as a religion of state. Although this shift followed a turn toward forced religious centralization initiated by the emperors during the crisis of the third century, the choice for Christianity represented a momentous departure from Roman tradition. I will argue that the intolerance and violence it engendered upset the equilibrium of Mediterranean diaspora trade, producing an institutional shock.

Religion played a prominent role in how diaspora groups operated. Through the worship of their native gods, group members remained distinct from their hosts and connected to their place of origin, both necessary ingredients for successful intercommunity trade. Equally important, acts of religious devotion signaled commitment and loyalty to the group, encouraged collective action against defectors and fostered economic trust and collaborative behavior. Religious "honest signaling" was also helpful at the intercommunity level. It allowed diasporas to connect to other groups and to their hosts. By setting up inscriptions with religiously inspired wishes of well-being for reigning emperors, they displayed adherence to a shared imperial ideology,

---

113. On emergent properties, see Harré 1985: 145–46; Checkland 1999: 50; Ober 2015: 45.

thereby lowering intergroup social barriers and signaling their trustworthiness as commercial partners.

But this complex system of socioeconomic interaction came under pressure when emperors began legislating against pagan cults. Groups involved in long-distance trade could no longer employ their native religious practices to engage in internal "honest signaling," nor could they insert their religious practices into an imperial ideology as external "honest signals."[114] To investigate the institutional upset that these changes produced, the chapter will examine two well-documented instances of religious violence against pagan sanctuaries in Gaza and Alexandria, and one lesser known one in the city of Rome.

The Epilogue, chapter 6, will briefly discuss a topic mentioned in chapter 5 but not fully explored there: the weakening of the Roman state. In the third century CE the Roman empire began having trouble maintaining its geographical integrity, a problem that would grow noticeably worse thereafter. The split between an eastern and western half in 395 CE was the most dramatic manifestation of that decreasing ability. After the empire split in two, especially the west in the course of the fifth century saw the abandonment of peripheral areas, although signs of declining state power appeared in the east as well. But as the western half eventually disintegrated, the eastern half recovered. In the sixth century it managed to extend its rule over parts of the west, including the Italian heartland. But even with this westward expansion, and even allowing for healthy economic activity in some eastern regions, as a military and economic organization the Roman empire was nothing like the mighty state it once had been. A separate section will discuss the effects of the empire's disintegration on human welfare, the topic of current research based on archaeological data including skeletal remains.

Finally in the Concluding Remarks, chapter 7, I will offer some tentative thoughts on the impact of Roman imperial rule on the impetus toward innovation. I propose that although the political and economic unification of the Mediterranean reduced transaction costs, it may also have reduced the drive toward innovation in both a technological and an institutional sense.

114. On signaling, see Posner 2000: 18–27; Bulbulia and Sosis 2011; Leeson 2014.

2

Public Institutions and
Phoenician Trade

THE ABSENCE OF THIRD-PARTY ENFORCEMENT was a central problem for premodern trade, especially if it took place over long distances. A historically well-documented way to overcome that problem was to rely on so-called trade diasporas, a term coined by Abner Cohen. In a seminal study Cohen defined a trade diaspora as an overseas commercial network centered on its members' shared geographical or ethnic origin. It typically

> has an informal political organization of its own which takes care of stability of order within the one community. . . . It tends to be autonomous in its judicial organization. Its members form a moral community which constrains the behaviour of the individual and ensures a large measure of conformity with common values and principles.[1]

Because diasporas expand the possibilities of long-distance trade, they provide a valuable service to their members, making the fear of partial or complete exclusion an effective deterrent of misconduct. Punishment can follow misbehavior against the in-group but also against outsiders, whether they be traders of the host community or members of other diasporas.[2] The rule-setting aspect of diasporas renders them institutions in the abstract, while individual historical ones are organizations.[3] As they are self-enforcing, they are what Douglass North, John Wallis and Barry Weingast have called "adherent" organizations, within which cooperation "must be, at every point in time, incentive-compatible for all members."[4]

---

1. Cohen 1971: 267.
2. Greif 1989; 2006; 2012; Terpstra 2013.
3. Institutions distinct from organizations: North 1990: 3–6.
4. North, Wallis and Weingast 2009: 16.

Trust in diasporas' ability to achieve collective action against cheaters, opportunists and freeriders is critical for their success. Charles Tilly has therefore classified them as "trust networks," which "consist of *ramified interpersonal connections, consisting mainly of strong ties, within which people set valued,
consequential, long-term resources and enterprises at risk to the malfeasance, mistakes, or failures of others.*" Trust networks, including trade diasporas, can
be sustained because "they build controls over malfeasance and safeguards
against consequences of mistakes and failures into their routine operation. For
members of trade diasporas . . . the threats of shunning, shaming, and denial
of reciprocity loom much larger than in everyday social networks."[5]

The institution of the trade diaspora is a well-observed, global historical
phenomenon. It operated in Africa, the Americas, Europe and Asia, in some
cases in the remote past, in others in more recent history.[6] Trade diasporas are
known to have tied together also the Mediterranean of the Iron Age and the
classical Greek period. But their importance for the Hellenistic era and
Roman imperial period has been undervalued or missed altogether. In a land-
mark book, *Cross-Cultural Trade in World History*, Philip Curtin wrote:

> With Alexander's conquests, the problems of political jurisdiction weak-
> ened, and trade became still more open in the Mediterranean world. In the
> eastern basin of the sea, Greek became the international language of trade,
> as Latin was to be in the west. With these developments, trade diasporas . . .
> ceased to exist as a major factor in Mediterranean commerce. They had
> contributed greatly to the homogenizing of Mediterranean cultures, but
> the very fact of cultural convergence meant that they were no longer re-
> quired as they once had been.[7]

This view is fundamentally wrong. A degree of cultural convergence certainly occurred—the treacherous terrain of Hellenization and Romanization—but the process did not make the trade diaspora redundant. For that to
happen the conditions of the industrial world needed to obtain, including the
existence of a fast, reliable communication technology and the establishment
of third-party enforcement. The usefulness of the trade diaspora is underscored by the fact that it continued to live on for some time even when such
conditions did obtain. It was an influential institution still in the "first global
economy," ca. 1870–1914.[8]

5. Tilly 2005: 12–13, italics in original. On ancient trading associations and trust, see Gabrielsen 2016.

6. Cohen 1971; Curtin 1984; Stein 1999: 46–55; Brubaker 2005; Tilly 2005: 65–69; Jones 2007:
146–47.

7. Curtin 1984: 80–81.

8. Jones 2007: 146–47.

In light of the trade diaspora's centrality for premodern trade, a key question to address is how it interacted with the organization of the state. On the face of it, the impact of state formation on ancient Mediterranean diasporas might perhaps not be expected to have been particularly profound. After all, trade diasporas were private, self-policing organizations that existed precisely because state-provided enforcement was unavailable. At first glance it would thus seem that the public and the private realm occupied separate or perhaps rather complementary societal spaces. But drawing a neat line between the two risks losing sight of the fact that they interacted all but inevitably.

A promising theoretical avenue to address the question of how public and private institutions communicated is through North, Wallis and Weingast's concept of the natural state. As discussed in chapter 1, an essential element of that concept is that natural states are non-Weberian in nature. They rely on private-order solutions, as only "elite groups are able to use the third-party enforcement of the coalition to structure contractual organizations."[9] But despite natural states' non-Weberian institutional structure, they do interfere in the private economy, a characteristic captured by North, Wallis and Weingast in a "postulate" or "prediction": "All natural states control trade." Given my subject matter, this idea seems highly relevant. However, the broad-brush way in which it is presented renders it confusing and unhelpful. Do all natural states control all trade all the time? If that is the prediction's intended meaning, it obviously cannot be accepted. Unfortunately, its authors offer little explanation, in a footnote only adding: "Natural states always control who trades, and may also control the places they trade and the prices at which they trade."[10] But even qualified this way, the postulate is problematic. It seems hard to accept the premise that all states before the early nineteenth century always controlled who traded, and that the majority are still always doing so today.

But if the phrasing of the postulate is too unequivocal, the basic logic behind it, as it emerges from the overall narrative of *Violence and Social Orders*, makes sense. Governing coalitions in natural states are incentivized to promote trade because it enhances productivity and increases the potential for rents. At the same time, promoting trade means that outside groups have to be allowed access to tradable surplus, which bears the risk of diluting power. The resulting "schizophrenic relationship" of dominant coalitions of natural states to commerce, division of labor and specialization creates an ongoing source of tension.[11] In natural states "economics is politics by other means,"

9. North, Wallis and Weingast 2009: 30.
10. North, Wallis and Weingast 2009: 38 with n. 8.
11. North, Wallis and Weingast 2009: 41–51. Quotation on p. 41.

hence the prediction.[12] I think that the general idea has merit, but that it should be applied loosely, and not rigidly as North, Wallis and Weingast seem to have thought.[13] I further propose that we rephrase their postulate into a less pithy but more workable one: "All natural states desire to control trade where it has the potential to affect the governing coalition's hold on power."

Such a desire for control could manifest itself in civic bodies exercising authority over the overseas trade of their subjects, whose activities could be highly lucrative to the state and greatly beneficial to its governing coalition.[14] The operation of the Dutch East India Company (VOC) is one of the best known examples where the state played such a managing role. As Douglas Irwin has argued, the fact that the VOC enjoyed state backing gave it an advantage over its English rival, which was not under government control: "When the Dutch States General helped form the VOC in 1602, created managerial incentives in the charter to increase shipping volume, and insulated its managers from the demands of investors, it institutionalized a contractual incentive mechanism enabling the company to commit to a higher level of trade."[15]

If long-distance trading organizations could to a greater or lesser degree be controlled by their native public bodies, they were inevitably under the authority of the rule-setting institutions they encountered overseas. Cooperation with those institutions was critical to the effectiveness of trade diasporas, which by their nature had to straddle a divide. Of necessity they had to cultivate their distinctiveness from their hosts. Only by staying a separate entity and preventing dilution of their group could they remain a self-policing unit, able to overcome enforcement constraints. At the same time, to facilitate commercial exchange they obviously needed to be able to cross the boundary between them and their hosts. The nature of the interaction between foreign merchants and the civic institutions of host communities could vary widely. As Tilly observed, trade diasporas "generally make their peace with governments en route and at their destinations; relations between diasporas and regimes typically range from evasive conformity with existing governments through patronage by regional power holders to direct licensing or sponsorship by governments."[16]

12. North, Wallis and Weingast 2009: 72.

13. Cf. how North, Wallis and Weingast 2009: 57–58 present, e.g., the Aztec empire's alleged control over trade as an encompassing, top-down affair.

14. See Ogilvie 2011: 160–91 for medieval and Early-Modern ruling elites benefiting from merchant guilds.

15. Irwin 1991: 1308. For a more critical view of the VOC, see Ogilvie 2011: 114–15, 118, 131, 228–29.

16. Tilly 2005: 66.

To investigate these matters in the ancient Mediterranean, I will have to reduce the vast amount of source material to a manageable level. In what follows I will therefore focus on only a single diaspora, the Phoenician, which can be traced through centuries of time. Phoenician traders operating far from their homeland appear in our earliest literary sources and can still be found in the evidence from Roman imperial times. They can thus serve as a gauge for how state formation and the accompanying increase in sociopolitical complexity affected the way long-distance intercommunity trade was conducted.

Public involvement of Phoenician city-states in their native diasporas is visible in our oldest written evidence and continues to be traceable in later sources. In Hellenistic and Roman times, at least Tyre and Sidon, though incorporated into larger political units, still claimed authority over their native trading associations overseas. To be sure, not all Phoenician trade was under some form of public control. Literary evidence suggests that already some of the earliest Phoenician overseas merchants conducted their business in Mediterranean waters without any apparent connection to their native civic bodies.[17] Nonetheless, the evidence for public interference in diasporas shows that a strict division between a "private economy," driven by utility-maximizing individuals, and a "state economy," driven by governments spending tax revenue, leaves the picture incomplete. The way the economy of the ancient Mediterranean developed was characterized by more complex public-private interplay.

Public-private interaction can be seen equally in the intercommunity dynamic of Phoenician diasporas negotiating their position within their host societies. In all cases to be discussed, the state's role in trade dovetailed with merchants' agency in shaping the institutional environment. An emblematic institution enabling such fluid interaction was "public friendship" (*proxenia*), which was a way for Greek city-states to regulate access to their societies. Public friendship was a durable institution creating steady diplomatic and economic relations between two distant communities. Through its conferral city-states provided selected foreigners with special privileges, thus controlling who traded preferentially. The title of "public friend" (*proxenos*) was a powerful one. It gave its holder generationally transferable access not only to concrete rights but also to community-wide esteem in a foreign society. It thereby provided recipient diaspora traders with considerable social leverage and the incentives to use it dutifully, with the result that private-order enforcement strengthened.

By the time of the Roman empire, public friendship had lost the significance it had possessed previously, but another institution had emerged to serve as a public-private communication and cooperation mechanism. The

17. See Hodos 2006: 3–4 for a similar observation about the Iron Age generally.

social norms of Rome's imperial ideology aided diaspora groups in their co-ordination of collective action, once more strengthening the private order that underpinned trade. As with Greek "public friendship" of the preceding centuries, the process was reciprocal and mutually beneficial. Trading groups publicly displayed adherence to the state's ideology and expressed consensus with its rule, thereby contributing to the stability of imperial governance.

Phoenician Migration and Trade

The history of Phoenician interaction with the Mediterranean is usually divided into three blocks. First comes the period from the ninth to the sixth century BCE, when Phoenicians settled in the west. Next comes the period from the sixth century BCE to 332 BCE, when Carthage eclipsed its former metropolis of Tyre in economic and political importance. Finally, there is the period from 332 BCE and beyond, when Phoenician cities were incorporated into first the Hellenistic kingdoms and then the Roman empire. Within the last block, a separate narrative is usually reserved for the period between 264 and 146 BCE, when Carthage came into conflict with Rome, ultimately to be destroyed by it. Carving out such chronological blocks is not conducive to the clarity of my discussion. I will therefore treat the preclassical and the Greco-Roman period in an unbroken sequence, but limit my study to diasporas from Phoenician cities in the Levant, adding only a few remarks on pre-Roman Carthage in an appendix.

A few preliminary words are necessary here on the terms "Phoenicia" and "Phoenicians," which are not unproblematic. Both are geographical terms that also have chronological connotations. The coastal territory of Syria-Palestine is commonly called the land of Canaan in the Hebrew Bible.[18] Although the origins of the word are obscure, the name goes back at least to the Middle Bronze Age, as shown by the Ebla clay tablets (ca. 2500 BCE). Today the name Canaan is used to refer to the area from the mouth of the Orontes River in the north to Egypt in the south for the phase preceding the Iron Age, which started around 1200 BCE in the Near East.[19] A land of city-states, Bronze-Age Canaan was dominated by the powerful urban centers of Byblos, Tyre and Ugarit (fig. 2.1). It maintained intensive political and commercial relations with both Egypt and Mesopotamia.[20]

The transition from the Late Bronze Age to the Early Iron Age was a period of upheaval, population drift and societal collapse, affecting the region deeply.

18. Astour 1965; Markoe 2000: 10; Aubet 2001: 9–11; Hodos 2006: 3–4.
19. On the shift from the Bronze Age to the Iron Age, see Broodbank 2013: 445–505.
20. Markoe 2000: 15–17, 21–22; Aubet 2001: 13–25.

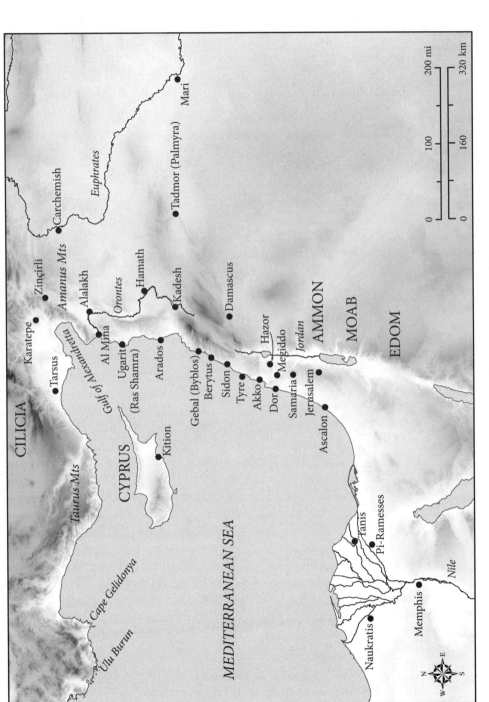

FIG. 2.1. The East Mediterranean with major Bronze Age and Iron Age cities.

Geopolitical shifts at the end of the Bronze Age reduced the size of the land of Canaan by two-thirds. The Israelite conquest of the south, the occupation of the southern coast by the Philistines and the settlement of the Aramaeans in the north claimed more than half of its coastline and much of its hinterland. These territorial losses left it a narrow coastal fringe from the isle of Arados in the north to Akko (Hellenistic-Roman Ptolemais) in the south, a strip of land just surpassing modern Lebanon in length.

For the ensuing period the remaining area is usually referred to as "Phoenicia" in the scholarly literature to distinguish it from Bronze-Age "Canaan," although there are problems with that convention. The word "Phoenicia" is not of Semitic but of Greek origin, and the inhabitants of this stretch of land never called it by that name, nor did they refer to themselves as "Phoenicians."[21] Individual cities always remained the focal point for self-identification and self-representation, an aspect related to the second problem with the designation "Phoenicia." The term appears to imply that the area was a unified state like Egypt or Assyria, which it was not. Phoenicia consisted of a patchwork of regions separated by river valleys and mountain spurs, a geography that hindered political coalescence.[22] Its coastal cities were also in constant competition for maritime trade, producing another impediment to interregional state formation. Both geographical and socioeconomic factors favored the concentration of power in the hands of autonomous city-states that shared a language and material culture but that were not centrally ruled.[23]

In the early ninth century BCE, Phoenicians spread to areas immediately surrounding their homeland, mainly to the north, where they began appearing around the Gulf of Alexandretta (fig. 2.1). Inscriptions in their language, dedications to the Tyrian ancestral god Melqart and passages in Assyrian annals show their presence also in Samaria, Neo-Hittite cities, Cilicia and on the banks of the Euphrates River in northern Syria.[24] Eventually they moved toward the west, far into the Mediterranean. But our literary and archaeological sources are not in agreement on when the process might have begun.

Classical authors hold that during the time of the Trojan War the maritime enterprise of the Phoenicians led them to Cyprus, Greece and farther west to Spain and Africa (Vell. Pat. 1.2.3; Strabo *Geogr.* 1.3.2; Pliny *NH* 16.216, 19.63; Sil. Ital. *Pun.* 3.241–42). According to the literary tradition, the oldest settlements were Utica (in Tunisia), Gadir (on the Atlantic coast of southern Spain) and Lixus (on the Atlantic coast of Morocco), all said to have been established

21. Aubet 2001: 6–13; Prag 2014; Xella 2014; Bell 2016: 92.

22. Marfoe 1979; Wagner and Alvar 1989: 63–64; Fales 2017: 207–08.

23. Pappa 2013: 1–3; Xella 2014.

24. Aubet 2001: 47–51; 87–88; Fales 2017: 193–96.

between 1110 and 1100 BCE. But so far the literary evidence has not been confirmed by the archaeological data. The earliest Phoenician material found at those sites dates to some four centuries later.[25] Still, it is worth noting that at Huelva, southern Spain, Levantine ceramics, balance weights and scraps of graffiti have recently been found in a layer from ca. 900 BCE.[26] Those finds open up the possibility that at Gadir, Utica and Lixus as well the archaeological dates may eventually be pushed back closer to the ones suggested by the written sources.

What prompted the Phoenicians to settle west as far as the Atlantic seaboard of Spain and Morocco is a debated question. Both overpopulation in the Levant and the allure of trade seem to have played a significant role in the push toward migration. In any case, there is little doubt that access to metals formed one of its driving forces.[27] Key supply areas where we see Phoenicians appearing are Cyprus (copper), Sardinia (silver, lead, copper, iron) and southern Spain (silver, gold, tin).[28] In antiquity the Phoenicians' attraction to metals was recognized as a motivation for their migration. Diodorus Siculus (5.35.4) comments that a search for silver had led them to Sicily, Sardinia, Spain and North Africa.

A Phoenician quest for metals in response to demands of tribute from the Assyrian empire is the theory traditionally put forward to explain this phenomenon. But Eleftheria Pappa has recently argued that this reading puts the cart before the horse: "Tribute would not have been imposed on the Phoenicians on the expectation of them reaching the other end of the known world and finding rich resources of silver and exotic products."[29] Phoenician involvement in the western metals trade must logically have developed prior to, and independently from, payments to Assyria, only subsequently to have provoked demands for tribute. New pottery and radiocarbon dates confirm that the Phoenicians were expanding westward before the Assyrian empire put pressure on their homeland.[30]

But although Pappa appears to be right in her revision both of the sequence of events and of cause and effect, she seems to assume that Phoenician sailors going west ventured into the great unknown. That, however, seems unlikely. They probably had a fairly accurate idea of what resources the west had to

25. Negbi 1992; Markoe 2000: 181, 187–88; Aubet 2001: 70–71, 161–65; Pappa 2013: 3–8.

26. Aubet 2008: 247–49; Broodbank 2013: 483–84; Bell 2016: 98–100.

27. Niemeyer 1990; Aubet 2001; Neville 2007; Pappa 2013. See McConnell et al. 2018 for evidence of Phoenician metallurgy in the Greenland ice sheet.

28. Giardino 1992; Pérez Macías 1996–97; Aubet 2001: 80; Gómez Toscano 2002. On Sardinian trade with the East Mediterranean, see Holt 2014: 5543.

29. Pappa 2013: 177–78. For the traditional view, see, e.g., Hodos 2006: 26–27.

30. Aubet 2008. See Fales 2017: 268–73 for a summary of the debate on Assyria's role.

offer. Bronze-Age societal collapse had produced severe and prolonged turbulence in the period before their migration. But a collective memory that had developed during centuries of Mediterranean interconnectedness seems to have stayed alive. In the words of Cyprian Broodbank, the Phoenicians at the time of their westward ventures were the "inheritors to a mass of orally transmitted, often mythologically encoded, knowledge about navigational conditions and hazards, memorized sequences of land- and seamarks, significant places, people and resources, and the intricacies of local custom, all accumulated by a multitude of anonymous Mediterranean seafarers."[31]

Whatever the nature of push and pull factors might have been, and whatever the balance between them, Phoenicians were notable participants in Mediterranean commercial exchange by the late eighth century BCE. Aside from the trade in metals and high-end goods with which they are mostly associated, they were capable agriculturalists who in their new environments cultivated staple foodstuffs, in some cases introducing new crops into their settlement areas.[32] Archaeological data show that they spread out from their nuclear settlements, working the surrounding fields. They established economies based on exchange with the indigenous populations and maintained both local and regional networks of trade in agricultural products.[33]

In the late seventh and early sixth centuries BCE, Phoenician cities came into conflict first with the Assyrian and then the Babylonian empire. Many Phoenician settlements lost their political connection to the Levantine homeland, even if cultural affinities continued to be felt. Carthage after its independence from Tyre in the sixth century acquired control of the Phoenician settlements in the west, eventually to become the heart of a naval empire controlling Spain, Sicily, Sardinia and stretches of the North African coast.[34] Independence from its metropolis had probably occurred before 525 BCE. In that year the Persian king, Cambyses, planned a naval attack on Carthage and ordered the Tyrians to join him. This they refused, as Herodotus tells us: "They were bound, they said, by a strict treaty, and could not righteously attack their own sons" (3.19).[35]

Contacts between Levantine cities and Carthage by no means ended, but the west became a separate entity from the metropolitan homeland. The word "Punic" is usually applied to this Carthaginian-controlled world, a term that is artificial yet useful for separating east and west, highlighting that the two

---

31. Broodbank 2013: 494.
32. Neville 2007: 116, 122.
33. Whittaker 1974; Wagner and Alvar 1989; Neville 2007: 105–34.
34. Neville 2007: 164–70; Ameling 2013; Bondì 2014: 61–62. See also the Appendix.
35. Tr.: A.D. Godley, *LCL* 1921.

had become culturally and politically distinct.[36] The strengthening interconnectedness in the west is interesting in its own right. But rather than trace
continued Punic connectivity I will focus here on the persistence of mercantile organizations from the east. The practice of trading through permanent
overseas settlers lived on in Phoenician cities in the Levant, even if the shape
and the settler-host dynamic of the networks changed in response to a changing political and economic landscape.

The independence of Carthage coincided with a general economic decline
of Phoenician cities. In 604 BCE the Babylonian king, Nebuchadnezzar II,
initiated a series of military campaigns, which would lead him west as far as
the Levantine coast. Encountering resistance at Tyre, he put up a land block-
ade around the city, a siege that we hear about from Ezekiel (29:18) and that
lasted thirteen years, according to Flavius Josephus (*C.Ap.* 1.156; *A.J.* 10.228).[37]
The Babylonian annexation of Palestine, the Transjordan and Cilicia blocked
both Arabian and Anatolian trade, and under Babylonian rule Phoenician cities seem to have reached a commercial low point.[38]

In 539 BCE, Babylon fell to King Cyrus of Persia, who incorporated the
territory of the Neo-Babylonian kingdom into his empire.[39] Active cooperation with the Persians in their war efforts won Phoenician cities not only Persian trust but also renewed commercial opportunities. Greek merchants had
meanwhile penetrated traditional Phoenician trading areas, including Cyprus,
Egypt and Rhodes, even reaching the northern Levantine coast.[40] It was presumably for this reason that, according to Herodotus (6.6.1), the Phoenicians
were eager for battle when in 494 BCE King Darius I planned a naval attack
on Miletos. Phoenician fleets also joined in the Greek invasions that the Persians undertook in the subsequent decades. Especially during the first half of
the fifth century, Greek feelings toward the Phoenicians cannot have been
particularly warm, and Greek texts indeed betray a negative attitude toward
them.[41] Nonetheless, trade with the Aegean did not cease. Fifth-century Attic
pottery has been found at Phoenician sites, as have coins from Athens and
other Greek cities. The coins were probably at least in part imported for their
metallic content. Phoenician cities began issuing their own currencies in the
mid-fifth century BCE and needed precious metals to do so.[42]

36. Bondì 2014.

37. On both texts, see Katzenstein 1997: 322–26, 330–32.

38. Markoe 2000: 47–49.

39. Wiesehöfer 2013: 199–202.

40. Markoe 2000: 49–52.

41. Mazza 1988: 559–60; Jigoulov 2010: 36–38.

42. Jigoulov 2010: 73, 100, 102–03, 117. Imitation Athenian coins identifying the issuing Phoe-

Throughout the period of Babylonian and Persian domination, Phoenicians appear to have remained a presence in some of the areas where they had landed at an early date, such as Cyprus and Rhodes. But in the fourth and third centuries BCE, they also began to settle in new centers of economic power, most notably Athens and Delos. For centuries they remained engaged in trade over long distances. Their merchants appear in Greek literary and epigraphic sources, and traders from Tyre and Berytus can still be found in the epigraphic record from Roman imperial times. In the troubled world of the fifth century CE, Tyrian merchants were apparently still a conspicuous presence. In his commentary on Ezekiel, written around 410 CE, the Christian scholar Jerome noted that up until his day,

> an ingrained passion for trade abides among the Syrians, who rush throughout the whole world out of the desire for profit, and their madness for trading merchandise is so great that . . . they seek riches in the midst of swords and the killing of wretched people. . . . It is businessmen of Tyre of this sort who are the ones who trade woven cloth, *purple, and embroidered works*, and they set out *fine linen too, and silk, and chodchod in* its *market*. (*Comm. Ezech.* 27.15–16)[43]

The Phoenician diaspora was shaped by specific cultural and historical factors that in many ways made it unique. But its chronological depth and geographical reach also provide it with singular historical relevance. As Fergus Millar observed,

> we really could now write a Phoenician-Punic oriented history of the Mediterranean from the eighth century onwards, which would focus on the nature, spread, survival, and decline of Phoenician-Punic culture in Phoenicia itself, in Cyprus, in North Africa, in Sicily, in Spain, in Sardinia, and marginally in Italy. We are not talking about an insignificant or short-lived phenomenon.[44]

I will study the influence of emerging public institutions on overseas trade, not the spread of Phoenician-Punic culture, as Millar suggested. But precisely the aspects of longevity and geographical range that he emphasized render the Phoenician diaspora well suited as a focal point for such a study.

---

nician workshops may have been the first runs of newly operating mints rather than counterfeit currency.

43. Tr.: Scheck 2017: 306, italics are Scheck's. Jerome writes that he was unable to find the meaning of the word *chodchod* in Ez. 27:16. *NRSV*: "rubies."

44. Millar 2006: 35.

Phoenician Trade and Domestic Institutions

Biblical texts provide much of the literary evidence for early Phoenician history. They contain hints that by the beginning of the first millennium BCE Phoenician royal houses were engaged in maritime affairs.[45] The treaty between the Tyrian king Hiram I and the Israelite king Solomon mentioned in the first book of Kings suggests that Tyre's royalty controlled a labor force of sailors. Promising to supply Solomon with cedar and cypress wood, Hiram declared: "My servants shall bring it down to the sea from the Lebanon; I will make it into rafts to go by sea to the place you indicate" (1 Kgs 5:6–11).[46] Another passage relates how Hiram and Solomon embarked on a joint maritime venture. Reportedly the two monarchs built and outfitted ships to sail to what the Biblical text calls "Ophir," a land with unknown whereabouts but probably either in East Africa or the southwestern Arabian Peninsula.[47] The passage says that Hiram contributed his personal specialists in sailing and navigation to the project: "Hiram sent his servants with the fleet, sailors who were familiar with the sea, together with the servants of Solomon" (1 Kgs 9:26–28).[48]

The single most important written source for the history of the area during this period is a papyrus text in the late Egyptian language, written in Hieratic script and dating to ca. 1000 BCE. It contains the first-person account of Wen-Amon, who claimed to be an Egyptian envoy sent to the Phoenician city of Byblos to obtain timber for a ceremonial barge for the god Amon. It is often regarded as a piece of fiction rather than an actual travel diary, but there is little doubt that its portrayal of the political and economic relations between Egypt and Byblos is essentially accurate.[49]

Just as the Biblical passages, the story provides information on Phoenician seafaring enterprise under royal management. To accomplish his mission, Wen-Amon approached King Zakar-Baal of Byblos. The king told him that the royal house possessed fifty coastal ships anchored in Sidon and another twenty seagoing ones anchored at home. Moreover, Zakar-Baal specified that the twenty ships in Byblos were in what the text calls a ḥbr, meaning an "association" or "trading partnership," with the Egyptian ruler Smendes.[50] The

45. Bondì 1978; Aubet 2001: 114–19.

46. Tr.: *NRSV*.

47. Katzenstein 1997: 109; Beitzel 2010: 37. Cf. Lipiński 2004: 191–202, who argues for a Mediterranean location.

48. Tr.: *NRSV*.

49. On Wen-Amon, see Greig 1990: 336–42; Egberts 1991; Katzenstein 1997: 71–73; Markoe 2000: 26–28.

50. On the meaning of the word ḥbr, see Katzenstein 1983; 1997: 70; Krahmalkov 2000: 175–76.

arrangement of a fleet run jointly by two monarchs is reminiscent of the partnership between Hiram and Solomon. King Jehoshaphat of Judah and King Ahaziah of Israel are later also said to have cooperated in this way in an (ill-fated) attempt to revive the Ophir trade (1 Kgs 22:48; 2 Chron. 20:35–36).

The phenomenon of Phoenician monarchs managing their personal merchantmen was not limited to tenth-century Byblos. A clay tablet from 676 BCE contains the text of a treaty between the Assyrian king Esarhaddon and the Tyrian king Baal. A clause stipulated that if Tyrian ships were to go down in Assyrian-controlled waters, ownership of the cargo would fall to Esarhaddon. The treaty specified that the clause would apply to either "a ship of Baal or the people of Tyre," making a distinction between the royal fleet and ships of the city's private citizens.[51]

To return to the Wen-Amon papyrus, the text says that fifty of King Zakar-Baal's ships were anchored in Sidon and were managed together with an otherwise unknown man named Werket-El. He is said to have lived in Tanis, Egypt, but there is general agreement that his name suggests a non-Egyptian origin. His ethnicity is unclear.[52] If he did indeed exist, he may have been the Sidonian king sojourning overseas, although the text does not provide any evidence for that hypothesis. More likely he was a Sidonian merchant, perhaps residing in Egypt for reasons of business. If so, he must have been an exceedingly wealthy individual possessing an economic power not far removed from that of royalty. Werket-El may or may not have been a fictional character, but several Biblical texts suggest that Phoenician cities had an influential socioeconomic stratum of such men. Isaiah describes a Tyre "whose merchants were princes, whose traders were the honored of the earth" (23:8). Ezekiel, in a prophecy against the same city, speaks of the "princes of the sea" who at the day of reckoning he foretells "shall step down from their thrones; they shall remove their robes and strip off their embroidered garments" (26:16).[53]

Wen-Amon mentions a Byblian assembly, which King Zakar-Baal convoked on meeting with the Tjekker people who were demanding the extradition of the Egyptian envoy. The El-Amarna tablets as well refer to such royal counselors, showing that they were a presence in Byblos, Simyra and Arados by the fourteenth century BCE.[54] These "lords of the city" or "city rulers" seem to have been members of a powerful elite advising the king on military

---

51. Parpola and Watanabe 1988: no. 5, col. 3, l. 15–17. See also Bondì 1978: 142–43; Katzenstein 1997: 272–73; Aubet 2001: 119; Fales 2017: 241–43.

52. On Werket-El, see Katzenstein 1983: 601–02; 1997: 60–61; Manfredi 2003: 341–42.

53. Tr.: *NRSV*.

54. *EA* nos. 138 (Byblos), 157 (Simyra) and 149 (Arados). On such counselors, see Katzenstein 1997: 30–31.

matters. A Tyrian council of elders also appears in that role in the above-mentioned treaty between King Baal of Tyre and King Esarhaddon of Assyria.[55] The common scholarly view is that the mercantile "princes" of Ezekiel and Isaiah comprised the majority of those elders and that Tyre and the other major Phoenician cities were ruled by "merchant oligarchies."[56]

All the same, not all Phoenician traders were associated with their city-states' governing elites. The ones we encounter in the Homeric epics seem to have been operating in Mediterranean waters without any connection to the royal houses or political bodies of their native cities. In one of the lengthier passages where they appear, the swineherd Eumaeus, an aristocrat by birth, tells the tale of how he ended up a slave in Odysseus' palace (Hom. *Od.* 15.415–84). Phoenician traders had come to his father's house bringing pretty objects and jewelry, which they sought to exchange for goods to bring back to their homeland. On discovering that a slave woman working in the palace was originally from Sidon, the Phoenicians proposed to return her to her native city. She agreed, offering to steal as much gold as she could in recompense and promising to bring them the child Eumaeus to sell into slavery. Few specifics are given on the merchandise that the traders either bought or sold; the items they carried with them are only referred to as "beautiful objects" (*athyrmata*). Some details are provided further on in the story, where one of the sailors is described as showing the ladies of the palace a necklace in gold and amber, which the women admiringly fondled and offered to buy.

Though fictional the story suggests that Phoenician itinerant traders sailed around the Greek islands on long journeys—they stayed for a year at the palace of Eumaeus' father—seeking principally to barter jewelry and other decorative artifacts, but not eschewing the opportunities of the slave trade if and when they arose.[57] Another passage in the *Odyssey* (14.287–309) points in the same direction, at least where impromptu slave trading is concerned. In Egypt Odysseus met a Phoenician merchant, a man "well skilled in beguilements."[58] The man convinced Odysseus to accompany him to his homeland, where he had a house and other possessions. After a year had lapsed the Phoenician sent a cargo to Libya, putting Odysseus aboard the vessel under false pretenses, in reality intending to sell him into slavery on arrival in Africa. Odysseus narrowly escaped that fate when the ship went down in a storm brought on by Zeus.

It should be noted that the second Homeric story presents a fundamentally different kind of Phoenician trade from the first. The mendacious merchant

55. Parpola and Watanabe 1988: no. 5, col. 3, l. 7.

56. Katzenstein 1997: 272; Markoe 2000: 87–88, 91; Aubet 2001: 145–46.

57. Sommer 2007: 100.

58. Tr.: Richard Lattimore, 1965. New York: Harper and Row.

sent a shipment directly from his homeland to Libya, suggesting that he was involved in business affairs distinct from ad hoc trading with multiple stopping points. Phoenician shipping of that nature finds confirmation in maritime archaeology. Two eighth-century BCE Phoenician shipwrecks found off the coast of Ascalon were carrying mainly wine amphorae.[59] That type of cargo implies point-to-point shipping rather than *cabotage,* and in any case economic activities different from the peddling of metalwork described in the story about Eumaeus.[60] But one way or the other, the Homeric epics suggest the existence of Phoenician private traders doing business independently from any royal palace. "Phoenician city-states possibly were dependent on a mixed economy of state intervention and private entrepreneurship, a distinction that remained fluid."[61] How much overseas trade had some public involvement and how much relied entirely on private enterprise the sources unfortunately do not allow us to determine.

A question related to the one about Phoenician ruling coalitions' intervention in maritime trade is how much control they had over their overseas settlements. Evidence is thin, but the available epigraphic and literary sources do suggest that Phoenician royalty exercised a measure of authority. Early on, Tyre seems to have governed directly several colonies on Cyprus.[62] Fragments of two Cypriote bronze bowls show mutilated inscriptions dated to the mid-eighth century BCE. Both contain honorific dedications to Baal Libnan by a *skn,* meaning "governor" or "representative," who in one of the texts proclaims himself to be a servant of King Hiram.[63] An inscription on a sarcophagus attests to the presence of a Tyrian government official (*skn ṣr*) at Kition still in the fourth century BCE, suggesting that the settlement remained connected to Tyre, despite having long since become independent from it.[64] Tyre's desire for a continued political influence on Cyprus is understandable given the island's geographical location and metallic resources. Not only is it the first stopping point going west from the Levantine coast but it is also a major source of copper.

Apart from founding settlements in metal-rich areas, Phoenicians established trading posts in Greek city-states, which emerged in a process of state

59. Stager 2003.

60. On *cabotage,* see Horden and Purcell 2000: 133–52.

61. Pappa 2013: 183. Similarly, Bell 2016: 94.

62. Yon 1997; Smith 2008.

63. *KAI* no. 31. On the inscriptions, see Cooke 1903: no. 11; Masson and Sznycer 1972: 73–74, 77–78; Katzenstein 1997: 207–10; Krahmalkov 2000: 342–43; Manfredi 2003: 339–41, 348; Smith 2008: 272–73.

64. Masson and Sznycer 1972: 69–76; Guzzo Amadasi and Karageorghis 1977: no. F6.

formation between the eighth and sixth centuries BCE.[65] Resident trading groups seem initially to have been limited in number, due perhaps to Greek distrust because of the Phoenician cities' military collaboration with the Persians. But eventually Phoenician trading groups became a noticeable presence in the Greek world. By the fourth century several of them were firmly established at Athens, as demonstrated by the city's epigraphic record. A number of inscriptions contain hints that they were connected to the governing bodies of their native cities.

One such inscription, dating to the 360s BCE, shows that a political decision by the Sidonian king Straton (Abdashtart I) had positively affected the economic conditions under which his subjects at Athens operated. The text contains an Athenian public decree honoring Straton for the diplomatic help he had provided Athenian ambassadors on their way to meet with the Persian king.[66] A rider to the decree, proposed by a certain Menexenos, granted Sidonian merchants at Athens exemption from the foreign-resident poll tax, the liturgy for festival choruses and property taxes.

We do not know who Menexenos was, although he may have been the man by that name involved in financial affairs mentioned by Isocrates (*Trap.* 9). If so, he may have been a local Athenian business contact of the Sidonians. True or not, the question is why he proposed the rider. He may have intended this step as a reward for King Straton's assistance. The key issue would then be whether Straton had anticipated the response, in which case we would be witnessing a Sidonian public policy of sorts aimed at promoting trade. But Darel Engen has suggested a different scenario: Menexenos saw the public decree to honor Straton as "a good opportunity to grant privileges to Sidonian traders in order to encourage them to continue to trade with Athens."[67] One way or the other, the diplomatic help of a Sidonian monarch to Athens had resulted in his subjects enjoying a favorable fiscal position there.

A marble altar with a mid-third-century BCE date provides more epigraphic evidence for ties between a group of Phoenician settlers at Athens and their native political institutions.[68] The altar is inscribed with two lines in Phoenician saying that it was commissioned by one Ben-Ḥodeš and

65. Mediterranean state formation: Osborne 2009; Terrenato and Haggis 2011; Hansen 2013; Morris 2013.

66. *IG* 2.2.141, l. 29–36. See Schürer 1986: 109–10; Grainger 1991: 205–06, 212; Engen 2010: 321–22; Jigoulov 2010: 64–65; Demetriou 2012: 206–08; Reger 2013: 149.

67. Engen 2010: 321. On the economic significance of public grants of tax exemptions (*ateleia*), see also Gabrielsen 2011: 235–38.

68. *CIS* 1.118 (= *KAI* no. 58; Cooke 1903: no. 34). See also Baslez 1986: 289; Lipiński 2004: 170–71.

consecrated to Sakun, a god equivalent to the Greek Hermes. Ben-Ḥodeš' father is identified as a judge or magistrate (*špṭ*) and his grandfather as a seal-keeper (*ḥtm*), meaning perhaps some type of notary.[69] The dedicant thus seems to have come from a family with a tradition of holding official positions of governance, although in what city we do not know. The titles may in fact not even refer to domestic administration. Ben-Ḥodeš' father could have been the head of one of the Phoenician trading associations at Athens, and could for that reason have been called a *špṭ* or *suffete*, as the word is usually transcribed. But more likely he had been a magistrate in the homeland. *Suffetes* are mostly attested in the Punic world, specifically at Carthage, but they existed in Phoenician cities as well.[70] Josephus (*C.Ap.* 1.21) mentions sixth-century BCE Tyrian *dikastai*, the Greek translation of *suffetes*; a *dikastês* appears in a third-century BCE Greek inscription from Sidon; and the word *suffete* is also listed in a similarly dated Phoenician inscription from Tyre.[71]

The question of what the magistracy entailed by the time Ben-Ḥodeš set up his altar is not easy to answer. By then a radical constitutional change had taken place in Phoenician cities: the abolition of kingships in favor of republican forms of government.[72] This change was precipitated by Alexander's conquests, but much about how it unfolded is lost to time. It seems to have taken some fifty years to complete, probably starting with Byblos and ending with Arados.[73] In 259 BCE, Arados started minting coins counting from a new era, perhaps commemorating the start of republican rule. This theory is based solely on the numismatic evidence, though, and is not supported by any other source. Alternative explanations are possible. It could be, for instance, that Antiochus II, about to embark on the second Syrian war around that time and in need of local allies, had conferred a special status on the city.[74] But either way, when in 218 BCE Antiochus III marched along the Levantine coast, "the people of Arados came to him asking for an alliance," as Polybius (5.68.7) recounts.[75] By that year at least, there no longer was an Aradian sovereign to represent the city.

A second-century CE Italian inscription, discussed farther down, together with Roman-era epigraphic evidence from Phoenicia itself shows that eventu-

69. See Krahmalkov 2000: 200, 477 on the meaning of the Phoenician words.

70. Punic *suffetes*: Cooke 1903: commentary to no. 42; Markoe 2000: 88–90.

71. Sidonian *dikastês*: Moretti 1953: no. 41; Tyrian *suffete*: Cooke 1903: no. 8. See Bikerman 1939: 97–99 and Teixidor 1979 for a discussion of Phoenician *suffetes*.

72. Grainger 1991: 55–66; Millar 2006: 41–43.

73. No king of Byblos is recorded after Enylos, mentioned by Arrian (*Anab.* 2.20.1): Grainger 1991: 58.

74. Seyrig 1951: 213–16; Grainger 1991: 56.

75. Tr.: W.R. Paton, *LCL* 1923.

ally the systems of government that replaced the monarchies were in the Greek mold of a city council and people's assembly.[76] But it is unclear how closely Greek-style constitutions were followed, nor is it clear whether they were adopted wholesale or introduced piecemeal. By the Hellenistic period Phoenician public officials with Greek titles were active. A Sidonian chief magistrate (*archon*), for instance, appears in a document on papyrus dated 260–256 BCE.[77] However, we know next to nothing about such magistrates, and deciding on their competences based on possible Greek parallels is risky.

A mid-third-century BCE inscription from Athens suggests that Phoenician city constitutions had changed, or were in the process of changing, into Greek-style ones with city councils and assemblies. It contains an honorary, bilingual decree in Phoenician and Greek. According to the Phoenician text, "it was resolved by the Sidonians in assembly" that a certain Šama'baal, a superintendent of a body of men "in charge of the temple and in charge of the buildings in the temple court," be awarded a gold crown for his services.[78] What deities the Sidonians in Athens were venerating at their temple is not stated, but it is a safe assumption that the god Nergal was among them. A mid-third-century BCE Athenian grave inscription mentions a Sidonian priest of that deity.[79]

The crucial question for my purposes is who "the Sidonians in assembly" were. Below the text in Phoenician a single line in Greek reads: "the *koinon* of the Sidonians (for) the Sidonian Diopeithes," a personal name that is an approximate Greek rendering of Šama'baal. On the analogy of the later Phoenician trading associations (*koina*) on Delos, the word *koinon* here almost certainly refers to the Sidonians established at Athens. It could have been this group who in a local gathering had voted to honor one of their own.

However, Javier Teixidor has argued that the phrase "the Sidonians in assembly" is unlikely to have indicated the group of migrant settlers.[80] First of all, the ethnic identifier is too broad for such a restricted group. In addition, in

76. Sartre 2005: 158, pointing also to officials with Greek titles, e.g., gymnasiarchs at Arados and Byblos.

77. *P.Mich.Zen.* 3 (= Moretti 1953: no. 41). See Bagnall 1976: 22–23; Durand 1997: no. 40; Bonnet 2014: 294–96.

78. *KAI* no. 60 (= *IG* 2.2.2946; Cooke 1903: no. 33). Tr.: Gibson 1982: no 41. The date is either 96 BCE or, more likely, the mid-third century BCE: Teixidor 1980: 457–60. On this inscription, see also Schürer 1986: 109; Ameling 1990; Lipiński 2004: 171–72; Millar 2006: 40; Jigoulov 2010: 63–64; Demetriou 2012: 209–11.

79. *RÉS* no. 1215 (= *CIS* 1.119; *IG* 2.2.10271; Cooke 1903: no. 35). On this text, see Demetriou 2012: 208–09.

80. Teixidor 1980: 454–55, 460. Note that he interprets *koinon* as referring to the Sidonian citizenry; cf. Ameling 1990.

an inscription from Sidon dating to the third or second century BCE, the word "assembly" (*'spt*) refers to a municipal legislative body.[81] In Teixidor's reading a general assembly in Sidon had decreed that the community living in Athens should honor one of its members. Such a decision implies that a political body in the homeland possessed information on the performance of an overseas trading group and had the authority to act on that information. The mention of compensation for services rendered suggests that the assembly members were aware of the usefulness to Sidon of the Athenian settlers.

Walter Ameling has contested Teixidor's reading, attributing the decree for Šama'baal to the Sidonians established at Athens. But it would be highly unusual for a diaspora group to grant an honorand a gold crown by vote in a formal gathering and to record the decision in a public inscription. By contrast, it was common for the Athenian assembly to do so (some examples are in the section on Athens below). It seems to me more plausible that what we are seeing is a newly minted Sidonian public body emulating the Athenian practice. Moreover, Ameling's interpretation is in large part based on an alleged absence of other instances of Phoenician municipal institutions exercising authority over their overseas trading groups. But he dismisses an inscription from Puteoli, Italy, which Teixidor in my view correctly presents as a parallel.

The Puteolan inscription is much longer than the one from Athens and much richer in historical detail. It says that in 174 CE a group of men from Tyre domiciled in Puteoli sent a letter to the public authorities of their native city.[82] The reason for their missive, they explained, was to request help with rent payments for a communal building that they were leasing. Strictly speaking they were asking that Tyre take over the annual rent, presumably from the city's public purse. But they also reminded the council and assembly that their station, unlike its counterpart in Rome, did not receive fees from shipowners and merchants, which suggests that they were in reality thinking of a different solution. The reply they received is also inscribed, and it would seem that the city council picked up on the hint and gave them what they were angling for. It decreed that the Tyrians in Rome were to pay the rent for the building in Puteoli. It seems unlikely that the Roman-based Tyrians, who seem not to have been consulted on any of this, could have ignored the council's decision against them.[83] Their Puteolan colleagues inscribed the decree in stone and evidently considered the matter settled.

81. Cooke 1903: no. 7 with Teixidor 1979.

82. *IG* 14.830 (= *OGIS* 595; *IGRR* 1.421). On this inscription, see Terpstra 2013: 70–84.

83. Ameling 1990: 193–94 overlooks this sign of the council's authority.

An important question that unfortunately has no obvious answer is what means the council might have had to enforce its decision. The Tyrians in Puteoli claimed that "our fatherland provides for two stations" (l. 40–41). Based on that phrase, we can speculate that public money went to Italy and that cutting off funding might have been an option. But no mention of such funding is made in the inscription, and it is clear that lease sums were not paid by Tyre. Perhaps we should instead be thinking of coercion through the threat of ending agency relations. The councilors might have had shared interests with the agents' principals; it is equally conceivable that some of them *were* the principals. But regardless of how the decision was enforced, a hint of what was at stake is a mention of the advantage to Tyre that the overseas group provided. The councilors in their discussion of the request proclaimed that a continued presence of the Puteolan station was "to the benefit of the city" (l. 37), which seems to have been more than rhetoric. In all likelihood they based their assessment on accurate information. The petitioners wrote that there were many establishments in Puteoli similar to their own, "as most of you know" (l. 6).

If details escape us, the conclusion must be that well-informed civic bodies in Tyre cooperated with, and had authority over, agents stationed overseas and that this arrangement was perceived to be in the city's interest by its governing establishment. Of course, Roman-era Tyre was no longer an independent city-state. But the Roman empire was not, and could not be, centrally ruled from the capital. The imperial state left much day-to-day administration to local urban governments, especially in domestic affairs such as this one.

Phoenician Trade and Greco-Roman Institutions

Regardless of any control from their domestic civic bodies, diasporas were under some form of political control from their hosts. Cooperation with their host societies was essential to their success as trading organizations, and they had to take care in navigating the public institutional environment they encountered overseas. In the Aegean, Phoenician traders were confronted with increasingly mature political institutions following the process of state formation there starting in the eighth century BCE. They had to adapt to the sociopolitically complex environment that eventually emerged, but could also turn it to their advantage.

Many Greek cities were generally wary of foreign elements, as Alain Bresson noted in a study on the right of entry into Greek harbors: "Greek political thought . . . in different forms displays a permanent concern for keeping foreigners at bay, especially merchants. . . . In the classical period the prototype of a city generous with its access to foreigners was Athens. . . . Still, even in the most open of cities their potential closure to strangers remained a basic principle of sovereignty."[84] Such restricted access and desire for control over trade and traders seems to agree with the fundamental logic of the natural state. However, classical Athens had a democratic form of government and was not ruled by a small coalition of rent-seeking elites held together by a need for conflict control. The question thus inevitably presents itself: Does it qualify as a natural state?

Oddly enough, given the importance of that question for the validity of their framework, North, Wallis and Weingast have little to say on the matter. In an aside they call Athens a "mature natural state," and thus ultimately an oligarchy, although one that was "on the doorstep of the transition" to an open-access society.[85] Broodbank's assessment of classical Athens in his study of Mediterranean *longue durée* history seems broadly in agreement with that view. In his judgment the city represented the far side of a sliding scale of oligarchies typical of the contemporary Greek world. The "creation of several tens of thousands of adult male citizens throughout Athens and Attica (at best a fifth of the total population, and, of course, excluding all women, slaves and foreigners) simply represented one end of a spectrum that ran through large, inclusive oligarchies such as Sparta's."[86] By contrast, Josiah Ober firmly rejects the notion that Athens might have been a natural state. Accentuating the city's democratic credentials, he judges that it "diverged markedly" from the model: "Natural states are not democratic; they seek to restrict access to institutions; they tend not to extend rights to secure possession of property or other privileges beyond the small and tightly patrolled ambit of the ruling coalition."[87]

This is a complex issue, partly because North, Wallis and Weingast's binary framework is too rigid, partly because at the most basic level valuating Greek democracy is a matter of seeing the glass as half full or half empty. The true depth of classical Greek democracy is too big a topic to be treated satisfactorily here. But an exhaustive discussion is also not necessary. What matters for my purposes is that Greek city-states, including Athens, displayed natural-state behavioral characteristics in desiring to control trading access to their societies.

In developing procedures for selected outsiders to acquire publicly conferred status, they both facilitated and regulated foreign merchants' interaction with their communities. An important civic institution of that type involved awarding a noncitizen the honorific title of "public friend" (*proxenos*),

84. Bresson 2007: 39–40.

85. North, Wallis and Weingast 2009: 150, 195.

86. Broodbank 2013: 583.

87. Ober 2015: 10–11. See Zuiderhoek 2017: 79–80 for a brief, general discussion with references on the debate about Greek democracy.

a grant that entailed not only rights but also duties. A public friend provided services to the city-state that honored him, receiving privileged status there in return.[88] He was also expected to represent the interests of that city-state in his home community. A public friend, who could but need not reside in the granting city, performed an intermediary role between two distant polities, tying them together through his benefactions and position as representative. Through such men, cities maintained networks of cooperation that could encompass diplomatic and political but also economic and trade-related matters.[89]

To remain meaningful, the grant of public friendship must have been subject to rigorous supervision by city-states' political institutions. But its controlled conferral by no means rendered it a marginal phenomenon, as shown by the roughly 2,500 securely identified decrees voted on over a span of about five centuries, starting around 500 BCE. Moreover, inscribing a decree in stone and putting it up in a public space was supplementary to the status it already provided an honorand. The implication is that many, if not most, decrees will never have been inscribed. We can only guess at what we are not seeing, but in William Mack's "very conservative" estimate the sum total must have been in the vicinity of 1.2 million, which, if anywhere near the mark, is a staggering number indeed.[90]

The fact that not all decrees were inscribed also means that the first epigraphic attestations of public friendship almost certainly postdate its genesis as an institution. For Greek city-states, extending the honor was an expression of what it meant to act as a political entity. The emergence of the practice seems to have had deep historical roots and seems to have been intimately related to early state formation. As Malcolm Wallace wrote, "Few aspects of Greek inter-state relations . . . so graphically illustrate the detailed workings of the slowly widening archaic political consciousness."[91] His study of early evidence for public friendship suggests that the institution dates back to the mid-sixth century BCE and had fully developed by the start of the fifth. It probably originated in mainland Greece and from there spread quickly to the larger Greek world, including Sicily and the southern Italian mainland (see the Appendix for a fourth-century BCE example also from North Africa).

In the standard granting procedure, the city council and people's assembly of a city-state decided to elevate a foreigner to the status of public friend on

88. *Proxenoi* were almost without exception male. To date, only eight *proxenia* decrees for women are known: Mack 2015: 25 n. 8.

89. Mack 2015: 32–43, 59–64.

90. Mack 2015: 14–15 with n. 35: eighty *proxenoi* in 1,000 *poleis*, renewed three times a century, 500 to 1 BCE.

91. Wallace 1970: 189.

the recommendation of one of their citizens. Typically the grant was made hereditary, applying also to the honorand's male offspring. Greek political bodies thus provided selected foreigners with not only personalized but also multigenerational privileges. The institution of public friendship was a powerful device that could be greatly beneficial to diaspora trade. It gave foreigners both the means and the incentives to act as "cross-cultural brokers," enabling them to establish intercommunity relations that were more encompassing than personal business connections, which by their nature were socially restricted and ephemeral.[92]

The award of public friendship was almost always accompanied by the grant of the title *euergetês* or "benefactor." But the honor of being named a benefactor was also regularly granted in isolation. This distinct use of the two terms is indicative of the different meanings they carried. Men who were public friends were considered to be benefactors as well, but of a specific kind. Men who were solely benefactors, on the other hand, had done well for a city in ways that did not warrant the grant of public friendship.[93] In the classical Greek period, being named a benefactor was an honor almost exclusively restricted to foreigners. The reason for denying citizens the opportunity to distinguish themselves in this way was probably a desire not to disrupt the egalitarian ethos of the city-state.[94] But in any case, with its restriction to foreigners, the honor, like public friendship, constituted an institution dedicated to the construction of intercommunity ties.

The number of public friendship decrees along with other grants of interstate honors decreased markedly in the second half of the second century BCE, to go into precipitous decline after ca. 100 BCE. The institution can still be traced in the second-century CE epigraphic record, but by that time it was no more than a faint echo of what it had been.[95] As public friendship was a means of regulating interstate affairs—both diplomatic and economic—its disappearance seems to be indicative of more general changes in the way states interacted.

Mack indeed places the dissolution of the institution in the context of larger interstate developments in the ancient Mediterranean. He argues that the weight of the Roman republic as the increasingly authoritative source of state prestige led to a reduced emphasis on Greek intercity connections. The pro-

---

92. "Cross-cultural brokers" is the term Curtin 1984: 2 introduced to explain the function of diaspora traders.

93. Mack 2015: 38–43.

94. Engen 2010: 148 makes that argument for classical Athens. For the different kind of *euergetism* operating under the Roman empire, see Zuiderhoek 2009.

95. Mack 2015: 233–81.

cess of institutional redirection continued under the empire, when Greek cities began to compete for new, Rome-oriented honorary titles such as "provincial center of the imperial cult" (*neôkoros*).[96] As Mack explains it, what happened is that the complex of Greek interstate honorific institutions had been

> a pluralistic system in which authority was dispersed, albeit never evenly, between the state-actors within it. . . . Rome's rise to a position of domination first reduced the importance for *poleis* of advertising or commemorating these social networks in that it constituted a higher and more final authority. Eventually, by monopolizing authority within the interstate system in ways which had been beyond the Hellenistic kings, and thereby monopolizing also symbols of prestige, it undermined the euergetical basis of these institutions. . . . Some of the institutional effort which cities had previously placed into establishing and maintaining links with peer-polities was now redirected to Rome.[97]

This explanation seems convincing to me, although I think that the Hellenistic kingdoms' limited effect on public friendship was not due solely to their inability to exert their authority Mediterranean-wide. In my view the successor states could well have assumed the same prestige-monopolizing role that Rome would later possess, certainly for urban trade networks falling within their respective borders. I suggest that under Hellenistic rule the style of royal governance was an equally significant factor in the continuation of public friendship. Hellenistic kings presented themselves as the champions of Greek freedom, leaving cities a large degree of autonomy not only for reasons of expediency but also of ideology and rule legitimization.[98] All the same, in my view Mack is right in pointing to Rome's growing hegemony as the determining factor in the decline of public friendship.

The increasing Roman influence on Mediterranean institutional development after the mid-second century BCE is reflected in the operation of the Phoenician trade diaspora. First of all, when the center of economic power shifted westward to Italy, the diaspora's settlement pattern changed accordingly. Phoenicians did not abandon the Greek world, but evidence suggests that Rome and Puteoli became the main focus of their activities. Second, with the geopolitical focus shifting away from Greek cities, the settler-host dynamic changed. Public friendship decrees for Phoenicians disappear from our evidence. What we witness instead is Phoenicians publicly showing allegiance to the power of Rome in general and, under the principate, specifically the

96. Mack 2015: 276. On *neôkoreia*, see Burrell 2004.

97. Mack 2015: 277–78.

98. On Hellenistic kings and Greek cities, see Strootman 2011.

person of the emperor. In so doing they followed an emerging practice of emperor worship, which would eventually grow into what is commonly called the "imperial cult."

That phrase is useful as a shorthand, although it should be emphasized that there was never a single entity identifiable as "the" imperial cult practiced uniformly throughout the empire. Rather "there was a series of different cults sharing a common focus in the worship of the emperor, his family or predecessors, but ... operating quite differently according to a variety of different local circumstances."[99] Still, I propose that emperor worship constitutes what Arthur Denzau and North have called a "shared mental model." Such a model facilitates group coordination by providing "those who share it ... with a set of concepts and language which makes communication easier."[100] Despite its different outward forms, emperor worship provided the inhabitants of the empire with a common ideological language, conceptually connected to the authority of the central state (see also chapters 4 and 5).

With the consolidation of the imperial cult into an established shared mental model, diaspora traders were handed a new way to connect to their host communities. The dynamic of engaging in imperial cult practices obviously differed from the dynamic of engaging in the intercity relations that had governed public friendship. All the same, in both cases the outcome was that overseas traders utilized a public institution to bridge the divide between them and their hosts to create a more secure economic environment.[101] This development is already visible in the evidence from Hellenistic Delos and on full display in the evidence from imperial-era Italy.

In the sections to follow I will trace the changing role that public institutions played in the interaction between Phoenician diaspora traders and their Mediterranean host societies. My discussion will be roughly chronological, starting with Rhodes and Cos, where Phoenicians were present already before the classical Greek period, and then moving on to Athens, where as far as we can tell they arrived only later. I will proceed to discuss subsequent developments on independent and then Athenian-controlled Delos, ending with second-century CE Puteoli.

Rhodes, Cos and Athens

Phoenician contacts with Rhodes seem to have begun already in the mid-ninth century BCE, perhaps unsurprisingly given the island's location as a

99. Beard, North and Price 1998: vol. 1, 318.

100. Denzau and North 1994: 18.

101. For this argument, see also Terpstra forthcoming.

gateway into the Aegean for sailors coming from the Levant. Votive objects and burials together with archaeological evidence for workshops attest to settlements of Phoenicians dating back to the late eighth century BCE.[102] The intensity of their interaction with Rhodes started to decline in the seventh century, and by the sixth the Greek influence on the island had become dominant. But the memory of early contacts between Greeks and Phoenicians lived on in the classical literary tradition, preserved in stories betraying mostly the territorial rivalry between the two groups.[103] Ergias of Rhodes, for instance, recounted how in some unspecified, remote past Phoenician settlers got tricked by the Greek commander Iphiclos into vacating the island under terms of a truce (Ath. *Deip.* 8.61).

Regardless of whether the Phoenicians abandoned Rhodes altogether, as Ergias would have us believe, in the mid-third century BCE their activity definitely picked up again. By that time Rhodes was still independent, but Phoenician cities were not. In the course of the third century they would fall to first the Ptolemaic and then the Seleucid kingdom.[104] However, as explained above, the rise of the successor states did not fatally weaken the Greek complex of honorific institutions originally established by autonomous city-states. Under Hellenistic rule, public friendship continued to be a way for distant communities to maintain bilateral ties.

Hellenistic-era Rhodes was a wealthy island and a vibrant center of seaborne commerce, attracting large numbers of foreigners.[105] Men and women from several Phoenician cities were among those, as the epigraphic record shows. At Lindos on the island's east coast an inscription dating to around 225 BCE contains a dedication to Zeus Sôter (likely the Greek rendering of a version of Baal) made by one Zenon from Arados. An Aradian by that name, probably the same man, also appears in another dedication from Lindos, made this time to the local deity Athena Lindia.[106] Both inscriptions are short, but what makes them interesting for my purposes is Zenon's identification as a public friend. Although the honor was a typical Greek affair, the fact that an Aradian could receive it shows that the web of intercommunity relations it wove included non-Greek cities.

Also at Lindos, an Aradian named Dionysios and his sister Phila ca. 215 BCE set up a statue of their mother, Astis, which they dedicated to Athena

---

102. Markoe 2000: 171; Kourou 2003; Lipiński 2004: 145–49.

103. Ribichini 1995.

104. The exception is Arados, which was never in Ptolemaic hands: Bagnall 1976: 11–13.

105. Morelli 1956; Gabrielsen 2001; 2013; Manning 2015a: 116–18, 128–29.

106. *IG* 12.1.32; *I.Lindos* 120. See Morelli 1956: 148. The cult of Zeus Sôter was widespread among Phoenicians overseas: Baslez 1986: 292.

Lindia and Heracles.[107] Dionysios presented himself as a local benefactor, al-though his donations to Rhodes are not specified. But whatever they might have been, we may see here more than an isolated case where a man from Phoenicia had acquired local status through a Greek honorific institution. Dionysios' father was named Zenon, the inscription documents. Given the find location and date of the inscription, he seems likely to have been the son of the Rhodian public friend Zenon recorded in the two dedications just men-tioned.[108] The grant of public friendship was intended to create intergenera-tional ties of mutual trust and benefit, and Dionysios was thus a natural heir to the position of Rhodian benefactor.

Communities from the other main Phoenician coastal cities were also pres-ent on Rhodes. The Rhodian benefactor Dionysios and his sister Phila counted as citizens of Arados, but their mother, Astis, had come from Sidon. Several inscriptions suggest that she formed part of a larger Sidonian enclave, at least one of whose members also managed to attract public honors. A Sido-nian named Protimos appears in two inscriptions as a Rhodian benefactor.[109] The other two large Phoenician cities, Berytus and Tyre, were represented on the island as well.[110] A number of their citizens are listed in inscriptions as *metoikoi*, official permanent residents. Most of our evidence on *metoikia* comes from classical Athens. Whether it carried the same meaning on Rhodes is unknown, but it is clear that the Phoenician recipients possessed an offi-cially recognized status on the island.[111]

A particularly informative Greek honorific inscription was found a little to the north of Rhodes on the island of Cos, where a certain Theron, son of Boudastratos from Tyre, was made a public friend sometime in the fourth or third century BCE.[112] Coan city officials declared that the marble stele with the granting decree was to be set up in the "Temple of the Twelve Gods," augmenting the already considerable public honor. The inscription gives de-tails on the rights conferred. It says that Theron could freely enter and exit the Coan harbor, whether in times of peace or war, adding that this privilege would apply to himself and his descendants, and to their persons and their possessions. As in the case of Zenon and his son Dionysios from Arados on Rhodes, we see here the intergenerational aspect of the institution of public

---

107. *I.Lindos* 132. The mutilated inscription *IG* 12.1.104c almost certainly also records Diony-sios the *euergetēs* setting up a statue for his mother, Astis.

108. Morelli 1956: 148, 170.

109. Sidonians on Rhodes, see Morelli 1956: 170. Protimos *euergetēs*: *NSER* 192–93.

110. Morelli 1956: 149–50 (Berytians), 174 (Tyrians).

111. For a discussion of the status of *metoikoi* on Rhodes, see Morelli 1956: 130–32.

112. *I.Cos* 54 (= Bresson 2007: no. 2).

friendship. The privileges that the Coans bestowed must have been attractive to someone sailing frequently turbulent and war-torn waters. Moreover, as Bresson observed, the grant of the rights to enter and exit and "import and export" demonstrates that such privileges were by no means a given.[113] Possessing them must have provided Theron with a substantial advantage in his maritime ventures.

In line with the trade-diaspora argument I am advancing, I propose that the benefits conferred on him were helpful to trade between Tyre and Cos more generally. Theron was incentivized to retain those benefits for himself and to secure them for his sons by acting as a dependable "cross-cultural broker." That behavior had positive effects on economic trust, especially by fortifying an intercommunity enforcement mechanism. Any Tyrian denounced by Theron as a cheater or shirker would have found himself barred from business on Cos. The threat of collective action provided a strong incentive to all Tyrians coming to the island to respect the rules of trade. Theron might also have warned Coans sailing to Tyre of unreliable business partners in his native city, promoting rule-compliant behavior there. While he obviously derived individual benefit from his position as a Coan public friend, he was expected to act in the shared interest of two connected societies. The same held true for the Aradian and Sidonian benefactors on Rhodes, who were also put in the position of trusted representatives between their own and a Greek community.

I add that the emphasis I place here on private order is not to deny the potential usefulness of well-functioning public institutions of adjudication. In the Greek world, as elsewhere, the resolution of commercial conflicts was doubtless overwhelmingly done informally.[114] Yet as a last resort it might well have involved the use of official courts of law, which provided a platform to broadcast perceived misbehavior and to receive a public endorsement of an aggrieved party's position. Rhodes seems to have possessed such institutions. Demosthenes (56.47) imagined Athenians litigating in a Rhodian court, which suggests that the Rhodian legal system was deemed to be dependable in settling intercommunity disputes.[115] Still, even if disputants went the route of official litigation, what made them abide by the verdict was private-order enforcement (see chapter 1).

---

113. Bresson 2007: 54–55; 2016: 286–93.

114. For better documented historical periods, see Ogilvie 2011: 296–300; Goldberg 2012: 159–62; Gelderblom 2013: 104–08. See also Posner 2000 and Ratzan 2015 with my remarks in chapter 1.

115. Cohen 1973: 69. The speech is usually attributed to Demosthenes, but its authorship is debated.

Hellenistic Cos and Rhodes were both wealthy maritime hubs, but Athens had already in the classical era established itself as the cultural and economic center of the Greek world. In the fifth and fourth centuries BCE the city, and especially its harbor area of the Piraeus, attracted many foreigners, who left a noticeable mark on the epigraphic record. Epitaphs commemorating people from overseas number in the thousands.[116] Phoenicians are among them: epitaphs for Sidonians, Berytians, Aradians and Tyrians date from the fourth century BCE to the time of the early Roman empire.[117]

Ancient authors as well give information on the presence of Phoenicians in the larger urban area of Athens, including the Bay of Phaleron. Dionysius of Halicarnassus (*Din.* 10) refers to a now-lost speech by the orator Dinarchus, written on the occasion of a lawsuit over a priesthood of Poseidon, brought by the Phalerians against the resident Phoenicians.[118] Scattered literary passages suggest that trade and finance were the Phoenicians' main activities. Isocrates (*Trap.* 4) tells of an occasion where one Pythodoros, a Phoenician, acted as a financial intermediary for the Athenian banker Pasion. Demosthenes (34.6) mentions a substantial loan of 4,500 drachmas extended to Phormio by a Phoenician named Theodoros, who operated in the Piraeus.

As on Rhodes and Cos, Phoenicians appear in public friendship decrees. One such decree dates to the 320s BCE and honors two Tyrians, father and son, named Hieron and Apses. The first lines of the text are fragmentary but may record that the honorands had brought grain to Athens from Carthage at a price lower than was available in Italy.[119] Athens had trouble with its food supply at the time, so the city had good reason to be grateful for the shipments, all the more so because the honorands reportedly continued to provide their services.[120] Noteworthy is the connection that Tyre evidently maintained with its former North African colony (more on that topic in the Appendix). For their benefactions, the honorands were awarded gold crowns as well as public friendship. The latter honor was to be hereditary, once more demonstrating the permanent, intergenerational bond between foreigners and a Greek city that it was meant to forge. Finally, the two men were given

116. Athenian grave stelae (most fourth-century BCE in date) of foreigners in Greek: *IG* 2.2.7882–10530. On the Piraeus, see Garland 1987: 58–100; Demetriou 2012: 188–229.

117. Sidon: *IG* 2.2.10265a-86, *CIS* 1.115 and *SEG* 51 (2001) no. 284; Berytus: *IG* 2.2.8407–08; Arados: *IG* 2.2.8357–58; Tyre: *IG* 2.2.10468–73.

118. Phoenicians in Phaleron: Baslez 1986: 291; Lipiński 2004: 172–73. On Phaleron, see Garland 1987: 10–14.

119. *IG.* 2.2.342 and 2.3.468; *SEG* 35 (1985) no. 70; *SEG* 54 (2004) no. 157 and Lambert 2006: no. 44; 2012: 122 (no. 44) with *add. corr.* 403. See also Walbank 1985; Culasso Gastaldi 2004: 193–203; Engen 2013: 306–07.

120. Fourth-century BCE food crises at Athens: Garnsey 1988: 150–64.

the formal right to own real estate at Athens, a privilege that for diaspora traders must have been extremely attractive, especially if we assume that this right was hereditary as well.[121]

Judging from the epigraphic record, the Sidonians were the most prominent Phoenician group established at Athens. I have discussed above the award of a gold crown by a Sidonian assembly to Šama'baal, and the Athenian honorary decree for the Sidonian king Straton, whose diplomatic help to Athens was rewarded with tax exemptions for his subjects. In addition, a Sidonian appears in a public friendship inscription. It honors Apollonides, son of Demetrios, much in the way that the Tyrians Hieron and Apses were honored in the roughly contemporary decree just mentioned.[122] In the case of Apollonides it is not made explicit what he had accomplished to be deemed worthy of the considerable honors bestowed upon him: public friendship for him and his children, a gold crown worth a thousand drachmas, the right to own Athenian real estate and a commemorative inscription set up on the Acropolis at public expense. But whatever benefit Apollonides may have provided the Athenians, it was surely trade related; he was honored on the recommendation of merchants and shipowners.

It was not lost on the Athenian historian and philosopher Xenophon that holding out such public honors to foreign merchants would strengthen commercial ties. He proposed measures in that spirit when Athens faced war-induced economic difficulties:

> It would also be an excellent plan to reserve front seats in the theater for merchants and shipowners, and to offer them hospitality occasionally, when the high quality of their ships and merchandise entitles them to be considered benefactors of the state. With the prospect of these honors before them they would look on us as friends and hasten to visit us to win the honor as well as the profit. The rise in the number of residents and visitors would of course lead to a corresponding expansion of our imports and exports, of sales, rents and customs. (*Por.* 3.4–5)[123]

Xenophon was proposing to grant foreign traders and shipowners formal hospitality in the magistrates' hall (*prytaneion*), the highest honor the Athenian state had to offer. Whether Athens was willing to go quite that far is debated, but it is clear that the stimulating economic effect of extending civic honors to foreign merchants was well understood at the public level.[124] The

---

121. On *egktēsis*, see Demetriou 2012: 215.

122. *IG* 2.2.343. See Culasso Gastaldi 2004: 183–92; Lambert 2006: no. 50; Harland 2009: 108; Engen 2010: no. 28.

123. Tr.: E.C. Marchant, *LCL* 1968.

124. Gabrielsen 2001: 221–22; Engen 2010: 172–73.

policy element of the practice did not end there. Stephen Lambert has emphasized that inscriptions with honorific decrees voted on by public bodies were "physical monuments deliberately placed in particular locations."[125] Such public display was intended to influence behavior more widely. Others were implicitly invited to win a similar distinction for themselves.

City-states had strategic goals in extending and displaying honors, including goals of an economic nature. But although city-states set the parameters and decided what privileges were conferred, the benefits allowed the recipients considerable leverage within their host and home communities alike. The honorands' position as esteemed benefactors to their hosts made them and their descendants pivotal men for intercommunity trust and enforcement. We thus see here a reciprocal and fluid process in which public authorities encouraged and regulated trade in ways that simultaneously strengthened the private order on which it relied.

I repeat that none of this is to deny the potential usefulness of public institutions of adjudication. Athens had a well-established court system that at least in theory was capable of handling intercommunity cases in an impartial manner. In practice, it seems things did not always work out that way.[126] But whatever the risk of suboptimal outcomes might have been, without much doubt courts were used strictly as a last resort, if for no other reason than to avoid legal fees.[127] As on Rhodes and Cos, a reliance on informal settlement remained the preferred option in trade disputes. Yet once again, even if official litigation was the route that disputants chose to take, private-order mechanisms provided the necessary enforcement.

Independent and Athenian-Ruled Delos

Public encouragement of and control over trade can also be seen on Hellenistic Delos, together with Athens the site that has yielded the most abundant epigraphic evidence for Phoenician commercial ventures in the Greek world. Phoenician activity on Delos increased significantly after the island became a duty-free entrepot in 167 BCE, but mercantile relations extended back in time by at least a century and probably even further. A bilingual fourth-century BCE Delian inscription commemorates Tyrian "sacred sailors" (*hieronautai*), who dedicated statues of Tyre and Sidon to Apollo.[128]

125. Lambert 2006: 116.

126. Thür 2015: 41–43. See Cohen 1973; Ober 2015: 243–48 for a more optimistic assessment of Athenian legal institutions.

127. Athenian legal fees: Thür 2015.

128. *ID* 50.

As the site of a celebrated Apollonian sanctuary, Delos' needs for long-distance trade prior to its position as a duty-free hub were in large part dictated by the temple economy. Accounts of the temple's revenues and expenditures were published annually in inscriptions, which provide us with precious information on what the sanctuary's administration bought and took in. Several Phoenicians are listed in the accounts. A Herakleides *Phoinix*, an artisan and metalworker, appears in the one from 276 BCE. If he is to be equated with the abundantly attested metals trader with the same name but unspecified origin, he had a fifty-year career on Delos.[129] Another Phoenician Herakleides, or maybe the same man yet again, appears in the temple account of 269 BCE. He is not labeled with the generic term *Phoinix* but identified as a man from Tyre. Herakleides, the account records, had sold two elephant tusks to the temple, a sale that fits a long tradition of Phoenician specialized trade in ivory.[130] Yet another Phoenician appears in the account from 192 BCE. This man, named Apollonios, must have enjoyed considerable social trust on Delos, as he acted as a guarantor in a lease agreement for "sacred houses" (*hierai oikiai*), temple property leased out to increase the sanctuary's revenue.[131]

Finally, a large body of evidence exists for Aradians on Hellenistic Delos. A third-century BCE inscription on an exedra displays a list of eight names, among them a Eukleia from Arados, the wife of Jason, and a Sillis from the same city; around 235 BCE a certain Straton from Arados donated a libation bowl to Apollo.[132] No fewer than three decrees record that Aradians were elevated to the status of Delian public friend. In the best preserved one, a Jason, son of Theogeiton, is honored for his services to the temple, the city and the Delian community. His benefactions seem in part to have consisted of extending help to Delian citizens in financial difficulties: "he works with all enthusiasm among those who should happen to have need," the decree reports.[133]

In a discussion of the Aradian inscriptions on Delos, Gary Reger has cautioned against the temptation of combining them to paint a picture of a multigenerational trading and banking enterprise. Such restraint seems prudent to me. However, given the economic activities of Phoenicians both on Delos

---

129. Heracleides *Phoinix*: IG 11.2.163.A l. 45–49. See Rey-Coquais 1961: 251 with n. 2.

130. *IG* 11.2.203.A l. 71. On Phoenician trade in ivory artwork, see Markoe 2000: 146–47 and (more critically) Fales 2017: 250–55.

131. Apollonios *Phoinix*: *ID* no. 400 l. 11. For the management of the Delian temple estate, see Kent 1948.

132. *IG* 11.4.1203; *ID* 313.A l. 9. On these Aradians on Delos, see Masson 1969: 682.

133. *IG* 11.4.601, 776 (cited, tr.: Reger 1994: 57) and 816. In the mutilated inscriptions the word *proxenos* does not appear, but their formulas all conform to what Mack calls the "*proxenos* paradigm": Mack 2015: 22–49, 81–89.

and elsewhere in the Greek world, concluding that the Aradians' "dealings with Delos had political or religious significance" and that it "was Delos's sanctity, not its economy, that generated the respect it received" strike me as overcorrections.[134] I am inclined to think that the decrees of public friendship for the Aradians point to an economic relationship that was well understood to be mutually beneficial, as was the case on Rhodes, on Cos and at Athens. As in those places, public friends had the means and motivation to act as gatekeepers in trade relations between their home and their host communities. The Aradians' position as honored representatives and trusted intermediaries provided them with incentives to sustain private-order enforcement, which discouraged opportunistic behavior within Aradian-Delian trade.

If Phoenician ties with Delos predated 167 BCE, they grew appreciably stronger after the island became a duty-free emporium under Athenian management. Rome had granted it that status to punish Rhodes, which had had the temerity to show independent diplomatic initiative after the conclusion of the Third Macedonian War.[135] The step was effective in dealing a painful blow to the commercial position of Rhodes where, according to Polybius (30.31.10–12), revenue from harbor dues dropped by 85 percent. For a period of about eighty years Delos became the leading East-Mediterranean entrepot, attracting a geographically wide range of traders, including southern Italians. It abruptly lost its central position when in 88 BCE it was raided by the Pontic king Mithridates, a shock from which it would never recover.[136]

All the most prominent Phoenician cities were represented on Delos between 167 and 88 BCE. A large number of individuals from Tyre, Berytus, Sidon and Arados appear in funerary stelae, ephebes' lists, temple records and religious dedications.[137] Not all those people were long-distance traders—some were artisans—but considerable segments of certainly the Berytians and Tyrians were involved in overseas commerce. Both groups maintained associations that ranked among the most active on Delos. In a well-known study of Delian trade, Nicholas Rauh wrote: "The groups making the most frequent dedications, constructing the most permanent installations, and hence playing the greatest role in the community, tended to organize themselves according to ethnically cohesive religious associations of a distinctly fraternal type."[138] That description, practically the definition of a trade diaspora, certainly applies to the Tyrian and Berytian groups.

134. Reger 1994: 56–58. Cf. Baslez 1987: 275–76, 280–81.
135. Rauh 1993: xi–xvii; Reger 1994: 20, 270–71; Kay 2014: 198–99.
136. Rauh 1993: 68–74.
137. Baslez 1987: 270, 282. Grave stelae (Sidonians): MF 314, 386, 476.
138. Rauh 1993: 29.

In the Delian epigraphic record, no single instance can be found after 167 BCE of Phoenicians receiving a grant of public friendship. One reason why might have been the island's social makeup, which in the Greek world was wholly unique. Because of Delos' establishment as a freeport, the foreign population there swelled in number to the point where it became larger than the native.[139] In addition, our sources are incomplete because not all inscriptions survive and, moreover, most decrees were never inscribed in the first place. Those circumstances may provide part of the explanation for the lack of evidence for Phoenician public friends on Delos after 167 BCE. But the rise of Rome as the dominant state in the Mediterranean seems likely to have been the main reason, especially as Delos' emporium position was a product of that rise. Other signs that the political center of gravity in the Mediterranean was shifting westward are the appearance of epigraphic expressions of loyalty to Roman power made by Phoenician diaspora groups.

Emblematic are the inscriptions and honorific monuments set up by the association (*koinon* or *synodos*) of the *Poseidoniastai* from Berytus, worshippers of Berytian Baal, a deity equated with Poseidon. The merchants, shipowners and warehousemen who made up this association possessed a building on Delos, a structure both epigraphically and archaeologically attested.[140] Its physical remains show that its core consisted of banqueting rooms, a peristyle courtyard, a vestibule and a multiroom "sacred area" (fig. 2.2).

One of the inscriptions set up by the Berytian association records how its members in their meetings had honored the Athenian people with crowns; a second documents how they had erected a public monument to the Athenians.[141] Both dedications were overt expressions of loyalty to Athens, but in the end also to Rome. Athenian authority over Delos squarely depended on Rome's say-so. Polybius (30.20.2) reports how the Athenians had begged the Roman senate to be placed in possession of the island.

Displays of loyalty directly to Rome as the dominant political power on the Delian scene are also manifest in the evidence from the building of the Berytians. The four cell-like rooms on its western side were given over to religious practices. Unsurprisingly, one of the rooms (no. ii) was dedicated to the group's patron deity Poseidon (Berytian Baal), shown by an inscribed statue base found still in its original location. The adjacent room (no. iii) was reserved for the Semitic goddess Astarte, while the most southern one (no. iv)

---

139. Errington 1988: 144–45.

140. Bruneau 1970: 622–30; Robert 1973a; Rauh 1993: 45; Gabrielsen 2007: 195; Harland 2009: 111–12; Trümper 2011: 53–58; Reger 2013: 149–50.

141. *ID* 1780 and 1777. On these inscriptions, see Robert 1973b: 476; Harland 2009: 112; Trümper 2011: 57.

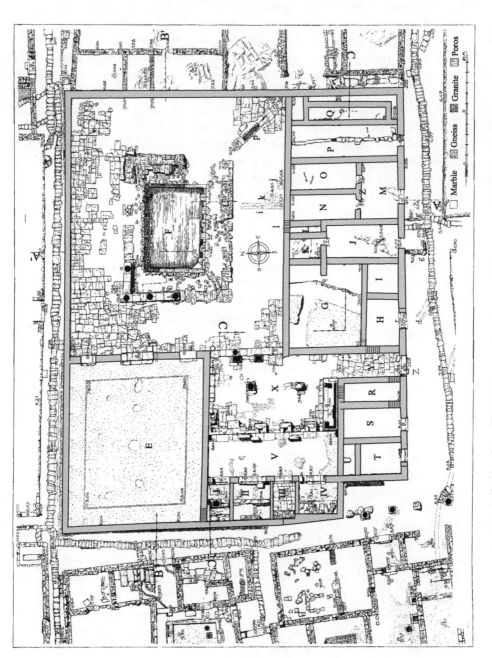

FIG. 2.2. Delian building of the *Poseidoniastai* from Berytus. Image courtesy of Monika Trümper.

was either dedicated to another Phoenician god, Eshmun, or used as a kind of vestry.[142]

Room no. i, meanwhile, was dedicated to Rome personified as a goddess, once more shown by an inscribed statue base. In the northwestern corner of a forecourt (X) an altar to the same goddess, Roma, was set up.[143] Furthermore, around 90 BCE the building received an honorary statue of the Roman military commander Gnaeus Octavius. This was a powerful man to be affiliated with, belonging to a three-generation line of consuls and high-ranking officers.[144] The inscribed base praised him as the association's benefactor, suggesting that the Berytians enjoyed friendly relations with members of the Roman ruling elite.[145]

The statue of the goddess Roma in the sacred area would not have been visible looking in from the street through the narrow hallway beyond the doorway, and neither would the altar to the goddess in the forecourt. This architectural arrangement implies that shows of adherence to political authority were meant to be seen only by association members and visitors to the building. In Monika Trümper's view, the

> various measures used to show the Poseidoniasts' reverence to Athens and Rome inside the clubhouse were most likely not intended to constantly remind and assure the Poseidoniasts of their loyalties to these "superpowers"; instead they suggest that Athenian and Roman representatives were invited to the clubhouse on specific occasions or even on a regular basis.[146]

This is speculation of course, but I think Trümper is right in assuming that the multiple displays of political loyalty were not meant for private consumption, an idea corroborated by the public monument that the *Poseidoniastai* set up to honor the people of Athens.

A second Phoenician association of merchants and shipowners, from Tyre this time, is known through only a single inscription.[147] The text uses a variety of ways to refer to the Tyrians as a collective—*koinon, synodos, thiasos*—terms that may have been synonyms but that may also have indicated subsections

---

142. Bruneau 1970: 623, 628; 1978; Trümper 2011: 54.

143. *ID* 1778 (base) and 1779 (altar). See Bruneau 1978: fig. 2 for the position of the altar, indicated with *b*.

144. Bliquez 1975. The Cn. Octavius in the Delian decree probably held the consulship in 87 BCE.

145. *ID* 1782; Bruneau 1978: 183.

146. Trümper 2011: 58.

147. *ID* 1519. See Bruneau 1970: 622; Rauh 1993: 45; Harland 2009: 111; Reger 2013: 150.

with different tasks. Even from the sole surviving epigraphic source it is evident that the Tyrians maintained an elaborate organization, likely not dissimilar to the one of the Berytian *Poseidoniastai*. It centered on the worship of Heracles, the Greek rendering of the Tyrian ancestral god Melqart ("the cause of the greatest good things that happen to people and the founder of our original homeland," the text solemnly declares).[148] Like their Berytian counterparts, the Tyrians maintained a building on Delos. So far, no architectural remains of this structure have been identified, a situation that will hopefully change one day as Delos' rich archaeology continues to be explored.

The inscription records how ca. 153 BCE the Tyrian association had dispatched an embassy to Athens, led by Patron, son of Dorotheos, one of its members. The aim of this mission was to obtain permission from the Athenian authorities to build a sacred enclosure to Heracles. As Patron was honored as a benefactor he obviously succeeded. It would be interesting to know if the Berytians had taken a similar step before constructing their communal building, but unfortunately we do not know. Either way, evidently the Tyrian organization of traders and shipowners engaged politically with the civic institutions in charge of Delos, just as their Berytian counterparts did.

What we are witnessing in the interaction between the Phoenician associations and the public authorities ruling Delos is a double-sided process: first of all, Rome as the now-dominant state in the Mediterranean exercising control over trade, and, second, diasporas turning that control to their advantage. Rome had made Delos a freeport nominally in Athenian charge, thereby immediately interfering in Mediterranean commerce. Through its military and political might it was redirecting trade flows, allowing access to business to whomever it favored. Diaspora traders, including Tyrians and Berytians, sought the endorsement of the public authorities of their host community, not unlike what they had done before through public friendship. Because a dominant imperial state had superimposed a layer of political power on local civic bodies, that is where they directed their efforts.

The official stamp of approval of the public rule-setting institutions on Delos elevated the Phoenician organizations' standing and heightened their perceived trustworthiness within the Delian community. As a result, their members acquired a stronger bargaining position in trade, an advantage they were incentivized to maintain by engaging in ongoing behavior as reliable business partners and loyal supporters of the dominant state. Their display of cooperation with political power, in other words, encouraged rule-compliant behavior, fostered economic trust and strengthened private order.

---

148. Tr.: Ascough, Harland and Kloppenborg 2012: no. 223 (l. 14–16). For the assimilation of Melqart with Heracles, see Bonnet 2014: 286–87.

At the same time, the fact that the Phoenicians expressed political allegiance rendered the process reciprocal and mutually beneficial. They sent loyalty signals to high Roman officials and displayed their adherence to Roman rule. They thus acknowledged the state's legitimacy, thereby reinforcing its hold on power. What all this demonstrates is that, as with public friendship in the Greek world of the preceding centuries, the Roman state's role in trade was not a top-down or unidirectional affair. It allowed merchants to manipulate state power, giving them an important degree of agency, while simultaneously satisfying the state's need for rule legitimization. The evidence from Puteoli shows the continuation of that double-sided process under the Roman empire.

Imperial-Era Puteoli

After Mithridates' attack on Delos, the island began a rapid descent into mercantile obscurity. Much of its business relocated to Puteoli, an Italian port city already called a "lesser Delos" by the second-century BCE poet Lucilius (Paul. *Festi* 88.4). The current state of our evidence does not allow us to say if Phoenicians were established in Puteoli before 88 BCE. They certainly were by 174 CE, though. From what we gather from the lengthy inscription discussed above, the Tyrians had by that time been maintaining a Puteolan presence for a considerable while.

Other Phoenician groups were active in the city as well. An unfortunately rather mutilated wax tablet dating to 57 CE probably records the arrival of a ship there from Sidon.[149] Berytians as well were present in Puteoli. In a short inscription, the worshippers of Jupiter Heliopolitanus, the great god of Baalbek, stated the rules governing access to their Puteolan burial site.[150] From the viewpoint of internal group governance, the most informative line is the closing one. It says that only organization members "who will have continued doing nothing against the law and statute of the corpus" could enter through the gates of the necropolis and have access to its streets. Here we see a foreign community established overseas for generations that was engaged in religious "boundary maintenance" and that was self-policing. The group appears again in an inscription from ca. 115 CE as the "worshippers of Jupiter Heliopolitanus, Berytians, who live in Puteoli." The text records that they honored Trajan with a dedication, which contains a full list of the emperor's official titles.[151]

---

149. *TPSulp.* 106. See Terpstra 2013: 64.
150. *CIL* 10.1579 (= *ILS* 4291). See Tran tam Tinh 1972: 149–50; Terpstra 2013: 84–85.
151. *CIL* 10.1634 (= *ILS* 300).

By the time of Trajan, the incremental shift in the Mediterranean from a pluralistic political landscape to a unipolar world in which a single state wielded ultimate power had long been completed. In the latter constellation it was still possible for diaspora traders to engage with their hosts at the local civic level, as they had done before in Greek city-states as benefactors and public friends. The Tyrians did not miss an opportunity to do so, as we will see below. But a different way of building a position favorable to trade within their host society had also become available: displays of allegiance to the overriding authority of the central state. A development in that direction had already been manifest on Delos. The Puteolan evidence shows its continuation and logical terminus: public expressions of loyalty to the emperor as the embodiment of state authority.

We know from the inscription discussed above that a group of Tyrians resided in Puteoli in the second half of the second century; in 174 CE they wrote a letter to their native city to request help with the rent payments for their communal building.[152] The costs incurred for the maintenance of the cults of their fatherland and expenditures for the Puteolan "Ox-Sacrifice Games" had depleted their budget, they explained (l. 9–12). Adding to their financial burden was a building refurbishment they had undertaken in honor of the "sacred festival days of the emperor" (l. 13–15), probably a recurring celebration of either the birthday or elevation to the purple of Marcus Aurelius.[153] These three budgetary items are worth examining in detail.

Worshipping ancestral deities was a typical diaspora activity, part of the "boundary maintenance" visible with both Phoenician and many other diaspora groups in the ancient Mediterranean.[154] The Tyrians remarked that the service to their native gods, one of them almost certainly Melqart, took place in shrines or temples (*naoi*). No details are given on those spaces, but it does not seem unreasonable to imagine something similar to the "sacred area" in the building of the Berytians on Delos. But whatever the architectural arrangement might have looked like, the Tyrians' religious activities generated necessary internal cohesion while at the same time creating an equally necessary boundary between them and their hosts.

By contrast, the other two projects to which they had directed financial resources were aimed not at maintaining but at crossing the boundary between their own and the Puteolan community. The first was sponsoring the "Ox-Sacrifice Games," a benefaction to the city of Puteoli. Nothing further is known about this festival, either about how it was celebrated or how it was

---

152. *IG* 14.830 (= *OGIS* 595; *IGRR* 1.421).

153. See Rives 1999: 144–45 for such celebratory practices.

154. Terpstra 2013; 2015; 2016.

financed. However, the language of the inscription hints at a way of funding that may not have been entirely voluntarily. The costs of the festival had been imposed upon them, the Tyrians wrote (l. 12, 26–27). Perhaps the task of financing the Ox-Sacrifice Games was a rotating liturgy to which foreign resident groups were also subject. If that was the case, then the Tyrians' turn to sponsor it must have come at an inconvenient time given the financial strain they were apparently under. All the same, sponsoring a public municipal festival obviously created goodwill with the host society, an effect they were surely aware of. The fact that they mentioned it twice in their public inscription is telling in that regard.

Equally telling is the mention of the costly refitting of their communal building initiated in celebration of the emperor's reign. Whatever the result might have looked like, it doubtless contained festive references to imperial rule, highlighting the Tyrians' loyalty to the central state and its governance. Nor was this the only way in which they communicated their allegiance. The opening line of the letter to their native city, subsequently immortalized in a public inscription, reads: "By the grace of the gods and the good fortune of our lord the emperor" (l. 5). Other evidence adds to the picture of a publicly expressed Tyrian reverence for Roman rule and rulers. A wax tablet from 52 CE records that a local Puteolan banker and a man from Tyre had entered into a process of dispute settlement. The location for their rendezvous was the "Hordionian altar of Augustus" in the Puteolan forum, a public monument serving the imperial cult.[155] This location was chosen because it added gravitas to the occasion and expressed the litigating parties' loyalty to the central state and their trustworthiness as actors within the state's legal framework, a topic I will explore further in chapter 4.

Groups from Phoenician cities were not unique in showing imperial-cult-inspired expressions of loyalty to imperial rule. In chapter 5 we will see more examples of trading communities making religious dedications for the good fortune and well-being of emperors and their families. Such acts made eminent sense for heterogeneous diaspora groups wishing to interact. Expressing loyalty to the state through the imperial cult allowed them to connect to their host society and establish economic trust with their business partners.[156] The imperial cult was an ideal vehicle for such trust-building behavior. Traders could participate in its rites regardless of their geographical origin or religious persuasion, and without having to make any compromise to the piety they owed their native gods. The cult was neutral in that respect, excluding no one, yet accessible and meaningful to all subjects of the empire. Intimately related

155. *TPSulp.* 4.
156. For this argument, see Terpstra forthcoming. On "economic trust," see also chapter 5.

to whoever was in power in the physical, not the metaphysical world, it was as much an ideological as a spiritual affair.

In the absence of third-party enforcement, collective action against cheaters, freeriders and opportunists formed the bedrock of trade. A public ideology shared by different communities ensured that coordination problems could be overcome and that effective private order could be established. Such an outcome is precisely what North predicted would emerge following the internalization of social norms and their consolidation into an interpretative cognitive framework:

> Shared mental models reflecting a common belief system will translate into a set of institutions broadly conceived to be legitimate. Consensual political order requires that, in equilibrium, all members of society have an incentive to obey and enforce the rules and that a sufficient number are motivated to punish potential deviants.[157]

For the imperial court and its governing apparatus, receiving pledges of adherence from mercantile groups was obviously beneficial as well. Such pledges signaled consensus with imperial governance, enhancing its stability. The Roman state never forced merchants publicly to express their allegiance the way it did with its soldiers, who had to take an oath of loyalty on recruitment and then twice annually throughout their time of service.[158] But the state's concern for a similar civilian consensus with its rule is evident from the communal vows made annually on January 3 throughout the empire on behalf of the emperor's well-being.[159] From the viewpoint of Rome's public authorities, loyalty signals received through a self-sustaining, private-order practice were as good as, and arguably better than, loyalty signals received in officially organized ceremonies. The evidence from imperial-era Puteoli thus points to an essentially reciprocal dynamic that was fluid and in which both traders and the state were agents and stakeholders.

Concluding Remarks

To discuss ancient Mediterranean diaspora trade in a single chapter, I have focused on the Phoenicians, but of course they were exceptional. Few if any of their commercial rivals and partners could match their overseas trading heritage. We lack the evidence necessary to determine how representative

---

157. North 2005: 104–05. On shared mental models, see also Denzau and North 1994.
158. Breeze 2016: 76.
159. On the *vota pro salute principis*, see Rives 1999: 144–45; Ando 2000: 359–62.

they were in interfering with the activities of their native diasporas. It seems probable that throughout the Greco-Roman period, a good number and perhaps the majority of Mediterranean overseas trade networks were entirely private, functioning independently of the civic bodies of their home communities. After all, already in Homer we encounter also Phoenician traders operating without any apparent connection to their native royal houses or governing institutions.

Still, public involvement in diaspora trade had a wider diffusion. Evidence can be found, for instance, in the Syrian city of Palmyra, whose political bodies during the first three centuries CE lent esteem to domestic benefactors of the Arabian diaspora. From a study of the city's epigraphic record, Michal Gawlikowski concluded that many caravans bringing goods through the desert "were manifestly of major public interest and supported by the [Palmyrene] municipal authorities. Indeed, the city council voted several times the highest honours for those who had helped the caravans."[160] Clearly we need to incorporate this element of public involvement in trade into the larger picture of ancient economic development if we aim to understand it.

That picture equally needs to include the mirrored process of governments exercising authority over the diasporas they hosted. State formation led to an institutionalization of the interaction between Phoenician diaspora groups and their host societies. Greek political bodies conferred multigenerational privileges and status on foreign merchants, allowing them to occupy well-defined and mutually beneficial positions within their communities. The enhanced ability of the recipients to act as cross-cultural brokers increased the effectiveness of diaspora networks and facilitated the establishment of private order. Subsequently, Roman imperial ideology supported the coordination of collective action between heterogeneous trading groups, which also had the effect of strengthening private order. In all situations discussed, the way in which hosts and diaspora groups positioned themselves was characterized by an essential fluidity, giving both sides a measure of agency in regulating trade.

One important point remains to be made. The positive effect of Greek public friendship and Roman imperial ideology on diaspora trade disincentivized state representatives from investing in a public enforcement infrastructure. I propose that this was a self-reinforcing dynamic: a lack of third-party enforcement had led trade to rely on private order. State formation and the emergence of public institutions allowed that private order to strengthen, which further discouraged investment in third-party enforcement. I emphasize that

160. Gawlikowski 1994: 31.

I do not see this outcome as the result of a calculated strategy by public servants on how best to allocate resources. Instead, it was the unintended result of long-term cultural, political and ideological developments.

Appendix: Carthage

Because in this chapter I chose to focus specifically on Phoenician cities and their trade diasporas, I have largely ignored the Punic Mediterranean. Another reason for me to leave the west to one side is that studying the influence of public institutions on Punic economic performance is all but impossible given the dearth of local written sources. But the spread of Carthaginian power is an integral part of the ongoing process of state formation and consolidation that I propose had an aggregate positive effect on the economy of the ancient Mediterranean (see chapter 1). A brief discussion of western developments is therefore in order. In what follows I give a summary overview of Carthage as the center of the Punic world, discussing the aspects of its pre-Roman economy that are most relevant to my overall narrative: its harbor infrastructure, its coinage, foreigners residing there and archaeological evidence for its overseas trade relations.

The rise of Carthage is reflected in the works of Roman authors, who list a succession of Roman-Carthaginian treaties.[161] Polybius (3.22.4–13) claimed that the first of those was drafted in 509 BCE, a date so early as to be suspicious, all the more so because it coincides with the conventional date of birth of the Roman republic. Livy (7.27.3) and Diodorus Siculus (16.69.1) date the first treaty to 348 BCE, which seems altogether more plausible.[162] The treaty's terms show that Carthage considered especially the West Mediterranean, including Sardinia, to be its exclusive domain. But it also stipulated that the Romans avoid Libya, and in a follow-up agreement of 306 BCE, it declared Sicily off-limits.[163]

Archaeology shows the growing economic integration of those areas in the course of the fourth century. Ceramic data from the Libyan site of Euesperides (modern Benghazi), for instance, provide "evidence for extensive trade between Cyrenaica and the Punic world, and also with southern Italy and Sicily," as Andrew Wilson notes. Public friendship played a connecting role

---

161. See Serrati 2006 for a discussion.

162. But cf. Cornell 1995: 210–14.

163. Polybius (3.26.3–7) emphatically denied the existence of the 306 BCE treaty; its terms would have made Rome the aggressor in 264 BCE. On the war's causes, see Harris 1979: 185–90.

here as well, demonstrated by a mid-fourth-century BCE decree for two men from Syracuse by the city council of Euesperides. In the combined evidence from the site, Wilson sees "a foreshadowing of the long-distance trade flows that are characteristic of the Roman world."[164] Excavations at Carthage confirm that notion, revealing that east and west were not separate economic zones and that a comprehensive connectivity had been emerging well before Rome unified the Mediterranean politically.[165]

Archaeological data show long-standing Carthaginian trade relations extending farther west than Libya and encompassing the Greek world. At Kerkouane on the tip of Cap Bon, the oldest layers produced sixth-century BCE Attic, Ionic and Corinthian wares. Subsequent layers contained an abundance of fifth-century BCE Greek pottery, especially Attic.[166] At Bir Massouda about a quarter of the pottery from a waste pit consisted of imported ceramics. Attic wares from the late fifth to the late fourth centuries BCE formed the largest portion, just over a quarter. Sherds from eastern Greece were also well represented, forming the second largest category.[167] Excavations have also produced large amounts of Attic black glaze wares, imports of which seem to have begun in the fourth century BCE, reaching a peak in the second half of that century.[168] More evidence on growing overseas shipping activity is provided by transport containers found at various excavations in the Carthage area. The fourth century BCE saw a noticeable increase in the number of imported amphorae as a percentage of all amphora types, from about 20 percent to 30 percent. Nonlocal wares arrived from territories controlled by Carthage, including Sicily and Sardinia, but also from other areas such as Calabria and the North Aegean.[169]

To facilitate imports, Carthage seems initially to have relied on natural lagoons rather than a constructed harbor. Appian (*Pun.* 96), in a famous passage, described how at the time of the Roman siege of 146 BCE the city possessed impressive basins for its naval and commercial fleets. Archaeology has confirmed the accuracy of his description. But perhaps surprisingly given Carthage's reputation as an ancient trading center, stratigraphic excavations have shown this infrastructure to be late in date—the second half of the third century BCE at the earliest. Near the coastline, southeast of Koudiat el Hobsia, a ritual burial site (*tophet*) was maintained by the mid-eighth century

164. Wilson 2013: 153. *Proxenia* decree: p. 124.

165. See Broodbank 2013; Manning 2018 for the preclassical history of that development.

166. Morel 1969: 494–500.

167. Docter et al. 2006: 50–54.

168. Chelbi 1992: 17; Docter et al. 2006: 57–58; Bechtold and Docter 2010: 96.

169. Bechtold and Docter 2010: 88 with fig. 3, 96 with fig. 8.

BCE, but no port infrastructure of a remotely comparable age has so far been discovered. It has been suggested that an archaic harbor might be buried to the south or west of the *tophet*, but this remains a hypothesis.[170]

As far as we know, the first detectable, large-scale intervention in the marshy coastal landscape was the excavation of a navigational or drainage channel, about 15 to 20 meters in width and 2 meters in depth, which has been traced for about 400 meters along the coastline (fig. 2.3: shaded area north of the *tophet*). Where it led and whence it came is unknown, although sediments with marine mollusks demonstrate that it had a connection to the open sea. The channel was a major work, but it was not architectural, lacking any stone lining to its sides and floor. Whatever purpose it may have served, it was filled in sometime after the mid-fourth century BCE, and certainly before the facilities described by Appian were built.[171]

The channel, its associated occupational level and the *tophet* have given us precious information on Carthage's agricultural, industrial and mercantile economy. As to the first, the channel fill contained an abundance of ecofacts. Henry Hurst and Lawrence Stager, who explored the harbor site in the 1970s, summed up the rich macrobotanical finds: "The fruits included pomegranate, fig, grape, olive, peach, plum, melon, Cyrenean lotus; there were also the remains of almonds, pistachios and filberts. . . . Particularly striking is the horticultural component, including many fruits which are best propagated by grafting."[172] Such finds demonstrate the advanced level of Punic agriculture, which built on a Phoenician and more generally a Levantine heritage.[173]

Also part of that heritage was metalworking, evidence for which was found to the west of the channel in an occupational level dating to ca. 400–350 BCE. Slags rich in iron oxide, terracotta tuyeres and pieces of fired mudbrick and fused sandstone—the likely remains of furnace walls—suggest iron smelting or processing. Finally, at the *tophet*, offerings of necklaces and amulets in amber, gold, silver, carnelian and steatite accompanied some of the cremated human remains, imported materials that give us an idea of the range of Carthage's overseas trade connections.[174]

Whatever port facilities—if any—were used for anchorage during the first centuries of Carthage's existence, eventually imports went through the city's new harbor, the remains of which are still a recognizable feature of the mod-

170. Lancel 1992: 192–211.

171. Hurst and Stager 1978: 338.

172. Hurst and Stager 1978: 340.

173. Broodbank 2013: 570–71.

174. Hurst and Stager 1978: 339–40.

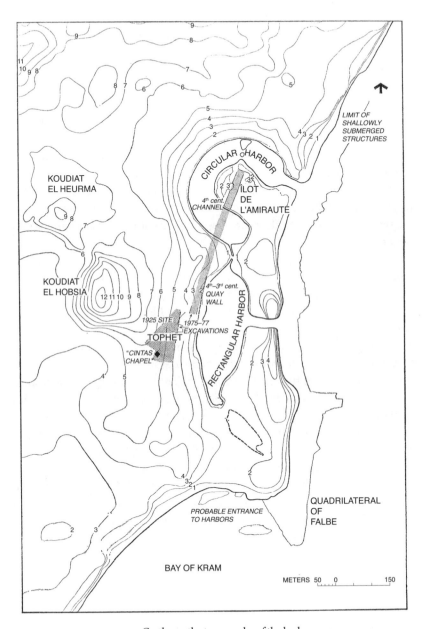

FIG. 2.3. Carthage: the topography of the harbor area.

ern coastline. Several seasons of excavation by British and American teams have established that it was constructed between the mid-third and mid-second centuries BCE, perhaps in several phases rather than a single event.[175] A circular and a rectangular basin were dug out of the marshland, the first serving military purposes, the second purposes of trade. The earthmoving works undertaken to build the new port were impressive. An estimated 115,000 cubic meters of soil were removed for the naval basin and an estimated 120,000 cubic meters for its commercial counterpart.

The significance of the substantial shipping facilities emerging seemingly out of nowhere was not lost on Hurst and Stager. Such a massive expenditure of resources and effort, they commented, was "certainly an important decision of government . . . and should be revealing about the state of Carthaginian politics at the time."[176] If nothing else, public works on that scale are indicative of considerable state capabilities in taxation and labor coordination. But they may also be telling about the state's imperial ambitions, perhaps underscored further by its adoption of coinage. Carthage began minting coins late in comparison with the classical Greek city-states. As late as the fourth century BCE it seems to have operated without coins, even foreign ones. The suggestion has been made that military expenditure rather than reasons of commerce finally provided the impetus to produce a currency which, if true, would be telling about Carthage as a nascent imperial power.[177]

Carthage attracted an array of foreigners, mostly from either its West Mediterranean sphere of influence or cities in the Levant to which it had historical ties. Connections of the latter type are evident from a religious dedication made by a woman from Sidon.[178] Furthermore, a third-century BCE inscription marks the tomb of a certain Amran, whose wife had come from Arados, while a grave stele with a similar date commemorates the last resting place of a man from Kition.[179] As for connections to the Punic world, Carthaginian necropoleis have yielded a number of fourth-century BCE lead discs inscribed in Greek and Punic, which probably served as ex-votos.[180] To what area of the Greek-speaking world these objects were related is uncertain, but Sicily is the most likely candidate. A grave inscription in Greek commemorates a certain Apollodoros from Heraclea, probably Sicilian Heraclea Minoa, a city men-

175. Lancel 1992: 195–202.

176. Hurst and Stager 1978: 344.

177. Frey-Kupper 2014. On Carthaginian imperialism, see Broodbank 2013: 580–82; Pilkington 2013.

178. *CIS* 1.308; Ferjaoui 1992: 176–77.

179. *RÉS* nos. 1225–26; Bénichou-Safar 1982: nos. 7, 82 (for the date, see ibid.: 325); Ferjaoui 1992: 176–78.

180. Berger 1903 (= *RÉS* no. 508); Delattre 1905: 175.

tioned in two other Carthaginian grave steles. In addition, at a sanctuary near the *tophet*, a woman who had come from the Sicilian city of Eryx made a dedication. More dedicants had come from a second large island dominated by Carthage: Sardinia.[181]

Unsurprisingly, the city's bond with Tyre seems to have been especially close, visible epigraphically in the number of settlers it received from its old metropolis.[182] Several dedicatory inscriptions dating to the third and second century BCE mention Tyrians.[183] Nine contain the phrase *bnṣr*, or "son of Tyre," in the patronymic lineup, an unusual phrase probably referring to the oldest ancestor mentioned, not the dedicant himself. If so, the memory of a Tyrian origin lived on for generations in some Carthaginian families. Literary sources as well show that a strong connection to Tyre continued to exist well after the sixth century BCE, when Carthage is thought to have become independent.[184] In the previously mentioned treaty that Carthage made with Rome in 348 BCE, Tyre entered as a party, according to the text that Polybius gives: "There is to be friendship on the following conditions between the Romans and their allies and the Carthaginians, Tyrians, and the people of Utica and their respective allies" (3.24.3–13).[185] At the time the treaty was drafted Carthage had become a much more powerful city than Tyre, which seems to have been included in the terms as an ally bound to its former colony by religious and historical ties.

Roman authors provide us with details on those ties. Diodorus Siculus (20.14.1–3) tells us that Carthage used to send tithes from the city's public revenue to Tyre for the upkeep of the ancestral cult of "Heracles," the Greek name of the Tyrian ancestral god Melqart. Over time Carthage's payments diminished, and when in 310 BCE Agathocles of Syracuse besieged the city, its inhabitants feared to have incurred the god's wrath. They promptly dispatched a large sum of money and the most expensive offerings to Tyre. Curtius Rufus (4.2.10) reports on religious affiliations between the two cities in the late third century BCE. According to his narrative, the Carthaginians used to send envoys to Tyre to participate in an annual religious festival there, almost certainly another reference to the cult of Melqart. The old metropolis and its former colony remained connected at the public level until at least

181. Chabot 1926; Lapeyre 1939: 296.

182. On the ties between Carthage and Tyre, see Millar 2006: 36–37; Bonnet 2014: 289–94.

183. Bordreuil and Ferjaoui 1988: 139–42; Ferjaoui 1992: 175–76.

184. Markoe 2000: 54–63. Cf. Ameling 2013, who argues that Carthage was autonomous from its founding.

185. Tr.: W.R. Paton, *LCL* 1922. For a discussion of the treaty, see Serrati 2006: 118–20.

Hellenistic times and probably well beyond. Polybius (31.12.11–12) mentions a sacred boat bringing first fruits from Carthage to Tyre, showing that the practice of sending offerings lived on still in the mid-second century BCE. Such spiritual and diplomatic bonds probably explain the inscription dating to the 320s BCE, discussed above in the section on Athens, in which the Athenians honored two men from Tyre as public friends for bringing in Carthaginian grain. The strong historical connection of the honorands' native city to Carthage seems to have translated into beneficial trading conditions for them there, allowing them access to grain at a favorable price.

3

King's Men and the
Stationary Bandit

WITH HIS INVASION OF THE Achaemenid realm in 334 BCE, Alexander briefly managed to unite a vast territory under Macedonian rule. However, that unification would not outlive him by much. His early death in 323 precipitated a period of energetic warfare among his former commanders, who fought for control over the Macedonian heartland and the territories won by conquest.[1] By 277 BCE, the dust had settled and the main shape of the Hellenistic world had emerged. Three main royal houses had been established: that of the Ptolemies in Egypt, the Seleucids in Asia and the Antigonids in Macedonia.

The Ptolemaic and Seleucid kingdoms were openly favorable to migration, at least of a particular kind. Their rulers aimed to attract settlers from the Greco-Macedonian world, including Thrace and western Asia Minor. To encourage migration, Ptolemaic kings offered lots to military settlers, while dynasts in the vast Seleucid empire founded Greek-style cities that provided newcomers with opportunities of agricultural exploitation and trade.[2] In both states the governmental structures also offered career paths in civil and military service. The opportunities on offer enticed large numbers of inhabitants of the Greco-Macedonian world to pull up stakes and move to the new kingdoms. Meanwhile, forced migration was becoming a major factor in the Mediterranean. A growing slave trade moved people around in increasing numbers, the mass sale of prisoners of war leading to occasional spikes.[3]

Among the effects of these migratory flows were a more ethnically mixed populace in many urban centers and the growth of a number of megacities,

---

1. Mooren 1983: 205–08; Adams 2006.

2. Cohen 1983; Adams 2006: 39, 43–45; Davies 2006: 82–83; Bingen 2007: 83–121.

3. Gabrielsen 2003; Davies 2006: 83–84.

most notably Alexandria and Antioch. A profound and enduring cultural effect was the enormous enlargement of the Greek-speaking world.[4] Local languages like Aramaic, Elamite, Egyptian, Phrygian and Persian continued to be spoken, but Greek became the universal vehicle of communication for urban elites and state bureaucracies. Along with the Greek language, Greek ways of cultural, artistic and religious expression were assimilated by native elites in Asia Minor, Egypt, Syria and lands farther to the east. The integrating effects of this cultural and linguistic convergence can be seen in a salient counterexample: Hasmonean Judea after ca. 140 BCE. Fiercely resistant to Greek culture, the Hasmonean dynasts promoted the use of Hebrew as the language of state. As an even stronger signal, they destroyed the Greek cities of Samaria and Marisa. Archaeological evidence shows the economic result of this deliberate separatism in the cessation of Greek amphora imports. Omnipresent in the predestruction layers at Samaria and Marisa, Greek amphorae are all but absent from the archaeological record of Hasmonean Jerusalem.[5]

The changes brought about by the creation of the Hellenistic world were momentous, yet have so far not been much discussed in this book. The reason why is the institutional developments that I chose to focus on in chapter 2. Control over trade diasporas always remained a local-level affair of municipal administrations, even after cities were incorporated into the Hellenistic kingdoms and then the Roman empire. Furthermore, the institution of Greek public friendship lost its significance only when Rome's authority became supreme. Diplomatic shows of allegiance to state authority, including ruler worship, had been a key feature also of the Hellenistic world:

> The success of ruler cult both as a medium for the communication between ruler and subordinate civic community and for the legitimation of monarchical power can be best seen in the fact that it continued long after the end of the Hellenistic period as part of the ideology of the Principate.[6]

Yet the birth of the successor kingdoms did not lead to the terminal decline of Greek interstate honorific institutions, which "persisted throughout the Hellenistic period, despite the appearance of much more powerful kings."[7]

But if up to this point I have largely ignored the Hellenistic states, in my overall narrative their emergence deserves a dedicated discussion. To repeat one of the central tenets of this book: state formation and consolidation had an aggregate positive effect on the economy of the ancient Mediterranean, starting in the Late Iron Age and peaking sometime in the Roman imperial

4. Adams 2006: 45; Bresson forthcoming.
5. Rotroff 2006: 143; Bresson forthcoming.
6. Chaniotis 2003: 442.
7. Mack 2015: 277.

period. What then of the Hellenistic kingdoms? The first thing to note is that Hellenistic state formation led to a more economically integrated East Mediterranean, assisted not only by the use of the Greek language but also by the unification of monetary standards based on the Attic drachma and the Alexandrian tetradrachm.[8] In addition, because of their size, the successor kingdoms were ruled by men with a control over resources going far beyond that of city-state elites.

Three institutions formed the heart of state power in the Hellenistic kingdoms: the monarchy, a small circle of royal associates and the army.[9] As the center of the state the king acted as its main driver, setting the wheels of government in motion through leadership in war, royal ordinances and gift-giving. Closest to the king as his collaborators in government were his "friends," *philoi* in Greek. The use of this word for members of the royal court is a sign of the strong personal character of Hellenistic kingship. Selected by the ruler, the "friends" served as a board of advisors and close confidants.[10] Finally, the army consisted of, first, a core of standing infantry and cavalry recruited from Macedonian-style royal cities and military colonies; second, temporary forces made up of levies from the local population; and third, mercenaries often recruited from the old Greek world.

The king's inner circle of "friends"—together with other high-ranking officials and the military—were all stakeholders in, and beneficiaries of, state power. Receiving salaries and rations but also gifts and bonuses like grants of royal land, these various groups were allowed access to agricultural surplus within the state's structures. In John Ma's characterization, "The Hellenistic state was run by and for a ruling group—which was not quite an economic class of the wealthy, but rather a political elite of state's men at various socioeconomic levels."[11] Ma does not couch his description in the social-order language of Douglass North, John Wallis and Barry Weingast, but what he paints is a picture closely conforming to their concept of the "natural state." As explained in chapter 1, in such states a dominant coalition

> limits access to valuable resources ... or access to and control of valuable activities ... to elite groups. The creation of rents through limiting access provides the glue that holds the coalition together, enabling elite groups to make credible commitments to one another to support the regime, perform their functions, and refrain from violence.[12]

8. Davies 2006: 80–81; Thonemann 2015: 111–27.

9. Ma 2013: 336–38. On the Ptolemaic army, see Fischer-Bovet 2014.

10. Local oligarchs, not present at court, could be *philoi*, too: Strootman 2011: 148–49.

11. Ma 2013: 339–40. On the structure of the Ptolemaic state, see also Manning 2004.

12. North, Wallis and Weingast 2009: 30.

High levels of taxation allowed for substantial military expenditure, no doubt the largest item in the budget of Hellenistic states.[13] Success on the battlefield lent legitimacy to royal rule, leading kings to engage in frequent campaigning. But warfare was not the only instrument used to validate kingship. Conspicuous consumption by the monarch and his retinue also projected power and legitimate rule to both the autochthonous and the Greco-Macedonian population.[14] Such elite spending drew on a variety of cultural sources—Macedonian, Achaemenid, Near Eastern, Egyptian—and ranged from monumental architecture to high art and literature. The celebration of luxury by the ruling group served to distinguish members from nonmembers, exercising a strong attraction on urban elites desirous of emulating the upper-class lifestyle. As Ma noted, the operation of the Hellenistic states likely "had a generally expansionary effect, notably by encouraging consumption by a whole class closely linked with the state, and invested in the state's ethos of superior lifestyle and display."[15]

But if elite conspicuous consumption drove economic development, it also potentially favored state predation. In a recent comparative study, Andrew Monson indeed argued that Ptolemaic rulers (about whom we are best informed) were motivated by predatory, short-term fiscal policies similar to those of the Roman late-republican elite:

> As Rome's political instability intensified, culminating in the civil wars, it was economically rational for Rome's rulers to ignore or partake in the exploitation of its provinces for immediate gain. The Ptolemaic rulers and their agents, especially during the revolts and dynastic conflicts of the second and first centuries BCE, arguably had similar incentives.[16]

The Roman elite's exploitation of the provinces that Monson refers to can be called "roving banditry," a phrase coined by Mancur Olson to describe the conduct of state actors intent on the immediate extraction of resources without regard for long-term economic productivity.[17] Its opposite is what Olson termed "stationary banditry," in which rulers invest in public goods as long as marginal returns outstrip the cost of the original investment. In the latter model, rulers are still not motivated by a desire to maximize the welfare of their subjects. But their interests are more in line with those of the governed,

---

13. Davies 2006: 81; Fischer-Bovet 2014: 71–83; Monson 2015.

14. Mooren 1983: 207–09; Reger 2003: 346; Davies 2006: 81–82, 86–87; Ma 2013: 343–44.

15. Ma 2013: 348. For a similar argument applied specifically to the Ptolemaic economy, see Von Reden 2011.

16. Monson 2015: 172.

17. Olson 1991; McGuire and Olson 1996; Olson 2000.

and their behavior creates fewer incentive problems. Their aim is to allow the people under their control to be economically productive so as to be able to reap more of the benefits themselves. Their policies are less extractive than those of roving bandits, and the result of their actions can be net-positive for economic development. The planning horizon of rulers and their representatives is a critical factor in predicting their behavior. In that context it is worth spending a few more words on the later Roman republic.

In 133 BCE, Rome inherited the Attalid kingdom (western Turkey) by royal bequest. The rights to collect taxes in the new possession were auctioned off to Italian tax farmers, who received short-term contracts of fixed duration. The winning bidders' profits would increase if they extracted dues in excess of the official rate, and they thus had every motivation to squeeze as much money out of the area as they could. Officials on temporary overseas appointments equally were incentivized to enrich themselves.[18] No rival polity with a power comparable to that of the Roman existed in the immediate vicinity of the former Attalid realm. Fear of a takeover by a competitor state fueled by popular discontent seems therefore not to have provided a check on abuse; unwisely, as it turned out. Rome's predatory behavior made its administration extremely unpopular. In 88 BCE anger boiled over, leading to a revolt stirred up by King Mithridates of Pontus. By the end of it, scores of Romans lay dead (Appian *Mithr.* 22–23; Plutarch *Sulla* 24.4). With an insufficiently long planning horizon, even the representatives of well-established states can evidently engage in roving banditry that is not in their own or indeed anyone's long-term interest.

Another factor to consider in evaluating a state's surplus taking is its penchant for warfare, especially if informed by considerations of rule legitimization. Thomas Wilke has sensibly proposed that the capital-destroying force of warfare needs to be taken into account in the stationary versus roving bandit dichotomy, which he criticized as too basic.[19] If stationary bandits are "belligerent dictators," he argued, it is still possible that they engage in behavior detrimental to long-term productivity, under certain conditions even extracting resources at a higher rate than roving bandits. These ideas have great relevance for the study of the Ptolemaic state, given its nature and rule-legitimizing ideology.

Were Ptolemaic kings involved in the roving banditry that typified the Roman administration of the later republic? Or, to phrase the question in Wilke's terms, were they belligerent dictators whose military endeavors were consistently hampering the productivity of the population they controlled? In

18. Tan 2015: 215–16. See also Terpstra 2013: 217–19.
19. Wilke 2002.

formulating an answer, we first of all need to be careful in how we evaluate the effects of warfare. As John Davies has pointed out, Hellenistic military pursuits were not necessarily negative for economic development:

> Not all military investment and expenditure, by land or sea, is predatory and destructive: some of it can be seen as protection and insurance against damage to persons or animals or property from brigands by land or pirates by sea. . . . The costs of such security could be seen as acceptable insurance premiums, and in any case comprised of redistribution of resource (to suppliers, crews, soldiers) rather than a destruction of resource.[20]

Moreover, Davies continued, most Hellenistic wars were only brief, and many were fought between "opposing teams of professional and mercenary soldiers whose interest was not so much in annihilating the enemy as in well-pensioned survival—a military atmosphere more redolent of European wars of the eighteenth century than of twentieth-century World Wars."[21]

One way to approach the question of where to place the Ptolemaic kingdom in the framework of Olson and Wilke is to analyze the incentives and behavior of individual actors operating at the highest levels of government. Because of the strong personal nature of Hellenistic kingship, an analysis of the actions of "king's men" can reveal how the state behaved generally. Although such a microhistorical approach has the drawback of a limited chronological scope, it has the major advantage of getting economic incentives and outcomes into sharper focus, providing us with a point of reference.

If the rule of Ptolemaic kings fit the stationary-bandit model, we would expect to see (1) some measure of concern for the long-term sustainability of that rule and (2) some investment in public goods. As for (1), fostering economic success was rational behavior if rulers expected to remain in power long enough to reap the benefits. As for (2), to promote economic success, rulers had an incentive to invest part of the extracted resources back into tax-paying societies. Resources could be directed toward the construction of a physical infrastructure—including canals, roads and harbors—but also toward the promotion of public order.

I will investigate these matters by studying the third-century BCE "Zenon archive." Its documents largely pertain to the activities of a certain Apollonios, the finance minister of Ptolemy II and a man who surely counted among the king's "friends."[22] Besides being a royal official, Apollonios was a private businessman with financial interests in Syria-Palestine, an area that formed part of

---

20. Davies 2001: 37.

21. Davies 2001: 38–39.

22. On Apollonios as finance minister (*dioikêtês*), see Edgar P.Mich.Zen. 1931: 5–15.

the Ptolemaic kingdom during his tenure. We know about the operation of his overseas network through the documents kept by one of his top-ranking agents, a man named Zenon. The documents shine a rare spotlight on the inner workings of an ancient long-distance business network. As we will see, its internal cohesion was based on ethnicity, peer monitoring constrained agents' behavior, and information was freely shared.

The archive shows a complex mix of official and entrepreneurial affairs, once more underscoring the point made in the previous chapter about the essential fluidity between ancient Mediterranean public and private economies. The Ptolemaic kingdom levied taxes in its overseas territories through a state infrastructure, for which Apollonios was responsible as finance minister. At the same time, his position as one of the Ptolemaic kingdom's highest-ranking representatives gave him substantial leverage in conducting his private business ventures. We might be inclined to separate the two sides of his professional life, conceptualizing them as discrete economic spheres. But in doing so we may be introducing a division that contemporaries would not have recognized. As Roger Bagnall observed, we "have great difficulty . . . in distinguishing between the activity of Apollonios as finance minister of Ptolemy Philadelphos and that of Apollonios the wealthy entrepreneur. It is perhaps doubtful that Apollonios, Zenon, or the king himself could have drawn a clear line of demarcation."[23]

Apollonios could have abused his dual position for his own immediate benefit, but there were incentives for him not to do so. First of all, the policy of the king was aimed at retaining Ptolemaic control over Syria-Palestine. As a royal representative with an open-ended tenure, Apollonios thus had an infinite planning horizon in his economic management of the area.[24] Allowing exploitation to exceed what the local economy could sustain in the long run would have been counterproductive. Second, Syria-Palestine had strategic and prestige value, and was continuously eyed by the neighboring Seleucid kingdom. Defusing this potential source of interstate tension formed part of Apollonios' mandate. The archive shows him personally involved in the top-level diplomacy following King Ptolemy's peace agreement with the Seleucids in 253 BCE.[25] In line with the king's external policy, Apollonios had to keep Syria-Palestine economically productive and socially stable. Discontent would

23. Bagnall 1976: 18. In the same sense: Rostovtzeff 1922: 26–27; Von Reden 2007: 282–83.

24. Apollonios seems to have remained in Ptolemy II's service until the king's death: Edgar *P.Mich.Zen.* 1931: 6–7.

25. *P.Cair.Zen.*2.59242 and *P.Cair.Zen.*2.59251 (= Durand 1997: no. 32; Bagnall and Derow 2004: no. 24), dated to November or December 253 BCE and April 252 BCE respectively. On both texts, see Orrieux 1983: 49–50.

have undermined Ptolemaic rule there and would have played into the hands of the Seleucids. Affairs of state aside, Apollonios had private business interests in Syria-Palestine, importing into Egypt both locally produced goods and products transshipped from farther east. He also possessed vineyards and other farmland overseas, which would yield a return only if managed carefully over time.

In his roles as entrepreneur and finance minister, Apollonios had a stable and encompassing interest in Syria-Palestine, and we would therefore expect to see him and his men engage in stationary-bandit behavior. The evidence indeed suggests that they did. At the same time, if the Ptolemaic kingdom acted as a stationary bandit in its overseas possessions, promoting public order there, this behavior did not extend to the enforcement of private property rights. As we will see, the absence of third-party enforcement is clear from the Zenon documents.

Zenon and the "Zenon Archive"

Sometime in the years preceding World War I, Egyptian farmers found a large cache of papyri at the site of the ancient city of Philadelphia in the Fayum region, west of the Nile Valley (fig. 3.1). Decomposing organic material makes the soil of Egyptian archaeological sites rich in nitrate and useful as fertilizer, which is why the farmers were mining the area. Recognizing the value of the papyri as archaeological artifacts, they sold sizeable batches to Western antiquities dealers. The separate purchases fragmented the find, and although the greatest number ended up in Cairo, large collections now reside in a variety of countries outside Egypt, including Italy, France, Germany, Britain and the United States.

Because of the illicit nature of the sales, and doubtless also because the importance of archaeological context did not register much with contemporary scholarship, the exact find location was never recorded.[26] We can reasonably speculate that the papyri were discovered in a midden, deposited there when they were no longer of use to their onetime owner. This was the fate of many papyrological texts, and is the reason why we possess a number of so-called archives, a somewhat misleading term for related documents fortuitously discarded together.[27] But there is no longer any way of knowing if this was the case also with the papyri found at Philadelphia. Their archaeological context is forever lost, depriving us of information that might have been helpful in interpreting their content.

26. Edgar *P.Mich.Zen.* 1931: 1; Durand 1997: 13–14.
27. See Terpstra 2014a.

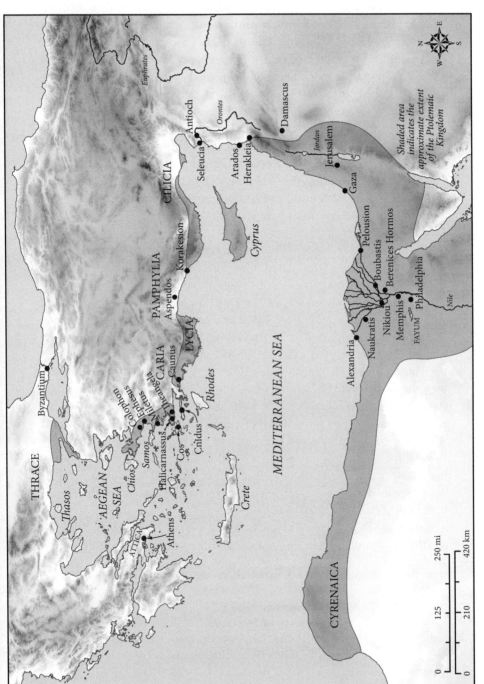

FIG. 3.1. The Ptolemaic kingdom in the mid–third century BCE.

About 1,750 legible texts comprise what is now commonly called the "Zenon archive."[28] Its eponymous protagonist, an enterprising Greek from the small coastal city of Caunus in Caria (Asia Minor, see fig. 3.1), had a most interesting and multifaceted career. Sometime before the end of the 260s BCE, Zenon must have left his hometown and headed for Egypt, more specifically its royal capital of Alexandria. The fact that he relocated and sought professional opportunities in the new Egyptian metropolis is emblematic of the world that the Hellenistic kingdoms had created. In a variety of configurations throughout its history the Ptolemaic state controlled extensive overseas territories: Cyrenaica, Syria-Palestine, Cyprus, Lycia and parts of Cilicia, Pamphylia and Caria (fig. 3.1).[29] During Zenon's lifetime his native region was under Ptolemaic control, and he thus remained within the boundaries and political structure of a single state, despite having moved across the Mediterranean.

The first secure evidence in the surviving corpus of texts of Zenon as Apollonios' employee is a letter dated November 260 BCE, although an older, damaged document suggests that the relationship went back at least a year.[30] There is unfortunately no way of knowing how Zenon became acquainted with the king's finance minister. Based primarily on the number of Carians that Apollonios employed, it is often thought that he was of Carian origin himself. If so, we may see a Carian network active in Egypt, providing men from the area with job opportunities. However, a reinterpretation of a dedicatory plaque to Apollo Hylates, a god unique to Cyprus, has recently led to the suggestion that Apollonios might have been a Cypriot.[31] But either way, Apollonios and Zenon formed part of a group of men from the Greek world who had permanently moved to Egypt and had forged professional careers there. If for Apollonios this meant a position within the Ptolemaic governmental hierarchy, Zenon never formed part of the royal bureaucracy and always remained a private agent, even if he met and transacted with officials both in Egypt and overseas.

Late in 260 BCE, Zenon was sent on a long journey around Syria, Palestine and the Transjordan, where he conducted business on his principal's behalf.[32]

---

28. For general introductions, see Edgar *P.Mich.Zen.* 1931: 1–50; Orrieux 1983: 16–20; Clarysse and Vandorpe 1995.

29. See Bagnall 1976; Fischer-Bovet forthcoming.

30. *P.Cair.Zen.*1.59002 (November 23, 260 BCE) and *P.Cair.Zen.* 5.59801 (October/November 261 BCE). In *PSI* 4.324 and 325, dating to May 30, 261 BCE, Zenon himself does not appear, but the inclusion of both letters in the archive almost certainly means that he was by then working for Apollonios.

31. Rigsby 2010: 131–36.

32. A departure in the winter of 260/259 BCE is implied by the dates mentioned in *P.Cair.*

In the spring of 258 BCE he returned to Egypt, although his traveling days were not over. He accompanied Apollonios on inspection tours through the Egyptian countryside, acting as the minister's personal secretary. Two years later, Zenon's position changed again when he was put in charge of a large Fayum estate, a gift by revocable title (*dôrea*) to Apollonios from King Ptolemy.[33] His tenure as estate manager was to last nine years, a period in which he also began developing his own agricultural business. In 248 BCE he retired from Apollonios' service and devoted himself exclusively to managing his personal business ventures in Philadelphia, which included leasing out farmland, lending money at interest, running bathhouses and raising livestock. The surviving documents become sparser for those years, and Zenon finally disappears from our surviving evidence altogether after 229 BCE. The archive thus spans about thirty years and consists of two sections, the first pertaining to Zenon's service as an aide to Apollonios, the second to his activities as an independent entrepreneur. We are less informed about the second part of Zenon's life, the number of documents relating to it making up only about a quarter of the total.[34]

The most extensively documented period is the time when Zenon served as the head manager of Apollonios' Fayum estate. This section of the archive has received the lion's share of scholarly attention. But the archive's earlier documents, if fewer in number, have the distinct advantage of recording not only agricultural production but also large-scale Mediterranean trading ventures. In addition, they provide insight into the management of an overseas territory by an imperial state. For those reasons, my discussion will focus on the older part of the archive.

The exact date Zenon left Egypt is recorded nowhere in the extant papyri, but we do know that he did not wait out the winter months. He set sail perhaps in December of 260 BCE, probably from the harbor of Pelousion in the northeastern Nile Delta, the regular point of departure for Gaza-bound ships (fig. 3.1). He spent at least some time there, making preparations for his voyage. A provisioning list records foodstuffs already bought and others still to be procured: flour, wine, honey, oil, olives and salted fish.[35] A large amount of food was evidently brought along from Egypt. But given the number of people

---

*Zen.*1.59004 (= Durand 1997: no. 4). Zenon stayed overseas at least until March 5, 258 BCE, as shown by *P.L.Bat.*20.32 (= Durand 1997: no. 10). On the dates of Zenon's travels, see also Tcherikover 1937: 11–12.

33. Rostovtzeff 1922; Manning 2005: 172–75; Bingen 2007: 192–93.

34. Orrieux 1983: 20. See Pestman 1981: 171–83 for the phases in Zenon's career and the accompanying documents.

35. *P.Mich.Zen.* 1.2 (= Durand 1997: no. 2), undated.

listed as fellow travelers, and the quantities of food that must have been needed to sustain them, provisions were likely also acquired locally overseas. Another six provisioning accounts indeed postdate Zenon's departure. They contain lists of foodstuffs for human consumption (flour, wine, fish) but also fodder for pack animals. Both types of provisions were to be distributed among the travelers.[36]

Some of the accounts mention place names, allowing us largely to reconstruct the route Zenon took. The itinerary shown in figure 3.2 is based predominantly on the information in the accounts. Apart from providing geographical data, the lists show us that Zenon traveled with a large entourage. One segment likely formed a permanent core consisting of Apollonios' agents and their attendants, including cooks, bakers, secretaries and clerks. The rest of the traveling company constantly changed composition. Not all the men (and two women, identified only by their husbands' names) we encounter were travelers from Egypt. Some were local chiefs and their retainers (donkey drivers, coachmen, horse grooms) providing services to the passengers and receiving sustenance in return. Others, such as the actor (*hypokritês*) Kleon and the officer (*hegemôn*) Nikias, seem to have been entirely unrelated to the expedition. They were probably joining the group only for a longer or shorter stretch for reasons of traveling convenience. Given that they received food rations as well, they must have had some connection to Apollonios.

It is clear from the correspondence in the archive that Zenon's position within Apollonios' network was exceptional. Higher-ranking and closer to the principal than many or perhaps all other men, Zenon handled a wide variety of business matters. But perhaps surprisingly, it is not clear what his mission was. His voyage may have had something to do with the recently concluded wars for control over the Levant that the Ptolemies and Seleucids had been fighting. If so, Apollonios may have dispatched Zenon as part of a political and economic reorganization and consolidation effort.[37] But Zenon does not seem to have had a precise task to accomplish or directive to follow. He at least makes no mention of any in his correspondence with his principal. Rather, he seems to have been sent overseas to manage Apollonios' multifaceted business generally, acting with a good deal of discretionary leeway.

Agency, Monitoring and Punishment

It is evident from the documents that Apollonios had already positioned a large number of men overseas by the time Zenon embarked on his tour of

36. *P.Cair.Zen.*1.59004–6, 4.59673, 5.59802, and *P.Lond.* 7.1930 (= Durand 1997: nos. 4–9).
37. Orrieux 1985: 157–58; Durand 1997: 37–40.

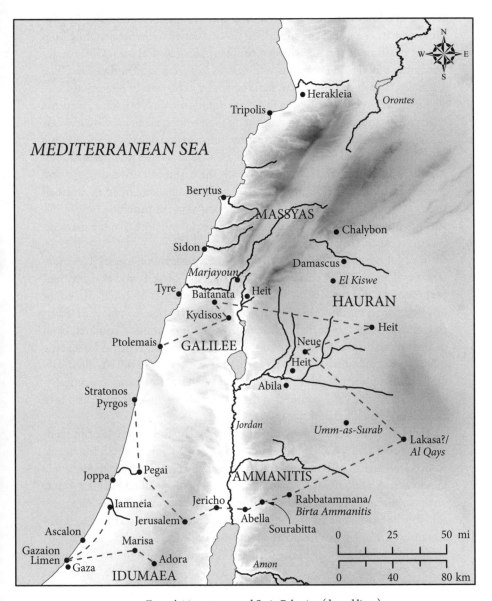

FIG. 3.2. Zenon's itinerary around Syria-Palestine (dotted lines).

Syria-Palestine. Those overseas agents seem to have stood in a hierarchical relationship. Some clearly possessed greater authority than others, having the power to overrule decisions made by their fellow agents. At the same time, we hear nowhere of titles suggestive of a formal chain of command. Authority was likely informal, based on seniority rather than a standardized ranking system.

It may, in addition, have been territorial and occupational. Many of Apollonios' men, it seems, had circumscribed tasks assigned to them, operating from
a fixed position or staying within a confined geographical area. Of those we
encounter a Zoilos in Ptolemais, a Menekles in Tyre and a Diodoros in Gaza;
a certain Ariston seemingly had Syria generally as his area of operation.[38]

As we will see in greater detail below, Apollonios' agents were entrusted
with money and authorized to transact on their principal's behalf. Their access
to the resources of an extremely wealthy individual may have tempted some
to embezzle goods, skim profits or cheat in other ways. The number and complexity of their transactions together with the distance between Egypt and
Syria-Palestine made it impossible for Apollonios personally to monitor all
their actions. He thus encountered the principal-agent problem: how to ensure the honest behavior of his men when they potentially had different interests from his and information was asymmetrical.[39]

In all probability, Apollonios relied to some measure on formal documentation and accountancy checks to verify his agents' honesty and evaluate their
performance. But the Zenon archive demonstrates that he could also count
on informal peer monitoring within his overseas network. A number of letters
show how his men reported on each other's failures of good conduct, from
incompetence and indecency to outright theft and fraud. With at least some
of his men Apollonios used a salary structure with delayed full payment, giving him the option of withholding pay if an agent's performance was unsatis-
factory.[40] But one case recorded in the archive shows that he could also take
considerably harsher, punitive measures.

Two letters to Zenon dated March 257 BCE relate the tragic tale of an agent
whose career was derailed, one can only imagine definitively.[41] The agent,
named Demetrios, had been sent by King Ptolemy on a short trip to Herakleia
in northern Phoenicia (figs. 3.1 and 3.2) for some unspecified business.[42] But
on his return to Egypt he had been apprehended by order of Apollonios, presumably because of some wrong he was suspected of having committed. He
was thrown in jail, while his possessions were confiscated and put up for public auction to the benefit of the treasury.[43] We would like to know what he

---

38. Zoilos: *PSI* 5.495; Menekles: *P.Cair.Zen.*1.59093; Diodoros: *PSI* 6.628, *P.Cair.Zen.*1.59009,
*P.Cair.Zen.*4, *add. et corrig.* 59009 p. 285; Ariston: *P.Cair.Zen.*4.59672.

39. Rees 1985a; 1985b.

40. *P.Cair.Zen.*1.59002 (= *P.Edgar* 1918: no. 2; Durand 1997: no. 1). See farther down for a
discussion.

41. *P.Cair.Zen.*1.59038 (= *P.Edgar* 1923: no. 80); *P.Cair.Zen.*1.59044 (= *P.Edgar* 1923: no. 81;
Durand 1997: no. 52).

42. *P.Lond.* 7.1933 (= Durand 1997: no. 51).

43. On Ptolemaic public auctions, see Manning 2015b: 104–05.

had done to deserve that treatment, but no details are offered in either letter. But whatever it might have been, he was not the only agent to get into trouble for the affair.

The letters were written by a certain Amyntas, an employee in Apollonios' household and a friend of the disgraced Demetrios. As we learn from Amyntas' first letter, not everything that Demetrios had with him belonged to him. Some of the objects he was carrying had been sent to him by Amyntas in response to a request for money. Those objects were valuable household items— silver drinking vessels—probably intended as pawns for cash.[44] Amyntas asked Zenon to halt the confiscation and public sale of those items, as Demetrios did not own them. But this was still not the whole story, as we learn from the second letter sent some three weeks later.

The valuables that Amyntas had lent Demetrios were not his property either but his employer's. He had helped himself to them and forwarded them to his cash-strapped friend without asking for permission. Realizing the gravity of the matter, he had drafted a letter to Apollonios asking for forgiveness. But before sending it, he thought it wise to consult with Zenon and the physician Artemidoros, two men close to the finance minister. Was it—yes or no—a good idea to send this letter?

> Amyntas to Zenon greeting. We wrote you lately about Demetrios, to whom on his return from Herakleia we lent some small drinking cups. And now since he is in prison and his belongings are being sold up we have written a letter to Apollonios of which a copy is written below for you, too. You would do well by taking counsel with Artemidoros the physician whether you think it advisable to deliver the letter to him or to let it go. . . . But if you think it best not to deliver the letter you will do me a favor by looking after Demetrios, for we hear he is now being neglected. Farewell.

A copy of the letter that Amyntas considered sending to Apollonios and on which he was soliciting advice then follows:

> To Apollonios. Demetrios, the checking-clerk appointed by you in the Prosopite district, having left home without intending to be long away and having moreover been robbed of his travel allowance and his servant by the pirate Lysimachos, when he was being detained by you begged us to advance him a little cash so that he might provide himself with the necessities of life. Money we had none to advance him, but we lent him some of the small drinking cups which you left abroad in the hands of Tryphera. . . .

44. Reekmans 1996: 91, 136.

Will you kindly grant us pardon, for we never dreamed that he would so shortly have come to grief. Farewell.[45]

How Demetrios, a checking-clerk (*antigrapheus*) not particularly high up in the royal bureaucratic hierarchy, had come to be sent on an overseas mission by the monarch is an intriguing question.[46] The answer perhaps lies in the fact that he had written to a household employee of Apollonios after pirates had robbed him of his travel money. Demetrios was evidently acquainted with the finance minister, who had appointed him to his official position, and also with the minister's men. All this suggests that he had in the past worked for Apollonios, perhaps as an overseas agent. He may through those connections have come to the attention of the king. But however that may be, the most significant aspect of the story for my purposes is Demetrios' imprisonment. Evidently Apollonios could utilize the state's public-order apparatus to punish his agents, incarcerating them and auctioning off their possessions if he saw fit to do so. If penalties of such severity were without a doubt rare, they were apparently what Apollonios' men could ultimately expect if they did not respect the rules.

Whatever Demetrios' misdeeds may have consisted of, they might have been brought to the attention of his principal through reports by agents who were in a position to observe the offending behavior. Several documents in the archive show evidence for such internal monitoring and reporting. An example is provided by a letter describing how an agent traveling around Syria-Palestine and the Aegean had embezzled goods. The extant text is missing its introduction, so we do not know the name of the perpetrator, although he may have been the Herakleides mentioned in the last sentence:

> And in Caunus he exchanged a pillow, a new one for an old, and he took the money ... (belonging?) to Nikanor's man and two more, old ones for new, belonging to the slave Troilos. He has money also from what he writes is in Hermokles' possession: a bedcover and one pillow. These things he sent from Miletos to Halicarnassus when he sent the bedsteads and the carpet. And he also exchanged the bedframe for his own; his wife now has it in Alexandria. And more: the bedcover he claimed he had lost in Gaza. And more: having bought some mattresses cheaply from Stachys for six drachmas he sold them for a high price in Rabbatammana. And more: what he said he had lost in Halicarnassus he has not lost but has himself. Force him to swear also about the bedstead-strap that he lost in Ptolemais, if you

45. Tr. (with modifications): *P.Edgar* 1923: no. 81.
46. For the position of *antigrapheus*, see Bagnall 1976: 3. The term is generic, though, and could well have been used also for controllers in the bureau of the *oikonomos*, men in positions higher than district checking-clerks.

want. About the rest the slave boy will inform you when you question him. And if Herakleides were there, he himself would have informed you about the bedcovers.[47]

We do not know who the addressee of this letter was, but from the inclusion of the document in the archive it is a safe assumption that it was intended for Zenon's eyes. We also do not know who the author was, but he was likely reporting on the misbehavior of someone whose actions he could observe and thus someone in the same line of work. So what was the occupation of the man denounced as a liar and embezzler? The large geographical range of his operations—from the Aegean down to Alexandria—suggests that he was someone working on ships.[48] That he was a man involved in maritime activities is suggested further by the nature of the goods he is said to have pilfered. Mostly those were beds and bed linens, which were probably not cargo but part of the standard equipment of long-haul ships.

In a document from the archive listing imported goods we find household items—stove burners, braziers and a couch—that were exempt from taxation. Almost certainly those goods were carried onboard for the use of the crew and passengers, and we can imagine a similar purpose for the bedding material.[49] Such items were not without value. Mattresses could fetch close to sixty drachmas apiece, as a papyrus in the archive informs us.[50] The embezzler, then, had likely been stealing ship furnishings, in part for his own use, in part to sell for profit. A colleague of his had become aware of this thieving and had decided to report it. Unfortunately, we do not know what action might have been taken by Apollonios or his higher-ranking agents in response to the account.

The letter revealed fraud and theft, but apart from such serious transgressions, Apollonios' men also reported a lack of due diligence by their fellow agents. A message to Zenon from a certain Krotos, an agent operating in or around Joppa, presents an example.[51] Krotos complained about the general incompetence of a man named Alexis, who seems to have been a subordinate of his.[52] Allegedly Alexis had failed to collect a sum of money from a group

47. *PSI* 6.616 (= Durand 1997: no. 28). See also Orrieux 1983: 45.

48. A captain named Herakleides is known from the archive: *P.Cair.Zen.*1.59012–13 (= Durand 1997: nos. 12–13).

49. *P.Cair.Zen.*1.59013 (= *P.Edgar* 1923: no. 74; Durand 1997: no. 13).

50. *P.Col.Zen.* 1.15: mention of seven mattresses for 400 drachmas total. On this text, see Orrieux 1983: 75.

51. *P.Cair.Zen.*1.59077 (= *P.Edgar* 1919: no. 12; Durand 1997: no. 49).

52. Krotos appears also in *P.Cair.Zen.*1.59093 and 5.59804 (= Durand 1997: nos. 45 and 44). Alexis appears in *P.Lond.* 7.1932 (= Durand 1997: no. 26) and *P.Cair.Zen.*1.59008 *verso*.

of oil transporters, although a slave girl had been given as a pledge for the debt. Through his bumbling he had let not only the money but also the slave girl slip through his fingers. He had, in addition, let a sailor escape from prison; the man was now nowhere to be found. In all likelihood the sailor belonged to the crew of one of Apollonios' ships.[53] The reason for his incarceration is not stated, but we can speculate that he was guilty of embezzlement of the kind described above. A public-order offense is also possible, although if that was the case, it is unclear why Krotos would have concerned himself with the matter. At any rate, if Alexis' actions did not constitute fraud, they were still failures to perform professional duties. Presumably Krotos wrote to Zenon to deflect blame for the incidents and to create a record of who was responsible for them.

Yet more evidence for internal monitoring is provided by a letter from one Herakleides, a coachman known also from other Zenon papyri. In a rather elliptical and rambling report, he described the behavior of two men operating in the area between Joppa, Ptolemais and Pegai (fig. 3.2).[54] He did not specify their profession, but a reference to the neglect and sale of animals under their care suggests that they were colleagues of his. A coachman with the same name as one of the alleged culprits appears also in another document, providing further support for that hypothesis.[55] Herakleides accused the two of running a prostitution ring, wasting money, neglecting their duties and probably also of selling their principal's property. He listed a number of shady transactions that they were involved in, including the sale, purchase and exploitation of female slaves. To discredit the duo further, he added that one of them had been dragged off to prison and shackled for seven days after a disturbance of some sort had erupted. He concluded by summing up the wrongdoings he had either witnessed personally or heard mentioned:

> For each day they went out onto the streets and made a splendid profit. And because they were doing this they did not keep their mind upon the livestock but Drimylos each day warmed two bronze cauldrons of water for his sweetheart. And he sold the female ass and the onager. And there are witnesses of these events. Concerning more of these affairs, if you ask me, you will find the whole truth.[56]

53. A sailor with the same name (Theron) as the one mentioned in this letter appears in *P.Cair.Zen.*4.59677, a list of grain allowances for a crew on what was likely one of Apollonios' ships.

54. Herakleides also appears in *P.Cair.Zen.*1.59006 and 59008 *recto* (= Durand 1997: nos. 9 and 16).

55. *P.L.Bat.*20.59 (= Durand 1997: no. 58).

56. *PSI* 4.406 (= Scholl 1983: no. 6; Durand 1997: no. 27). Tr.: Rowlandson 1998: no. 207.

Some of the actions on which Herakleides reported were not so much fraudulent toward the principal as unseemly: landing in prison after a brawl, squandering money on a girlfriend's bathing habits. We could see these additions simply as an attempt at character assassination, but one wonders if Herakleides was not also worried about the social position of Apollonios' agents—himself included—in Syria-Palestine. If so, his reporting may betray an awareness that to function properly, the network needed to observe reasonable bounds of decency. Many of Apollonios' men stationed in the area were originally from Greece or western Asia Minor, were recent arrivals from Egypt and were thus easily identifiable corporately. Misbehavior of even one would reflect negatively on the group, and a bad collective reputation would make it harder for all agents to operate effectively. To prevent unnecessary difficulties, it was best for the collective to restrain improper conduct.

As the ultimate beneficiary of the network Apollonios as well was incentivized to curb any misbehavior of his men toward the local population. That held true especially for his agents' treatment of local collaborators, who were indispensable for the smooth running of business. Concern for the ongoing cooperation of such collaborators probably explains the presence of a letter in the archive from a man who was evidently a non-Greek. He complained bitterly to Zenon about the treatment he had received, first at the hands of a certain Krotos and then of a certain Jason.[57] The author had worked for Zenon in Syria, probably as a transporter; "I did everything that was ordered with respect to the camels," he declared. But after Zenon's return to Egypt he had been regarded with contempt by Krotos and had not been paid his salary, despite repeated requests. A similar episode had then followed with Jason. According to the author he had suffered the described injustices because of his non-Greek ethnicity:

> They have treated me with scorn because I am a "barbarian." I beg you, therefore, if it seems good to you, to give them orders that I am to obtain what is owing and that in future they pay me in full, in order that I may not perish of hunger because I do not know how to speak Greek.[58]

Because the first words of the text have faded, we lack the author's name, making it impossible to determine his ethnic background. Given that he had been employed by Zenon in Syria, it seems reasonable to assume that he was

57. *P.Col.Zen.* 2.66 (= Durand 1997: no. 50). See also Orrieux 1983: 132–33; Reekmans 1996: 80–81.

58. Tr.: Bagnall and Derow 2004: no. 137. The word *hellenizein* might mean "to speak Greek" but also "to act like a Greek," as both Durand and Bagnall and Derow point out in their commentaries.

a local Arab, but this can be no more than conjecture. The language of the letter also gives no indication of his ethnic identity. It is written in decent Greek, but was likely composed by a scribe rather than the nameless "barbarian" in person. This transmission through an intermediary has made it impossible to judge how weak the protagonist's Greek was in actuality. He presumably knew enough to communicate with Krotos and Jason, despite his claim that he did not speak the language at all. But whatever his Greek language proficiency might have been, his non-Greek ways had apparently been reason for Apollonios' men to treat him with disdain.

Yet the insults and injustices were clearly not the end of the affair. The maltreated "barbarian" wrote to Zenon directly and evidently got his complaint across. We would like to know if any action was taken to right the alleged wrongs and if it included not only the overdue salary payments but also a reprimand (or worse) for Krotos and Jason. No evidence exists allowing us to say what happened next, but the fact that the letter was filed in Zenon's records does suggest that the complaint was taken seriously. We can conclude that when Apollonios' men employed external labor and treated it unfairly, complaints could reach the highest rungs of management, pointing to checks on abuse. More information on such checks is provided by the documentation related to the running of Apollonios' agricultural business in Syria-Palestine.

Apollonios' Baitanata Estate

A number of papyri provide information on the management of an estate that Apollonios possessed at Baitanata, southeast of Tyre (fig. 3.2).[59] An undated document records gifts sent on behalf of Apollonios to both Zenon and a certain Kriton, probably to be identified with the frequently mentioned commander of Apollonios' commercial fleet in the Nile Delta.[60] The presents were all foodstuffs (Chian cheese, olives, fish and meat) and included wax-sealed jars of wine from Baitanata's vineyards. Apart from telling us that the wine must have been of high enough quality to serve as handouts, the text provides us with information on the status of the land. The Zenon archive makes it clear that the large Egyptian domain that Apollonios would later receive from the king was a so-called *dôrea*, a gift by revocable title. By contrast, the papyri refer to Baitanata only with the generic term of *ktêma*, "estate," suggesting that it was not royal but private land. If so, it must have been acquired

---

59. See Durand 1997: 67–68 for a discussion of the location.

60. *PSI* 6.594 (= Durand 1997: no. 38; Kloppenborg 2006: no. 4). On Kriton, the position of commander (*stolarchês*) and Apollonios' Nile Delta fleet, see Hauben 2006.

by Apollonios personally, although we do not know how or when it might have come into his possession.[61]

We get some information on the size of the vineyards in a letter dated May 9, 257 BCE.[62] It was written by a man named Glaukias and addressed to Apollonios directly. Glaukias is recorded nowhere else in the archive, but his letter confirms that he was an agent sent from Egypt to inspect matters at Baitanata and to settle some other Syrian affairs, which remain vague. From his message we learn that the vineyards had 80,000 vines, which, depending on the spacing between plants, probably meant a plot size between 18 and 44 hectares.[63] The letter reports on the work done on the estate—a well struck, a dwelling constructed—and the quality of the vintage. According to the upbeat assessment of Glaukias, the wine produced was so excellent that it could pass for Chian, one of the most prized wines of the Hellenistic world. "Your business is flourishing and fortune is favoring you in all things," he concluded brightly.[64]

Yet from a third and only fragmentary papyrus, it seems that some fifteen months earlier trouble had been brewing at Baitanata.[65] Because of the lacunae in the text, much remains uncertain, but it is obvious that the farmworkers had lodged a complaint and that the estate manager, Melas, had been communicating with them about their grievances. A higher-ranking but now anonymous third party had then intervened and drawn up a report. This third party was for certain not Zenon, who at the time of these events was about to return to Egypt. The author of the report, by contrast, had just arrived from Egypt, as he notes in passing. Perhaps he was the inspector Glaukias who would visit the area in May of the following year. But whoever wrote the report, from the last lines it would seem that the document was intended for Apollonios, even if he is not explicitly identified as the addressee:

> I asked them (i.e., the workers) to stay and to put things in order. If they do this they will receive all kindness from you. Having made these recommendations, I dispatched them. Melas thought it right that I write to you in regard to all these matters. Therefore I have written to you so that you will know.[66]

61. Durand 1997: no. 38, but cf. Tcherikover 1937: 45–48, who maintains that Baitanata was royal land.

62. *P.Lond.* 7.1948 (= Durand 1997: no. 36; Kloppenborg 2006: no. 3).

63. Although much higher numbers up to 112 hectares are also possible: Kloppenborg 2006: no. 3 n. to l. 7.

64. Tr.: Kloppenborg 2006: no. 3.

65. *PSI* 6.554 (= Durand 1997: no. 22; Kloppenborg 2006: no. 1).

66. Tr. here and below (with small alterations): Kloppenborg 2006: no. 1.

The workers were complaining about three seemingly unrelated issues, though all to do with the estate's harvest. First, they objected to a claim of arrears on payments for some unknown crop, probably grain.[67] Whether the complaint concerned taxation or rent is unclear, as is the function of the *kômomisthôtês* making the request for outstanding payments. The title appears only once elsewhere in the papyrological corpus in an equally ambiguous context, and could indicate a private tax farmer but also a Ptolemaic public official.[68]

Second, the workers protested that solid cakes of grape skins and seeds, the residual material from the grape pressing process, had been taken away from them while they had a dearth of such leftovers. They probably considered compressed grape skins to be valuable as foodstuffs, and perhaps also as medicine.[69] Finally, they seem to have been complaining about a tax on figs, although the text is too fragmentary to say much beyond that. Whatever the nature of the last complaint, it at least suggests that in addition to vineyards and likely grain fields the estate included orchards:

> Regarding the grape pressings that were taken away (?). Melas acknowledged to have taken them, because the place suffered from a lack of water and they ruined the grape pressings. He needed (it) for the workers he had in the city and most of (the tenants) owned their own vineyards from which they could get pressings. To those who did not own vineyards he promised that he would provide sufficient (pressings). But they also complained about the figs because he had collected the three ... from the crop ... injustice ... that they have produced the figs in the 27th year and that they also have paid to ... from the fruit they had produced.

Melas' mention of provisions for his workers in the city—Tyre presumably—tells us that his responsibilities extended beyond Baitanata, and that his principal's business affairs in the area had longer branches. His remark that most of the farmers could get grape pressings from their own vineyards further shows us that many of them were landowners who worked at Apollonios' estate as either leaseholders or wage laborers. Baitanata thus seems to have depended on the surrounding farming community for its economic success.

My concern is what the report reveals about the behavior of Apollonios and his men toward the local population. If the farmworkers were complain-

---

67. The harvest is expressed in the Syrian *koros*, a measure used mainly for dry goods: Tcherikover 1937: 45; Durand 1997: 154–55. *P.Cair.Zen*.1.59004 mentions Baitanata flour, further suggesting that Apollonios' estate produced grain.

68. See Kloppenborg 2006: no. 1 n. to l. 13 for a commentary. A *kômomisthôtês* also appears in *P.Tebt.* 1.183.

69. Nutritional and medicinal properties of *stemphula*: Hp. *Morb.* 2.69; Gal. 6.576.

ing, they seem not to have been cowed into submission. They evidently did not lack means of redress when they felt they were being unfairly treated, and it seems that their petition eventually reached Apollonios personally. A year later things had apparently calmed down completely, and the estate was thriving. Glaukias, in his report on the situation there, makes no mention of any further trouble with the laborers. Moreover, given the reportedly high quality of the vintage, careful work must have been done on the vines in the intervening months. Whatever the nature of the dispute in 258 BCE, it seems not to have been indicative of ongoing, abusive exploitation.

The episode and its aftermath suggest that Apollonios and his local agents were motivated by stationary-bandit considerations. They were incentivized to prevent a rebellion or more passive resistance by the agricultural workforce at Baitanata to ensure the estate's long-term productivity and profitability. Of course, Apollonios was not acting in his capacity as finance minister in his dealings with the laborers on his personal estate. But as noted above, his behavior was informed by a complex blend of public and private incentives. An attempt to study his activities based on a clear distinction between the two is all but impossible, as we will see in the next section.

Trade, Taxation and Diplomacy

The first time we see Zenon personally conducting business overseas is in a document dating to April or May of 259 BCE and drawn up in the village of Birta in the Transjordan (fig. 3.2). It records the sale of a seven-year-old Babylonian slave girl. The Syrian slave trade is frequently attested in the archive, and the document suggests that Apollonios had a stake in it not only as a government official but also as a businessman and consumer. Given the private nature of the recorded transaction, the girl was in all likelihood destined for Apollonios' personal household.

The sale took place on behalf of a certain Toubias, a local chieftain and Ptolemaic vassal.[70] The cosmopolitan character of the Hellenistic world is on vivid display in the contract. Toubias' transacting agent was a Cnidian Greek, while a military settler in his service is identified as a "Persian," likely a Jew judging from his father's name, Ananias. On Zenon's side the witnesses included a geographical variety of Greeks: a Milesian, an Athenian, a Colophonian and an Aspendian.

What makes this contract typical of the Zenon archive is the fluidity between private and public economies it displays. Toubias was a local ruler in

---

70. *P.Cair.Zen.*1.59003 (= *P.Edgar* 1918: no. 3; Durand 1997: no. 3; Bagnall and Derow 2004: no. 143). See Harper 1928: 6–17; Tcherikover 1937: 52–53; Orrieux 1983: 42–44; 1985: 158–62.

Ptolemaic-controlled territories and as such ultimately subject to royal power. His position as a political stakeholder is highlighted in a letter of his to Apollonios, in which he mentioned having followed Apollonios' suggestion of sending gifts to the king, clearly as a diplomatic gesture. From another one of his letters we know that he sent gifts also to Apollonios personally.[71] Toubias and Apollonios thus engaged in public diplomacy while at the same time transacting privately through their business agents. Such a combination emerges also in other documents, for instance in a list of goods that Zenon shipped from Ptolemais to Pelousion, ranging from crab and Sicilian salted fish to rose oil and live goats. Those goods were gifts made by two men with Phoenician names: Balmalakos and Mattanit(?) son of Tibelos, the first declaring himself to be on familiar terms with Zenon.[72] Here as well we are likely seeing diplomatic gestures of local power-holders, at least one of whom had transacted some private business with Apollonios' agent.

As noted above, the slave trade often appears in the archive, and it is clear that not just Zenon but also many of his colleagues were engaged in it. As far as we can tell the slaves making their way to Egypt were predominantly children, mostly girls like the Babylonian girl that Zenon bought from Toubias. We possess little information on how they were employed, but in all probability they were destined for household work, not heavy labor on the farm.[73] The import of slaves was motivated by financial considerations. Relatively plentiful and cheap in Syria-Palestine, slaves were scarce and expensive in Egypt, and the price difference fueled a lucrative Levantine export business.[74]

But although Syrian slaves were an attractive commodity to markets in Egypt, a tax had to be paid to get them there. Given Apollonios' dual position as an importer and the king's finance minister his agents' activities in this economic area are interesting to observe. Two letters in particular are worth discussing. The one cited below dates to September 6, 257 BCE, at a time when Zenon had already returned to Egypt. Evidently his colleagues thought it expedient to keep him abreast of goings-on overseas. The interpretation of the document is not straightforward because, as is often the case, pieces of the

71. *P.Cair.Zen.*1.59075–76 (= *P.Edgar* 1919: no. 13 and 1923: no. 84; Durand 1997: nos. 29–30; Bagnall and Derow 2004: no. 65). Both letters are dated May 13, 257 BCE.

72. *P.Lond.* 7.2141 (= Durand 1997: no. 15). Another Phoenician (Milkias) appears in *P.Cair. Zen.*1.59008 recto.

73. This has to remain conjecture, as "we are ignorant of the function of at least 90% of slaves attested in papyrological sources": Straus forthcoming.

74. Tcherikover 1937: 16–18. The slave trade figures prominently in a royal ordinance of ca. 261 BCE; see Liebesny 1936. Syrian slaves exported to Egypt, see also *PSI* 6.648 and *P.Cornell* 1, l. 222–24 (= Durand 1997: nos. 53–54). On slavery in the Zenon papyri generally, see Scholl 1983.

puzzle are missing. Nevertheless, it is obvious that a certain Apollophanes, an agent of Apollonios, had clashed with the custom officials in Gaza:

> Philotas to Zenon, greeting. Krotos requested us to write to you concerning the slaves who ran away from the harbor of Gaza. For I happened to be called in by Apollophanes and him (i.e., Krotos) in order to work with them on matters with the tax collectors and (to recover and send the slaves?) quickly to them. Therefore, having proceeded to Herodes the tax collector, I found that Apollophanes had made an agreement with him for a tax of eighty drachmas in the name of Apollonios. Whereupon I annulled that (agreement) and made another in the name of Apollophanes and decreased the tax agreed upon by forty drachmas. And I brought the slaves back to the harbor and we brought them to Herakleides (i.e., the boat captain) and handed them over to Apollophanes. And he said that he himself would guard (them) and he did not let us concern ourselves with it although we were willing to assist in watching (the slaves). Therefore, I wrote to you that you would know.[75]

The runaway slaves mentioned by the letter writer Philotas seem to have been captured or at least detained by the customs authorities at Gaza. This is not stated in so many words, but implied by the fact that Philotas went to see the tax official Herodes to arrange matters and bring the slaves back to the harbor, doubtless the place from where they had made their bid for freedom. The listed sum was probably not a regular tax but an exceptional surcharge for capture and detention, which would explain why it was negotiable.[76] So far, the reading of the papyrus poses few problems.

However, the role of the agent Apollophanes is difficult to assess. Why had he made an agreement in his principal's name for a sum of eighty drachmas, and why was it then transferred to his own name for half that amount? To my mind the most plausible explanation is that Apollophanes, while carrying out a slave shipment for Apollonios, had charged his principal's account for the unforeseen cost he had incurred.[77] His senior colleague Philotas had subsequently reassessed and renegotiated the deal, transferring the charge to Apollophanes personally as the agent responsible for letting the slaves escape. Still, he did lend his fellow agent a hand by arranging a much reduced sum.

---

75. *P.Cair.Zen.*5.59804 (= Scholl 1983: no. 2; Durand 1997: no. 44). Tr.: White 1986: no. 9.

76. For demands of money for the capture of slaves, see the discussion below of *P.Cair. Zen.*1.59015 *verso* (= *P.Edgar* 1923: no. 76; Scholl 1983: no. 3; Durand 1997: no. 42).

77. Cf. Durand 1997: no. 44: Apollophanes was transporting his own slaves and had attempted to defraud his principal. This seems an implausible interpretation given the tone of the letter.

How Philotas had managed to convince the Gazan tax official to break open the contract and cut the charge by half is unclear, although his senior position within the agent network must have helped. It seems doubtful that anyone unconnected to a man as influential as Apollonios would have had the leverage that Philotas apparently enjoyed. Apollophanes had initially made a contract in his principal's name, so there can be no doubt that all involved knew perfectly well who the interested party behind the shipment was. Moreover, the Ptolemaic finance minister was by no means just anyone to the tax collectors operating in the Gazan harbor. The dynamic at work here, which is difficult for us fully to appreciate, was thus that two groups of men who served different immediate interests but who were ultimately subordinate to the same powerful individual attempted to get the best arrangement possible.

The agent Apollophanes' performance in this affair had hardly been outstanding. Despite his errors, there were still people willing to assist him, but one cannot help but wonder if his conduct damaged his standing with his peers. An undated letter mentioning a conflict between him and one of Apollonios' ship captains does indeed hint at such damage. It tells us that the captain had refused to take Apollophanes on board (here as well, a third party came to the rescue), although no details are given on why.[78] Whatever might have made Apollophanes objectionable as a passenger, that he had a history of causing trouble for those around him is suggested further by another letter dating to 257 BCE.

Once more he had been shipping slaves, out of Tyre this time, and once more some wheeling and dealing with custom officials had ensued. The question of what exactly transpired has been debated in the scholarship, but evidently Apollophanes had attempted to export slaves out of Phoenicia without possessing the necessary papers. Confronted by the Tyrian taxmen, he had turned to a certain Menekles and claimed to be handling Zenon's merchandise. This assertion had prompted Menekles to intervene on Apollophanes' behalf, probably with the outcome that the shipment was allowed to proceed:

> Herakleitos to Zenon, greetings.... Apollophanes also came to Syria, and while we were on the way to Massyas we met him in Sidon.... And Menekles, the man in Tyre, related that he (i.e., Apollophanes) transported slaves and goods from Gaza to Tyre and transshipped them in Tyre without having notified the custom officials and without having an export license for the slaves. And they (i.e., the custom officials) noticed this and confiscated his goods. Apollophanes then appeared before Menekles and said that the slaves and goods belonged to you; therefore, Menekles also

78. *P.Cair.Zen.*1.59019 (= *P.Edgar* 1922: no. 70; Durand 1997: no. 24).

defended his interests. I am writing it to you now so that you order Apollophanes that he should enter nothing in your name except when it appears to be useful to you. . . . Farewell.[79]

Menekles is a key figure in this story, but we do not know what his function might have been. He could have been a Ptolemaic custom official, although the way he is described in the text, "the man in Tyre," suggests otherwise. He was obviously in close contact with the letter writer Herakleitos, to whom he had reported Apollophanes' actions. Moreover, he was ready to assist when goods said to belong to Zenon were impounded, by implication suggesting that he was protecting the business interests of Apollonios as his principal. These circumstances would lead to the conclusion that he was yet another one of Apollonios' ubiquitous overseas agents. If so, he was evidently superior in rank to Apollophanes. Just as Philotas in the letter cited above, he apparently had a good deal of power, enough to challenge the custom house in Tyre. We thus get the impression that here as well the crux of the matter was state affairs somehow intersecting with private enterprise. The question is to what degree—if any—Apollonios was involved in the events described here. He is not mentioned anywhere in the extant correspondence, and in contrast to the previous episode no agreements were made in his name.

Michael Rostovtzeff thought that we are witnessing a shady business from the top down. In his interpretation of events, the agents were shipping slaves from Phoenicia to Egypt for Apollonios, using his high position to influence officials and evade taxes, presumably with his tacit consent.[80] But Victor Tcherikover challenged that reading, providing a more plausible interpretation. The slaves, he argued, were probably not destined for Egypt at all. They were brought to Tyre from Gaza, which shows that they were on a northerly, not a southerly route. It therefore seems more likely that Apollophanes intended to ship the slaves beyond the borders of the Ptolemaic kingdom, which would also explain why he needed an export license. The finance minister could surely have produced such a license, and the fact that none was issued implies that the agent was acting without his principal's knowledge and permission.

In this reading only Apollophanes had acted in a less than upright manner. Found out, he did not want Apollonios to learn of the affair, which is why he invoked not the name of his principal but Zenon's when appealing to Menekles for help.[81] Menekles came to his defense, so it would seem that this plan

79. P.Cair.Zen.1.59093 (= P.Edgar 1919: no. 14; Scholl 1983: no. 5). Tr.: Tcherikover 1937: 69–70. Cf. Rostovtzeff 1922: 33–34 and Bagnall 1976: 20, who propose that it was Menekles who had attempted to export slaves, with Apollophanes coming to his aid.

80. Rostovtzeff 1922: 33–34. In this sense also Bagnall 1976: 19–20; Orrieux 1983: 45–46.

81. So Tcherikover 1937: 18–20, 68–72, followed by Durand 1997: no. 45.

worked, at least initially. Herakleitos on hearing all this thought he should warn Zenon that merchandise was being shipped under the false claim that it belonged to him. We would like to know what happened next and if Apollonios eventually took disciplinary steps against Apollophanes, something he was perfectly willing to do, as we have seen above. Unfortunately, we do not know how the affair ended.

Regardless of whether this reconstruction is correct in every detail, both cited letters on slave exports illustrate how Apollonios' private business inevitably crossed paths with the tax gathering machinery that was also under his supervision. Some scholars have doubted if he always walked a straight line in this area. Bagnall thought that it "appears at times as if Apollonios was, through Zenon, busy evading the laws that he was responsible for enforcing."[82] Rostovtzeff harbored similar suspicions, as we have seen. However, no concrete evidence exists to support that view. Campbell Edgar, in an extensive survey of the archive, found no indication of dishonesty, unscrupulousness or cheating of the treasury, concluding that "nothing recorded of [Apollonios] leads us to suppose that he was not a faithful servant of the king."[83] Evidence on the importing side of Apollonios' shipments is in line with that assessment.

Direct information on his handling of Ptolemaic taxation is provided by custom declarations made at Pelousion, Egypt, for goods coming in from Syria-Palestine, probably included in the archive because Zenon was involved on the forwarding end. One long papyrus dating to May or June of 259 BCE lists the cargo of two ships. The text shows us both the variety of goods for personal use that Apollonios shipped in from overseas and the tax he paid on those goods.[84] All imported products appear to have been of high quality. Some were luxury goods, such as wine from dried grapes, Attic honey, Chian cheese, game meat (wild stag and boar) and "white oil," a prized commodity produced in a special manufacturing process.[85] The varying quantities listed—low for oil, much higher for wine—suggest that some imports were intended for Apollonios' own household while others may have been intended for retail, or perhaps to serve as handouts.[86]

---

82. Bagnall 1976: 20.

83. Edgar *P.Mich.Zen.* 1931: 15.

84. *P.Cair.Zen.*1.59012 (= *P.Edgar* 1923: no. 73; Durand 1997: no. 12).

85. See Bresson 2012.

86. Edgar points to a consignment of oil as a possible parallel (*P.Edgar* 1923: no. 75). That shipment was almost certainly intended for retail within Egypt. There is no reason, as Orrieux 1983: 58 does, to see the imported goods as gifts. Cf. *P.Lond.* 7.2141, where the nature of the goods as gifts is made explicit.

Import duties were high on the products coming in: as much as 50 percent on white oil, special wine and high-quality vinegar, 33 percent on more common wines and dried figs, 25 percent on honey, meats, fish and cheeses and 20 percent on wool. On top of the import duties, minor taxes included a naval tax on oil and a 1 percent harbor levy. But contrary to what we might expect, little if any special treatment is detectable. The Egyptian custom house applied only a minimal deduction of 0.25 percent to the large sum due, and it is not even certain if it did so because of Apollonios' position as finance minister.

The goods listed in the cargo inventories all originated in the Aegean, Asia Minor and Syria. But a document drawn up in Gaza provides evidence also on Apollonios' trade with the Arabian Peninsula and India.[87] The nature of the text—assembled from ten damaged papyrus fragments—is not clear. It could be listing exquisite presents sent to him in the service of diplomacy, the kind of gift-giving we have seen Toubias and two Phoenicians engage in. But a more likely explanation is that it records market purchases. The text opens with a mention of a certain Diodoros, who served as a "supervisor in charge of frankincense production" (*tou epi tês libanôtikês*). The title shows that Apollonios had an agent stationed in Gaza with the specific task of overseeing the movement of aromatics. Such permanent oversight makes more sense for regular, commercial shipments than for occasional dispatches of presents.

Further supporting that view is that the quantities listed seem to have been on the large side for gifts: one entry is for thirty talents (ca. 900 kilograms) of incense, another for an equal amount of myrrh.[88] A list dated 261 BCE shows that Apollonios had appreciable quantities of Arabian aromatics stored in his Egyptian warehouses (at least ten talents' worth), so he evidently had a high demand for such products.[89] In that light, it should not surprise us that he had a man stationed permanently in Gaza. The city was a major transit point for perfumes, flavorings and spices, which were carried there through the Arabian Peninsula to be shipped to Mediterranean destinations (see also chapter 5).

The Gazan shipment inventory shows the large geographical range of the areas feeding the eastern supply lines. Goods included Minaean incense from south Arabia (present-day Yemen), frankincense from Gerrha on the Persian Gulf, henna and myrrh, both products of Arabia or India, and finally cinnamon oil, cassia and nard, all Indian products. Some of the fragrances and

87. *PSI* 6.628; *P.Cair.Zen.*1.59009; *P.Cair.Zen.*4, *add. et corrig.* 59009 p. 285 (= Durand 1997: nos. 19–21).

88. But cf. the texts listed in Durand 1997: 149 n. 118, putting these quantities in perspective.

89. *P.Cair.Zen.*4.59536.

unguents were transported in alabaster jars, valuable containers in keeping with their expensive content. Such precious, unguent-filled jars were still traded much later in second-century CE Palmyra, as we know from its famous tax law.[90] In Zenon's time the Palmyrenes were not yet of any great commercial consequence, and they do not appear in the archive.[91] But the papyri do refer to another people who were on the cusp of becoming instrumental in the steadily growing and highly lucrative east-west caravan trade, the Nabataeans.

A passage from Diodorus Siculus (19.94–100) places the rise of the Nabataeans in the late fourth century BCE. At that time they were beginning to grow rich by transporting Arabian aromatics and spices through the desert to their capital city, Petra, and on from there to Gaza. By the mid-third century they seemingly were not yet the prominent merchants and caravaneers they would become, but the Zenon papyri do contain hints of their ascent. The Gazan shipment inventory mentions a man with the Arab name of Malichos, the name of later Nabataean royalty. He lived in the Moabite region (modern Jordan) and may have been a trading agent. It is possible that he belonged to a nascent trade diaspora that would fully develop in the subsequent centuries and into the Roman period, when Nabataean merchants settled as far west as Puteoli in Italy.[92]

Elsewhere in the Zenon papyri as well, men with Nabataean names appear: Obanes, Rabbelos and Zaidelos. Finally, the word "Nabataeans" itself occurs in the archive, its oldest known attestation in the Greek language. A group of men labeled thus are described as being commercially active in the Hauran region (modern Jordan and Syria), which adds to the picture of a growing Nabataean mercantile presence in the area.[93] Given the demand structure of the Hellenistic states, the appearance of the Nabataeans in our sources is not surprising. Much about the economic impact of the successor kingdoms on contemporary Arabia remains unknown, but that their formation spurred long-distance, desert trade in luxury products is not in doubt. In the third century BCE several Arabian dynasties adopted coinage based on the Attic drachma, a testament to the radiating economic influence of the Hellenistic states.[94] A process of monetization also occurred in the Ptolemaic kingdom

90. Matthews 1984: 172, 176. An inscribed, third-century BCE alabaster jar is discussed by Nachtergael 1998. On Palmyrene trade in the Roman Empire, see Terpstra 2016.

91. See Kaizer 2015 for an evaluation of the recently discovered third-century BCE archaeological evidence from Palmyra.

92. Terpstra 2015.

93. *P.Cair.Zen.*1.59004, 59006, 59015 *verso*; *PSI* 4.406. See Orrieux 1983: 44–45; Durand 1997: 173.

94. Kitchen 2001; Thonemann 2015: 37–39.

itself, which brings me to the evidence for banks and financial transactions in the Zenon archive.

Banks and Finance

In the earliest two documents from the Zenon archive, dated May 30, 261 BCE, Zenon does not himself appear. Both are official letters that were probably filed in Zenon's documentation because he performed a courier service. They were written by Apollonios and contain instructions to one Apollodotos and a Hikesios, who were Carian crown officials on a visit to Syria-Palestine.[95] As the letters must have been given to Zenon for him to pass on, it seems strange that they are preserved in the archive. It is possible that the extant documents are copies that Zenon made for his personal administration. But it is also possible that they are the originals, which he kept after relaying Apollonios' instructions orally or after changed circumstances obviated the need for delivery.[96] In any event, the text of both letters is identical save for the name of the intended recipient:

> Apollonios to Apollodotos greeting. If anyone exporting grain from Syria pays you either the price or a deposit, receive it from them through the bank and give us double-sealed receipts, writing the name of the payer and the amount of money and whether he is paying on behalf of another. Farewell.[97]

We do not know the destination of the Syrian exports alluded to here. Tcherikover thought that the grain was being shipped from Syria to Egypt, but given the coals-to-Newcastle flavor of such an activity, shipments to Caria or even somewhere beyond the borders of the Ptolemaic kingdom seem more plausible.[98] We also do not know from what type of plot the grain originated. It could have come from royal land or alternatively from a personal estate of Apollonios. As we have seen, the finance minister's fields at Baitanata, though predominantly producing grapes, probably also produced some amount of grain. But given that no estate is specified by name or owner, it seems more likely that the grain came from land not exploited by either the Ptolemies or their officials. Both the producers and the exporters were probably private entrepreneurs whose business the Ptolemaic government regulated and taxed.

95. *P.Cair.Zen.*1.59036–37 (= Bagnall and Derow 2004: no. 118 and no. 67).

96. Rostovtzeff 1922: 24–25; Harper 1928: 2–5.

97. *PSI* 4.324 (Apollodotos) and 325 (Hikesios) (= Durand 1997: nos. 33–34). Tr.: Bagnall and Derow 2004: no. 66. *P.Lond.* 7.2022 (= Durand 1997: no. 35) probably also belongs to this dossier.

98. Tcherikover 1937: 20–22. Cf. Orrieux 1983: 41; Durand 1997: nos. 33–34.

The existence of a financial infrastructure overseas is evident from the reference to a Syrian bank, which served as an intermediary facilitating transactions between Egypt and Syria. If the payments to be made were indeed public revenue from exports, then this was a "royal bank" (*basilikê trapeza*) and thus a state institution. Ptolemaic royal banks were operating at least as early as ca. 265 BCE, when one is first attested in a papyrological text.[99] They facilitated payments on behalf of the king, received money due to him, including taxes, and were managed by government officials. But they also functioned as general financial institutions handling private accounts. They may have been a Ptolemaic invention but may also have been based on an older model from Athens, where there seems to have been a "public bank" (*dêmosia trapeza*) already in the classical period.[100] But one way or the other, the concept of a bank as a financial institution was almost certainly imported into Hellenistic Egypt from the Greek world.

Private banks initially operated in the Ptolemaic kingdom as well, starting in or before ca. 270 BCE, the date of their first attestation in the papyri.[101] But they disappeared sometime after 259 BCE, when the government created a banking monopoly by leasing out the right to change money to a limited number of concession holders. These concessionary moneychangers existed alongside royal banks, the relationship between the two being the subject of debate. But if the exact nature of the arrangement escapes us, the firm hold of the Ptolemaic kingdom on banking activities betrays both a keen public interest in, and a clear understanding of, monetary affairs. The Romans considered the Ptolemaic financial infrastructure to be useful enough to maintain it, and most royal banks continued to operate as public institutions (*dêmosiai trapezai*) under Roman rule.[102]

The earliest known message from Apollonios to Zenon personally, dated November 23, 260 BCE, also concerned financial matters. It was likely sent while Zenon was still in Egypt but already preparing for his journey. The letter contains instructions about logistics and salary payments: Zenon was asked to arrange transport and pay for two men named Nikomachos and Zoilos, both en route to Syria-Palestine. One would like to know who these men were and why they were traveling. Although we cannot be sure about the details, it is likely that, in contrast to the crown officials in the letters cited above, they were Apollonios' private agents. Nikomachos is only mentioned here, but Zoilos appears in a letter from two years later, revealing him to have been

99. *P.Hib.* 1.29, l. 39–40. See Bogaert 1981: 89–90.

100. Bogaert 1981: 87, 90–91; Bingen 2007: 183–88.

101. *P.Hib.* 1.110 *recto*, l. 30. See Bogaert 1983: 15–16.

102. Bogaert 1981: 89–90, 97; 1983: 19–23.

stationed in Ptolemais, south of Tyre (fig. 3.2).[103] About these two men Apollonios wrote:

> Apollonios to Zenon greeting. We have sent to you Nikomachos and Zoilos. Therefore place them on the fast sailing ship or the merchant galley, and may they receive the same salary that is paid to the others. Each of them has twenty drachmas advance payment from us. Goodbye.[104]

A striking aspect of this letter is how few specifics Apollonios cared to provide. He obviously expected Zenon to be able to do what was asked of him without needing any great deal of instruction. Agents were apparently paid a standard compensation, which Apollonios assumed he need not specify. He also did not bother to state when and where the new arrivals were to be paid. As he had already given them an advance sum he must have intended full remuneration to take place somewhere in Syria after the agents had performed whatever task they had been given. Obviously he took it for granted that his intentions in all this would be self-evident to Zenon. Although we are deprived of information on agents' salaries, we do learn that the pay structure of at least some of them was set up to incentivize them to perform their duties properly. If they did not, their salaries could be withheld.

To make the requested payments, Zenon must have had access to his principal's funds in some way, but how we are not told. There can be little doubt that he had been entrusted with a sum in cash for his expedition. We have already seen the case of the disgraced agent Demetrios, who had been robbed of such travel money by pirates; in a letter cited farther down, a scribe touring Phoenicia also explicitly mentions a travel allowance. Several other papyri refer to such funds. One message lists a sum of a hundred drachmas, but whether that amount was typical or not, there is no way of knowing.[105]

Either way, Zenon did not in all likelihood need to carry all the necessary funds with him from Egypt. Given his principal's authority as finance minister over the Ptolemaic banking system, it seems reasonable to assume that he could draw on accounts at one or more branches overseas.[106] During the years after 257 BCE, when he had returned to Egypt, he arranged both his own and

103. *PSI* 5.495 (= Durand 1997: no. 46).

104. *P.Cair.Zen*.1.59002 (= *P.Edgar* 1918: no. 2; Durand 1997: no. 1). Tr. (with modifications): Harper 1928: 5.

105. *P.Lond*. 7.2086 (= Durand 1997: no. 55). The word also appears in *PSI* 5.495, l. 16 and the fragmentary *P.Cair.Zen*.4.59558, l. 13 (= Durand 1997: nos. 46 and 56). See also *P.Cair.Zen*.1.59044, l. 25 (*methodion*). On travel funds, see Reekmans 1996: 59–61.

106. See *P.Cair.Zen*.1.59021 (= Bagnall and Derow 2004: no. 102; Panagopoulou 2016) for Apollonios' authority over the money supply.

Apollonios' affairs through no fewer than nine banks, so at that time at least such financial management was standard practice for him.[107] But if Nikomachos and Zoilos were not paid out of a strongbox, what bank was to be used is not stated, and neither is a location or banker's name. The brevity of the letter is telling about the amount of information residing with Zenon and—given the involvement of at least two other agents, a ship's captain and perhaps a Syrian banker—within the wider network.

A letter dated December 30, 259 BCE, tells us about the kind of cash that Zenon must have received for his trip. It was written by Demetrios, a scribe stationed on the island of Cyprus (a Ptolemaic possession at the time) but on a journey along the Phoenician coast:[108]

> Demetrios to Zenon greeting. I have spent my travel allowance because of some purchases in Tyre. Therefore, you would do well to give 150 drachmas to Nikadas who has brought the letter to you. Charmos finished before me and went ahead, otherwise I would have sent him along (with Nikadas). Make certain too that you send Nikadas to Berytus safely. Also, write to me where the money must be sent. Goodbye:[109]

We do not know what Demetrios had bought in Tyre, but given the source of the money, the purchases must have been made in the service of either the governmental duties or the business ventures of Apollonios. Both seem equally possible. The only other letter in the archive where Tyre appears is the one that describes the dubious activities of the agent Apollophanes.[110] From that document it appears that the city played a role as both a trading hub and a place where custom officials were busy checking export licenses. But regardless of whether the scribe's expenditures were made for private affairs, public affairs, or some combination of the two, Apollonios' men apparently enjoyed some flexibility in how they spent their travel funds. In all likelihood they had to produce a formal expense report subsequent to their expeditions. But from Demetrios' request, it would seem that it was perfectly ordinary for them to tap the network for cash when money ran short. It is worth noting in this regard that the letter does not mention interest payments.[111] The loan was not a commercial transaction but a temporary reallocation of internal funds.

107. Bogaert 1991.

108. On Ptolemaic Cyprus, see Bagnall 1976: 38–79.

109. *P.Cair.Zen.*1.59016 (= Durand 1997: no. 25). Tr.: White 1986: no. 5. See also Tcherikover 1937: 11; Orrieux 1983: 55.

110. *P.Cair.Zen.*1.59093. Tyre might also be mentioned in the fragmentary *P.Cair.Zen.*4.59558, l. 11.

111. Cf. *P.Cair.Zen.*1.59010, l. 7–8.

Zenon evidently had access to financial resources he could use to respond to requests for bridge funding. Almost certainly, he sent Demetrios the 150 drachmas in cash, but it cannot be deduced whether he took the money out of a strongbox or drew on a bank account. Seeing how Demetrios asked Zenon to specify where he should send repayment Zenon was obviously on the move at the time and would have had difficulty operating through a single banking house. On the other hand, it is not unthinkable that several banking establishments were available to him overseas, allowing him to withdraw and deposit money while on the road. In Egypt the network of royal banks was widely spread out over towns and villages.[112] If the situation in Syria-Palestine was not necessarily identical, it seems likely that more banks existed than the one we happen to know about through the letters to the two Carian officials. Regardless, Apollonios' overseas business network clearly was firmly plugged into the monetary economy.

The wide geographical spread of royal banks over Egypt and their establishment also in the Ptolemaic overseas territories brings me to an important point. In constructing a financial infrastructure, the state had in effect created a public good. Of course, royal banks served the interests of the state first and foremost, facilitating tax payments to the treasury, which is why they were kept under public management. In addition, the sophistication of the Ptolemaic banking system in the mid-third century BCE should not be overstated, as it was still in development at the time. Sitta von Reden, in a thorough survey of the role of money in early Ptolemaic Egypt, lists both the financial capabilities and limitations of banks:

> Account holders could advise bankers by written order to pay out to, or accept money from, third parties. Yet no giro transfer of money from one account to another, or between accounts in different banks, is so far attested. Royal bankers seem to have been able to set off payments into one account against expenditure from another, and thus in practice transferred money between accounts. But this is attested only in connection with royal deposits and was not a normal procedure.[113]

All the same, the economic effect of the development of a financial infrastructure was profound. Although Egypt knew rudimentary forms of coinage already in the seventh century BCE, its economy went from being largely unmonetized to largely monetized in the course of the third century BCE.[114]

112. Bogaert 1981: 99; 1983: 23; Von Reden 2007: 258–68.
113. Von Reden: 2007: 254. But cf. Von Reden 2010: 118.
114. Manning 2008: 85–86; 2018: 198–99; Von Reden 2010: 41–47.

How far the use of coins and banks trickled down the socioeconomic ladder is a matter of debate, but undeniably the overall effect was to allow an increasing number of Ptolemaic subjects access to financial institutions. The expansionary effect will have been comparable to the one that Rome experienced after its rise in monetary liquidity, a topic discussed extensively by David Hollander and Philip Kay (see chapter 1).[115] Certainly in this area, the Ptolemaic kingdom engaged in behavior that was both beneficial to the state and economic development generally.[116]

Public Order and Private Enforcement

The documents discussed so far suggest that Apollonios and his men treated the exploitation of Syria-Palestine as a going concern, behavior consistent with the stationary-bandit model. If they were representative of the Ptolemaic kingdom, we should expect to see state promotion of public order overseas, similar to that in Egypt. At the same time, we should not expect to see third-party enforcement, a public good unavailable even in the Egyptian heartland.[117] The Zenon papyri indeed show the state providing order, but not enforcement.

One document is particularly revealing about the lack of third-party enforcement, even if many details of the story remain blurry.[118] What we know for certain is that Jeddous, a local chieftain in a village somewhere in Judea or Idumea, owed Zenon money but had been unwilling to pay. Zenon had written to him warning that securities for the sum would be seized if payment was not forthcoming, but the threat had not had the desired effect. Confronting the debtor was then left to one of Zenon's assistants, a man named Straton, who was accompanied by a young helper sent as backup by a district official.[119] The official had given the young man a letter in which Jeddous was once more admonished to repay his debt. This step, too, did not resolve the situation. The document records that the two men returned empty-handed, having been violently ejected from the village. What happened next we unfor-

115. Hollander 2007; Kay 2014.

116. On Ptolemaic demand and consumption, see Von Reden 2011.

117. See Bauschatz 2007; 2013 with my remarks in chapter 1.

118. P.Cair.Zen.1.59018 (= P.Edgar 1918: no. 4; White 1986: no. 7; Durand 1997: no. 23; Kloppenborg 2006: no. 2). The date is April 4, 258 BCE, so the affair took place at a time when Zenon may already have left Syria-Palestine. See Harper 1928: 22–23; Tcherikover 1937: 51; Orieux 1983: 47–48.

119. On the position of this young helper (neaniskos), see Reinach 1908: 501–02; Robert and Robert 1983: 102.

tunately do not know. The affair is never mentioned again in the extant papyri.

How a local chieftain had come to be indebted to Zenon is an open question. As far as we know, Zenon did not have any assets in Syria-Palestine and traveled there only once in his lifetime. Maybe he had lent some money to Jeddous, as he had done with the scribe Demetrios some three months earlier (see above). But that explanation does not seem likely, as Jeddous obviously did not form part of Apollonios' network of agents. It seems equally unlikely that the debt consisted of tax arrears. Zenon was a private agent, not a government official, and nowhere else in the archive do we see him engaged in tax gathering. The most plausible explanation is, therefore, that he tried to collect a debt resulting from a private business deal of his principal.

As already mentioned, Apollonios was involved in the slave trade, transacting with local rulers like Toubias through his agents. A debt following a slave sale is therefore a distinct possibility. But whatever the nature of the debt might have been, the episode illustrates the limits of the Ptolemaic state in legal enforcement. Even a high-ranking agent of the finance minister could encounter difficulties in recovering a debt. Zenon largely had to rely on self-help. The district authorities did lend him a hand, but in an ad hoc fashion that turned out to be wholly ineffectual. If after Zenon's conspicuous lack of success they followed up with more forceful measures, we do not know about it.

Five letters drafted by Zenon on the back of an account for oil imports present another instructive case where the absence of third-party enforcement had to be circumvented.[120] The drafts show that Zenon intended to write to a number of men in a plot to recover some lost property. Many cancellations and corrections demonstrate that he had been laboring over his sentences. The pertinent lines of the first three letters read:

> To Pasikles. If you are well, it would be excellent; we too are well. Krotos informed me that you had written to him that the runaway slaves are reported to be with Kollochoutos and his brother Zaidelos and that they demand a hundred drachmas for returning them. Therefore, you would do well to make all effort that they be recovered and handed over to Straton who carries this note to you. For by doing this you would grant me a favor. And whatever you spend I will repay. . . . And if you have any need of anything from the country (i.e., Egypt), write to us, for we will gladly do it.

> To Epikrates. During our stay in Marisa we bought slaves out of Zaidelos' stock but, while we were on our way to Egypt, three of the slaves ran away,

120. P.Cair.Zen.1.59015 verso (= P.Edgar 1923: no. 76; Scholl 1983: no. 3; Durand 1997: no. 42). See Tcherikover 1937: 51; Orrieux 1983: 48–49.

two of them brothers; their names and descriptions I have written below. We were informed that they are with Kollochoutos. . . . Therefore, you would do well to make all effort that they be recovered and handed over to Straton.

To Peisistratos. If you are well, it would be excellent; we too are well. Krotos informed us that Pasikles had written that the runaway slaves, which we bought in Marisa from Zaidelos' stock, are being held for reward. Therefore, we wrote requesting that all care be taken that they be recovered and that he hands them over to Straton who is carrying these letters to you. Therefore, you too would do well both by reminding him and by zealously cooperating so that they do not get away. . . . And you too would favor us by writing if you desire anything from the country (i.e., Egypt), for we would gladly do it for you.[121]

What these letters reveal is that Zenon had bought a number of slaves in Marisa (east of Gaza, fig 3.2) from the brothers Kollochoutos and Zaidelos, and that part of his purchase had then fled. The escaped slaves had somehow ended up back with the sellers, who were demanding a fee of a hundred drachmas for their release.

Asking such fees was permitted under Ptolemaic law if done through local officials, as demonstrated by an inscription from Caria dating to ca. 200 BCE.[122] But in this particular instance, the demand was made by the same men who had sold the slaves. They were likely attempting to benefit twice from the sale in an underhanded way, which explains why Zenon wanted to take action against them. The drafts show him organizing support for his case. At the time of writing he had already returned to Egypt, which must be the reason why he intended to leave the execution of his plan to his assistant Straton, presumably the same man he had sent over to Jeddous in the failed attempt to recover a debt. Straton was to deliver Zenon's letters and was to act as the central figure in a group of hoped-for collaborators, who were to include the three addressees in the cited drafts: Pasikles, Epikrates and Peisistratos. The drafts not quoted here were addressed to two others, a certain Epainetos and Ammon, who were asked not to hinder Straton in the performance of his task.

Who were the five men to whom Zenon was writing? Little to no information is available on them, but Epikrates at least seems to have been an agent of Apollonios. A fragmentary papyrus, also mentioning slaves in Marisa and likely forming part of the same dossier, records him forwarding a shipment of

---

121. Tr. (with modifications): White 1986: no. 6.
122. Robert and Robert 1983: 102–03.

wool.[123] It is possible that the others were Ptolemaic officials, although the letters provide no evidence to suggest that they were. But even if some were in the service of the public authorities, Zenon's draft letters do not show that "from the mid-third century, Marisa (was) well under Ptolemaic control with a police or military presence, difficult to define but real," as Xavier Durand proposed.[124] On the contrary, what we are witnessing is an attempt at self-help. All letters give the strong impression that assistance was requested of the addressees as personal favors; the one to Pasikles in fact expressly says so. Moreover, Pasikles and Peisistratos were promised rewards in return for their aid. Both were asked if they desired anything from the homeland, which was probably an offer to supply them with goods that were scarce in Syria-Palestine but available to Zenon in Egypt. The promise of a recompense in kind shows the tit-for-tat nature of the solicited support. In short, Zenon was planning enforcement of his private property rights through personal connections.

The need to drum up support in such a manner was doubtless exceptional. Apollonios' men will mostly have relied on personalized pressure within socially restricted groups for enforcement. Such groups could span larger geographical areas, but then had to depend on relationships within which repeat dealings took place or a trading partner's public position was at stake. The first dynamic probably and the second definitely played a role in, for instance, the relationship between Toubias and Apollonios. It seems unthinkable that Toubias, who sold a slave girl to Zenon but who also sent diplomatic gifts to both the finance minister and the king, would ever have behaved as the Marisan slave dealers did. The implication is that the latter did not have strong ties to Zenon, Apollonios or the king, did not worry about their standing with any of them and did not care about missing out on future deals. Enforcement of private property rights under such conditions could evidently be problematic. Given the risks of entering into one-shot deals with less familiar overseas business partners, Apollonios and his agents must have kept such affairs to a minimum.

Caution of that kind must have been typical of long-distance traders in the ancient world. Still, Apollonios was no ordinary merchant but one of the highest-ranking officials in the Ptolemaic state. We might perhaps expect his men to have had access to public means of coercion unavailable to others. Yet Zenon in his conflicts with Jeddous and the Marisan slave dealers seems neither to have requested nor spontaneously to have received military support. This omission was not for lack of an army presence, as the main cities in Syria-Palestine were all garrisoned. Furthermore, the existence of a state coercion

---

123. *P.Cair.Zen.*4.59537 (= Scholl 1983: no. 4; Durand 1997: no. 43).
124. Durand 1997: 222.

apparatus is shown by a papyrus dated ca. 261 BCE. It contains the text of two royal ordinances issued to regulate taxes and slave registrations. The decrees declared that all residents of Syria and Phoenicia should report possession of both livestock and enslaved freeborn natives to their local financial officials. The penalties for noncompliance were harsh: unreported slaves would be confiscated and their owners fined a sum of 6,000 drachmas.[125] If nothing else, the decrees demonstrate that the state was perfectly ready to employ its means of force in tax and census matters.

Such force extended to maintaining public order, as shown by two letters from the Zenon archive discussed above. In the first letter we hear of a man who had stirred up a commotion, and who was then imprisoned and shackled for a week. In the second we learn of a sailor who had been incarcerated, although he managed to escape and disappear.[126] In both texts the word "prison" appears, called a *phylakê* in the original Greek of the one letter, a *desmôtêrion* in the other. John Bauschatz has argued that in Egypt those were technical terms referring to different buildings manned by different types of police forces.[127] Whether the distinction existed also in Syria-Palestine cannot be determined on the basis of the available evidence. But one way or the other, the letters show that as in Egypt, so in the Ptolemaic overseas possessions a public-order infrastructure existed.

As we have seen at the beginning of this chapter, Apollonios could and did imprison his own agents if he saw the need to do so. Taking that step was no doubt unusual for him, but it does show that the state's coercion apparatus stood at his disposal. We can therefore reasonably ask why he did not freely allow it to be turned on uncooperative business partners of his overseas agents. In formulating an answer, I suggest that we once again need to consider his position as the official of a stationary-bandit state, and an entrepreneur with an encompassing economic interest in Syria-Palestine. Third-party enforcement was not a public good that the Ptolemaic kingdom provided. If Apollonios had asymmetrically used state force for his own ends, this would have been seen by the local population as extralegal and extortionate. That perception would have, in turn, created incentive problems, an outcome that was not in Apollonios' personal interests nor in the interests of the state he served. Employing public means of violence had to be left strictly as a last resort to avoid damaging economic productivity and diminishing rent and tax revenue.

---

125. Liebesny 1936: right column l. 2–6. On these royal ordinances, see Bagnall 1976: 18–19.

126. *PSI* 4.406 (= Durand 1997: no. 27); *P.Cair.Zen.*1.59077 (= *P.Edgar* 1919: no. 12; Durand 1997: no. 49).

127. On *phylakai* and *desmôtêria*, see Bauschatz 2007: 11–16; 2013: 247–49.

Concluding Remarks

The papyri related to Zenon's tour around Syria-Palestine present only a snapshot of third-century BCE economic activity, covering no more than a couple of years. But their limited chronological scope notwithstanding, they provide valuable insight into the incentives and behavior of a high-profile Ptolemaic official and his agents, and by extension of the Ptolemaic state. As a private entrepreneur, Apollonios imported both staple and luxury goods from Syria-Palestine and managed an agricultural business there. As an eminent public official, he received expensive diplomatic gifts from local power-holders and controlled the region's tax and banking systems. He could have abused his dual position by evading taxes on his private ventures while engaging in predation to satisfy the state's fiscal needs. However, nothing in the evidence suggests that he did so.

The public and private sides of his activities are often impossible to disentangle, but we get the overall impression that he ran a carefully managed operation. I propose that his socioeconomic and political position explains that outcome. His encompassing and long-term interest in Syria-Palestine as both a businessman and a royal official of a state in constant competition with the Seleucids incentivized him to behave as a stationary bandit. His behavior was mirrored by the kingdom he served, which used some of the resources it extracted to provide public goods, including a banking system and an infrastructure to enforce public order. But third-party enforcement was not a public good that the state provided. Private-order enforcement remained necessary, and the Zenon archive allows us near-unique insight into how it was achieved by an ancient business network.

Finally, for perspective, it is worth returning to the later Roman republic and its fiscal regime, a topic touched on in the introduction. The Zenon documents show that Apollonios' management of affairs in Syria-Palestine was markedly different from how the Roman republican elite governed Rome's growing overseas empire. The republic was ruled by officials elected for only short periods of time, with enforced intervals between magistracies. As James Tan has argued, when the republic began receiving taxes from its expanding overseas domains, the surplus became a potential threat to the elite's monopoly on political power.[128] If the new resources had been allowed to flow into the treasury, the state could have become a donor of public goods and thus a rival to elite patronage. Paradoxically, curtailing state revenue was therefore in the interests of the ruling aristocracy. Short-term magistracies combined with cutthroat political competition further disincentivized officeholders from

128. Tan 2015.

maximizing state income. The public purse would be controlled by newly elected officials the following year, and inflating it bore the risk of handing political enemies an advantage.

The result was a fiscal regime in which provincial tax collection was farmed out—limiting the state's entitlement to revenue to a fixed amount—while Roman citizens were exempted from taxation. As Tan explains, this system had a number of interconnected consequences. First, the state could not increase its footprint in its provision of public goods, and the Roman citizenry thus remained locked into preexisting ties of elite patronage. Second, members of the elite became classic examples of roving bandits, treating overseas magistracies as personal money-making ventures. The conquered provincials could not resist, while tax-exempt Roman citizens had lost the right to protest. The process of personal enrichment of the few and socioeconomic lock-in of the many was thereby allowed to continue. Eventually the tax system changed when the republic collapsed, turning the Roman state into a monarchy in all but name and leading to a relaxation of fiscal demands.

4

Civic Order and Contract Enforcement

THE ROMAN EMPIRE WAS A successful political, military and economic organization. It was the largest state the ancient Mediterranean would ever know, ruling the entire Basin for centuries following an impressive series of military conquests. Archaeological work on the diffusion of transport containers and the development of harbor facilities is increasingly showing that connectivity within the state's confines was high.[1] Archaeological evidence is also providing an ever more detailed picture of Roman living standards, which in the first centuries CE were high as well (see further chapter 6). A general consensus seems to have developed that the Roman economy produced per capita growth, although the debate about when it might have begun and how long it might have lasted is likely to continue.[2] But at all events, current studies reveal that the empire attained remarkable achievements.

As in ancient economic scholarship generally, the work of Douglass North has been deeply influential in research on Rome's success. One item on the Neo-Institutional research agenda has been the organization of the state as a provider of public goods that facilitated trade. Keith Hopkins suggested that "Roman government and prolonged peace cut transaction costs; for example, the suppression of piracy made peaceful transport across the Mediterranean Sea possible, and so reduced the risks and costs of transport."[3] Elio Lo Cascio, in a similar vein, pointed to the "establishment of more peaceful and safer conditions at sea," listing further "the diffusion of a 'technology of measurement'

---

1. See, e.g., Bonifay and Tchernia 2012; Wilson, Schörle and Rice 2012. On Mediterranean connectivity generally, see Horden and Purcell 2000; Broodbank 2013.

2. Hopkins 2002; Saller 2002; Jongman 2006; 2007a; 2007b; Scheidel 2007: 43–44; Erdkamp 2016; Harper 2017: 29–38.

3. Hopkins 2002: 219.

and of common metrological systems, and above all the creation of a unitary monetary area and of common legal rules."[4] Not all those cost-reducing factors required a unified political sphere. After all, the adoption of Attic and Alexandrian monetary standards had facilitated the economic integration of the Hellenistic East Mediterranean, but that outcome had not resulted from political consolidation by a single state. Still, Hellenistic state formation had been the driving force behind the process. It seems an uncontroversial proposition that the ongoing unification of currency and metrological systems under the Roman empire further facilitated economic development.

The unification of legal rules had equal if not more potential in that regard, but its positive effect on economic conditions was more complex. In theory, parties drafting a contract did not have to investigate which sets of rules were available, nor did they have to reach agreement on which set to apply. But in practice things were not so simple. Access to Roman law was at least nominally restricted to citizens, and local customs remained in force throughout the empire. Because of those complicating factors, transacting parties could not avoid incurring information and negotiation costs in adopting a legal framework. But a much bigger concern was enforcement costs. Following North's work, Hopkins thought that the state reduced those costs, because its "enforcement of law secured relatively predictable and peaceful outcomes to contracts."[5] Lo Cascio, as well, argued that an "analysis of the state . . . becomes central, in so far as it is the state that, through what North calls its 'comparative advantage in violence,' can define and enforce the 'rules of the game,' in particular exclusive property rights."[6] As outlined in chapter 1, such views are incorrect. The Roman empire as a non-Weberian state did not claim a monopoly on violence, and consequently self-help "was vital in every era of Roman civilization and evident in every phase of Rome's legal history."[7]

That is not to say that courts lacked recourse to punitive measures. Juridical and literary texts say that they could brand someone with "infamy," a sentence applied mostly in what we would call criminal justice.[8] But there was no general "law of infamy" and, moreover, the "true impact of *infamia* as a legal penalty can only be fully understood in the context of Roman society where commerce and social progression was based on family and status connections."[9] Its efficacy, in other words, depended on mechanisms of reputation and social control, and thus ultimately on private order. In addition, one can

---

4. Lo Cascio 2006: 221–22. Similarly: Kehoe 2007: 543.

5. Hopkins 2002: 219.

6. Lo Cascio 2006: 219.

7. Fuhrmann 2012: 49.

8. On *infamia*, see Crook 1967: 83–85; Garnsey 1970: 189–90; Chiusi 2013.

9. Du Plessis 2015: 108.

question how much literary texts on infamy reflect Rome's lived historical reality, especially outside aristocratic circles. From an extensive analysis of petitions to officials in Egypt dating to ca. 30 BCE–ca. 284 CE and concerning violations of persons and property, Barbara Anagnostou-Canas concluded: "In almost all documents, civil blends with criminal, and sentences settle questions of procedure rather than substance; rare are any references to penalties following this type of offense."[10]

Of course Roman power was by no means toothless. The state involved itself in civilian policing and the maintenance of public order, just as the Ptolemaic kingdom had done (see chapter 3). The Roman state's police activities were studied comprehensively by Christopher Fuhrmann in a book covering roughly the same time period as the one by Anagnostou-Canas. Fuhrmann observed that in Roman Egypt, probably the most fully policed province of the empire, liturgies and corvée duties indicate what security tasks the public authorities deemed to be important: "We hear of field guards, guards of the threshing floor, sluice guards, . . . crop guards, prison guards, day guards and night guards, watchtower guards and lookouts, harbor guards, estate guards, river guards, guardians of the peace, . . . bandit catchers, and just plain 'guards.'"[11] Significantly, in the evidence for this wide range of police duties, we hear nothing of civil enforcement officers.

Given the limits of state help in enforcement, it is not immediately obvious why legal actors would have turned to Roman law in the first place. Of course the process of transacting could be facilitated by using template contracts and standard clauses, and Roman law's sophistication allowed it to be put to good use in moneylending and trade.[12] But tailored alternatives accepted as valid within a restricted socioeconomic circle would equally have served. As a hypothetical situation, we can imagine specialized traders in a particular commodity adhering to rules that were specific to their business and different in detail or substance from the ones provided by the state. They would have been free to do so, as the "Romans imposed their rule but not their law." We should therefore not overestimate the impact of imperial legal institutions on everyday economic life. "Although the Romans had developed a refined law of contracts and sat in judgment of provincial contract disputes across the empire, Roman law neither informed nor controlled the vast majority of those contracts."[13]

Transacting parties might of course want a Roman court to have jurisdiction over any dispute that might arise between them. Official adjudication

10. Anagnostou-Canas 1991: 126–27.

11. Fuhrmann 2012: 77.

12. Terpstra 2008; Kehoe 2015.

13. Ratzan 2015: 188.

followed standardized procedures, rendering the process predictable and thereby attractive. Formal litigation also held the promise for the winning side of receiving an authoritative, state-sanctioned imprimatur, enhancing the chances that successful collective action would be taken against his adversary. The potential for that outcome was likely the main reason why disputants invested in legal action (see chapter 1). If contracting parties had any thoughts of ever going the route of formal litigation, they would do well to draft their agreements in accordance with official edicts. However, business partners doubtless avoided lawsuits where they could, attempting if at all possible to resolve conflicts bilaterally or through private arbitration by their peers. We cannot know what percentage of Roman contract disputes were resolved informally and what percentage ended up in the courts. But evidence from better documented historical periods suggests that the balance was tipped heavily in favor of the first.[14]

A restriction of Roman law to citizens, the continued vitality of local customs, a lack of state-provided enforcement and routine avoidance of formal litigation all impeded the legal unification of Rome's vast empire. Yet where we catch a glimpse of the historical reality—in Campanian and Dacian wax tablets, in the Babatha archive from Arabia and in the papyri from Roman Egypt—we find a remarkable diffusion of Roman law.[15] In a case study of documents found in Pompeii but drawn up predominantly in the port city of Puteoli, I have explained that phenomenon by way of path dependency.[16] Roman law had deep historical roots, investments in legal knowledge created "sunk costs," and procedures requiring parties to reach consensus on the litigation terms produced satisfactory outcomes. Those factors made Roman law the default system for contracting and conflict resolution in Puteoli, I argued. But although I still think that this assessment is correct, I now also think that an element is missing.

In chapter 2, I discussed imperial ideology and the way it gave economic actors agency in shaping the institutional environment of the "natural state."[17] Publicly displaying adherence to a shared ideology allowed heterogeneous business communities to connect, while it also provided informal constraints and created social order, facilitating collective action.[18] In this chapter I will

---

14. Ogilvie 2011: 296–300; Goldberg 2012: 159–62; Gelderblom 2013: 104–08.

15. Campanian and Dacian tablets, see below. Roman law in the Babatha archive: Cotton 1993; in Egyptian papyri: Taubenschlag 1972. Roman law in the provinces generally: Galsterer 1986.

16. Terpstra 2013: 9–49.

17. "Natural states": North, Wallis and Weingast 2009: 30–109.

18. Informal constraints and social order: North 1981: 36–45; 2005: 103–08. See also Denzau and North 1994 on shared mental models.

study the microeconomic effects of imperial ideology more closely, focusing specifically on the intracommunity enforcement of contracts. I argue that using the imperial legal system had enforcement and transaction-cost advantages, despite the absence of state coercion. Roman witnesses expressed their social standing by signing documents on behalf of contracting parties, making contracts what I call "publicly embedded."

Within the ancient world, the practice of using witnesses to provide additional proof of transactions and to create community-wide knowledge of contracts was by no means unique to the Roman empire.[19] But what made the Roman practice exceptional was its deep connection to social status, reflected in how names were sequenced in witness lists. Crucially, the civic order created by the state was the main determinant of someone's ranking. Holding public office or having done so in the past provided the highest possible social standing, securing a claim to one of the top positions. Officeholding could mean service as a city magistrate but also as an official of the imperial cult. Such positions were few, and in Roman everyday business not all witnesses were or could be active magistrates or former officeholders. But Roman citizenship was another important status determinant, especially if acquired by birth.

These civic-order determinants were intertwined with an imperial ideology, in which legal actors engaged by expressing loyalty to the authority of the central state and more specifically the person of the emperor. Contracts drawn up following the precepts of the imperial legal system were thus tied to individuals' personal status, a civic order and an imperial ideology, which in combination decreased the chances of breach and reduced enforcement costs. This complex of interlocking factors gave Roman contract law a competitive edge over alternatives, making it attractive as an economic institution.

To produce that historical outcome, several discrete social, ideological and status elements had to work together in a specific way. I stress that I do not see either the process or the result as premeditated, whether by state representatives or private economic actors. The combination of ideological and civic-order elements happened to be beneficial to legal enforcement, but that effect was unintended and undesigned. It can thus be classified as an "emergent property," a phrase used frequently in the study of living organisms but also of decentralized, complex human systems. As Peter Checkland explains, emergence is "not a mysterious concept." He gives an example from genetics for clarification:

> For an observer to choose to see some complex entity as a whole, separable from its environment, it must have properties which (for that observer at

19. See, e.g., Manning 2015b: 110–12 on the act of witnessing demotic contracts in Ptolemaic Egypt.

least) are properties of it as a single entity: so-called *emergent properties*. These are the properties which make the whole entity "more than the sum of its parts." ... In the structure of DNA, the laws of physical chemistry allow any sequence of aminoacid residues along the double helix. In order to explain experimental findings we have to invoke the idea that certain sequences constitute a "code" which, in biological reproduction, results in our having red hair or a large nose. The "genetic code" is an emergent property of the aminoacid sequences.[20]

I suggest that the concept of emergence is useful also for our understanding of Roman contract enforcement. As a socioeconomic system, it was institutionalized but in an undirected way, while its efficacy was not to be found in any of the individual components constituting the ensemble.

To investigate how this system worked, I will study two sets of Roman documents written on wax tablets, the first from Campania, the second from the province of Dacia. In both cases it will appear that witness lists not only passively reflect a social-status order but also represent the active, ongoing shaping of that order. By signing Roman legal documents and listing their names according to their civic status, community members displayed their social standing and simultaneously reinforced it. They also put that reputation at risk, exposing it to the possibility that a formal contract to which they had added their names as a status marker might be breached. In addition, for all participants, witnessing was a time investment and a favor they were extending, one they expected to be reciprocated. Respecting the reputation of the witnesses and securing their future goodwill were serious factors to consider for the transacting parties. Both factors enhanced their incentives either to comply with the contract or to cooperate in dispute settlement, whether formally or informally. The combined effect was to create intracommunity webs of reciprocal obligations and trust that provided a way to enforce contracts in the absence of state coercion.

Witness Rankings in Roman Documents

The Campanian tablets I will consider first consist of three subsets, one from Herculaneum and two from nearby Pompeii (fig. 4.1). All were buried in volcanic debris during the famous eruption of Mt. Vesuvius in 79 CE that devastated the Bay of Naples. Both the Herculanean and the Pompeian collections contain witness lists, but they are not all equally usable due to damage and loss

20. Checkland 1999: 50, italics in original. On emergent properties, see also Harré 1985: 145–46; Ober 2015: 45.

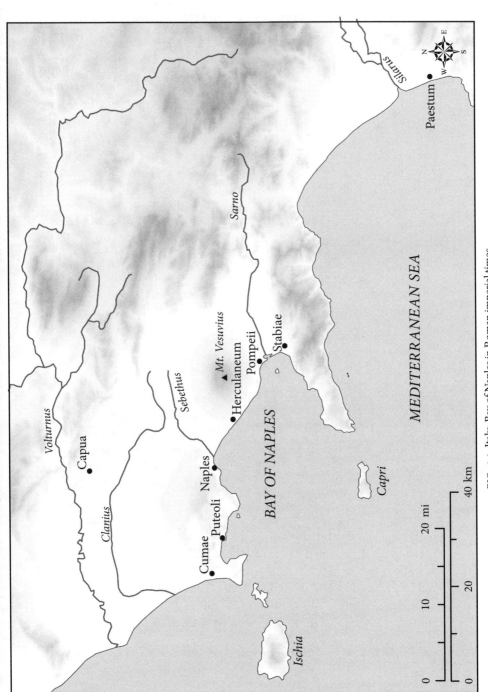

FIG. 4.1. Italy: Bay of Naples in Roman imperial times.

of evidence. Of the two Pompeian collections the so-called Jucundus archive, discovered in 1875, contains the largest number of lists, making it the most informative set on how the practice of witnessing worked.[21]

The Jucundus tablets were drafted between 15 and 62 CE, with the majority dating to Neronian times. They record mostly transactions for loans extended by one L. Caecilius Jucundus to buyers at Pompeian auction sales. In addition to providing his clients with credit, Jucundus probably kept money on deposit for them, making him a banker by profession.[22] The tablets were found in a wooden chest on the ground floor of a Pompeian house, known to modern archaeologists as number V.1.26. Almost certainly this urban villa was once Jucundus' domicile, although the dates of the documents suggest that he may no longer have been alive by 79 CE. A signed amphora, several mural inscriptions on the house's street-side walls and the tablets themselves show that when the building was buried it was still occupied by Caecilii Jucundi, perhaps by Jucundus' two sons. We know that Jucundus had succeeded one L. Caecilius Felix, who appears once in the oldest document from the archive and who might have been his father. Both the house and the banking venture thus seem to have been passed down through the generations, although we do not know if Jucundus' descendants had followed him and Felix in the banking business.[23]

Many of the surviving 153 documents of the Jucundus archive have legible witness lists. Careful studies of those lists have revealed that the way names were sequenced is not random but follows a finely calibrated status order. One of the first scholars to write about this social-status aspect of the tablets was Jean Andreau. He noticed that the witness lists followed certain regularities and that the order was corrected here and there, showing that the sequence mattered to people. It seemed unlikely that Pompeians had an exact mental map of the social status of every single individual within their urban community. Apart from being all but impossible to devise given the number of city inhabitants, demographic turnover and a wide variety of socioeconomic events would have constantly altered the landscape. Andreau recognized that, instead, general guidelines had to have been in force to help determine someone's status in a particular witness lineup. Understanding those guidelines would reveal a good deal about how Roman social hierarchy functioned.

His detailed study allowed him to formulate a number of general rules about what determined someone's ranking.[24] First of all, participation in pub-

21. On the find and its archaeological context, see Andreau 1974: 13–31; Jongman 1988: 212–15.

22. Andreau 1974: 38–39, 95–103.

23. Andreau 1974: 25–38; Jongman 1988: 214.

24. Andreau 1974: 170–76.

lic life correlated with elevated social standing. Holding a municipal magistracy assured that a witness occupied one of the top spots. Not actively holding office but having done so in the past, or belonging to a family whose members frequently did, also provided prestige.[25] Freeborn men universally enjoyed higher status than former slaves, an advantage enhanced by the fact that city magistracies were open only to men free by birth.[26] But freedmen could still increase their standing by becoming a member of the *Augustales*, public officials responsible for the maintenance of the imperial cult. Furthermore, Pompeii had a body of so-called *ministri Augusti* composed of slaves from prominent families. Their function is not fully understood, but they were probably also charged with imperial cult-related tasks.[27] Freedmen who had been *ministri* in their former lives as slaves derived prestige from their background, even if they stood a rung below the *Augustales*.

Andreau's analysis yielded a large amount of information on the determinants of social standing in the Roman world, but Willem Jongman realized that more still could be squeezed from the Jucundus archive. Many names appear in more than one tablet, making it possible to combine all 334 legible witness names into a single, ranked list. Having produced that list with the help of a computer program, Jongman combined it with all the available information on witnesses' municipal, *Augustalis* and *minister Augusti* positions, and with evidence on freed and freeborn status. Finally, he added data on personal wealth for those listed Pompeians with a known city address, assuming that a larger floor plan in general correlated with greater affluence.[28] The results confirmed Andreau's finding that ranking witnesses was done with great care. They also confirmed a strong correlation between holding civic office and occupying one of the top positions as a witness. But, perhaps surprisingly, the results did not establish a correlation between affluence and prestige ranking. To explain that outcome, Jongman proposed that wealth was a necessary but not a sufficient condition for social standing, providing status only "if it was transformed into a political role in the community."[29]

The number of people in the lists whose address can be established with reasonable certainty is low (n=22).[30] Because the sample is small, the possibility remains that there were men in Pompeii who enjoyed status simply by being rich. All the same, the idea that great value was attached to officeholding

25. Andreau 1974: 172 with n. 5, 215–17.

26. Freedman status is usually not listed and has to be deduced from *cognomina*. This method is reasonably secure, though. See Andreau 1974: 140–55; Jongman 1988: 242–43.

27. Andreau 1974: 205–07.

28. Jongman 1988: 230–73.

29. Jongman 1988: 263.

30. Jongman 1988: 238–41, 354–64.

is supported by a famous Pompeian inscription, set up for one N. Popidius Celsinus ca. 62 CE. It records that Celsinus at six years of age had been elected a member of the city council as a reward for rebuilding the temple of Isis, destroyed by an earthquake.[31] Obviously the boy was too young for either exploit, and his father, N. Popidius Ampliatus, must have been behind the arrangement. Ampliatus was a freedman. Not eligible for municipal office himself, he had secured a political position for his freeborn son, knowing this to be the most reliable route to social advancement.

Getting elected to a municipal magistracy was an assured way of gaining social status, but things are more nebulous when it comes to non-officeholders. We often do not know why one particular freeborn man not known to have held a magistracy was ranked above another, and similarly with freedmen. All the same, especially for freedmen we can guess at some of the rules with a fair amount of confidence. For instance, it seems logical to suppose that being the former slave of a freeborn man provided higher status than being the freedman of a freedman. It also seems likely that a freedman's status increased the further he moved away from the moment he was manumitted and the longer he had held Roman citizenship.

Rules similar to those observed by Andreau and Jongman applied in Herculaneum, judging from the documents found there.[32] Moreover, evidence suggests that listing witnesses according to their civic status was common practice in the Roman world generally, in private contracts as well as official documents such as military discharge certificates.[33] A fascinating example playing out at a social level far above Jucundus and his Pompeian clientele is provided by an inscription from Banasa in modern-day Morocco, dating to 177 CE.[34] It records a grant of Roman citizenship to a local chieftain and his family by the emperors Marcus Aurelius and Lucius Verus. No fewer than twelve witness names are listed, clearly according to a status pattern. All were eminent men belonging to the inner sociopolitical circle of the imperial capital: five consulars are followed by two former holders of senior equestrian posts, in turn followed by the two praetorian prefects in office. Concluding the list are the well-known Roman jurist Q. Cervidius Scaevola, at the time perhaps still chief officer of the night watch, and two more junior knights.

Confirmation that all these observations reflect a universal Roman practice can be found in the literary sources, which suggest that members of Rome's

---

31. *CIL* 10.846 (= *ILS* 6367), see Jongman 1988: 261. For N. Popidius Ampliatus, see *CIL* 10.847–48, 921.

32. Camodeca 1993: 343–45.

33. Camodeca 1993; Haensch 1996: esp. 463–64; Meyer 2004: 156.

34. *AE* 1971: no. 534. On the witnesses, see Williams 1975: 70–78.

high society were routinely asked to sign contracts and wills as witnesses. Martial (*Ep.* 10.70) claimed barely to get one book a year written because of the tasks he was constantly being asked to perform, the signing of documents among them. Seneca (*Ep.* 8.6) and Pliny the Younger (*Ep.* 1.9.2–3) as well intimated that such business could take up much of a man's time. Prestige and hierarchy were a matter of concern here, too, as we learn from one of Juvenal's satires (*Sat.* 3.81–83). The xenophobic protagonist, about to leave Rome because life there had become too unpleasant for his taste, complained that some Greeks got to write their names above his, despite the fact that he was of true Roman stock.

Witness Lists in the Sulpicii Archive

The most informative subset in the Campanian wax tablet collection for large scale trade and finance consists of 127 documents. It was found in 1959 in Pompeii, although it records mostly transactions that had taken place in Puteoli on the other side of the Bay of Naples (fig. 4.1).[35] What makes these documents particularly valuable as evidence for Roman socioeconomic history is that they display a far greater variety in their content than the Jucundus tablets, which almost exclusively contain receipts for loans.

The tablets were discovered during road construction outside the Pompeian city walls in a building that had been buried in the eruption of Mt. Vesuvius, just like Jucundus' villa. But unlike that villa the structure could be only partly uncovered because of the time pressure of the planned roadwork. The excavated section showed five decorated dining rooms opening up onto a small garden. A wicker basket containing the wooden tablets was found in one of those rooms. What had helped conserve organic material in the building—not just the tablets and the basket but also the latticework sliding doors of the dining rooms—was the wet condition of the soil. This area of Pompeii south of the Stabian gate probably once lined the bank of the river Sarno and formed part of the river harbor. The high water table in this low-lying area had created an anoxic environment that had sealed and preserved the ancient wood.

The tablets are the product of a banking venture run by three generations of C. Sulpicii and are for that reason usually referred to as the Sulpicii archive. They record an assortment of legal acts to do with finance and litigation, all showing that their drafters closely followed the rules of Roman law. The parallels they revealed between the writings of the jurists and daily practice delighted Roman legal scholars. As Joseph Wolf wrote triumphantly, the

---

35. On the discovery of the tablets, see Terpstra 2013: 11–15.

documents provide "irrefutable proof that Roman civil law, in all its complexity and in the way Roman jurisprudence had developed it, thoroughly obtained in everyday life."[36] The relevance of that finding for the question of how well the Roman economy performed is clear: the more widely Roman law was applied in contracting the more forceful its transaction-cost-reducing effect will have been.

Unfortunately, fewer than 30 percent of the documents still have their witness lists, a number far lower than for the Jucundus and Herculanean tablets.[37] In addition, many lists are barely legible. The mutilated state of the archive should at least in part be blamed on poor handling postexcavation, but it would also seem that many documents were already incomplete by the time they got encased in ash.[38] Whatever the main cause of the damage, only two of the 120 witness names recur, precluding the possibility of combining all names into a single list like the one Jongman produced for the Jucundus archive. The limited overlap not only results from the restricted number of lists but also from another factor: Puteoli was a substantially larger city than either Pompeii or Herculaneum.

No consensus exists on the size of Pompeii's population at the moment Vesuvius erupted, but most current estimates concentrate around 10,000. Herculaneum's population was significantly smaller, likely less than half that.[39] By contrast, Puteoli housed perhaps 30,000 to 40,000 inhabitants at its peak, which coincided roughly with the period 26–61 CE covered by the Sulpicii tablets.[40] When the documents were drafted, Puteoli was not yet experiencing major competition for its position as Rome's principal harbor, as the large basin at Portus would not get built until the early second century CE.[41] Given Puteoli's larger size relative to Pompeii and Herculaneum, the social group from which witnesses could potentially be drawn was larger as well, meaning that the chances of names recurring were lower.

At the same time, population size was not necessarily the sole determinant of the size of the witness pool. In all three cities, only a section of the group of

36. Wolf 2001: 131.

37. More than 73 percent for the Jucundus tablets: Jongman 1988: 234. The exact number is yet unknown for the Herculanean tablets, as Camodeca is still in the process of reexamining them, but it is comparably high: Camodeca 1993: 343.

38. *TPSulp.* p. 18–19; Wolf 2001: 78–79; Terpstra 2013: 14.

39. Pompeii: Lazer 2009: 73–76; Flohr 2017. Herculaneum: Camodeca 1993: 346.

40. Camodeca 1977: 89–90. For the date range of the tablets, see Terpstra 2013: 13 n. 12.

41. D'Arms 1974 has warned against exaggerating the negative economic effect of Portus' construction on Puteoli. All the same, the effect must have been felt.

free adult males might have been tapped to recruit witnesses.[42] Such a selection seems not to have affected the tablets from Herculaneum. Its sample of names seems to be more or less representative of the city's total free adult male population.[43] But in the Jucundus and Sulpicii archives freedman names are overrepresented, meaning that witnesses were drawn from more restricted pools.[44]

Like the owners of the respective archives, many members of both groups were probably involved in trade and finance, activities that in the Roman world were conducted predominantly within a freedman social milieu. Another reason why this milieu is overrepresented in the Sulpicii tablets was the nature of Puteoli as a mercantile harbor of Mediterranean significance and consequently with a freedman population larger than that of most Italian cities. Still, the percentage of freedmen in the tablets seems higher than the percentage of freedmen in the total urban population.[45] The Sulpicii archive thus appears to reflect the economic interaction of a particular social group, a business circle whose size can no longer be established. But although we remain ignorant of the group's numbers, it is evident from the information in the tablets that its members transacted repeatedly over the years.[46] Many of them must have been well acquainted.

Witnessing was a serious undertaking for this group, as is clear from how systematically the practice was followed. Apart from being done methodically, it was done extensively, involving large numbers of participants. The documents consist of two basic types: declarations written in the first person (*chirographa*), and statements written in the third person (*testationes*). The first type was signed by three witnesses together with the individual making the declaration. But the second type was signed by no fewer than seven, frequently nine and sometimes as many as eleven witnesses. The category of *testationes* is by far the most prevalent in the Sulpicii documents, constituting about two-thirds of the total. We do not know how many documents were drafted in Puteoli in any typical day, week or month, but given the numbers of participants needed, being called upon to witness a transaction must have been a common occurrence. It is probably safe to say that it was a routine activity for many members of the group represented in the tablets.

---

42. Women and (with some exceptions in *chirographa*) slaves were excluded: Camodeca 1993: 342–43; Meyer 2004: 159 n. 108.

43. Camodeca 1993: 345–47.

44. Jongman 1988: 271; *TPSulp.* p. 26–31.

45. Camodeca 1993: 348–49.

46. Repeat dealings in the Sulpicii tablets: Terpstra 2013: 21–23.

An example of the kind of information the tablets provide will be useful at this point. A particularly instructive one with a well-preserved witness list is a document recording that on August 21, 38 CE, a slave sale had taken place in Puteoli.[47] Unfortunately, the text of the contract itself is damaged, and we do not know the name of the purchased individual, although the Latin declensions show him to have been male. He was guaranteed by the seller to be neither a fugitive slave nor a slave prone to running away. An additional clause stipulated that the sale would be covered by the edict of the *aediles curules*, officials in Rome appointed annually and charged with the supervision of the capital's marketplaces. In all likelihood the reference to the curule edict was included in the contract to provide the buyer with additional protection against hidden defects, for instance the possibility that the slave had been attempting suicide or had committed a crime punishable by death.[48]

Mention of the edict shows that the transacting parties desired to bring their contract in line with rules and regulations promulgated by officials in Rome.[49] Doing so was entirely voluntary. Even in the imperial capital itself there was nothing inappropriate about deviating from the edict in contracts of sale, as the Roman jurist Ulpian emphasized (*Dig.* 2.14.31). Another clause in the contract confirms that the parties intended to adhere to Roman law and, moreover, that following official legal formulas was standard practice within their wider business circle. In the event that a third party should come forward to claim the slave, the seller promised to pay double the purchase price to the buyer as a penalty, a provision specified to be "in keeping with the *formula* in the way that is customary." The type of penalty referred to in the contract is well known from Roman juridical literature.[50]

The document presents one of the limited number of examples from the Sulpicii archive of a complete and clearly legible witness list. But before looking at the names appended to the contract, it will be useful first to get a sense of the kind of transaction we are seeing. Who were the transacting parties and what do we know about them? Both their names are preserved: the buyer was a Titus Vestorius Arpocra *minor* and the seller a Titus Vestorius Phoenix. Both men evidently belonged to the same *gens*, a word best translated as "clan." Our

47. *TPSulp.* 43, on which see Camodeca 1992: 141–55, 160–64; Wolf 2001: 112–13; Jakab 2015: 217–18.

48. *TPSulp.* p. 116; Camodeca 1992: 150.

49. This practice was followed more widely in the area, as we know from a tablet discovered at Herculaneum: *TH* 60. See Camodeca 2000: 55–63.

50. *Dig.* 21.1.21.20 (Ulpian); 21.1.58.1 (Paul); 21.2.16.2 (Pomponius). See Camodeca 1992: 150–55 for a discussion.

evidence on the Vestorii shows that its members had a history of involvement in moneylending and long-distance trade.

Vestorii are well attested in Puteoli and the area around Naples generally. From passages in Vitruvius (7.11.1) and Pliny (*NH* 33.162) we know that an entrepreneur named Vestorius had introduced a type of Alexandrian blue dye-stuff into Puteoli, eventually to invent his own blue dye called *vestorianum*. It seems likely that this dealer in colorings should be equated with the Puteolan C. Vestorius active in trade and moneylending who is frequently mentioned by Cicero as a close associate. In 56–55 BCE it seems to have been this Vestorius who extended the loan that allowed Cicero to rebuild his house on the Palatine Hill in Rome (*Ad Att.* 4.6.4).[51]

Archaeological evidence suggests that Vestorius' dyestuff trade included other colorings and encompassed exports to the west. A mid-first-century BCE shipwreck found at Planier at the mouth of the river Rhône contained the type of blue dye produced in Puteoli, and also a specific kind of friable volcanic rock and little cylinders of *cerusa cotta*, both raw material for red dyes. The ceramic wares in the ship's hold show that it had docked in Campania, supporting the idea of a connection to Puteoli and Vestorius' color-manufacturing business. In addition, some of the cargo consisted of amphorae stamped with the name of M. Tuccius Galeo, an associate of Cicero and a man almost certainly acquainted also with C. Vestorius.[52] Whether the Vestorii continued to be high-end moneylenders and traders in dyestuffs into the first century CE is unknown, but it is certain that in Puteoli they were still held in high esteem at that time. Their standing was such that it left a mark on Puteoli's urban landscape. An inscription dating to 93–94 CE informs us that a sector of the city was called the "Vestorianus quarter" (*vicus Vestorianus*).[53]

If the buyer and seller in the contract belonged to the Vestorii in 38 CE, they were likely not members by birth. Both their surnames (*cognomina*) suggest that they were former slaves.[54] The seller Phoenix's name was fairly common for a Roman slave and likely did not denote anything particular about him. By contrast, the buyer's name, Arpocra, is rare and strongly suggestive of Egyptian ties. It derives from Harpocrates, a deity representing the youthful form of the god Horus.[55] In light of the republican-era Vestorius and his trade in blue dyestuff from Alexandria, it is tempting to assume an ongoing commercial connection of the Vestorii to Egypt.

51. On Vestorius, see Sirago 1979; Andreau 1983.

52. Tchernia 1969; Camodeca 1977: 74 n. 52.

53. *CIL* 10.1631. See Camodeca 1977: 73–75.

54. On Phoenix and Arpocra, see Camodeca 1992: 148 n. 17.

55. Malaise 1972: 198–201; Frankfurter 1998: 133–34.

Phoenix and Arpocra drew up their contract in front of witnesses. Nine men confirmed that the slave sale had taken place as written in the document:[56]

C(aius) Julius C. f. Fal. Senecio
C(aius) Munnius C. f. Rufus
A(ulus) Fuficius Donatus
L(ucius) Pontius Philadelphus
T(itus) Vestorius Phoenix(?)
C(aius) Paccius Felix
C(aius) Claudius (?)us
C(aius) Mateius Primogenius
C(aius) Suettius Dama

The first two names stand out for the abbreviated phrase C(aii) f(ilius), "son of Gaius," through which the signatories signaled that they were freeborn citizens. Their surnames as well are indicative of freeborn status. Senecio and Rufus are proper Roman names, rare among slaves and freedmen and associated with the more elevated layers of Roman society.[57] The top-listed witness, Senecio, also added the specification Fal(erna) to his name, indicating the citizen subunit (*tribus*) to which he belonged.[58] But his emphasis on citizenship and freeborn status notwithstanding, his clan name, Julius, may betray descendance from an imperial freedman. As for Rufus, no other Munii appear in the archive, but they are well attested in Campania, especially in the area of Capua.[59]

Unlike the two signatories at the top, the other witnesses were former slaves, judging from their surnames.[60] Nevertheless, at least A. Fuficius Donatus and L. Pontius Philadelphus belonged to eminent local clans. The Fuficii were prominent in Puteoli by 105 BCE, when one of their members held a high municipal magistracy there. They are subsequently attested widely in Campania until the end of the second century CE.[61] L. Pontii are recorded in Puteoli in late-republican times, and appear among the urban elite of Cumae in the Augustan period.[62]

56. The names are written in the genitive in the document, but I give them in the nominative here for clarity.

57. Kajanto 1965: 229 (Rufus) and 301 (Senecio).

58. Camodeca 1992: 161 n. 51; Terpstra 2013: 20 n. 42.

59. Camodeca 1992: 161 and n. 52: the name is difficult to read, but *Munni* seems to be the most likely reading.

60. On *cognomina* as evidence for freedman status, see Andreau 1974: 140–55.

61. *CIL* 10.1781 (105 BCE). Other Campanian evidence for Fuficii, see Camodeca 1992: 162 n. 54–55.

62. *CIL* 10.1589. Evidence for L. Pontii at Cumae, see Camodeca 1992: 162 n. 57.

The surname of T. Vestorius, who is number five on this list, cannot be read with certainty, but he was in any case a member of the Vestorii, just as the contracting parties. If the reading "Phoenix" is correct, he might have been the seller, although he seems more likely to have been a third party.[63] Number six below him has a name with a strong local flavor. "Paccius" is Oscan in origin, and C. Paccius Felix thus seems to have belonged to an old bloodline with pre-Roman roots. Though not frequently attested in Puteoli, the Paccii were well known in Campania. They counted several officeholders among their ranks, including eventually a proconsul in the 70s CE.[64] The surname of the seventh witness can no longer be read, but the Claudii were certainly prominent in Campania, as scattered evidence shows. C. Claudii are attested as city magistrates at Paestum in the mid-first century BCE. Two of their most eminent members are also known to have possessed real estate in Herculaneum and Liternum at the time of the late republic.[65] We can say far less about the next witness listed, C. Mateius Primogenius. The Mateii are rarely attested, appearing only once in Pompeii and once in Herculaneum.[66]

Finally, C. Suettius Dama unquestionably belonged to a clan that ranked among the Puteolan elite. In Cicero's letters (*Ad Att.* 13.12.4), a certain Suettius appears as coheir to an estate in the vicinity of Puteoli.[67] The wax tablets show how the Suettii were still prominent in the city during the Julio-Claudian period. From two documents we learn that they had built an altar to Augustus in the Puteolan forum. An inscription further refers to a colonnaded vestibule that they had constructed there. The vestibule and the altar had likely been built together as a single public monument.[68]

What does the list reveal about the witnesses' social standing? We can first of all be confident that Senecio and Rufus received the top two positions because of their freeborn citizen status, which both emphasized by adding their patronymic. But what factors determined their relative status relationship remains unclear. If Senecio was the descendant of imperial freedmen, it did not prevent him from having a higher standing than Rufus. We can even speculate that this aspect of his lineage, if indeed it existed, might have been the source of his superior prestige. No certainty can be had here, unfortunately. As for the

63. Sellers do appear elsewhere in lists of signatories, but only in the bottom position. See below.

64. Camodeca 1992: 163 n. 59–60. C. Paccius Felix also appears as a witness in *TPSulp.* 23.

65. On C. Claudii, see Camodeca 1992: 163 n. 61.

66. Camodeca 1992: 164 n. 62.

67. If, that is, we should read S. Vettius as Suettius: Camodeca 1992: 164 n. 65.

68. *AE* 1974: no. 256 (*chalcidicum Suettianum*); *TPSulp.* 9 and 18 (*ara Augusti Suettiana*). On these structures, see Camodeca 1979: 20–23; 1982: 32–33 n. 27. Suettii as witnesses: *TPSulp.* 90, 91, 122.

seven men listed lower down, if all were freedmen, some belonged to eminent and politically active clans, which must have influenced their ranking. But relative clan prominence does not appear to explain everything. It would seem, for instance, that C. Suettius Dama belonged to a more prominent clan than at least some of the six men listed above him. Other factors of his public persona—an only recent manumission and acquisition of citizenship perhaps—must have determined his bottom position.

We would much like to know not only what determined these men's rankings but also why specifically they acted as witnesses to the recorded slave sale. It is evident from the tablets that witness selections followed at least a number of rules. As with the hierarchy rankings, many details about those rules elude us, although the cumulative data do provide some clues. For instance, it is surely not by coincidence that in documents recording loan payments in cash, members of the creditor's clan never appear among the witnesses while the debtor or a representative is always listed.[69] All the same, apart from the total number of signatories, which seems to have been dictated by the type of document to be drafted, the process of witness selection does not seem to have been subject to many restrictions. Selections seem largely to have been a matter of the transacting parties' free choice.

As for the question of who was asked to appear, or voluntarily chose to do so, in all probability some of the witnesses were personally involved in the agreements they signed, even if indirectly. We can, for example, imagine a scenario where a regular trading partner of one of the contracting parties appeared because the transaction had external benefits for his own business. But if scenarios of that nature are plausible, we lack the data necessary to verify them. All the same, such a dynamic is insufficient to explain all selections or self-selections. As contracts were witnessed by anywhere from three to eleven men, all but inevitably some of the signatories had no economic interests in the contracts whatsoever. Personal connections, friendships and chance circumstances, such as whoever happened to be available at any given time, must also have determined many witness lineups.

The Stoic philosopher Seneca, in one of his essays, implies that in everyday business the contracting parties brought along their own witnesses, which supports the idea that selections were largely left to their personal discretion. He interprets the practice of witnessing in a moralizing way, inserting his musings on the phenomenon into a reflection on human nature:

> If only buyer and seller could dispense with formal commitments, and if only contractual agreements were not protected by wax seals! Better that our good faith and an attitude respectful of justice should be the safeguard.

69. Observable in both the Sulpicii and Herculanean tablets: Camodeca 1993: 343.

But people have put situational requirements ahead of ideals, and they would rather compel good faith than wait around for it. Witnesses are called by both parties. One man insists on supplementary guarantors and entries in several ledgers when making loans. Another won't settle for a verbal contract, but has the guarantor locked in with a written commitment. This is scandalous—an admission that human beings are crooks and that dishonesty is rampant. We put more faith in seals than in souls. (*De Ben.* 3.15.1–3)[70]

Seneca's point is, in an ideal world, witnessing would not be necessary, which leads to a key question. What was its social purpose? A related and equally important question also presents itself: What was the purpose of the painstakingly precise status rankings?

"Publicly Embedded" Contracts

Neither question has so far been addressed in any detail by Roman scholarship, which has studied witness lists chiefly from the viewpoint of social stratification.[71] The lack of attention to the first question is perhaps understandable, as the answer seems self-evident. The Seneca passage cited above provides strong pointers to the direction in which we should be thinking. A contractual partner might renege on his promises, denying that a transaction had taken place and declaring the written contract a forgery. A safety mechanism against such behavior was provided by drafting a statement in the presence of witnesses and having them sign their names. But witnessing did more than provide evidentiary support for written statements, and the practice had wider socioeconomic effects. A comparison with a better documented historical situation will be useful here.

A chance find in Fustat (old Cairo) of medieval letters has given us firsthand evidence on the business ventures of a community of Jewish traders active in the eleventh-century Mediterranean.[72] The members of this community are now often called the "Geniza" merchants, after the room in which their letters were discovered: a Geniza (synagogue depository) for documents written in Hebrew letters.[73] Contrary to the situation under the Roman empire, no single state controlled the entire Mediterranean in the eleventh

70. Tr.: Griffin and Inwood 2011: 68.

71. Andreau 1974; Jongman 1988. Older literature discussed the legalistic aspects of witness lists: Bruns 1882: 37–49; Mommsen: *CIL* 3 p. 922–23.

72. On the find, the documents and the Jewish trading community, see Goitein 1967–88; Greif 1989; Goldberg 2012.

73. An alternative name is "Maghribi traders": Greif 1989; 2006; 2012.

century, although the Fatimid caliphate dominated a large part of the eastern half. Because of the political fragmentation of their area of operation, the Geniza merchants had to deal with officials from a number of different states, which presented them with problems that Roman traders did not face.[74] But what they shared with their Roman counterparts was that the states under whose rule they fell did not provide contract enforcement. In a recent, extensive study of the Geniza business letters, Jessica Goldberg noted that a lack of public institutions in support of trade forced the Jewish mercantile group to rely on private coping mechanisms:

> Maintaining market order and reputation was ... a burden that the state placed on the shoulders of the local business community. Part of the working day for a merchant at home was to attend the market as a witness—monitoring the opening of and dispersion of packages, attesting to market prices, observing sales and agreements, formally witnessing written contracts. Merchants made up the pool of reputable locals who sustained the reputation and functioning of the market.... The business community was also expected to be a source of knowledge on local market law, both informing judges and negotiating dispute settlements.[75]

For the Geniza merchants, witnessing formed an essential part of the social dynamic that sustained their business. Traders rendered service to the collective with their input, and markets depended on it to function properly. As Goldberg observed, "Witnessing took up the valuable time of fellow merchants during the marketing and shipping seasons, but was a public good that the local community provided."[76] Like their medieval counterparts, the people listed in the Roman tablets invested time in the practice of witnessing. How much time we do not know, but if even elite men like Martial, Seneca and Pliny remarked on how frequently they were being asked to participate, then surely the time commitment was large for members of Campanian mercantile communities.

The Geniza archive contains private letters that allow us to reconstruct the individual relationships between traders. By contrast, the Campanian tablets preserve almost exclusively formal contracts revealing little of the interpersonal relations behind them.[77] It is therefore all but impossible in individual

74. For example, Geniza merchants had to establish ties with semi-independent officials, who could turn on them and threaten violence and even death: Goldberg 2012: 175–76.

75. Goldberg 2012: 170. On the importance of witnessing for the Geniza merchants, see also Goitein 1967: 196; Greif 2006: 65.

76. Goldberg 2012: 159.

77. A rare exception is *TPSulp.* 80, a letter concerning a shipping arrangement, unfortunately badly damaged. On this letter, see Terpstra 2013: 90–92; 2017: 51–52.

cases to establish why the witnesses appeared. As discussed above, it seems unlikely that all were screening transactions that affected them personally. Some and perhaps most were extending favors to friends and associates by attending. But whatever their individual motivations might have been, we can safely say that having multiple people witness one's contracts, and being ready to do the same for others, created a social fabric that fostered trust and ensured the steady operation of business. Witnessing wove a fine web of reciprocal obligations, and seen in that light the practice facilitated economic interaction in more profound ways than it would seem taking into account only the need to produce proof of contracts.

In both the medieval and the Roman situation, the absence of the state provided the impetus for the development of private-order mechanisms that underpinned commercial exchange. But in the Roman case, the influence of public institutions is also manifest to a remarkable degree. Contracting parties voluntarily employed the rules of Roman law, a choice that was not self-evident, as explained above. The question of what motivated them to adopt the rigorous framework of the imperial legal system deserves further consideration.

Elizabeth Meyer has provided an interesting answer, asserting that "Roman law initially drew its authority from outside government and outside itself, from the wider world of belief in which it was embedded."[78] A social-consensus element was added to this spiritual one during the "self-assertive" time of the late republic and early empire. By writing legal acts down in wax tablets, individuals could express their personal good faith. Eventually the state imposed systematizing requirements on legal tablets. A technical measure of 61 CE, for instance, prescribed a particular way of sealing them (Suet. *Nero* 17; Paul. *Sent.* 5.25.6).[79] The state's de facto endorsement of legal tablets further enhanced their authority. These factors led to the legal system's continuous use, a process that became self-perpetuating: "The more ways in which legal acts followed widely accepted, formalized techniques . . . the more likely their users were to believe in their efficacy and, therefore, the more believable and efficacious legal practice in general would be."[80] In my view this explanation has much to recommend itself, even if Meyer moves too easily here between the use of wax tablets and the use of the legal system, two practices not to be equated.[81] Yet I also think that factors beyond a path-dependent trajectory initially determined by religious significance rendered the Roman legal system attractive and efficacious.

78. Meyer 2004: 294.
79. Meyer 2004: esp. 125–68.
80. Meyer 2004: 295.
81. See my path-dependency analysis of Meyer's argument: Terpstra 2013: 35–36.

The question of what those factors might have been brings me to the purpose of the meticulously executed status rankings. The Campanian communities visible in the tablets differed from the community of Geniza traders, who did not list witnesses hierarchically.[82] It follows that the purpose of ranking witnesses went beyond facilitating the smooth running of business, which the Geniza traders also achieved. To understand the significance of the rankings we need to shift our perspective away from the one adopted so far by Roman scholarship, which has studied witness lists primarily as passive reflections of social hierarchy. Instead, we need to conceive of the act of witnessing as an active, performative gesture that confirmed and even created standing.

Social status is not something static and immutable, a secure possession to be quietly enjoyed. Once acquired it needs constantly to be reaffirmed. If gaining access to public institutions of officeholding most securely conferred social status, then it should come as no surprise that reaffirming that status was preferentially done through public institutions as well. Participating in drafting documents that followed the provisions of the imperial legal system was attractive from that point of view. For the most distinguished community members, it was a way of endorsing the civic order from which their prestige derived. They claimed and reasserted their status by the solemn act of witnessing a transaction and by prominently writing their name in a formal document. They may, in addition, have enhanced their standing, as by acting as witnesses they displayed their importance to the proper functioning of the local economy. It seems likely that the witnesses listed below the top positions were motivated by similar considerations. If they could not lay claim to a position in the social top tier they, too, were endorsing the prevailing civic order and were showcasing their relevance to the socioeconomic life of their community.

City magistracies were positions of local government, but the position of *Augustalis*—a status marker significant especially within a freedman social milieu—was associated with the overarching ideology of the imperial state. The tablets contain several indications that using Roman law formed part of that ideology. Agreements to initiate litigation were held at locations with imperial-cult significance: in Rome in the Forum of Augustus, in Puteoli at either one of two altars of Augustus located in the central forum.[83] Five documents, all related to financial litigation and loan agreements, record how the contracting parties had sworn oaths on "the divine power of the deified Au-

---

82. The oral nature of many Geniza traders' contracts of sale made systematically ranking witnesses impossible. On oral Geniza contracts and how they were witnessed, see Goitein 1967: 196.

83. Forum of Augustus in Rome: *TH* 15, *TPSulp.* 13–15, 19; Puteolan altars: *TPSulp.* 1–11, 16–18.

gustus"; two formulas included the "divine spirit" of the current emperors (Gaius and Claudius, respectively).[84] Such oaths can be found also in official declarations filed with the governmental bureaucracy in Roman Egypt.[85] Swearing on the emperor's divine spirit to attest to the veracity of official statements was apparently a standard requirement for citizens interacting with the state. The Pompeian wax tablets suggest that the practice partly carried over to private contracting.

The conclusion from the prominent imperial-cult elements in contracting, witnessing and dispute settlement must be that the use of Roman law should be understood in a larger ideological framework. Setting contracts in that framework embedded them not only in Meyer's "wider world of belief" but also the wider social order that structured Roman society. Contracts drawn up according to the precepts of the imperial legal system and witnessed by men ranked according to their civic status were in that sense "publicly embedded." Their civic order and ideological embeddedness increased their enforceability and reduced enforcement costs.

To see how that effect emerged, we first need to realize that conflicts were resolved informally whenever possible. Commercial partners in disagreement over a contract and bargaining "in the shadow of the law" had every incentive to avoid a trial. Because of legal fees, the costs of delays and the potential for a financially suboptimal outcome, the surplus from cooperation was usually obvious.[86] Furthermore, official litigation could jeopardize valuable business connections. Especially for members of close-knit mercantile groups, resolving a dispute on friendly terms was almost always preferable. The dearth of personal letters in the Campanian archives deprives us of evidence for such unofficial dispute settlement.[87] But more informative documentation from the eleventh to seventeenth centuries shows us that within medieval and Early-Modern business communities, settling conflicts out of court was the preferred option. The Geniza merchants avoided lawsuits where they could, despite the availability of both Jewish and Islamic courts.[88] In Bruges and Amsterdam during the 1400s to 1600s attempting to resolve disputes through mediation was traders' first course of action, as Oscar Gelderblom has shown.[89]

84. *TPSulp.* 29, 54, 63, 68, 117. On the significance of the imperial cult for trade and business, see Terpstra forthcoming.

85. Ando 2000: 359.

86. Cooter, Marks and Mnookin 1982: 228.

87. But cf. *TPSulp.* 2, 3, 27 and *TPSulp.* 25, 34–39, two "dossiers" pertaining to out-of-court settlements reached after official litigation had been initiated.

88. Goldberg 2012: 159–62.

89. Gelderblom 2013: 104–08.

Compared to members of those groups, Roman traders had an additional incentive to reach settlements informally: retaining the future goodwill of witnesses by respecting their social standing. By listing their names in an official contract, the signatories had not only reaffirmed their social status but had also staked that status. If a contract to which they had added their names was breached, their reputation could be negatively affected. By not honoring an agreement, a contractual party therefore risked irking the witnesses on the opposite side. In addition, he risked embarrassing the men he himself had asked to appear. A desire not to imperil the relationship with the witnesses increased the pressure on contractual partners either to comply with the agreed-upon terms or to cooperate in informal settlement. Either way, enforcement costs would be reduced.

Of course, litigation could not always be avoided, and both our literary and documentary sources show that the social standing of witnesses was central also at that stage. In court the litigating parties might make official statements, which would be recorded in written documents and witnessed in the same way as private contracts. A particularly well-preserved example from the Sulpicii archive documents that a defendant had made a declaration on the plaintiff's request.[90] At the time of the lawsuit, which occurred in 55 CE, the two men had been commercial partners for at least seven years. What prompted them to go to court remains unclear, but their dispute for certain concerned financial transactions. It was probably related to damage caused by two slaves who had been conducting business as agents. In any event, nine men added their names to the document, confirming that the defendant had made the statement as recorded. It is unclear for whose side they were signing, but as the plaintiff had requested that the declaration be made, one imagines that they were acting on his behalf.

Apart from validating official declarations made during legal proceedings, witnesses played another role in court. They could be summoned before the bench to make individual statements under oath to clarify matters relevant to the dispute. Agreeing to perform that task was not to be taken lightly. Promising to appear and subsequently backing out diminished one's standing and led to legal ostracism. The archaic law of the Twelve Tables already contained a provision to that effect, according to Aulus Gellius: "Whoever shall allow himself to be summoned as a witness . . . if he does not give his testimony, let him be regarded as dishonored and incapable of giving testimony in the future" (NA 15.13.11).[91] A litigating party might contest a witnessed contract by calling counterwitnesses and having them give oral testimony in court. The

90. *TPSulp.* 25, on which see also Wolf 2001: 99–100; Terpstra 2013: 22, 38.

91. Tr.: J.C. Rolfe, *LCL* 1927.

question of what evidence would then prevail depended on the circumstances of the case, and lawyers might argue both ways, as the first-century CE rhetorician Quintilian explained: "Written evidence and oral evidence often conflict. There are general arguments on both sides. One party relies on the oath, the other on the agreement of the signatories" (*Inst.Or.* 5.7.32).[92]

In litigation proceedings as well, status rankings played a significant role, whether in lists attached to official declarations or in oral testimonies. As the provision in the Twelve Tables shows, preoccupation with honor and status in things legal had been pervasive in Roman society from at least the time of the early republic. In a survey of inequality in legal matters, Peter Garnsey concluded that "although Roman legal institutions underwent transformation to suit the needs and attitudes of the new [imperial] regime, there was a fundamental continuity from Republic to Empire in the spirit in which the law was administered."[93] That spirit included the way in which the testimony of witnesses was evaluated. Having prominent witnesses on one's side provided an officially sanctioned advantage, according to a large body of Roman juridical literature.[94] The Roman jurists clearly say that higher social rank translated into greater credibility in court. Of the various terms that they employed for high status, to be taken into consideration during legal proceedings, "dignity" and "authority" were especially closely associated with officeholding.[95]

Some examples of legal opinions will elucidate the point. The third-century CE jurist Modestinus declared: "The value of testimony depends on the dignity, faith, morals, and gravity of witnesses" (*Dig.* 22.5.2).[96] Callistratus, another third-century jurist, cautioned that the "reliability of witnesses must be carefully assessed. One must first inquire into their status. Are they decurions or plebeians?" (*Dig.* 22.5.3.*pr.*). The concept that higher status meant greater value as a witness in court was applied to the administration of the law in the provinces as well. According to Callistratus, the emperor Hadrian had written a rescript to Vibius Varus, the legate of the province of Cilicia in the early 130s CE, explaining that "you know best what weight to attach to witnesses, what their dignity and reputation is" (*Dig.* 22.5.3.1). In another rescript to Valerius Verus, the governor of an unknown province, Hadrian wrote: "Sometimes the number of witnesses, sometimes their dignity and

92. Tr.: J. Henderson, *LCL* 2001.

93. Garnsey 1970: 3.

94. See Meyer 2016: 275–78 for a discussion.

95. *Dignitas* and *auctoritas*. On the legal significance of these terms, see Garnsey 1970: 224–25, 227.

96. Tr.: Watson 1998: vol. 2, 192. On the first passage, see Garnsey 1970: 211–12, 231.

authority, at others common knowledge settles the truth of the matter in issue" (*Dig.* 22.5.3.2).[97]

If the testimony of high-status men had greater weight in court, then securing their presence increased the enforceability of one's contracts. Both witnesses and transacting parties were thus invested in the reputational element of witnessing, not only in contracting but also in a court setting. For witnesses, signing agreements was a way of displaying their importance to economic life and thereby a way of reaffirming and potentially enhancing their community standing. For contractual partners, engaging high-profile witnesses was a way of increasing the enforceability of their agreements.

The Dacian Wax Tablets

Hadrian's rescripts show that social rank was taken into consideration in the evaluation of witness testimony also in the provinces. Men who possessed greater dignity and authority through their participation in public life were credited with greater credibility. If that was the case, then the practice of ranking witnesses might also have been adopted by provincial communities. By implication, their agreements might have been similarly "publicly embedded," increasing the enforceability of contracts and decreasing enforcement costs. Unfortunately, that hypothesis is not easy to test. No collection of wax tablets exists that can compare in size with the Campanian archives and that would have allowed for a neat comparison. Although Egypt has provided us with large quantities of wooden writing tablets, they come from a number of dispersed sites and remain poorly studied.[98]

But a reasonably large alternative set from a single site does exist. It consists of twenty-five tablets containing documents dating to 131–67 CE. Those tablets were found in the Apuseni mountains of Transylvania, far removed from Campania in both a geographical and a socioeconomic sense. The Apuseni mountain range is one of the richest metallogenic regions in Europe for both gold and silver. Between 106 and 271 CE it formed part of the Roman province of Dacia, and unsurprisingly given its metallic wealth, it was predominantly a mining district.[99] The settlement of Alburnus Maior was once located there (fig. 4.2), right in the heart of one of the world's largest gold deposits.

The information in the wax tablets teaches us much about the socioeconomic life of Alburnus Maior and its surrounding area. But before analyzing the tablets' content, it is worth spending a few words on their find history.

97. Tr.: Watson 1998: vol. 2, 192–93. On these passages, see Garnsey 1970: 153–54 n. 3.

98. Brashear and Hoogendijk 1990; Terpstra 2014a.

99. Mrozek 1977; Hirt 2010: 41–44; Cauuet 2014.

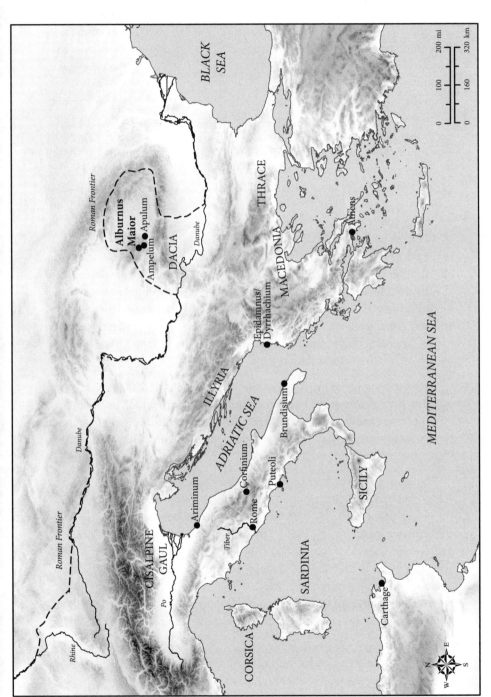

FIG. 4.2. The central Mediterranean and Dacia in Roman imperial times.

They entered the archaeological record through a depositional process different from that of the archives from Campania. But like the Campanian tablets, they were discovered in a primary context, which greatly enhances their historical value. The find context of the tablets is indicative of the substantial importance they must have had in antiquity.

In 1847 the German jurist *cum* travel writer Ferdinand Neigebaur visited Transylvania on the trail of classical antiquities, recording his findings in a diary that he would publish four years later. During his stay in the Apuseni mountains, he spent part of his time investigating several Roman wax tablets discovered in the ancient mining galleries in the decades before his visit.[100] He gathered what information he could find on the circumstances of the discoveries, going over local records and interviewing the population in the surrounding villages.

What he conveys in his diary is that little care had been given to the preservation of the tablets. Many were destroyed or had somehow vanished shortly after being found. The process of destruction had already begun with the first two, found in 1786, only one of which survived. A total of seven more were discovered in 1788 and 1790, of which four had disappeared for nebulous reasons. A find from 1820 allegedly contained several tablets, but only one was extant. In a particularly intriguing report about yet more vanished tablets Neigebaur relates how a local resident

> in the mining pit of his father in the year 1791 found in a recess or room filled with deadly air or bad fumes an old man with a long beard and by appearance about forty years of age, who crumbled to dust when touched. Not far from him lay six Roman wooden tablets of which, however, nothing further is known.[101]

The story about the body may have been no more than local folklore, but it is certain that the climatic conditions of the mines are highly conducive to the preservation of organic material. The tablets are not the only archaeological evidence bearing testimony to that fact. Explorations of the network of galleries have revealed Roman-era wooden drainage channels, ladders, support struts and the remains of waterwheels, equipment providing excellent evidence on ancient mining techniques.[102]

The largest cache of tablets was found several years after Neigebaur's visit, in 1854–55.[103] At that time as well, the careless handling of the artifacts led to

100. Neigebaur 1851: 187–91. See also Mommsen's summary of when the various finds were made: *CIL* 3 p. 921.

101. Neigebaur 1851: 191.

102. Cauuet 2014.

103. See Érdy 1856; Seidl 1856: 318–20.

much loss of evidence. According to the Austrian antiquarian, writer and poet Johann Seidl, reporting to the Viennese Imperial Academy of Sciences in 1856, one find had originally consisted of several dozen tablets. Nine were sent to the National Museum in Budapest, but of the rest, only fragments remained because "an incompetent hand . . . to scrub them down and clean them from dust had not only erased whole lines of the delicate Roman cursive script . . . but had moreover dried the wet tablets by a stove so that the wax flaked off."[104] Little could be learned from what was left of the tablets other than their size, shape and general character, Seidl concluded ruefully.

The overall treatment of the artifacts may have been regrettable, but that we possess information on where and how they were found is a blessing to Roman scholarship. The tablets were likely hidden deep in the mines because the Marcomannic Wars (167–82 CE) threatened to engulf the area, and were then never retrieved when peace returned.[105] They could have been left underground for any number of reasons. It is possible that their owners were no longer alive by the time the fighting ended or that they had left Alburnus Maior never to return. However, it seems unlikely that all listed individuals had died or moved away. Alburnus Maior was by no means depopulated by the wars, and epigraphic evidence suggests vigorous economic activity there in the early third century CE.[106] Alternatively, the recorded agreements might have expired in the course of the years and might not have been considered worth recovering. But even if time had voided the contracts, the tablets would still have been useful as writing material. Wax tablets were intended for reuse and designed with that purpose in mind.[107]

From the information on the finds gathered by Neigebaur and Seidl, it would seem that the tablets were discovered when renewed mining activities opened up collapsed or flooded Roman galleries. The most plausible explanation, then, for the tablets' abandonment is that their retrieval had become too difficult or dangerous. If that was the case, then the sample we have might be only a fraction of what was originally carried down the shafts. All tablets stored in galleries that were still accessible after the conclusion of the Marcomannic Wars presumably would have been brought back up.

It is surprising that no high-value objects are ever reported to have been found alongside the tablets. The population of a region bracing for warfare would surely have had other valuables worth hiding, such as coins, jewelry or precious-metal tableware, but none of the stories about the various find

---

104. Seidl 1856: 318.

105. MacKendrick 1975: 206; Pólay 1982: 510. Cf. Piso 2004: 301–02.

106. Mrozek 1977: 97–98; Mihailescu-Bîrliba 2011: 13–15, 67–76.

107. Meyer 2004. On the importance of wax tablets for "everyday writing," see Terpstra 2014a.

incidents mention any. We can think of several scenarios. The least satisfying from an archaeological perspective would be that such artifacts were in fact found but were kept by the miners, who reported only on objects that to them seemed to be of little value. Other explanations are, of course, possible, but all will have to remain speculative.

Regardless of whether metal valuables were ever concealed in the mines, the wax tablets were obviously of considerable importance to the people who had gone through the trouble of hiding them. They were discovered in different findspots and do not form a single archive, meaning that several individuals working independently had been responsible for their deposition. Given that the oldest surviving document dates to 131 CE, collectively those individuals had been keeping a written record of socioeconomic life going back at least thirty-six years. Moreover, the investigative work of Neigebaur and Seidl shows that an unknown but certainly large number of tablets were lost postdiscovery. More still are likely to have been retrieved in antiquity, so the complete record will have been considerably more extensive than what we have now.

Roman Dacia and Alburnus Maior

The province of Roman Dacia was created in 106 CE after the emperor Trajan had invaded and subjugated the area, an endeavor that had taken him five years to complete. A detailed pictorial narrative celebrating his military exploits still exists, carved into one of Rome's most famous monuments, Trajan's Column.[108] The area across the river Danube that was to become Roman Dacia seems to have been thinly populated before Trajan's campaigns and even more so immediately afterward, when many native Dacians had been killed, chased out or shipped to Italy as slaves. A considerable number apparently were also recruited into the Roman army and dispatched to Egypt, some shortly after 106 CE, as indicated by ostraca found in the Eastern Desert bearing the names of Dacian soldiers.[109]

To raise the population numbers in the new province, the emperor encouraged large-scale immigration. People moving in consisted of nearby ethnic groups such as Illyrians and Thracians, both native to the Balkans, but also of Greeks from Asia Minor, Italians and Syrians.[110] A large military force brought to Dacia to keep the peace consisted of legionaries and auxiliary troops from all over the empire, contributing to the province's demographic rise and its ethnic diversity. Apart from soldiers on active duty, military veterans settled

108. For a discussion of the Dacian wars following the narrative on the column, see MacKendrick 1975: 71–94.

109. Pólay 1982: 511; Dana 2003; Mihailescu-Bîrliba 2011: 31–35.

110. See Pólay 1971; Mihailescu-Bîrliba 2011; Varga 2014.

as colonists.[111] Roman culture spread rapidly in Dacia, perhaps unsurprisingly given the immigration of large numbers of civilians from other provinces and of soldiers and veterans accustomed to a rigid Roman institutional environment. Immigrants took with them the practice of commemorating events in inscriptions, the "epigraphic habit," as Ramsay MacMullen has famously called it, "part of the package that we call Romanization."[112] A Roman material culture emerged as well, and the archaeological record shows aqueducts, amphitheaters and public baths going up.[113]

Mining formed a large component of the economy of Roman Dacia generally and of the area where the wax tablets were discovered in particular. The mines around Alburnus Maior were a state asset, and their exploitation was overseen by a public official with the title of "procurator of the gold mines" (*procurator aurariarum*). Ten such officials are known to us through inscriptions dating from the reign of Trajan to the early third century CE.[114] Some of the procurators were imperial freedmen, suggesting that the emperor's court kept a close watch on the process of gold extraction in the new province. But although state involvement in the exploitation of the mines is certain, the details about the organizational logistics are blurry. Three of the wax tablets from Alburnus Maior preserve labor contracts.[115] They show that the workforce down in the pits consisted not, or at least not solely, of slaves and convicted criminals, the type of labor force frequently found at Roman mines elsewhere. The state itself may have contracted free workers, but the documents contain no language that points in that direction. Rather than the state exploiting the mines directly, it seems more likely that sections were sold or leased out to private companies or individual entrepreneurs, who would then attract the necessary manpower. In that scenario, the imperial procurators would have been in charge of subcontracting and revenue collection.[116]

However that may have been, Alburnus Maior—recently Romanized, peripheral, landlocked, mountainous, heavily dependent on mining—is in all respects just about as far removed from the Bay of Naples as one can get. In addition, Alburnus Maior was not an urban environment like Puteoli, Pompeii or Herculaneum. It was only a small settlement forming the center of a constellation of connected villages, some of whose names appear in the

111. MacKendrick 1975: 134–37, 142–43; Pólay 1982: 511; Varga 2014: 87–98.

112. MacMullen 1982: 238.

113. MacKendrick 1975: 107–43.

114. Mrozek 1977: 97; Hirt 2010: 41–44, 126–30.

115. *CIL* 3 p. 948–49 nos. 10–11: explicit mention of mining work; *CIL* 3 p. 948 no. 9: nature of work uncertain. On these contracts, see Mrozek 1977: 102–06; Ciulei 1983: 39–60.

116. Pólay 1982: 519–21; Hirt 2010: 232–35. For this practice in the Lusitanian mines, see Wilson 2002: 24–25; Kehoe 2007: 568.

tablets.[117] As one would expect based on the historical, geographical and socioeconomic differences between the Bay of Naples and the Transylvanian mountains, the Campanian and Dacian documents present different pictures of Roman life. Yet in many ways their similarities are also remarkable, as the discussion below will show.

Of the twenty-five Dacian tablets, only fourteen can be read with enough certainty for us to know what they documented. Fortunately they display a great variety in their content, ranging from the labor contracts mentioned above to loans and other financial agreements, the sale of a house, the sale of slaves and the dissolution of a funerary association. An outlier in the collection is a ledger recording money received for foodstuffs—pork and lamb meat, white bread, salt, onions and vinegar—providing us with precious information on local food prices. Incense is included in the ledger, suggesting that it records purchases made in preparation for a banquet to be held at a religious festival.[118] Apart from giving us an idea of the local economy of Alburnus Maior the tablets provide us with evidence on its ethnic makeup. Illyrian names are especially well represented, but Greek and Latin names are frequently attested as well.[119] Finally, the strong military presence in Dacia is reflected in the tablets. Veterans and soldiers of the *XIII Gemina* legion, headquartered in nearby Apulum (fig. 4.2), appear in some of them, and two documents were drawn up in the soldiers' camp.[120]

Witnesses Rankings in the Dacian Tablets

Unfortunately for my purposes the tablets contain only ten witness lists, of which one is now also missing its main text.[121] But although the number of lists is low and the recurrence of names rare, the evidence is highly instructive about the practice of witnessing contracts. One of the most informative documents from that point of view records a slave sale that had taken place at the settlement of Kartum on March 17, 139 CE. The skeleton text reads:

Maximus son of Bato has bought and accepted . . . a girl by name Passia . . . more or less around six years old . . . for 205 *denarii* from Dasius son of

---

117. Piso 2004: 299; Ciongradi 2009: 14–15. Place names mentioned in the tablets apart from Alburnus Maior: Kartum, Deusara and Immenosus Maior, together with the camp of *legio XIII Gemina*.

118. Mommsen speculates on the festival of the *Laralia*: CIL 3 p. 953 no. 15 n. 1.

119. Mrozek 1977: 99; Mihailescu-Bîrliba 2011: 67–79; Varga 2014: 122–26. On Illyrian names, see Wilkes 1992: 74–87; Piso 2004.

120. See Pólay 1971: 73.

121. Witness lists: CIL 3 p. 924–32, 934–48, 956, 959 nos. 1–3, 5–8, 10, 20, 25.

Verzo, a Pirustian from Kavieretium. It is vouched for that she is a physically sound girl, not charged with theft and damage, is not a fugitive truant. But if anyone shall have claimed back this girl ... as a result of which it is not legal for Maximus son of Bato ... to hold and possess her rightfully, in that case Maximus son of Bato demanded that the exact sum and an equivalent amount be paid in good faith.[122]

A complete and clearly legible list of seven names is appended to this contract. The first six men down from the top are witnesses, while the signatory in the bottom position is the seller, Dasius:

Maximus son of Venetus, *princeps*
Masurius son of Messius, *decurio*
Anneses son of Andunocnes
Planius Sclaies son of Verzo
Liccaius Marciniesus son of Epicadus
Epicadus son of Plares, also known as Mico
Dasius son of Verzo, the seller

A striking aspect of the contract text is its close adherence to Roman legal concepts. It employs the formulaic language of imperial law, familiar to us from a large body of Roman juristic writing. That the text was composed of boilerplate phrases from that repertoire is suggested further by a reference to the girl as "him" in a subordinate clause, a type of mistake found in several more of the Dacian documents.[123] But if stock formulas taken from Roman contract law were not all modified correctly, they seem not to have been uncritically copied either. Two more of the Dacian tablets record slave sales, and a comparison between the three contracts shows that some thought had gone into tailoring the texts to the case at hand.[124]

Because of the legal mold in which the contract has been poured, we hear strong echoes of the Puteolan slave sale discussed above: the seller Dasius guaranteed that nothing in Passia's personal history made her a liability, furthermore guaranteeing that she was neither a runaway nor prone to becoming one in future. As the Puteolan seller had done, Dasius promised to pay double the purchase price in case a third party should come forward to lay a claim of ownership.[125]

---

122. *CIL* 3 p. 936–39 no. 6 (= *FIRA* no. 87). Tr.: Meyer 2004: 57.

123. Tab. 1 l. 9. On such mistakes, see Mommsen *CIL* 3 p. 923.

124. Ciulei 1983: 21.

125. For a more detailed comparison between the Puteolan and the Dacian contract, see Jakab 2015: 217–22.

But just as striking as the Roman flavor of the contract is the decidedly non-Roman flavor of many names. Moreover, it seems highly doubtful that any of the men involved possessed Roman citizenship, contractual parties and witnesses alike. None used the traditional Roman triple name, and even the ones with Roman-sounding names identified themselves as "son of" in a way typical of noncitizens (*peregrini*). Yet the text explicitly says that the sale was concluded through *mancipatio*, the official procedure required for the transfer of slave ownership.[126] According to standard legal doctrine the use of Roman law was not available to noncitizens, so the contract presents us with a historical problem. That problem becomes even more acute considering that most people appearing in the Dacian tablets seem to have lacked citizenship, probably some 75 percent.[127]

In the past the issue has much exercised Roman legal scholarship, but a consensus on how to resolve it seems not to have emerged. Perhaps the most attractive solution proposed so far is that the population of Alburnus Maior might have possessed the "right of commerce" (*ius commercii*), which included the right to use Roman law.[128] However, nothing in the tablets or other epigraphic evidence provides any support for that hypothesis. In my view we would do better simply to accept the contradiction and conclude with Elemér Pólay that the "imperial law of sale by means of the Romans' documentary formulas had almost completely entered into the legal practice of the settled *peregrini*."[129]

The adoption of Roman law by noncitizens was hardly a phenomenon unique to Dacia. Hartmut Galsterer, in a general survey of the reception of the legal system in the provinces, surely had it right when he wrote that "juridical status in the principate was increasingly defined by social relationships and ties rather than by the type of citizenship one enjoyed. . . . It did not count so much whether one was a Roman citizen or not, but whether or not one belonged to a superior status group."[130] In line with the point made above about witnessing as a performative gesture, I would add here: or whether one desired to be seen as belonging to a superior status group.

All this leaves unresolved what seems to be the central problem, namely the question of the contracts' legal validity. But although that question appears to be key, it might be merely a distraction. Ultimately a contract is as good as its enforceability, and on that aspect we should focus our attention. First of all, it is likely that in Alburnus Maior, as in other historical societies we know of,

---

126. See Gaius *Inst.* 2.14a, 2.22.
127. Pólay 1982: 513.
128. See Ciulei 1983: 26–29 for a summary of the discussion.
129. Pólay 1982: 523.
130. Galsterer 1986: 26–27.

most disputes were preferably resolved out of court by informal settlement. With such outcomes no magistrate would ever evaluate the legal merits of written agreements, and it did not much matter how they were phrased. But even if a dispute had to be resolved in court, in the end it all depended on what a local community and the judges serving it would find acceptable. As to what that might have been in Alburnus Maior, I suggest that contracts were publicly embedded in a way similar to the Campanian ones, lending them social respectability and legal strength.

A closer look at the men appearing in the contract will clarify the point. The seller Dasius was of Illyrian origin, as was his father Verzo, in both cases shown by their names.[131] In addition, Dasius identified himself as belonging to the Pirustians, an Illyrian tribe known to us through the works of the geographers Strabo (*Geogr.* 7.5.3) and Ptolemy (*Geogr.* 2.15). Kavieretium was his hometown, and he had clearly come to Dacia as an immigrant.[132] He appears once elsewhere in the documents as a party to a contract concluded in 131 CE, although the text is too badly damaged to determine what it entailed.[133] The buyer Maximus was of Illyrian ethnic descent as well, despite his Roman personal name, as shown by his patronymic.[134] As for the witnesses, their names suggest that all were Illyrians, with the possible exception of Masurius son of Messius, who might have been a Thracian.[135]

The non-Romanness of the witnesses aside, what jumps out is that Maximus and Masurius added titles to their names, in both cases indicating that they had attained official positions. Given what we know from the Campanian tablets, it is unlikely to be a coincidence that they were the top two witnesses listed. Because we lack information about the other four men, it is impossible for us to say why their names were sequenced as they were. Nevertheless, based on the data from the Campanian tablets and other Roman documentary evidence it is a legitimate inference that here as well their place in the local social hierarchy determined their position in the list. By contrast, the seller Dasius' bottom position was likely not the result of his social standing (or lack thereof), but the result of sellers customarily signing last, below the witnesses proper. Three other contracts of sale from Dacia and one more from Herculaneum provide parallels for that practice.[136]

---

131. Mihailescu-Bîrliba 2011: 72; Varga 2014: p. 122 no. 105.

132. Pólay 1971: 78; Piso 2004: 293.

133. *CIL* 3 p. 954 no. 17.

134. Mihailescu-Bîrliba 2011: 73; Varga 2014: p. 123 no. 110.

135. Illyrians all: Pólay 1971: 78–79; Mihailescu-Bîrliba 2011: 71–74. Masurius either Thracian or Illyrian: Varga 2014: p. 123 no. 109.

136. Dacia: *CIL* 3 p. 940–47 nos. 7–8, p. 959 no. 25 (= *FIRA* nos. 88–90); Herculaneum: *TH* 61 (on which see Camodeca 2000: 66–70; Jakab 2015: 218–19). Sellers among the signatories in the Dacian tablets: Ciulei 1983: 15.

The titles with which Maximus and Masurius presented themselves are worth examining in detail. A *princeps* was a member of the traditional Illyrian tribal aristocracy who had become a local governor in the Roman provincial administration. During the time of the early empire the Romans had placed Illyria under the authority of their own prefects, who were mostly military men. But in the course of the first century CE they gradually ceded control to the *principes*, co-opting them into their administration as trusted local collaborators and granting citizenship to a selected few.[137] It is possible that the position was introduced into Dacia as well and that Maximus held it locally, but he may also have been referring to a previous appointment in his native region.[138] Either way, given the large-scale Illyrian immigration into Dacia, clearly reflected in the slave sale document, many of the inhabitants of Alburnus Maior will have been familiar with the position of *princeps* and with the authority it carried. As for Masurius, he was or had been a *decurio*, a member of a local municipal council. He may have held that position at Alburnus Maior, provided it had a council, or else perhaps at another Dacian settlement such as nearby Ampelum (fig. 4.2). But it is also possible that in a previous life he had served as a councilor in an Illyrian or Thracian town.[139] One way or the other, a *princeps* was without doubt a higher-ranking official than a *decurio*, a status differential reflected in the relative position of Maximus and Masurius in the list.

The practice of ranking witnesses can also be observed in other Dacian documents. One of those, dated May 6, 159 CE, is a contract for the sale of a house in Alburnus Maior.[140] The building was located in what is called the "quarter of the Pirustians," a sector named after the Illyrian tribe already mentioned. Evidently substantial Illyrian migration to Alburnus Maior had occurred, and many of the original settlers had apparently come from a specific area. The two neighbors of the property to be sold are identified in the contract. One sure enough had an Illyrian personal name, Plator, although his patronymic was Roman.[141] The background of the second neighbor is murky, but he was probably not of Illyrian but of Greek origin.[142] Finally, the property's seller was likely of non-Illyrian ethnic descent and may have been an Italian. All in all, the neighborhood rather seems to have changed character

---

137. Wilkes 1969: 189–90, 193, 240–41, 266–67; 1992: 237–38.

138. *CIL* 3.1322 (= *AE* 1968: no. 443) (*princeps* T. Aurelius Afer) is unfortunately also ambiguous on this point. Maximus as a local Dacian *princeps*: Pólay 1971: 80.

139. Pólay 1971: 80–81.

140. *CIL* 3, p. 944–47 no. 8 (= *FIRA* no. 90).

141. Mihailescu-Bîrliba 2011: 74; Varga 2014: p. 122 no. 98. See Kajanto 1965: 281 on the name Acceptianus.

142. Mihailescu-Bîrliba 2011: 72; Varga 2014: p. 122 no. 97.

since receiving its Pirustian moniker. In any event, the description of the house shows it was what we would call a semi-detached today:

> Andueia son of Bato bought and received in ownership half a house, on the right hand as you go in, which is in Alburnus Maior in the quarter of the Pirustians between the neighbors Plator Acceptianus and Ingenuus son of Callistus, for three hundred *denarii* from Veturius Valens. Andueia son of Bato shall lawfully hold that half of a house which is in question with its walls, fences, boundaries, entries, doors and windows, as it is secured with nails and in the best condition. If anyone shall evict Andueia son of Bato from that house or part of it, so that he and those whom it concerns are not allowed properly to hold, possess or occupy it, then Veturius Valens promises in good faith to give to Andueia son of Bato such sum as he in good faith claims to be properly given, in as much as he is not allowed so to do. And for the half of the said house Veturius Valens has received from Andueia son of Bato, and acknowledges that he holds, the price of three hundred *denarii*.[143]

A list of seven names follows. As in the slave sale cited above, the seller appears in the bottom position, here again almost certainly because it was customary for sellers to sign last:

L. Vasidius Victor signed
T. Flavius Felix
M. Lucanus Melior
Plator son of Carpus
T. Aurelius Priscus
Bato son of Annaeus
Veturius Valens, seller

The seller, Veturius Valens, seems to have been a Roman citizen, judging from his name. Moreover, he seems to have been one from birth, as his surname was a respectable one, not associated with a freedman social milieu.[144] Given his pure Roman name, and given the large-scale and geographically wide-ranging migration into Dacia, he may well have come from Italy.[145] However, as the document postdates the creation of the province of Dacia by over half a century, it cannot be ruled out that he was locally born. The buyer, Andueia son of Bato, on the other hand, was all but certainly a noncitizen.

---

143. Tr. (with modifications): Jones 1970: 261.
144. See Kajanto 1965: 66 on the name Valens.
145. Mihailescu-Bîrliba 2011: 77 in any case seems to think so.

As demonstrated by the slave sale discussed above, in Alburnus Maior it was socially acceptable for noncitizens to transact business using the imperial legal system. The contract between Andueia and Valens shows that no local custom prevented men of different civic status from doing the same. Ownership is stated to be transferred through *mancipatio*, which according to official legal doctrine applied not only to slaves but also to provincial real estate.[146] However, because Andueia lacked citizenship, ownership of the house strictly speaking could not be transferred to him that way. The contract thus provides another example of an incongruity between civic status and legal practice.

A mix of citizen and noncitizen names is presented also by the witness list. Two men were without much doubt noncitizens: Plator and Bato, both Illyrians.[147] The four others carried a Roman triple name and were most likely citizens.[148] Just like the seller Veturius Valens, they may have come from the Italian peninsula, although the possibility of a provincial origin cannot be excluded. As to their positions in the witness list, the fact that three of them occupied the top three positions seems to suggest that citizenship provided social status. But if that was the case, it did not necessarily trump the social standing of noncitizens, seeing how Plator son of Carpus was listed above T. Aurelius Priscus. We can think of a variety of reasons why that might have been the case, but no information on the men's personal background is available, and no conclusions can be drawn.

From the perspective of social status and how it was expressed, the most interesting individual on the list is L. Vasidius Victor, the man in the top position. Several indicators show that he was held in high regard. Most importantly, he appears as the first witness listed not only in this document but also in two later ones, documenting a loan agreement and the dissolution of a funerary association.[149] In each case the witness lineup is entirely different, so it would seem that Victor's status in the local community surpassed most everyone else's. The three documents in which he appears were drafted in 159, 162 and 167 CE, so he was evidently able to maintain his high standing for a good number of years.

Apart from Victor's top position, there is another indication of his special status.[150] All other men's names are entered in the genitive, the usual way for

---

146. That is, provincial real estate on soil with the *ius italicum*. Whether or not Alburnus Maior possessed that right is unknown, further complicating the legal dimension of this story: Ciulei 1983: 27.

147. Mihailescu-Bîrliba 2011: 71, 74; Varga 2014: p. 122 nos. 93, 99.

148. But cf. Pólay 1971: 81–82, who remains skeptical about their citizenship.

149. *CIL* 3 p. 934–35 no. 5, p. 924–27 no. 1.

150. Pólay 1971: 76; Mrozek 1977: 101–02.

witnesses to be represented. But Victor's name is written in the nominative and followed by the word *sig(navit)*, meaning "he signed," further setting it apart from the five names listed underneath. With this addition Victor conceivably intended to emphasize that he was sufficiently literate to sign his own name. If that was his motivation it was in any case still part of status display. What lay behind his social standing is unfortunately impossible for us to determine, but a tantalizing glimpse of what it might have been is provided by the tablet from 162 CE in which he also appears as a witness. Added to Victor's name is a word or phrase that unfortunately cannot be deciphered.[151] However, we can safely assume that it indicated a magistracy or other official position, in line with the general Roman practice of listing witnesses according to their rank in public life.

As discussed above, using Roman law in contracting was optional. If transacting parties chose to employ it, they had incentives for their behavior. That held true for citizen communities such as those of Puteoli and Pompeii, and therefore all the more so for a largely noncitizen community such as that of Alburnus Maior. I propose that in Dacia as well, the ranked witness lists point to why the Roman legal system was preferred over alternatives based on local, ethnic or occupational custom. Participation in public life and the acquisition of official titles translated into the highest possible social standing. Individuals having attained such high standing needed to maintain it in a way consonant with it. Contributing to the smooth running of the local economy using the legal institutions of the imperial state provided a natural way for them to do so. As in Campanian cities, so in Alburnus Maior the process of ongoing status affirmation and reaffirmation produced a self-reinforcing dynamic. In Dacia as well, both the contracting parties and the witnesses were invested in the ranked listings. The practice made contracts publicly embedded, which increased their enforceability and decreased enforcement costs.

The surviving Transylvanian tablets do not contain any evidence for litigation, making it impossible for us to determine how local magistrates treated contracts drawn up completely or partly by noncitizens. But the question of whether such contracts, strictly speaking, possessed legal validity must have been a non-issue in everyday practice. It would have been extremely disruptive to the local economy if agreements for the sale of slaves and real estate were not considered solid. Logic dictates that they were enforceable, and I suggest that what made them so was their public embeddedness. Declaring them void would have meant challenging the civic order in which they had been set. None of this means that citizenship did not matter in the provinces. It obviously did and was taken quite seriously, as is made

---

151. Mommsen reads: —*ctati-as*: *CIL* 3 p. 935 with n. 8.

plain by the second-century CE inscription from Banasa, mentioned above, recording a grant of citizenship to a North-African tribal chief and his family.[152] But noncitizen status did not prevent members of Alburnus Maior's community from using Roman law and from positioning themselves in the civic order that structured Roman socioeconomic life.

In Puteoli, the legal system was intertwined with an imperial ideology. Litigation agreements stipulated that parties meet at locations with imperial-cult significance, and a number of contracts contain oaths sworn on the divine power of the emperors. We do not know where parties at Alburnus Maior met to initiate dispute settlements, nor do we know if swearing oaths on divine imperial power formed part of the legal practice there. But if public institutions were attractive in part because they allowed community members to embed their contracts in the state's civic order then evidence for the imperial cult is relevant in that larger context. At Alburnus Maior such evidence is limited, yet worth discussing briefly.

Of the modest epigraphic corpus from the site only five inscriptions are related to the imperial cult, a small number but showing a notable consistency. All are dedications inscribed on votive altars, and all are for deities bearing the epithet "Augustan." The inscriptions are hard to date, but probably belong to the late second or early third century CE. None of the dedicants seem to have been Roman citizens. Four had Illyrian names or at least an Illyrian patronymic, as was the case with one Fronto son of Plares. He dedicated an altar to Asclepius Augustus on behalf of an association, about which he unfortunately gives no specifics.[153] The other Illyrian dedicants were a Panes son of Epicadus, a Panes son of Noses and a Plator son of Sarus, who respectively set up altars to Diana Augusta, Apollo Augustus and Fortuna Augusta.[154] The only non-Illyrian dedicant so far known is Hermes son of Myrinus, probably a man of Greek origin, who set up an altar to Silvanus Augustus.[155]

Four of the altars were found out of context. Only the one to Fortuna Augusta was discovered in its original location, allowing us to get a sense of what its ancient setting might have looked like. It was placed in an area surrounded by an enclosure wall, roughly square in shape with inner dimensions of about 20 by 18 meters.[156] This area was unroofed and unpaved and may in antiquity

152. *AE* 1971: no. 534.

153. Beu-Dachin 2003: no.1 (= Ciongradi 2009: no. 42; Varga 2014: p. 125 no. 154).

154. *AE* 1944: no. 21 (= Ciongradi 2009: no. 27; Varga 2014: p. 126 no. 176); *AE* 1960: no. 236 (= Ciongradi 2009: no. 55; Varga 2014: p. 126 no. 177); *AE* 2003: no. 1492 (= Zirra et al. 2003: no. 1; Ciongradi 2009: no. 8; Varga 2014: p. 126 no. 189).

155. Ciongradi 2009: no. 67 (= Varga 2014: p. 125 no. 158).

156. Zirra et al. 2003: 337 with fig. 1.

have presented a garden-like appearance. It seems to have served as a sacred precinct of sorts containing a large collection of altars, at least fourteen in number, most of them inscribed.[157] The altars had all been dedicated by different individuals, the majority with Illyrian names such as Beucus, Dasius and Panes, some with Roman names including a man bearing a traditional Roman triple name, M. Ulpius Clemens. These men had set up their altars to a variety of gods, some well known such as Asclepius, Apollo and Mercury, others obscure such as the Artani deities, probably of Illyrian extraction.[158] The variety in gods and personal names shows that the precinct served an ethnically and religiously diverse community, suggesting that it was not a private sanctuary but a public or at least semi-public space.

The excavators proposed that Plator had placed his altar to Fortuna Augusta in this communal area as an expression of his "loyalty to the Roman Empire and the Emperor," an interpretation in line with evidence from elsewhere in the Roman world for "Augustan gods."[159] By the late second century CE the practice of labeling deities "Augustan" stood in a long Roman tradition of applying epithets that specified a divinity's peculiar powers. This custom came to include the addition of clan names, indicating that their members had a privileged association with a particular deity and enjoyed his or her special protection. Applying the epithet "Augustan" was in turn a continuation of that tradition. As Duncan Fishwick explained,

> the original intention of the epithet *Augustus/a* will have been to personalize the deity, to appropriate its powers for the emperor and his family. . . . Whether they understood it or not, then, those using the epithet were loyally asking the deity to bless the emperor. . . . But what one suspects is that in the great majority of cases this was simply not understood and the adjectival form . . . came as a result to mean simply "Royal" or "Imperial." Thus the habit of making a god "Augustan" must be viewed as little more than a mechanical process, a conventional gesture that flattered the emperor or expressed passive sympathy with the state and its policies.[160]

Of course we do not know if the dedicants of the Augustan altars in Alburnus Maior intended to invoke the blessing of particular gods for the reigning emperor or if they intended more generally to express their sympathy with the state. But the question of whether that distinction existed and what exactly the

---

157. *AE* 2003: nos. 1492–99, 1501, 1503, 1508 (= Zirra et al. 2003: nos. 1–10, 13).

158. The epithet *Artani* might be related to an Illyrian word for "king": Schmidt Heidenreich: *AE* 2003: no. 1503.

159. Zirra et al. 2003: 339. On "Augustan gods," see Fishwick 1991: 446–54.

160. Fishwick 1991: 448.

Dacian dedicants had in mind is irrelevant for my purposes. In either case the authors of the inscriptions presented themselves as faithful subjects of the emperor, engaging in imperial-cult activity to express their loyalty to the central authority that governed the empire.[161] Evidently an imperial ideology formed part of the lived historical experience of the population of Alburnus Maior. Its inhabitants employed imperial institutions, legal, political, ideological and religious, to position themselves in public life. All the elements that in Puteoli and Pompeii produced the emergent property of a system of contract enforcement were thus in place here as well.

Concluding Remarks

It is tempting to assume a priori that the Roman legal system as a public good reduced transaction costs in contracting. Negotiation and information costs could indeed be lowered through the use of standard clauses, but the highest potential costs will have been for enforcement. On the face of it the imperial legal system was of little help in that area. But despite the lack of a public coercion infrastructure, Roman law did provide transacting parties with enforcement advantages. Witnesses were ranked according to their social standing, allowing contracts to be "publicly embedded." That practice did more than create the conditions for a smooth running of business, as shown by the example of the Geniza traders, who also relied on witnessing but who did not adopt hierarchical rankings. The added effect in the Roman case was to insert contracts into a wider world of status and ideology, which increased their strength and reduced the costs of enforcing them.

A key component in producing that effect was the civic order of Roman society, which largely determined someone's social standing. Acquiring a public position in political or religious life conferred the highest possible prestige. Other determinants of rank were civic-order dependent as well, such as freeborn citizen status. Individuals sought to emphasize and maintain their standing within their particular social group by engaging in public behavior consonant with it. In witnessing contracts drawn up according to the precepts of the imperial legal system, they on the one hand displayed their importance to economic life and on the other endorsed the civic order from which their individual status derived. This behavior was intimately connected to an imperial ideology, visible in expressions of loyalty to the state through engagement in the imperial cult. The social arrangements that defined Roman society thus combined to create an effect that was more than the sum of its parts and that gave Roman law an enforcement-cost advantage. This outcome of unplanned

161. On imperial ideology and provincial loyalty, see Ando 2000.

and undirected institutional developments can be classified as an "emergent property."

As we saw in chapter 2, the operation of regular, intercommunity commerce over long distances was made possible by trade diasporas, which under the Roman empire employed Rome's imperial ideology to support private order. That same ideology was a key ingredient also in the emergent property of intragroup contract enforcement. Because the enforcement mechanism worked well in sustaining economic life, there was no need for the Roman state to invest in a coercion infrastructure. Taking that step would have had a high fixed cost and little to no expected payoff, so state representatives were not incentivized to do so. It probably bears repeating that I do not see that outcome as the result of a public policy based on a conscious cost-benefit analysis but as the result of stochastic, historical developments.

5

Economic Trust and
Religious Violence

IN A LONG AND CAREFULLY argued chapter in the *Cambridge Ancient History*, Bryan Ward-Perkins explored economic decline in late antiquity, approaching the subject from—as one would expect of him—an archaeological perspective. He makes the seemingly obvious yet important observation that the way in which the Roman economy unraveled reveals how it worked previously, in its untroubled state:

> In order to begin to understand its decline, I find it necessary to believe, first, that the Roman economy (through both commerce and the state) linked local, regional and overseas networks of specialization and distribution into impressive but fragile overall structures. It is then possible to investigate a number of different factors that may have weakened these structures.[1]

Ward-Perkins is right to emphasize that we should not attribute Rome's economic decline to a single factor. Several separate ones were at work, although some reinforced one another. Ecological change, writ large, is increasingly being recognized as one of the main drivers.

Kyle Harper, in a well-informed book on that subject, has recently argued that high connectivity had created an integrated disease regime in the area covered by the Roman empire at a moment when the climate there was becoming less favorable to agriculture. Lethal waves of endemic disease followed, starting in the second century CE. In addition, the empire began to suffer foreign invasions triggered by the westward migration of nomads on the Eurasian steppe, an area that was also experiencing environmental stress. The resulting economic degradation and political instability continued to worsen,

1. Ward-Perkins 2000b: 390.

and ultimately the downward drag proved to be too much for the Roman empire. This way of thinking is markedly different from the traditional approach, characterized by an emphasis on moral decay, political dysfunction and military mismanagement. Harper by contrast contends that the "fall of Rome's empire was not the inexorable consequence of some intrinsic fault that only worked itself out in the fullness of time. Nor was it the unnecessary outcome of some false path that wiser steps might have circumvented."[2]

In my view Harper is right in saying that we should not be looking for a fundamental flaw that from days of old had been woven into the fabric of Roman society and that in the end had to lead to its undoing. As noted in chapter 1, Daron Acemoglu and James Robinson's idea of Rome's "extractive institutions" reaching their limit is an example of such a misguided explanation.[3] I also agree that we should not be searching for a catastrophic and ultimately fatal misstep to explain Rome's demise. Yet I also think that Harper underplays the contribution of human agency to Rome's downward spiral. To the degree that the human element factors into his story at all, it appears mostly as resilience in the face of adversity.[4] But human actions had negative effects as well. Some of those actions seem initially to have been a response to the exogenous headwinds described by Harper. They may not have provided the initial impetus for Rome's downhill turn, but they had severely damaging and entirely avoidable consequences, aggravating an already adverse situation. In line with the theme of this book I will focus here on damaging human action at the state level: a change in official religious policy.

Participating in religious rites forms a powerful way of promoting collaborative conduct, enabling what the anthropological and economic literature has labeled "honest signaling." As Richard Sosis explained, the "performance of . . . costly behaviors signals and engenders commitment and loyalty to the group and the beliefs of its members. Trust is enhanced among adherents, thereby facilitating cooperative pursuits."[5] In-group trust does not depend on the belief in an omniscient, metaphysical being meting out punishment, although such notions may well heighten a cult's honesty-generating effect.[6] Instead, the value of religion in business lies in its ability to delineate membership, foster strong ties, reduce monitoring costs and facilitate collective action against defectors. The harshest economic punishment that a group can impose is the permanent exclusion of an individual from all further trade,

2. Harper 2017: 286.

3. Acemoglu and Robinson 2012: 158–75.

4. E.g., Harper 2017: 20.

5. Sosis 2005: 9.

6. See Mokyr 2016: 128–29 for a discussion of that effect.

although shunning can take many milder forms. In addition to economic penalties, religious groups are frequently able to impose social penalties on their members, for instance diminishing the marriage prospects of transgressors and their relatives.

Although trust in an interpersonal sense can increase the economic advantages of religious group membership, it is not necessary to produce them. The enhanced effectiveness of collective action in itself provides the main benefits. Confidence in private order possibly enhanced by justified faith in interpersonal honesty based on communal cult practice is what I will call "economic trust." Its beneficial effects can be illustrated with a well-known modern-day example. Multiple case studies have shown how ultra-orthodox Jewish diamond dealers in Antwerp, Amsterdam, London, New York and Tel Aviv enjoy enforcement and transaction-cost advantages as members of tight-knit religious communities.[7]

During the first centuries of its existence, the Roman empire adopted a generally relaxed, hands-off attitude toward the religions of trading groups.[8] It allowed those groups to engage in their individual cult practices, thereby allowing them to build internal cohesion and establish the type of private order described above. Of course the Roman world was polytheistic in nature, characterized by a multiplicity of nonexclusionary cults, and the influence of religion in most cases will not have been as strong as in the example of the modern-day Jewish diamond dealers. Nonetheless, the basic effects were the same.

The state's lack of intrusion into private cultic life had positive effects on diaspora trade, but its presence in the public religious sphere had positive effects as well. The state's religiously tinted ideology promoted society-wide private order, as we have seen in chapters 2 and 4. To encourage gestures of imperial consensus, the Roman authorities created occasions allowing the population of the empire to express their loyalty to the state and its governance. Some of those occasions were ad hoc, celebrating an imperial accession or a notable victory; others were fixed, celebrating anniversaries and birthdays of former and reigning emperors. To the category of fixed, recurring occasions belonged the collective vows on behalf of the emperor's well-being, made annually on January 3 in public ceremonies around the empire.[9]

In creating an imperial ideology with religious overtones the state had in effect created an honest-signaling device at the intergroup level. Intercommunity signaling, in which members of a heterogeneous population adopt

---

7. See Sosis 2005: 11–12 for a discussion with references.

8. An attitude not to be confused with a policy of religious toleration: Garnsey 1984.

9. Rives 1999: 144–45; Ando 2000: 359–62.

"degrees of homogeneity," can be a highly effective way of promoting intergroup trade, as Peter Leeson has argued. "The use of social-distance-reducing signals separates cheaters from cooperators ex ante, ensuring that in equilibrium only cooperators exchange."[10] As with in-group signaling, to be considered meaningful such acts need to consist of publicly observable and sufficiently costly up-front investments.[11] If investments are credible as cooperation signals they can allow intercommunity trade to occur even under "anarchy," a situation loosely defined by Leeson as the absence of formal government.

A common way for Roman trading groups to signal their trustworthiness was to set up inscriptions with religious vows that invoked their gods and that expressed wishes of well-being for emperors and their families. Acts of that nature were not only entirely consonant with the state's desire to receive token gestures of consensus with its rule but also credible as social distance-reducing signals. Religious vows involving public display were highly visible investments that could also be costly. Of course, rather than a situation of "anarchy," this was a situation in which the state acted as the provider of the ideology that served as a signal. But otherwise the process of heterogeneous groups adopting "degrees of homogeneity" is similar to the one described by Leeson.

The private-order dynamic of Roman trade diasporas fostering ties of economic trust internally through native cult activities and externally through religious vows of adherence to a state ideology seems to have functioned well in supporting intercommunity trade. Little to no sign of strain is evident, such as religious violence between diaspora groups or between diaspora groups and their hosts.[12] But the polytheistic environment that had sustained this complex system of socioeconomic interaction came under increasing pressure after Constantine's conversion to Christianity in 312 CE. The state turned progressively hostile to pagan cults, embarking on a process of forced religious unification that provoked violence and bloodshed.

According to a theory posited recently by Polymnia Athanassiadi, the turn toward religious coercion had antecedents going back some sixty years, to the reign of Decius. In 249 CE, Decius ordered all inhabitants of the empire on threat of penalties to offer public blood sacrifice for the safety of the Roman state. The order appalled the Christian community, still a minority at the time. Athanassiadi sees Decius' remarkable edict as the first step toward the establishment of a compulsory state religion, a development of

10. Leeson 2014: 17.

11. Leeson 2014: 22–24.

12. Clashes between Alexandrian Jews and Greeks (see below) may be an example, but if so represent the exception.

which the harsh persecution of Christians by Diocletian would be another early manifestation.

As to the larger context of that general drift, Athanassiadi explicitly cites the severe and prolonged crisis that afflicted the empire after the end of the Severan dynasty in 235 CE.[13] In the roughly fifty years following, there were invasions, usurpations, secession attempts in both east and west, outbreaks of disease, bouts of inflation and rapid successions of emperors, whose reign in some cases lasted mere weeks. The Roman state, as Athanassiadi sums up the situation, was "surrounded by energetic enemies and overwhelmed by social ills and natural calamities. According to the celebrated phrase of a fifth-century historian, in the mid-third century the empire found itself 'leaderless and helpless.'"[14] Faced with this dire state of affairs, Decius' aim was not to sniff out Christians, assumed by some scholars to have been his motivation. Instead he intended to appease the gods and unite the Roman citizenry in what had become a precarious moment in the empire's existence.[15]

Distressing the Christians was probably an unintended consequence of his edict, but a following one issued by Valerian in 257 CE did deliberately target them. It ordered the arrest of high-ranking members of the church, requiring them to offer sacrifice to display their allegiance to the state and its religious rites. "In so doing," David Potter notes, "it represents the ongoing tendency toward centralization of all activity around the will of the palace, and an insistence upon conformity among members of the ruling class."[16] Attempts at the restoration of imperial control through novel ways of centralization, including in the area of religion, thus appear to have been a response by emperors who had seen their grip on things slipping. Such a reaction to instability agrees with the general idea of the natural state, which is "sensitive to changes that alter elite interests and capabilities," as Douglass North, John Wallis and Barry Weingast wrote. "The limited access order is stable as a social order, but each natural state is subject to constant change; and because natural states rely on an interlocking system of elite interests, they are not always robust to changing circumstances."[17]

The edicts by Decius and Valerian suggest that the religious coercion of the fourth century CE had its roots in the crisis of the third century. Constantine

---

13. See Liebeschuetz 2015: 19–28 for a discussion of why it is appropriate to call the third-century situation a crisis.

14. Athanassiadi 2010: 49. The historian is Zosimus, the passage 1.37.1.

15. Along similar lines, Ando 2000: 206–09 with n. 5; Potter 2014: 237–39.

16. Potter 2014: 251.

17. North, Wallis and Weingast 2009: 254.

deviated from his predecessors by favoring Christianity over the traditional Roman cults, but in his religious policy he was less of an innovator than he appears.[18] Already decades before his reign, a sociopolitical undercurrent was pushing the Roman state in the direction of religious exclusivism and intolerance. Still, if Constantine's attempts at religious unification followed a turn taken earlier, it was the more momentous development in the process. "The abandonment of long established cults surely does reflect a change of mentality that is very profound indeed."[19]

An important socioeconomic consequence of that change was the consolidation of a new Christian establishment and the growing public prominence of bishops. In 321 CE Constantine issued a law permitting property bequests to the church, and as a result ecclesiastical wealth began to accumulate over the generations (*Cod. Theod.* 16.2.4). Bishops could thus come to control substantial financial means on their appointment, making some of them extremely powerful men.[20] Because such men had public prominence, controlled resources and had access to military violence they can be considered part of the ruling coalition of the natural state.[21] Below, we will see several examples of influential bishops asserting their authority through the use of armed force.

The negative economic consequences of the state's hostility to cultic diversity went beyond the violent destruction of life and capital. An unintended effect of its policy was to undercut one of the foundations on which long established trading communities had built economic trust. The state's forced promotion of cultic uniformity made it increasingly hard for trading groups to maintain cohesion through engagement in their respective religions. It also made impossible the insertion of those religions into an imperial ideology as an intergroup signaling device. The combined effect was to produce a shock to the Roman system of long-distance commerce and an upset of the existing private-order equilibrium. The empire's "impressive but fragile" structures of economic interconnectedness weakened. In what follows, I will discuss that process through three specific cases, one of them a *cause célèbre* of late-Roman religious violence.[22] But first, a brief general outline of the larger fourth-century CE context will be useful.

18. Athanassiadi 2010. See also Rives 1999.

19. Liebeschuetz 2015: 26.

20. On episcopal power and status, see Cameron 1993: 71–73; Rapp 2000; Gaddis 2005: 251–82.

21. On violence control and elite privileges in the natural state, see North, Wallis and Weingast 2009: 18–21.

22. For the attack on the Alexandrian Serapeum as a *cause célèbre*, see Watts 2015b: 1–9.

Christianity, Violence and the State

With the exception of Julian, who briefly reigned in the early 360s CE, all Roman emperors after Constantine endorsed Christianity. This enduring shift in the religious outlook of the imperial court is Constantine's most important legacy. Imperial patronage of the church is a major reason, and arguably the main reason, that Christianity would rise to become a world religion. Allowing the new faith to triumph over the traditional cults represents an impressive intellectual, political and social achievement, the scale of which should not be underestimated: "In 312 it was as easy to conceive of a Christian Roman Empire as it was to imagine a Roman imperial rail network."[23]

After Constantine committed to supporting the church in 312 CE, he began issuing legislation condemning all forms of religious allegiance other than the officially sanctioned form of Christianity. His successors followed in his footsteps, issuing their own edicts and decrees in favor of the catholic faith. Many of those laws are included in Book 16 of the Theodosian Code, promulgated in 438 CE. They provide us with direct evidence on what emperors attempted to achieve.[24] The compilation of the Code shows that legislation was not necessarily effective. Repeated attempts to outlaw the same practices at any rate suggest otherwise.

The Christian scholar Eusebius mentions in several passages of his biography of Constantine that the emperor had issued a law that forbade making sacrifices to idols (*Vita Const.* 2.45, 4.23, 4.25). The text of that law is no longer extant, but an edict of 341 CE issued by Constantine's son Constantius II refers to the earlier ban. It aimed at the same goal.

> Superstition shall cease; the madness of sacrifices shall be abolished. For if any man in violation of the law of the sainted Emperor, Our father, and in violation of this command of Our Clemency, should dare to perform sacrifices, he shall suffer the infliction of a suitable punishment and the effect of an immediate sentence. (*Cod. Theod.* 16.10.2)[25]

Yet pagan sacrifice continued. A comprehensively worded law of 392 CE once again attempted to put it to a halt.

> No person at all, of any class or order whatsoever of men or of dignities, whether he occupies a position of power or has completed such honors, whether he is powerful by the lot of birth or is humble in lineage, legal

23. Watts 2015a: 197.

24. Cameron 1993: 74–75; Hunt 1993; Trombley 1993: vol. 1, 10–35; Noethlichs 2015; Watts 2015a: 203–10.

25. Tr.: Pharr 1952: 472.

status and fortune, shall sacrifice an innocent victim to senseless images in any place at all or in any city. He shall not, by more secret wickedness, venerate his protective deity with fire, his guardian spirit with wine, his household gods with fragrant odors; he shall not burn lights to them, place incense before them, or suspend wreaths for them. (*Cod. Theod.* 16.10.12)[26]

Several years later again, in 399 CE, the emperors Arcadius and Honorius thought it necessary to write about the matter to Apollodorus, the proconsul of Africa:

If any person should be apprehended while performing a sacrifice, he shall be punished according to the laws. Idols shall be taken down under the direction of the office staff after an investigation has been held, since it is evident that even now the worship of a vain superstition is being paid to idols. (*Cod. Theod.* 16.10.18)[27]

If the edict betrays a hint of exasperation, that is perhaps understandable. According to Keith Hopkins' estimate, about half the population of the empire was still non-Christian around 350 CE, although it is also possible that a more or less even Christian-pagan split was not reached until the early fifth century.[28] Even then it could legitimately be asked how many Romans were only going through the motions of Christian worship simply because it was the sensible thing to do in the face of religious violence and oppression. As the rhetorician Libanius warned the emperor Theodosius in 386 CE,

if they tell you that some other people have been converted by such measures (i.e., the destruction of pagan temples) and now share their religious beliefs, do not overlook the fact that they speak of conversions apparent, not real. Their converts have not really been changed—they only say they have. This does not mean that they have exchanged one faith for another— only that this crew (i.e., the Christians) have been bamboozled. They go to their ceremonies, join their crowds, go everywhere where these do, but when they adopt an attitude of prayer, they either invoke no god at all or else they invoke the gods. (*Or.* 30.28)[29]

Whatever the pace of religious change may have been, pagan beliefs and practices could not simply be legislated out of existence, that much is clear. But the repeated edicts against sacrifice and the strong language they employed show which way the wind was blowing at the state level.

26. Tr. (with modifications): Pharr 1952: 473.
27. Tr.: Pharr 1952: 475.
28. Hopkins 1998: 191, fig.1. Cf. MacMullen 1984: 81–83.
29. Tr.: A.F. Norman, *LCL* 1977.

By the time the renewed bans on sacrifice were issued, the religious atmosphere in the empire was turning increasingly nasty. Many cities were shaken by street fighting and riots, a situation that had been growing worse by fits and starts. Earlier in the century, violence against pagan sanctuaries had also occurred, but there is evidence of public disapproval by the ecclesiastical establishment. At the Synod of Elvira in 305 CE the southern Spanish bishops declared that anyone who broke idols and got killed doing so would not count as a martyr. They justified their decision by pointing out that such behavior was not found in the Gospels and had not been indulged in by the Apostles.[30] Of course the church was not yet operating from a position of strength, which might explain the bishops' caution and call for moderation. But judging by the stories of rumblings that begin appearing in the literary sources, things looked different once the church had court backing.

Before discussing the escalation of violence, it is worth spending a few words on Constantine's nephew Julian, a most interesting character who has left us a large corpus of his own writings. Julian would become known to posterity as "the Apostate," having been branded thus already by his contemporary, the bishop and theologian Gregory of Nazianzus (Or. 4.1). Brought up a Christian, he came under the influence of Neoplatonic mysticism while a student, eventually to embrace paganism.[31] He kept his beliefs hidden, not making them known until he became sole ruler in 361 CE on the sudden death of his cousin, Constantius II. Once in full control of government, he attempted to reverse some of the changes set in motion by Constantine. He removed the tax privileges of the clergy and forbade Christians to teach rhetoric and grammar, in effect barring them from teaching at all. Political miscalculations and the brevity of his reign, which lasted barely over eighteen months, prevented his policies from having long-term effect. But his accession and rule did have an impact on the contemporary religious conflicts that simmered and periodically erupted, especially in cities in the east.

The pronouncement of the Spanish Synod implies that by the early fourth century, religious violence was not unidirectional, deadly revenge potentially following the destruction of pagan shrines. Stories of later incidents as well show that once a first act of provocation had been committed, a cycle of violence could ensue. The church historian Sozomen (HE 5.7, 5.9), referring to incidents that had taken place in the 360s CE, mentions how in Gaza and Alexandria pagans had committed atrocities against Christians. In both cases, acts of insult and sacrilege against pagan cults had apparently provided the

---

30. Hefele 1907: vol. 1.1, 255 (Can. 60).

31. On Julian, see Cameron 1993: 85–98; Gaddis 2005: 88–97; Athanassiadi 2010: 80–94.

spark. Both Sozomen (*HE* 5.10) and Gregory of Nazianzus (*Or.* 4.88–91) relate how at Arethusa in Syria the local bishop Mark had demolished a pagan temple on authority of Constantius II. But on the accession of Julian, the non-Christian townsfolk saw a chance for payback, lynching Mark in most creative ways. In Caesarea, central Turkey, Christians had torn down two temples, one to the city's ancestral god Apollo and the other to its tutelary deity Jupiter. But when early in Julian's reign the Caesarean Christians unwisely went on to attack the sanctuary of Fortuna, state reprisals followed, including the enrollment of the clergy into the military (Soz. *HE* 5.4).

After this period of heightened tension and mutual acts of brutality, things seem to have calmed down. But the climate turned more openly violent again at the end of the fourth and beginning of the fifth century.[32] Major sanctuaries in Gaza and Alexandria were given over to destruction (more on both below), part of a larger sweep of temple razings taking place in the eastern provinces. Marcellus the bishop of Apamea sometime in the 380s or 390s CE destroyed the city's great temple of Zeus, having been sanctioned to do so by Theodosius I (Theodoret *HE* 5.20–21). Troops at his side kept the populace in check. He apparently was carrying out a more comprehensive program of temple destruction, which ultimately would not end well for him. While on his instructions soldiers and gladiators were busy smashing a pagan sanctuary in Aulon, the bishop, standing at some distance from the scene, was grabbed by an angry mob and burned alive. The perpetrators were eventually identified by the bishop's sons, who vowed to avenge their father's death. They were prevented from doing so by the provincial council, which no doubt hoped to prevent a blood feud from deepening a religious rift.

Sozomen (*HE* 7.15), who relates this story, mentions in the same passage how in many cities in Arabia, Syria, Palestine and Phoenicia, pagans were attempting to defend their shrines and temples against Christian assault. If the sources are not as informative on the west, probably in large part due to the manuscript tradition, similar attacks certainly happened there as well. Martin the bishop of Tours busied himself with demolishing ancient pagan temples, overturning altars and cutting down sacred trees, as Sulpicius Severus informs us (*Vita Martini* 13–15). Archaeological evidence fills out the incomplete literary picture. Scattered across the northern provinces are "broken buildings, burnt-out buildings, hastily buried icons and sacred vessels."[33] In 401 CE in Carthage, there apparently was enough left to smash to lead Augustine, the bishop of Hippo, to preach to a congregation in a fiery sermon: "For that all

32. Cameron 1993: 75–76; MacMullen 1984: 90–91.
33. MacMullen 1984: 101.

superstition of pagans and heathens should be annihilated is what God wants, God commands, God proclaims!" (*Serm.* 24.6).[34] The result may have been the religious riot in Sufetula that we hear about in one of Augustine's letters (*Ep.* 50), a confrontation that left sixty Christians dead.[35]

The conflict between paganism and Christianity has to be seen against a larger backdrop of religious frictions and power struggles within the church establishment. Christianity had not been a monolithic religion prior to Constantine's conversion and did not suddenly turn into one post–312 CE. Branches including Donatism, Meletianism and Arianism had large numbers of adherents, and members of the various groups were at each other's throats with righteous zeal. Ramsay MacMullen has emphasized the "intransigence, sometimes amounting to ferocity," with which Christian disagreements were argued, battles of words and vitriol that could turn bloody. Clashes over doctrinal differences were fierce, particularly in Egypt, which "echoed to the shouts of partisans, the din of violence, and laments for those robbed, stripped naked, flogged, imprisoned, exiled, sent to the quarries and copper mines, conscripted into the army, tortured, decapitated, strangled, or stoned or beaten to death. The express object was to make converts."[36]

Emperors were directly involved in those internal conflicts, aiming with varying degrees of success to achieve unity within the church.[37] Harsh threats of physical coercion were not eschewed in attempts to implement catholic doctrine. An egregious example of the severity that emperors reserved for their coreligionists is the law of 382 CE prescribing the death penalty for celebrating Easter on any day other than the officially authorized one (*Cod. Theod.* 16.5.9.2). Whether anyone was ever executed for that offense is perhaps doubtful, but the point here is the spirit that informed the law. Given the fervor shading into fanaticism with which disputes over doctrine were fought within the church community, it is not surprising that even greater antagonism was aimed at non-Christian cults.

The polytheistic nature of Greco-Roman religion made it apt at absorbing new gods by incorporating them into the existing pantheon. Out of that praxis a seemingly improbable gray area between Christianity and paganism developed, visible for instance in burial practices displaying a mix of pagan and

34. Tr.: MacMullen 1984: 95. For the date (June 16, 401 CE), see Lambot in *CCSL* 1961: vol. 41, 324–25.

35. See Brown 1972: 308 for the supposition. For the situation in North Africa, see Brown 1972: 237–331; Gaddis 2005: 103–30.

36. MacMullen 1984: 93.

37. Cameron 1993: 66–71; Beard, North and Price 1998: vol. 1, 369–71; Gaddis 2005: 68–75.

Christian iconography.[38] But ultimately, the monotheistic, exclusivist nature of Christianity made it incompatible with the Greco-Roman religious tradition on principle. As the discussion above has shown, for both emperors and the ecclesiastical establishment, principles mattered. Yet throughout the fourth century no policy was designed systematically to eradicate non-Christian cults, even if emperors repeatedly attempted to halt pagan sacrifice. Late in the century we still find evidence of non-Christians litigating to appeal laws for the overthrow of their temples. But in 407 CE after years of imperial ad hoc decisions and case-by-case treatment, a blanket decree for the destruction of pagan images and altars went out to the west from Rome (*Cod. Theod.* 16.10.19.1–2). By then "it could be fairly claimed that non-Christians were outlaws at last, and . . . that a state religion had at last emerged."[39]

Gazan Long-Distance Trade

By the time of the Roman empire Gaza was already an old city, having existed for at least a millennium and a half. Its first known mention occurs in an inscription on a temple wall in Karnak, Egypt, dating to 1468 BCE and listing the cities conquered by Tuthmosis III.[40] Gaza was a prized possession for the pharaoh because of its location on "the way of the sea" (Isa. 9:1), the trunk road along the coast between Egypt and the land of Canaan.[41] It would eventually grow into a trading post strategically placed on both a north-south and an east-west axis, connecting the Arabian Peninsula to the Mediterranean. How early that transformation had begun is unknown, although archaeological and numismatic evidence indicates that it dates back at least to the time of the Achaemenid empire.[42] A Plutarch passage (*Alex.* 25.4) also suggests that the city had consolidated its position as an emporium for high-value eastern goods before 332 BCE. Alexander captured Gaza in that year and is said to have sent his old tutor Leonidas five hundred talents of incense and one hundred talents of myrrh from the spoils of war.

Hellenistic-era documentary evidence confirms the picture of a city with valuable eastern trading links. As we have seen in chapter 3, Gaza was important enough for the Ptolemaic finance minister Apollonios to have an agent

---

38. MacMullen 1984: 78–79.

39. MacMullen 1984: 100–01.

40. Katzenstein 1982; Isaac in *CIIP* 2014: vol. 3, 409.

41. Tr.: *NRSV*. On early Gaza, see Glucker 1987: 1–4; contributions by Miroschedji, Burdajewicz and Giroud to Humbert 2000.

42. Glucker 1987: 86.

permanently stationed there to supervise shipments of Egypt-bound aromatics. Apollonios' business documentation shows the wide geographical range of areas sending goods to Gaza. Frankincense arrived there from Gerrha on the Persian Gulf, incense and myrrh from south Arabia, and henna, cinnamon oil, cassia and nard from India.[43]

During the Hellenistic and early Roman era the desert trade in such high-value goods allowed the Nabataeans to carve out a key position for themselves as transporters and middlemen. Originally a nomadic people, they increasingly became a sedentary society, occupying the area around Petra, their most important settlement. Operating from that strategic location they brought goods from India, the Persian Gulf and Arabia through the desert to Gaza, the nearest harbor on the Mediterranean.[44] The mercantile importance of Petra is often assumed to have declined after 106 CE when the Romans annexed the Nabataean kingdom, causing caravan routes to shift northward to Palmyra.[45] But if that was the case the process was slow, and the transport of eastern goods to Gaza over Petra did not cease until sometime in late antiquity. Archaeological evidence shows that the road between Petra and Gaza remained in use until at least the end of the third century.[46]

Late-antique, long-distance trade at an even later date is suggested by a passage from Timotheus of Gaza (*Peri Zoon* 24), an early-sixth-century CE author. Timotheus wrote that a trader in Indian goods had passed through Gaza with two Indian giraffes and an elephant. The destination of the exotic fauna was reportedly the court of the emperor Anastasius in Constantinople. What makes the passage puzzling and a bit suspicious is the fact that the giraffe is, of course, an African and not an Indian animal. The story seems not to have been fanciful, though. A contemporary work reports on the shipment's arrival at the emperor's court (Mar. Com. *Chron.* 496). Presumably the India merchant traveled to Gaza over Aela coming from the Red Sea, where he might have picked up the two giraffes at a harbor on the African coast.

Still, if movements of high-end goods continued well into late antiquity, it seems that the aromatics trade dried up. Textual evidence on Gaza does not allude to it anymore, indicating that the city had lost its prominence as a way station on the Arabian supply route. But what it lost in eastern trade it gained in exports of wine, which its hinterland started producing on a large scale. Literary sources first in their silence and subsequently in their effusiveness

---

43. *PSI* 6.628; *P.Cair.Zen.*1.59009; *P.Cair.Zen.*4, *add. et corrig.* 59009 p. 285 (= Durand 1997: nos. 19–21).

44. See Young 2001: 82–106; Terpstra 2015.

45. Although cf. Young 2001: 100–01.

46. Cohen 1982.

suggest that this economic shift was a development of the later empire. Pliny the Elder (*NH* 14), writing in the first century CE, makes no mention of Gaza in his long exposition of grape types, wine production areas and methods of vine cultivation. But Gazan wine does appear in the writings of several late-antique authors, who universally praise its high quality.[47] The anonymous author of a fourth-century CE geographical survey work, for instance, commented: "Ascalon and Gaza are distinguished cities full of commercial activity and having everything in abundance. They export an excellent wine all over Syria and Egypt" (*Exp. Tot. Mundi* 29).[48] Gazan wine amphorae are also a well-known feature of late-antique archaeological strata in the Mediterranean and beyond, appearing as far west as London and Trier.[49]

Gaza's commercial history doubtless explains the presence of its natives in the imperial heartland of Italy. We catch only a glimpse of a Gazan diaspora through two mid-third-century CE inscriptions, but its activities seem unlikely to have been limited to that narrow timeframe. Rome was the empire's largest market, generating about 8 percent of Roman GDP in Hopkins' estimate, in "great proportion" through trade in high-value products.[50] Given Gaza's long mercantile tradition and nodal position in the Mediterranean for Indian and Arabian goods, the city seems likely to have had a longer history of commercial exchange with Rome through overseas agents.

Regardless of when ties might initially have been established, during the reign of Gordian III (238–44 CE), Gazan natives were demonstrably active in Portus, the harbor at the mouth of the river Tiber serving Rome. An inscription found there tells us that the city of Gaza honored Gordian, "the most god-beloved ruler of the world," as its benefactor.[51] It had done so, the text clarifies, "at the prompting of its ancestral god and through Tiberius Claudius Papirius, keeper of the temple." In all probability Gordian had conferred special privileges on Gaza. In response, Papirius, on behalf of the city's trade diaspora at Portus, had publicly paid tribute to the emperor. The decree does not say to what god the temple overseen by Papirius was dedicated, but the reference to Gaza's ancestral faith provides a first clue that we should be thinking of Marnas, Gaza's tutelary deity.

47. Glucker 1987: 93–94; McCormick 2001: 35–37; Hahn 2004: 207–08; McCormick 2012: 54 n. 17; Isaac in *CIIP* 2014: vol. 3, 420–21.

48. Tr.: Isaac in *CIIP* 2014: vol. 3, 420.

49. Glucker 1987: 94. For examples of Gazan amphorae, see the contribution by Ballet to Humbert 2000; McCormick 2001: fig. 1.1: Type A *Gazition*.

50. Hopkins 2002: 222 with n. 73.

51. *I.Porto* no. 5, on which see Taylor 1912: 79–80; Floriani Squarciapino 1962: 63–65; Meiggs 1973: 394; Mussies 1990: 2423–24.

A second inscription from Portus confirms the god's identity. It is inscribed on a column of gray granite and says that Tiberius Claudius Papirius acting as the temple keeper had erected the monument from his own money. The dedicant was almost certainly the same religious official as the one honoring Gordian, and we can thus safely ascribe the artifact to the mid-third century CE. Carved above the inscription in Greek is the Aramaic *mem*, the initial letter of the name Marnas, frequently attested also on Gazan coin legends as a shorthand for the god.[52] A third Greek inscription contains Marnas' full name, but its use as evidence for the establishment of his cult at Portus is more problematic.[53] The stone on which it was inscribed is lost, and the renaissance-era transcription of the text is mostly unintelligible, having apparently been badly copied. Although an Italian provenance of the artifact seems certain, no information on its find location is listed. Nevertheless, as the Marnas cult is not recorded anywhere else in Italy, the third inscription as well likely refers to the god's worship at Portus.

The Marnas cult was strongly associated with the city of Gaza, as shown by an abundance of visual and textual sources. But although the evidence on Marnas is rich it unfortunately gives us little information on his origin and nature. The picture that emerges from the literary texts is that of a sky god who also performed oracles. Ancient authors equate him with Cretan Zeus, but that tradition seems to be Hellenistic in date. His name could possibly, though not unproblematically, be traced to an Aramaic phrase meaning "Our Lord."[54] If that reading is correct it would suggest that he had a Semitic origin. All the same, his surviving iconography is Greek in style. Depictions of him appear on various Gazan coin types, which, however, are not consistent in their portrayal of him. Some depict Marnas as a naked, bearded, Zeus-like figure either seated on a throne or standing and holding a lightning bolt. Others show him as a slender youth holding a bow in the manner of Apollo, standing in a pedimented temple and facing a female deity, perhaps a version of Artemis (fig. 5.1).[55] But although his visual representation varied, his depiction on coins shows that the citizens of Gaza considered him to be emblematic of their city.

Because of the centrality of Marnas to a Gazan civic identity, members of Gaza's trade diaspora could establish a connection to their homeland and engage in "boundary maintenance" through adherence to his cult. At Portus they did so by dedicating a sanctuary to him, while an official of their temple set up public inscriptions in Greek, the language of the East Mediterranean.

52. *I.Porto* no. 10. See Mussies 1990: 2424–27.

53. *I.Porto* no. 11.

54. See Mussies 1990: 2433–47 for a discussion.

55. Mussies 1990: 2447–49; Belayche 2009: 180–83.

FIG. 5.1. Bronze coin from Gaza, 132–33 CE, showing Marnas (right).
American Numismatic Society, no. 2012.71.163.

Both acts established them as a distinct group, separate both from their Italian host community and other diaspora groups. The mention in one of the inscriptions of costs incurred for a Marnas monument hints at another social benefit that his cult provided Gaza's diaspora: the opportunity for intragroup honest signaling. Devotion could take the form of publicly observable, costly upfront investments, which helped promote economic trust based on effective private order. Finally the Gazans at Portus engaged in intercommunity signaling. They honored the emperor in a religious vow that invoked their signature deity, thereby inserting their cult into an imperial ideology. In short, they engaged in activities that are familiar to us from other diasporas active in the Roman era. Their behavior resembles, for instance, that of the Tyrians settled in Puteoli, themselves typical of foreign groups there (see chapter 2).

The Destruction of the Gazan Marneion

The level of reverence for Marnas at Gaza and his high visibility on the city's coinage perhaps explain why he appears in Christian literature as a god whose downfall was devoutly to be wished. Ill will toward him is evident, for instance, in the works of Jerome, a prolific Christian author and scholar. In several stories from his *Life of St. Hilarion*, written around 390 CE, the Marnas cult is condemned as idolatry, while its Gazan adherents are denounced as enemies of God (*Vita Hilar.* 14, 20). Jerome displayed hostility toward the Marnas cult also in a letter from 403 CE addressed to Laeta, the daughter-in-law of his spiritual pupil Paula.[56] He assured Laeta that Christianity was on the ascent in public life, reminding her that "the army standards bear the emblem of the cross." Alluding to the recent destruction of the Alexandrian Serapeum by Roman troops he continued, "Today even the Egyptian Serapis has become a Christian; Marnas mourns in his prison at Gaza, and fears continuously that his temple will be overthrown" (*Ep.* 107.2).[57]

Violent destruction by military means was indeed to be the fate of the Marnas temple. We happen to have a particularly detailed and vivid description of that event, written purportedly by an eyewitness calling himself Mark the Deacon. His account of the temple's razing is included in his hagiography of Porphyry, an early fifth-century saint from Thessalonica. In Mark's telling, Porphyry, soon after his appointment as bishop of Gaza in 395 CE, saw himself confronted by a large crowd of angry Marnas faithful. They blamed a drought afflicting the area on the bishop's arrival, claiming it had been prophesied as bad luck by Marnas, Lord of the Rains. Offering numerous sacrifices, they begged their ancestral deity to help them in their misfortune, but to no avail. Porphyry and his flock then produced a multiday downpour through prayer, hymn-singing and other acts of Christian devotion, winning several converts in the process (*Vita Porph.* 19–21). After that episode Porphyry pondered what was to be done about the rampant idol worship in his diocese. He decided to petition the emperor Arcadius in Constantinople, requesting that Gaza's pagan temples be destroyed, including the oracle-giving Marneion (*Vita Porph.* 26).

His petition first reached the empress Eudoxia who, being "ardent in the faith," was receptive to it and passed it on to her husband. But Arcadius was hesitant to grant the request, worrying that it might imperil a source of state revenue:

> The emperor was displeased upon hearing this, saying: "I know that that city (i.e., Gaza) is prone to idolatry, but it is willing to pay its dues in public taxes, bringing in substantial amounts. Therefore, if we suddenly instill fear in them, they will take to flight and we will lose this great amount of tax income." (*Vita Porph.* 39–41)[58]

56. On Jerome and Paula, see Cameron 1993: 81–82.

57. Tr.: F.A. Wright, *LCL* 1933. The conventionally accepted year is 391 CE, but cf. Hahn 2004: 81–84.

58. Tr.: Rapp 2001: 64.

Undeterred, the empress told the bishop's delegation that she would not let them depart before they had accomplished their mission. She kept her word, organizing some stagecraft during the baptism ceremony of her new-born son, Theodosius II, heir to the throne. Through a trick she made it seem as if the baby Theodosius approved the petition, thus securing the still reluctant backing of Arcadius. The emperor wrote a letter ordering the destruction of Gaza's temples and sent a military detachment to help Porphyry's men execute that decree (*Vita Porph.* 42, 46–50). Jubilantly, the party returned to Gaza, publicly announced the emperor's decision and proceeded to raze seven pagan sanctuaries. Finally they turned to the Marneion, having left it until last because the temple's priests had barricaded it from the inside. The priests had fled through secret passageways, getting themselves to safety. But their barricades would not save the building:

> So having brought the raw pitch, and the sulfur, and the pork fat, and having mixed the three, they applied this to the inner doors, and after a prayer, set fire to them. Immediately the whole temple caught fire and burned. All those among the soldiers and the strangers who were able, wrested from the flames what they could find, either gold, or silver, or iron, or lead. (*Vita Porph.* 69)[59]

On the site of the Marneion, Porphyry built a church, the empress Eudoxia personally having provided him with a floor plan, funding and columns of expensive green marble (*Vita Porph.* 75, 84). Criticized by some of his flock for the outsize scale of the building, the bishop assured them that the Lord Jesus would multiply the Christian faithful at Gaza to the point where the congregation would outgrow the church (*Vita Porph.* 93).

This is an engaging story. But how much of it is true? Unlike many other saints who are more or less certain to have been historical figures, Porphyry is not mentioned by any other author, nor is he attested in inscriptions. Archaeology has so far also not produced evidence for the grand church he is supposed to have built. Textual problems and stereotypical accounts of conversions add to the suspicion of a largely invented narrative. Nevertheless, in Claudia Rapp's assessment, the "text abounds with such convincing historical detail and shows such an intimate knowledge of the region of Gaza in late Antiquity, that at the very least the general storyline merits our confidence."[60] What we can safely say is that Mark's account of events reflects the early-fifth-century historical setting. MacMullen, much more skeptical about the *Life,*

59. Tr.: Rapp 2001: 70.
60. Rapp 2001: 56. On the historicity of Mark's *Life of St. Porphyry,* see also Trombley 1993: vol. 1, 246–82.

concludes: "Intrigues and the pulling of the right strings in the capital . . . until at last a letter is obtained from the emperor himself to be read aloud to the populace of Gaza by a commander at the head of his troops—all this may be pure invention. But it fits the times."[61]

Whatever we may think of Porphyry as a historical figure, the destruction of the Marnas temple and its replacement by a church in the early years of the fifth century are known historical facts. In 403 CE the Marneion must still have been standing, as Jerome in his letter to Laeta spoke of its overthrow as an event yet to occur. But by 408–10 CE, the building had definitely been torn down. In those years Jerome wrote a commentary on the prophecies of Isaiah in which he noted with obvious satisfaction that "by the destruction of idol-worship the gospel is built up. We see it fulfilled in our day. The Serapeum in Alexandria and the temple of Marnas in Gaza have become churches of the Lord" (*Comm.Isa.* 7.3 on Isa. 17:1–3).[62]

Jerome was primarily interested in spiritual affairs and unfortunately did not comment on how the torching of the Marneion affected Gaza's society and economy. But although he stayed silent on the matter, it is hard to see how the incident could have been anything other than a major blow to the city. Gaza was doubtless not majority Christian in the early fifth century. For one thing, Mark the Deacon presents the Christian population there as tiny. He writes that halfway through Porphyry's episcopate the bishop had enlarged his flock from 280 to 847 souls, an impressive threefold increase. All the same, assuming that Gaza had about 20,000 inhabitants at the time, the Christian community was still only about 4 percent of the population.[63] Mark's numbers are without much doubt spurious. But as it fit his hagiographic purposes to present his saint Porphyry as a particularly successful proselytizer, they are all the more telling in their modesty.

Given the continued centrality of Marnas in the religious life of Gaza into the fifth century, we can imagine Gazan overseas traders around 400 CE still adhering to his cult. Of course if they did they had to have been keeping their heads down already for a considerable while. The razing of the Marneion would in that case surely have spelled the end for even such muted worship. Members of Gaza's diaspora would have been in effect deprived of a cultural marker, making the necessary boundary between them and their hosts harder to maintain. Equally if not more important, they had been deprived of a way to maintain cohesion and solidarity within their community. A way of "honest signaling" and promoting economic trust through costly behavioral patterns had been lost, and intragroup cooperation had become harder as a result.

61. MacMullen 1984: 88–89.
62. Tr.: Stemberger 2000: 197–98.
63. MacMullen 1984: 56; Trombley 1993: vol. 1, 223; Rapp 2001: 53–54.

The Marneion's destruction also negatively affected signaling in intercommunity trade. If we give credence to Mark the Deacon, the violence had occurred on direct order of Arcadius himself. True or not, one thing is certain. The ideological winds had shifted dramatically from the ones prevailing in the third century, when a Gazan community at Portus could legitimately honor the emperor by invoking an oracular pronouncement of its signature deity. To be sure, public expressions of religious attachment to the ruler did not cease after Constantine. But Christians appropriated the practice, importing into it the concept of sainthood and rendering it incompatible with pagan elements such as sacrifice and oracles.[64]

If the Marnas faithful ever needed a reminder that their cult had become incompatible with the new imperial ideology, the razing of the Marneion certainly provided one. It showed them that the state had gone from being mistrustful of their cult to being openly hostile to it. Gazans operating overseas could no longer slot their ancestral faith into the state's ideological framework. They thereby lost not only a device to foster intragroup but also intergroup bonds of economic trust. As a consequence it would have decreased the willingness of both Gazan merchants and their trading partners as members of "trust networks" to set their "valued, consequential, long-term resources and enterprises at risk to the malfeasance, mistakes, or failures of others."[65]

It is, of course, possible that some Gazan merchants had converted to Christianity before the Marneion was burned down, which would have at least mitigated those problems. Passages from Sozomen (*HE* 2.5) and Eusebius (*Vita Const.* 4.38) suggest that such might indeed have been the case. Both authors claim that the inhabitants of Maiumas, Gaza's harbor district, had turned to Christianity sometime during the reign of Constantine, for which their coastal settlement received independent city status as a reward. Maiumas would retain that status until the 360s CE, when it was made part of Gaza again by Julian (Soz. *HE* 5.3).[66] A passage in Mark's *Life* as well hints at a religious split between Gaza and its seaport (*Vita Porph.* 58). It says that Porphyry's delegation on returning victoriously from the court at Constantinople was met by the Christians of Maiumas, joined by some coreligionists from Gaza. But the group from the seaside was the larger one, having banded together with a number of wine merchants from Egypt. This passage seems to suggest that Christians in general were to be found predominantly in Gaza's harbor area, the native faithful there perhaps being wine dealers like their Egyptian brethren.

64. Bowersock 1982: 176–82.

65. Tilly 2005: 12. "Trust networks," see also chapter 2.

66. On Gaza and Maiumas, see Glucker 1987: 43–44; Trombley 1993: vol. 1, 191–93; Hahn 2004: 195–96; Isaac in *CIIP* 2014: vol. 3, 423–24.

But if that was the case, the situation looked only marginally better. Christian merchants from Gaza, whether operating domestically or overseas, would have been at odds with what around 400 CE was still the dominant religious culture of their hometown. If Gaza's mercantile community had converted ahead of the city, cheering on the destruction of places of worship dear to their fellow citizens, it would have increased preexisting animosity, rancor and resentment. Sozomen's mention (*HE* 5.9) of vengeful brutality in the 360s CE shows that religious hostility had been festering at Gaza for at least a generation.[67] The early-fifth-century violence can only have inflamed it further, tearing at the city's social fabric.

Gaza's pagans might have been forcefully barred from openly expressing their religious sentiments, but that seems unlikely to have turned them into enthusiastic Christians. A detail provided by Mark the Deacon indeed suggests that changes in their religious beliefs were slow to develop. He writes that Porphyry ordered the floor panels from the Marneion's inner sanctum to be used in a public street, "so that they would be trampled upon not only by men, but also by women, dogs, pigs, and beasts." Horrified, the people of Gaza continued to avoid stepping on the panels "to the present day" (*Vita Porph.* 76).[68] Memory of the Marneion lived on, as did reverence for its spiritual power. The conversion of Gaza's population beyond a begrudging acceptance of the new status quo will have required time, quite likely spanning generations. It might moreover have required the ongoing threat of military violence. Mark the Deacon reports that the soldiers sent by the emperor to enforce his decree were left behind after the pagan temples had been leveled, "for the sake of good order in the city" (*Vita Porph.* 77).[69]

None of this can have been conducive to creating stable trading conditions, and least of all can it have helped to foster the ties of economic trust on which Gazan commerce depended. The emperor Arcadius may in reality have expressed concern that destroying Gaza's temples would imperil a source of imperial tax revenue, or Mark the Deacon may have put those words into his mouth. One way or the other, that negative economic consequences would follow was entirely predictable.

Alexandria and the Serapis Cult

Founded by Alexander in 331 BCE, the city of Alexandria is considerably younger than Gaza, although as a place of human habitation it might be just as old. Literary sources say that the site where the city would rise was known

67. On the earlier hostility, see Hahn 2004: 196–97.

68. Tr.: Rapp 2001: 71.

69. Tr.: Rapp 2001: 71.

as Rhakotis, a name likely deriving from an Egyptian phrase meaning "mouth of the walls." If so, it might have been a fortified place, perhaps a pharaonic military post.[70] Archaeological evidence from underwater excavations as well suggests that it was originally a dynastic settlement. No surviving source tells us why Alexander chose the site of Rhakotis for his Egyptian namesake city. But if we cannot be certain about his motives, we can reasonably guess that the natural advantages of the location factored into his decision.[71] The site was close to the Canopic branch of the Nile, providing riverine access to the Egyptian interior. Equally important, at this westernmost point on the Delta, the prevailing eastward sea currents prevented the harbor from silting up by washing away the soil that the Nile continuously deposited into the Mediterranean.

It is unknown whether Alexander intended his new settlement to be primarily a military port serving his ongoing campaigns of conquest or whether he also had commercial designs for it. Regardless, in the Hellenistic era Alexandria would quickly grow into a harbor metropolis with a Mediterranean-wide mercantile significance. It exported grain from the Egyptian hinterland as well as manufactured goods including papyrus, glass and textiles. Furthermore, in a way not unlike Gaza, it served as a transit point for high-value goods from Arabia and India. Shipments from the east traveled from the Red Sea harbors of Berenice and Myos Hormos through the Eastern Desert to Coptos on the Nile, and from there downstream to Alexandria.[72]

Early in the Roman imperial period the city became of key economic and sociopolitical importance as the home base of the fleet that provided Rome with public grain. That importance remained unchanged until 617 CE, and Alexandrian tax grain continued to be shipped throughout Roman history. What did change was the destination of the grain. Starting around 324 CE, the emperors incrementally redirected the Alexandrian grain fleet to the new imperial center of Constantinople, which enjoyed the same privileges of state-subsidized food distributions as Rome.[73] The volume of public grain shipments remained impressive into late antiquity. Constantinople would still receive some 160,000 metric tons of state grain annually during the reign of the emperor Justinian (527–65 CE).[74]

But Alexandria's position as a key Roman shipping hub went well beyond the imperial grain supply. Its commercial activity under the emperors was as broad and diverse as it had been under the Ptolemies. In the late first century

70. On pre-Ptolemaic Alexandria, see Ashton 2004: 16–19.

71. Maehler 2004: 1–2.

72. On Egypt's Red Sea ports, see Young 2001: 35–40; Wilson 2015.

73. Durliat 1990: 42–45, 250–52.

74. McCormick 2001: 97.

CE the Greek orator Dio Chrysostom, in a speech delivered at Alexandria, described the mercantile dominance of the city in a flattering passage:

> Not only have you a monopoly of the shipping of the entire Mediterranean by reason of the beauty of your harbors, the magnitude of your fleet, and the abundance and the marketing of the products of every land, but also the outer waters that lie beyond are in your grasp, both the Red Sea and the Indian Ocean. . . . The result is that the trade, not merely of islands, ports, a few straits and isthmuses, but of practically the whole world is yours. For Alexandria is situated, as it were, at the crossroads of the whole world, of even the most remote nations thereof, as if it were a market serving a single city, a market which brings together into one place all manner of men (32.36).[75]

Documentary texts bearing out this literary account are unfortunately rare. The humidity of the Nile Delta is destructive to organic material, including papyrus, and the resulting disappearance of texts from the site has led Alexandria to be underrepresented in the papyrological corpus.[76] But where scattered documentary evidence does allow us to catch a glimpse of the city's long-distance trading activities, the picture conforms to Dio's description.

One of the most famous texts dates to the mid-second century CE and is commonly known as the Muziris papyrus.[77] It documents a loan and transportation agreement for merchandise coming from Muziris on India's southwest coast to Alexandria, where goods were to clear customs.[78] One side of the papyrus records part of an agreement covering transportation while the other lists amounts of nard, ivory and textiles, all typical Indian exports. The total after-tax worth of the shipment was almost seven million sesterces, seven times the minimum property qualification for a Roman senator.

Shipments of such high value were doubtless rare in the overall movement of goods, but they were by no means marginal to the Roman economy nor were the taxes levied on them a minor source of state revenue. We know that a 25 percent tax applied to imports going into the empire on the eastern frontier during the second century CE. As Andrew Wilson has pointed out, the tax revenue of only a hundred cargoes similar to the one listed in the Muziris papyrus would have paid for a third of Rome's estimated annual military budget. The number of sailings was in all probability higher in actuality. Strabo

75. Tr.: J.W. Cohoon and H. Lamar Crosby, *LCL* 1940. For a discussion of the moralizing context of this passage, see Trapp 2004: 117–20.

76. For a discussion of what does survive, see Rowlandson and Harker 2004.

77. *P.Vindob.* G 40822, on which see Casson 1990; Young 2001: 49–51.

78. On Muziris and the Roman trading colony there, see Terpstra forthcoming.

(2.5.12), writing a century before the Muziris papyrus was drafted, discusses the India trade of Alexandrian merchants, mentioning that as many as 120 vessels were traveling between Myos Hormos and India.[79]

Alexandria housed a large number of gods, as was to be expected given the city's size and cosmopolitan nature. A fourth-century CE building catalog lists around 2,500 temples, nearly one for every twenty houses.[80] But as was the case with Marnas at Gaza, only one god could lay claim to being the urban patron deity: Serapis. His origins are not as nebulous as those of Marnas, but they are not fully known. Serapis is not mentioned by any Greek author of the classical period, nor does he figure in ancient mythology. He first appears in scattered fourth-century BCE sources, suddenly to become prominent in those from the third. His spiritual sphere of influence seems to have been wide ranging. He was associated with the underworld and the realm of the dead. But his iconography typically depicts him wearing a grain or fruit basket head-dress (fig. 5.2), and he is frequently portrayed with a cornucopia, both indicators that he was also a god of abundance and fertility. To his followers he seems furthermore to have been a deeply personal god who answered prayers, appeared in dreams and gave oracles.

His variety of partly contradictory attributes was a puzzle to ancient authors, who give a confused account of his powers and origin. A passage by the second-century CE Christian writer Clement of Alexandria (*Prot.* 4.48) says that Serapis was a blend of the traditional Egyptian deities Osiris and Apis, and that his name was a compound: Osirapis. That theory has found support in modern scholarship.[81]

Serapis was the patron deity not only of the city of Alexandria but also of the Ptolemaic kings, who adopted him as a representation of royal rule.[82] Because the dynasty associated itself with the god, signs of piety could be used to curry royal favor, as can be seen in a document dating to 257 BCE from the Zenon archive (see chapter 3). It contains a letter by a certain Zoilos of Aspendus to the Ptolemaic finance minister Apollonios. Zoilos wrote that he had received dreams in which Serapis instructed him to build a Serapeum. With his letter he attempted to persuade the finance minister to establish and fund the temple, concluding "it would be good for you to heed the god's commands so that Serapis will be merciful to you and greatly enhance your status with the king."[83]

---

79. Wilson 2015: 23.
80. Watts 2015b: 18.
81. See Stambaugh 1972: 1–15 for a discussion of Serapis' attributes and origin.
82. Stambaugh 1972: 30–34, 93–98.
83. *P.Cair.Zen.*1.59034 (= Durand 1997: no. 31). Tr.: Renberg and Bubelis 2011: 174.

FIG. 5.2. Bust of Serapis, Greco-Roman Museum, Alexandria. Judith McKenzie/Manar al-Athar. See Alexandria—Serapeum—Sculpture.

Because of Serapis' symbolic importance to the ruling monarchy, resources were lavished on his central Alexandrian sanctuary, which was a magnificent structure already in the third century BCE. In contrast to the Marneion at Gaza, which has not been discovered so far, archaeological remains of the Serapeum at Alexandria are visible and accessible today. Analyses of the standing architecture together with extensive excavations have shown that its first

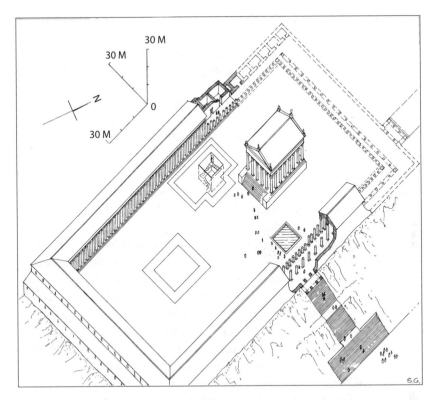

FIG. 5.3. Alexandria: Serapeum, axonometric reconstruction of Roman phase.
Image courtesy of Judith McKenzie.

building phase dates back at least to the reign of Ptolemy III Euergetes (246–222 BCE).[84] This large temple complex burned down sometime in 181 CE and was then rebuilt on an even grander scale.[85] Figure 5.3 shows the appearance of the new structure, giving an idea of its vast dimensions.

In this second, Roman phase the Serapeum consisted of a raised platform surrounded by a colonnaded enclosure that measured over 200 meters in length and over 100 meters in width. A monumental staircase gave access to the inner courtyard from the east. Visitors would first pass a square pool beyond which stood the central temple of Serapis, offset to the north from the platform's east-west axis. Opposite the monumental entrance, a T-shaped building surrounded the access to a stairwell leading down to a system of underground passageways, some 156 meters in total length. Across from the Serapis temple rose a square structure of unknown purpose. For the latter

84. McKenzie, Gibson and Reyes 2004: 81–84.
85. McKenzie, Gibson and Reyes 2004: 98–99.

two buildings, insufficient evidence survives to say what they might have looked like.[86]

The scale and splendor of the temple complex reflect the significance of the Serapis cult for Alexandria's civic identity. Both literary texts and documentary sources provide examples of that significance. Dio Chrysostom, in the speech already cited, showed himself to be aware of Serapis' centrality to the religious experience of his audience: "Here in Alexandria the deity is most in honor, and to you especially does he display his power through almost daily oracles and dreams" (32.12).[87] Papyrological evidence dating from the first to the third centuries CE underscores the preeminence of the Serapis cult in the religious landscape of Alexandria. Letters sent from the city and found in the Egyptian countryside almost invariably open with the stock phrase "I make supplication for you every day before the lord Serapis."[88]

Although the god was strongly associated with Alexandria, his cult spread more widely in the Hellenistic and Roman era, gaining non-Egyptian adherents in the Mediterranean and beyond.[89] This geographical diffusion seems to have been the result of an increasing commercial connectivity. The cult can be found moving along the maritime nodes of the Mediterranean and the artery roads of Italy.[90] The initial impetus seems to have been provided by Egyptians carrying the cult with them overseas to places frequented by traders. On the Greek island of Delos, for instance—in the second century BCE a commercial hub and tax-free emporium (see chapter 2)—no fewer than three Serapea were built. The largest and most richly adorned of those was public in nature.[91] The significance of this temple to the larger Delian community is evident from the dedications made there by non-Egyptians, Italian traders prominently among them.[92]

It might have been Italians active on Delos who introduced the Serapis cult to Puteoli, where a Serapeum existed already in the late second century BCE.[93] However, as Puteoli at the time served as Rome's principal harbor, it seems perhaps more likely that Alexandrian residents were responsible for the cult's establishment. We have no direct evidence for such residents, but the label of a "lesser Delos," applied to Puteoli by the second-century BCE poet

86. McKenzie, Gibson and Reyes 2004: 96–97.

87. Tr.: J.W. Cohoon and H. Lamar Crosby, LCL 1940.

88. Rowlandson and Harker 2004: 87–88.

89. See Malaise 1984.

90. Malaise 1972: 255–60; 1984: 1646–48.

91. Malaise 1972: 275–82.

92. Malaise 1972: 282–311.

93. *CIL* 10.1781 (= *ILS* 5317). See Dubois 1907: 148–52, 194–97; Tran tam Tinh 1972: 3–6, 58–62.

Lucilius (Paul. *Festi* 88.4), would make little sense if foreign groups had not settled there.

Irrespective of who took the initiative to erect the Serapeum at Puteoli, it was still a thriving cult center in the third century CE. A Latin inscription records how a certain Sextus Pompeius Primitivus and Marcus Virius Fructus had enlarged and beautified the temple in honor of the god.[94] The dedicants were almost certainly not Egyptians, as suggested by their names and their choice for an inscription in Latin. But it seems more than likely that Alexandrians also were venerators at the Serapeum. Ties between Italy and Alexandria strengthened considerably after 30 BCE, when Egypt became a Roman province and Alexandrian grain ships started arriving regularly in Puteoli.[95] Such strengthening ties might explain two Puteolan archaeological finds bearing inscriptions in Greek: a red glass amulet reading "great is the name of Serapis," and an oil lamp in the shape of a ship depicting Serapis and Isis and stamped with the word *euploia*, meaning "good sailing." The bottom of the lamp is also inscribed, displaying the words "take me Helio-Serapis." Probably Helio-Serapis was the name of the ship on which the lamp once traveled, meaning that the vessel had been put under the protection of Serapis, who on the lamp's decorated side is portrayed holding a rudder.[96] The artifact points to an important reason why the god was at home in a large harbor such as Puteoli. One of his spiritual attributes was that of patron of navigation and protector of seafarers.

The inscription set up by Primitivus and Fructus at the Puteolan Serapeum provides another indication of why the Serapis cult had power and appeal. It records that the dedicants had made a vow for the health of the emperor, probably Caracalla, who reigned from 198 CE to 217 CE. As the Ptolemies had done before them, Roman emperors incorporated Serapis into a public ideology. Caracalla had a Serapeum constructed in Rome, and may have been the initiator of an annual Serapis festival there, listed in a mid-fourth-century CE religious calendar.[97] An inscription from the city commemorates a prayer to Serapis for Caracalla's well-being made by a temple worker, presumably attached to the emperor's new building.[98] Caracalla moreover displayed an image of Serapis on his coinage, showing that he expressly intended to be associated with the god. He was by no means unique in that respect. Serapis appears also on issues minted by Domitian, Hadrian, Commodus, Gordian III,

94. *CIL* 10.1594. See Tran tam Tinh 1972: 62.

95. Garnsey 1988: 231–35.

96. Tran tam Tinh 1972: 51–54.

97. Malaise 1972: 440–41; Richardson 1992: 361; Beard, North and Price 1998: vol. 1, 382–83; Santangeli Valenzani in Steinby 1999: vol. 4, 302–03.

98. *IG* 14.1024.

Gallienus and Claudius Gothicus, as well as on a series of votive coins struck during the reign of Diocletian. The monumental arch of Diocletian's fellow tetrarch Galerius, constructed at Thessalonica in 303 CE, depicts the god in one of its sculptural reliefs.[99]

The situation in Ostia looked a little different from the one in Puteoli. The city had two Serapea that apparently were frequented by discrete groups of worshippers. First, there was one in the city proper. The town's records show that it had been consecrated on Hadrian's birthday, a choice of date pointing to the imperial-ideology aspect of the Serapis cult.[100] Both archaeological and epigraphic data inform us about the temple. Its associated inscriptions are mostly in Latin, implying a local following that might have been quite sizeable.[101] Serapis imagery seems to have been put up in public spaces in Ostia to be venerated by passersby, suggesting that the god had widespread appeal.

Minucius Felix provides that information in the *Octavius*, a fictional story set in Ostia and written in the first decades of the third century CE.[102] Its protagonists set out on an early morning saunter to discuss philosophical matters. As they went, one of them "noticed a statue of Serapis, and following the custom of the superstitious masses, he moved his hand to his lips and formed a kiss" (2.4).[103] Such popular veneration should come as no surprise given Ostia's nature as a major harbor. As in Puteoli, Serapis and other Egyptian gods were held in esteem in the city as the guardian spirits of sailors, shown by an Ostian oil lamp in the shape of a ship displaying Serapis together with Isis and Harpocrates.[104]

But if Ostians generally venerated Serapis, we know from a number of mostly third-century CE inscriptions that Alexandrians maintained their separate sanctuary to him in the harbor district of Portus. All inscriptions from that location are in Greek, an indication of the East-Mediterranean origin of the religious community.[105] Moreover, some of the people making dedications there were demonstrably either natives of Alexandria or involved in the city's economic activities. A father and son, members of the Alexandrian city council, dedicated a statue of an ancestor to Serapis, ca. 200 CE. We further hear of an administrator of the grain fleet who was also a Serapeum official at Portus and who in 201 CE made a vow there for the safe return from

99. Malaise 1972: 446–49; Manders 2012: 97–98, 235–40, 322.

100. Floriani Squarciapino 1962: 19; Malaise 1972: 421; Meiggs 1973: 367.

101. Floriani Squarciapino 1962: 24–25.

102. For the date of the *Octavius*, see Clarke 1974: 5–12.

103. Tr.: Clarke 1974: 52–53.

104. Floriani Squarciapino 1962: 32 with frontispiece.

105. *I.Porto* nos. 3, 12–13, 16–20. See Floriani Squarciapino 1962: 24 with n. 3; Meiggs 1973: 387–88.

Egypt of the emperor Septimius Severus and his family. The youngest inscription, also made by an official of the Serapis temple, dates to the reign of Severus Alexander (222–35 CE) and contains a wish of well-being for the emperor and his mother Julia Mamaea.[106] The last two inscriptions once again indicate the imperial-ideology significance of the cult.

Other evidence for Serapis worship at Ostia consists of a statue of the god unearthed near what archaeologists usually refer to as the "square of the corporations," a building where foreign trading groups met and did business.[107] The colonnaded structure has mosaic floors marking the rooms for each group, and one such room was assigned to Alexandrians. In all probability the Serapis statue found close by served their association. If that hypothesis is correct it would be another confirmation that Alexandrians overseas continued to claim Serapis as their identifying god, although his cult attracted considerable numbers of non-Egyptian adherents. The temple at Portus is an indication of that symbolic appropriation, as is a story in the *Acts of the Alexandrians*, a collection of partly fictionalized writings on city politics preserved on papyrus. The *Acts* contain an account of how a diplomatic delegation from Alexandria arrived at the imperial court of Trajan carrying a bust of Serapis as their civic identifier.[108]

Outside observers, as well, associated the god with Alexandria; an example is Libanius, a teacher of rhetoric from Antioch who ca. 386 CE spoke of the "mighty city of Serapis, with its fleet of ships whereby it makes the produce of Egypt common to all mankind" (*Or.* 30.35). The same oration also contains what seems like an eerie foreshadowing of what was to happen to the Alexandrian Serapeum within a few years. Libanius mentions a recently destroyed temple in a city "on our frontier with Persia" (perhaps Edessa), comparing its splendor to that of the Serapeum, "which I pray may never suffer the same fate" (30.44).[109] It is hard to judge from this single aside whether Libanius sensed that something was in the air in Alexandria. But if he did, he was right.

The Destruction of the Alexandrian Serapeum

At the end of the fourth century CE Alexandria had a long and ignominious history of undignified scuffles and street fighting. A notorious instance had occurred in 38–41 CE. Tensions between city Jews and Greeks had devolved

106. *I.Porto* nos. 3, 16–17.

107. Museo Ostiense, inv. no. 1210. On the *piazzale delle corporazioni*, see Terpstra 2013: 100–12; 2014b.

108. *P.Oxy* 1242 (= Musurillo 1954: no. 8). On the *Acta Alexandrinorum*, see Rowlandson and Harker 2004: 94–102.

109. Tr.: A.F. Norman, *LCL* 1977.

into violent conflict, which the emperor Claudius attempted to put to a halt. In an open letter to the Alexandrian citizenry, he darkly warned that the patience of even a man of his benevolent disposition had its limits.[110] Much later the fourth-century historian Ammianus Marcellinus would still allude to the unruly nature of the urban populace, characterizing Alexandria as "a city which on its own impulse, and without ground, is frequently roused to rebellion and rioting" (22.11.4).[111] Yet the violence that would lead to the military destruction of the Serapeum signified something altogether different and more profound, reflective as it was of tectonic, empire-wide religious shifts.

The assault on the temple is much better documented than the one on the Marneion at Gaza. We possess no fewer than five ancient accounts of the incident (Eunap. *VS* 472; Rufin. *HE* 11.22–23; Socr. *HE* 5.16–17; Soz. *HE* 7.15.2–10; Theod. *HE* 5.22). In addition, we can study the archaeology from the site, which can usefully be compared to what the literary sources are saying. But the relative abundance of evidence notwithstanding, much about how events unfolded remains obscure, down to the date and even year, which might have been 391 but also 392 CE.[112] More problematic is the fact that the surviving literary accounts present cause and effect in different ways. To reconstruct what happened, scholarship has generally favored taking the description by the church historian and theologian Rufinus of Aquileia as the lead narrative.[113] His account is the fullest and is also close to the event in time, published in 402 or 403 CE. The description by Eunapius is a few years older still, dating to 399 CE, but it is short, while the other three versions were written about half a century after the incident.

The history of the Serapeum's ruin ca. 391 CE had a prelude dating back some three decades. At that time the temple had been invaded and stripped of its statuary by the Alexandrian bishop George with the help of the Egyptian military prefect and his troops.[114] A response to the bishop's violation had not been long in the waiting. Incensed by the attack, the Alexandrian populace "grinding their teeth and uttering fearful outcries" had seized and lynched George at the first opportunity (Amm. Marc. 22.11.8).[115] Serapis was a god dear to the emperor Julian, who almost certainly had the cult artifacts restored. Still, he reportedly was willing to inflict the death penalty on the bishop's lynchers, only to be held back by his confidants (Amm. Marc.

110. *P.Lond.* 6.1912. For another papyrological reference to that conflict, see Terpstra 2017: 52–53.

111. Tr.: J.C. Rolfe, *LCL* 1940.

112. See Hahn 2004: 81–84; Dijkstra 2015: 35–36.

113. See Dijkstra 2015: 31–36 for a discussion. Cf. Hahn 2004: 85–97.

114. Thelamon 1981: 248–50.

115. Tr.: J.C. Rolfe, *LCL* 1940.

22.11.11). In the end all he did was send an open letter to the people of Alexandria reproving them for taking matters into their own hands. "The proper course was for you to reserve for me the decision concerning the offenders," he tut-tutted (*Ep.* 21.378D). His pagan sympathies played a key role in his decision to show leniency, as he himself admitted: "It is a fortunate thing for you, men of Alexandria, that this transgression of yours occurred in my reign, since by reason of my reverence for the god (i.e., Serapis) . . . I preserve for you the affection of a brother" (*Ep.* 21.380B).[116] Thus the murder of George had gone unpunished.

The Arian bishop had been a divisive figure within the Christian community. Ammianus Marcellinus (22.11.10) claims that the Christians did not come to his aid when he was being lynched, although they might have saved him. Nevertheless, the incident and its aftermath provoked antagonistic sentiments, which were stirred up again by the actions of another Alexandrian bishop, Theophilus (384–412 CE). The way Rufinus tells it, Theophilus had requested permission from the emperor Theodosius I to turn a neglected and derelict public building into a church. He received it and began construction. His workmen then hit upon an underground pagan sanctuary, perhaps abandoned like the building above it, although Rufinus does not say. He also does not give details on the nature of the temple, but in all probability it was devoted to Mithraism, a mystery cult characterized by its subterranean meeting places. Socrates (*HE* 5.16), in his alternative account, does indeed report that the bishop had been rummaging through a Mithraeum. In any event, the pagan community could not abide the discovery:

> The pagans therefore, when they saw the dens of their iniquity and caverns of sin being uncovered, could not bear to have exposed this evil which long ages had covered and darkness had concealed, but began all of them, as though they had drunk the serpents' cup, to behave violently and to give vent to their fury in public. Nor was it just their usual noisy demonstrations; they used weapons, battling up and down the streets. (Rufin. *HE* 11.22)[117]

The reaction seems excessive for a mere chance discovery of a single and possibly decommissioned temple to Mithras. Rufinus here probably glossed over a provocation by the bishop, which is preserved in the versions of Socrates and Sozomen. Both those authors say that Theophilus had the cult objects from the pillaged temple paraded around for public ridicule.[118]

---

116. Tr.: W.C. Wright, *LCL* 1923.

117. Tr.: Amidon 1997: 79.

118. A temple of Mithras in Socrates (*HE* 5.16), but of Dionysus in Sozomen (*HE* 7.15.2).

Riots ensued, leading to injury and even death. In the end the pagans barricaded themselves into the Serapeum, allegedly taking with them Christian hostages whom they ordered to offer sacrifice, torturing those who refused. On the face of it their retreat to the Serapeum makes little sense. After all, not Serapis but Mithras had been insulted. Moreover, not all pagan Alexandrians will have been initiated into the Mithraic mysteries, so the feelings of many will have been hurt only vicariously. To understand why events took this turn we should take into consideration that, as described above, to non-Christians Serapis was the religious symbol of the city. His centrality to a pagan civic identity meant that non-Christian Alexandrians of all stripes could rally around him. In addition, given the earlier episcopal attack on the Serapeum, and the unavenged but doubtless unforgotten assassination of George, the pagan citizenry had good reason to be fearful for the integrity of their iconic sanctuary.

A standoff followed during which the urban authorities repeatedly warned the pagan rebels fortified within the Serapeum that government action might be taken against them. However, they stopped short of ordering the temple to be stormed because it had meanwhile been turned into a formidable stronghold. Instead, they petitioned the emperor for help. Theodosius wrote back that the Christians killed were to be regarded as martyrs and that their deaths should go unavenged. But, Rufinus says, he did proclaim that "the cause of the evils and the roots of the discord . . . should be eliminated, so that once these were done away with, the reason for the conflict might also disappear" (*HE* 11.22).[119] The proclamation was read aloud at the temple, leading resistance to melt away.

With the Serapeum condemned by government decree, the end was as swift as it was predictable. A military detachment marched onto the temple grounds and smashed the enormous cult statue of Serapis. His limbs were dragged off with ropes to all corners of the city, where they were burned. His torso was carted off to the amphitheater where it, too, was torched, presumably as a public spectacle (Rufin. *HE* 11.23). As for the temple buildings, Rufinus reports that "on the site of Serapis' tomb the unholy sanctuaries were leveled, and on the one side there rose a martyr's shrine, on the other a church" (*HE* 11.27).[120] His contemporary, the non-Christian author Eunapius, whose sympathies clearly lay with the other side, also says that the temple buildings were demolished by the soldiers. He bitterly mocks them for making war on stones: "They won a victory without meeting a foe or fighting a battle" (*VS* 472).[121]

---

119. Tr.: Amidon 1997: 80.
120. Tr.: Amidon 1997: 85.
121. Tr.: W.C. Wright, *LCL* 1921.

According to Socrates (*HE* 5.16), the bishop Theophilus continued to level temples in the aftermath of the confrontation, helped in his exertions by the governor of Alexandria and the commander-in-chief of the troops in Egypt. Rufinus adds that

> another thing was done in Alexandria: the busts of Serapis, which had been in every house in the walls, the entrances, the doorposts, and even the windows, were so cut and filed away that not even a trace or mention of him ... remained anywhere. In their place everyone painted the sign of the Lord's cross on doorposts, entrances, windows, walls, and columns. (*HE* 11.29)[122]

Meanwhile, many pagan citizens, including members of Alexandria's intelligentsia, decided to flee the city. In a rare personal note Socrates (*HE* 5.16) remarks that two of the refugees had been his teachers at Constantinople. One of them, Helladius, was wont to boast in confined circles that he had killed nine men during the conflict. Socrates does not say so, but one imagines that he wrote his account of events in large part based on what he had heard from his mentors.

Serapis' large temple statue has disappeared without a trace, but the physical remains of the Serapeum site allow us to study what happened to the temple buildings. The archaeology does not show evidence of church construction on the platform itself. That finding accords with the accounts of all but one of the ancient authors (the exception is Sozomen), who indeed do not claim that any of the buildings were converted into places of Christian worship. The archaeology also confirms Rufinus' statement that a church was constructed beside the Serapeum. To the west of the platform, archaeological explorations have found a late-antique foundation wall and traces of a mosaic floor, interpreted as the remains of a church. Other Christian archaeological finds from that area include baptismal fonts and cisterns with inscribed crosses.[123]

As for the fate of the Serapeum complex, if the ancient authors are correct in claiming that its buildings were destroyed, they must have meant the central sanctuary, and possibly the square structure directly opposite and the T-shaped stairwell enclosure (fig. 5.3). But they cannot have been referring to the large colonnade, which several Arabic sources describe as a marvel to behold. By the tenth century it had lost its roof and may well have sustained other damage. But it remained a recognizable feature of the urban landscape until at least the twelfth century, giving the site its Arabic name of ṣawārī, or "columns."[124]

---

122. Tr.: Amidon 1997: 86.
123. McKenzie, Gibson and Reyes 2004: 107–08.
124. Hamarneh 1971: 82–83.

The importance of Alexandria for the economy of not just Egypt but the whole Roman empire is beyond discussion, and the question of what the impact of the religious clash might have been is not a trivial one. Broadly speaking, it is hard to see how the deadly violence, the destruction of an iconic monument with military force and the flight from the city of citizens on the losing side could have had anything but negative economic effects. But to focus here only on Alexandria's overseas trade, the destruction of the Serapeum deprived the city's diaspora of a cultic symbol that had been theirs to claim for centuries. Together with their cult, they had lost an instrument of boundary maintenance, "honest signaling" and economic trust building.[125]

Of course, here as at Gaza it is possible that by 391 CE some or even all the city's long-distance traders had converted to Christianity, although we have no way of knowing. But if that was the case, large numbers of citizens in their place of origin evidently had not. As at Gaza, religious tension had been building at Alexandria for decades, as the episode of George's lynching demonstrates. The eruption of a partisan showdown can only have exacerbated the preexisting enmity and acrimony. Citywide economic trust will have been in short supply, probably generationally. Despite all the brutality that had accompanied the Serapeum's destruction we know that the pagan population of Alexandria did not resign itself to its fate by turning Christian *en bloc*. Almost a century after the incident in another explosion of violence, a ransacking Christian mob tore through the city in search of pagan cult objects. It could still collect enough images to keep a bonfire going for a full day, according to a report by Zacharias, the bishop of Mytilene (*Vita Sev.* 33–48).[126]

The demolition of the Serapeum by Rome's legions underscored how dramatically the prevailing imperial ideology had shifted. That was true also at Gaza, but particularly salient at Alexandria. Marnas always remained a Gazan domestic god, but Serapis had been adopted as a symbol of imperial rule first by Ptolemaic kings and then Roman emperors. Until the early fourth century CE, the inhabitants of the Roman empire could turn to Serapis to display their allegiance to the ruler and his governance. Of course, emperors would never hear of most of the Serapis-inspired wishes of well-being they received, but reaching them was not the point of the gestures. The point was for the dedicants to signal to their social environment that they were loyal citizens of the empire and, if they were traders, trustworthy commercial partners. Whether

125. On "honest signaling" and diasporas as "trust networks," see Sosis 2005; Tilly 2005: 65–69; Bulbulia and Sosis 2011.

126. See Watts 2010: 234–43; 2015b: 23 on the event. For Zacharias and his *Life of Severus*, see Brock and Fitzgerald 2013: 15–23, 33–100.

for Alexandrian or other Serapis adherents, such signaling behavior was now no longer possible. Roman imperial ideology had made a complete U-turn on Serapis. The god had gone from a favored emblem of state power to a disgrace to the state's ideology, ending up on the receiving end of military violence.

The Syrian Temple in Rome

A question only touched on so far is until what date diasporas such as the Gazan and Alexandrian continued to center on their ancestral cults. That question, though not easy to answer, is worth exploring further. Late-antique evidence on the Serapis and Marnas cults is neither particularly revealing nor entirely consistent. In Rome a Serapis festival was still being celebrated in the 350s CE, so the god remained a feature of the public life of the imperial city decades after Constantine.[127] But the same may not have been true at nearby Ostia, where a tympanon from the Serapeum bearing the words "to Jupiter Serapis" was found reused in a late-antique floor.[128] As for the temple of the Alexandrian overseas community at Portus, lack of archaeological evidence prevents us from knowing what happened to it. But the absence of Serapis inscriptions past the third century not only at Portus but also at Ostia and Puteoli should perhaps be taken as evidence that in all three places the cult was abandoned during the reign of Constantine. There is also no epigraphic evidence for Marnas worship at Portus beyond the reign of Gordian III, seemingly warranting a similar conclusion for his cult.

However, the absence of inscriptions may not be as telling as it appears. We should first of all take into account that by the 250s CE, the practice of setting up inscriptions, religious or otherwise, had all but ceased empire-wide, never to regain its previous intensity thereafter. The third-century crisis best explains the downward turn, although it may also have been due to a changing "epigraphic habit," to use MacMullen's celebrated phrase.[129] Either way, we simply possess far fewer epigraphic data for late antiquity generally. Conclusions based on the absence of evidence are always risky, but particularly so here. In addition, if Gazan and Alexandrian trade diasporas were still venerating their native deities in the post-Constantinian empire, it was politic for them not to be overt about it. Setting up public inscriptions to pagan gods was ill advised, and we should therefore not necessarily expect to hear about further worship even if it did continue.

127. Beard, North and Price 1998: vol. 1, 382–83.

128. Floriani Squarciapino 1962: 21.

129. Liebeschuetz 2015: 25–26; MacMullen 1982; 1988: 3–7.

If epigraphic data alone are insufficient, archaeological evidence holds great promise. But as the Serapeum and the Marneion at Portus have so far not been discovered, and neither has the Serapeum at Puteoli, we need to look elsewhere for physical evidence of pagan religious activity by overseas communities. As we will see, archaeological data from Rome suggest that some groups continued to celebrate their ancestral rites well into the second half of the fourth century, terminating the practice only when forced to do so.

Late-antique Rome continued to have a highly symbolic status as the old imperial capital, even though the emperors had abandoned the city as a regular place of residence. Far into the fourth century, the traditional state cults were treated with respect. Public temples were restored by city officials, and until 382 CE a number of pagan rites still received public funding.[130] The power of a centuries-long tradition was evidently strong, and the city's religious heritage could not and would not be swept aside from one moment to the next. But for cults of private groups things looked decidedly more precarious. How much so is evident from the fortunes of a temple to Syrian gods on the eastern slope of the Janiculum Hill, a fascinating structure rich in evidence on the transformation of Roman religious life.

Excavations performed in the early twentieth century have shown that the sanctuary went through three building phases (fig. 5.4). The first seems to have consisted of only an enclosure, oriented on the points of the compass. Next to the enclosure was a reservoir interpreted as a pond for sacred fish, reminiscent of the lake mentioned by Lucian in his treatise on the temple at Hierapolis in Syria (De Dea Syria 45–47).[131] Little archaeological and no epigraphic evidence remains of this phase, which has tentatively been dated to the mid-first century CE.[132] Without any apparent interruption in cultic activity, phase two then turned the sacred space into a more substantial sanctuary, which followed the enclosure's original layout and maintained the reservoir. It is unclear when this rebuilding event occurred, but for certain it predates 176 CE.[133] A third phase dating to the fourth century saw a radical change in the temple's architecture. An elongated building of an unusual shape replaced

130. Beard, North and Price 1998: vol. 1, 373–88; Salzman 2011; Iara 2015.

131. On the sacred lake at Hierapolis, and others like it elsewhere, see Lightfoot 2003: 489–97.

132. Gauckler 1912: 249–53, 259, 263–69; Savage 1940: 45; Goodhue 1975: 47–48; Calzini Gysens 1982: 61–64.

133. Gauckler 1912: 202, 227–49; Savage 1940: 45–47; Goodhue 1975: 41–47; Richardson 1992: 219–20; Calzini Gysens in Steinby 1996: vol. 3, 138–39.

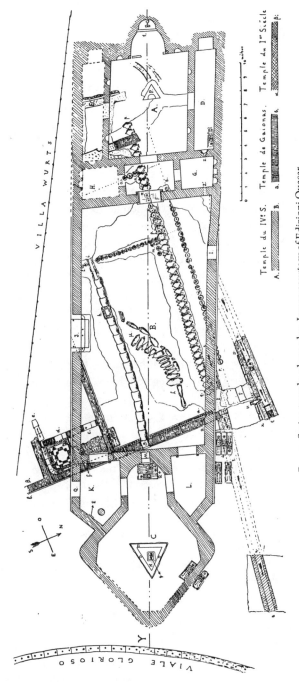

FIG. 5.4. Rome: Syrian temple, phase plan. Image courtesy of Edizioni Quasar.

the second-phase structure, not respecting its alignment on the compass but turning its orientation southeast by about 20 degrees.[134]

The excavations yielded a number of highly interesting inscriptions. A marble slab, which may have served as a table for offerings, had been engraved with a dedication to Jupiter Heliopolitanus, the great god of Baalbek, who seems to have been the chief deity venerated at the temple during the second phase.[135] The epigraphic evidence shows that other divinities receiving worship there at the time included Zeus Keraunios, Jupiter Maleciabrudes and Hadad Libaneotes.[136] All those gods are connected by their relationship to Berytus, and Federico De Romanis has therefore suggested that the sanctuary served mainly Berytian traders. In support of that interpretation he points to an inscription by Berytian Heliopolitanus worshippers at Puteoli, and a legal text concerning commercial shipments between Berytus and Italy.[137] Although two military officers are found among the Roman devotees, support for De Romanis' hypothesis is provided by a granite column from Portus, dedicated to Heliopolitanus by one M. Antonius Gaionas for the safety of Marcus Aurelius and Commodus.[138] This Gaionas was a prominent member of the religious community that centered on the Janiculum temple. We do not know what his profession might have been, but the fact that he erected a monument at Portus suggests that he had business interests down in the harbors.

Gaionas perhaps served as a priest at the temple, and he certainly acted as a benefactor to the faithful who congregated there. Though in no way belonging to the Roman elite, he seems to have been a man of some means and public standing, both of which he was keen to promote. The Heliopolitanus dedication on the offering table says that he had donated the artifact and dedicated it to the welfare and victory of the emperors. The inscription lists *cistiber* as one of his titles, which probably referred to a minor office involving responsibilities for nighttime security and fire patrol.[139] Gaionas was evidently proud of the position, mentioning it also in three other inscriptions including his

134. Gauckler 1912: 173–207, 222–27; Savage 1940: 47–49; Goodhue 1975: 24–41; Calzini Gysens in Steinby 1996: vol. 3, 139–43.

135. *CIL* 6.36793. On the artifact and the inscription, see Gauckler 1912: 84–85, 142–46; Savage 1940: 49; Goodhue 1975: 30–33.

136. *IGUR* 1.110, 111; *CIL* 6.36792.

137. De Romanis 2008. Inscription: *CIL* 10.1634 (= *ILS* 300); legal passage: *Dig.* 5.1.1.1 (Scaevola). On the latter, see also Terpstra 2017: 50–51.

138. Officers: *CIL* 6.423 (= *ILS* 4287) and *CIL* 6.36791 (= *ILS* 9283); column at Portus: *CIL* 14.24. On Gaionas, see Savage 1940: 37; Goodhue 1975: 7–10; Noy 2000: 240–42.

139. Savage 1940: 37 with n. 104; Moretti's commentary to *IGUR* 1.166, l. 13; Goodhue 1975: 79–89; Beard, North and Price 1998: vol. 1, 292.

epitaph. One of the inscriptions furthermore commemorates that he had been a member of the college of *Augustales,* public officials responsible for the maintenance of the imperial cult.[140] All the by-now-familiar elements of an imperial ideology are at work in these texts: wishes of well-being for the emperors expressed in religious dedications by a man who displayed his connection to the state by repeatedly emphasizing his civic status. Unfortunately we do not possess documentary evidence from Rome like we do for Puteoli, Herculaneum and Pompeii. Nonetheless, it seems a reasonable assumption that if Gaionas was ever asked to act as a witness to a contract he would have occupied one of the top spots in the witness list (see chapter 4).

The second-phase temple that had been standing since at least 176 CE was destroyed by fire, an incident that left burn marks across the area. A coin issued during the reign of Constantius II found at the floor level below the collapsed walls shows that the event occurred sometime after 337 CE.[141] The archaeology suggests that the destruction had not been an accident but a deliberate act of violence against the sanctuary. After the conflagration the reservoir was filled in, while the remaining walls were knocked down and surviving cultic objects were buried. Paul Gauckler, the original excavator, interpreted the destruction as the result of imperial legislation, specifically the edict of 356 CE in which the emperor ordered the closure of temples "so as to deny to all abandoned men the opportunity to commit sin" (*Cod. Theod.* 16.10.4).[142] The relationship need not have been so direct, but the razing of the Janiculum temple certainly fits the pattern of assault on pagan sanctuaries during the general timeframe.

The building still must have been in use when it was burned down. Torching and obliterating it would have made little sense if it had stood vacant inoffensively. The absence of any evidence for religious change would lead to the conclusion that a Heliopolitanus community from the general area of Berytus continued to congregate at the sanctuary until it was given over to the flames. Such ongoing adherence until at least the mid-fourth century is made credible by literary sources showing that in Syria the Heliopolitanus cult was practiced far beyond that time. John Malalas (*Chron.* 13.37) informs us that ca. 379 CE the great Heliopolitanus temple at Baalbek was destroyed by Theodosius I, who consecrated a church on the site. But the cult of Heliopolitanus proved to be tenacious, both at Baalbek and elsewhere in Syria. In 579

---

140. *IGUR* 1.166; Duthoy and Frel 1996: 294; *IGUR* 3.1157 (epitaph). On Gaionas' title of *Claudialis Augustalis,* see Goodhue 1975: 91–93.

141. Gauckler 1912: 146 n. 4, 202; Goodhue 1975: 41, 47; Goddard 2008: 165 with n. 7.

142. Tr.: Pharr 1952: 472. Gauckler 1912: 146 n. 4, 255, 270 with n. 2. For the date of the edict (356, not 346 CE), see Jones, Martindale and Morris 1971: vol. 1, 879–80.

CE, Tiberius II initiated a harsh persecution of the god's adherents, torturing and crucifying the obstinate faithful, according to John of Ephesus (*HE* 3.3.27).

Despite the gathering winds of religious intolerance, the site on the Janiculum Hill was given renewed religious significance not long after the second-phase temple was destroyed. Cultic rites centered on the enigmatic phase-three sanctuary. Compared to the preceding one, which the archaeological evidence shows to have been richly adorned, this was a rather poorly constructed edifice erected in part with reused building material and apparently in haste.[143] But even if it was only a modest building, the religious climate must have changed sufficiently for its donors to risk the expense and effort, pointing perhaps to a construction date in the early 360s CE during the reign of Julian "the Apostate."[144]

A key question for our understanding of the site is whether continuity existed in cultic activity from phase two to three, a matter that has elicited considerable debate.[145] The changes in architectural orientation and plan of the sanctuary suggest a break with the past, one way or another. In addition, the octagonal room on the new building's eastern side and its associated finds show that religious activity now included mystery rites, which as far as we know were not previously celebrated at the site. Cultic objects that do not fit the religious practices of the earlier phases, such as a partly gilded statue of Dionysus, also speak against continuity. The most likely hypothesis is that the phase-three building served syncretistic rites centering predominantly on the cult of Osiris.[146] What religious community might have congregated at the temple during its final stage remains unclear. However, the building housed two Heliopolitanus dedications salvaged from the phase-two temple, suggesting that Berytians might still have been among the worshippers.[147]

Either way, the third-phase temple would not be tolerated for long. A few years, or at most decades, after its construction it was violently attacked. Smashed statuary and cultic ornaments were found scattered about the rooms and buried in the soil.[148] The year in which religious activity at the Janiculum

143. Gauckler 1912: 222–27, 173–207; Goodhue 1975: 26–41.

144. Gauckler 1912: 206, 222, 255–56; Savage 1940: 47; Goodhue 1975: 41. Cf. Goddard 2008: 168, who interprets the building as a suburban villa with private sanctuary, hidden from view to avoid persecution.

145. See Goodhue 1975: 49–69 for a discussion.

146. Duthoy and Frel 1996: 292–93; Goddard 2008.

147. Goodhue 1975: 50–51, 53–54.

148. Gauckler 1912: 147 n. 2, 206–07, 256; Goodhue 1975: 36–38, 41; Savage 1940: 47–48; Calzini Gysens in Steinby 1996: vol. 3, 139–43.

site was definitively terminated can no longer be established, but may have been 377 or perhaps 391–92 CE following new imperial legislation. This time the temple was not set ablaze. Instead it was made permanently inaccessible and was then left to the elements. Its roof and walls slowly caved in. Unchecked vegetation and soil washing down the slope of the Janiculum Hill eventually withdrew it from view and erased it from memory.

Concluding Remarks

The successful implementation of a compulsory, monotheistic state religion was an impressive sociopolitical accomplishment. It was not the only factor profoundly affecting late-antique Roman society, but it was probably related to others, including the crisis of the third century, which in turn was probably related to environmental change.[149] Whether or not we accept that account, it seems clear that the process of forced religious change had a negative impact on the Roman economy. The loss of human life and the destruction of physical capital aside, the growing intolerance toward pagan cults damaged the institutional structure supporting trade. That structure had evolved and persisted for centuries. It had relied on cultic diversity and a complex interplay between private order and public ideology, making it fragile. The equilibrium it had reached was violently shaken under the new Christian regime.

Still, Roman long-distance trade did not grind to a halt in the course of the fourth century CE, and the question of what the newly emerging institutional framework might have looked like thus logically presents itself. The medieval Mediterranean is instructive here, presenting us with a picture that is both recognizable and different. To overcome adverse premodern trading conditions, Mediterranean merchants in the eleventh and twelfth centuries operated through overseas agents selected along religious lines, just as their Roman predecessors had done. Only now, as Shelemo Goitein noted, the main monotheistic religions were at the heart of socioeconomic life.

> Because of the general insecurity and the slowness of communications, international trade was largely dependent on personal relationships and mutual confidence. A man shipping goods overseas normally had to wait months before he could know what happened to them. He had to rely on his friends in the country of destination for the proper handling of his affairs. Mostly, although by no means exclusively, friends were chosen from one's own religious community. . . . The clubhouse of the Middle Ages where one met one's peers daily, or, at least, regularly, was the mosque, the

---

149. Third-century crisis and environmental change: Harper 2017: 129–59.

church, or the synagogue. . . . Thus, coreligionists became natural business friends.[150]

For medieval Christian, Jewish and Muslim traders, their faith was a common point of reference, providing them with a shared set of values that helped them establish economic trust. However, Christianity had a universalistic claim and had no association with any particular city, area or ethnic community. Moreover, in the Roman empire it eventually became the majority religion, probably at some point in the fifth century. Without serious organizational modifications it therefore could not replace pagan cults in support of diaspora trade. As Sosis noted, "It seems likely that when coreligionists constitute a majority, they will require additional identity information to narrow the individual's affiliation to a specific subpopulation within the majority culture."[151] Geographical origin may still have served as an identity marker, but trade in a specific commodity may also have served that purpose.

A hint that the latter may have been occurring with at least some Roman traders is provided by Mark the Deacon. As discussed above, Mark mentions the presence of Christian wine merchants from Egypt at the Gazan harbor of Maiumas, an area where most of Gaza's wine dealers were probably also to be found. This remark, if true, might suggest that traders were forming commodity-based Christian networks, which ultimately would have resembled the ones described by Goitein. But if a new equilibrium was eventually found and trade continued, the transition had been violent and slow. It was certainly still incomplete by the start of the fifth century. By that time additional factors were increasingly having a negative impact on the functioning of the Roman empire as a political, military and economic organization, a topic I will leave for the Epilogue.

150. Goitein 1973: 6–7.
151. Sosis 2005: 23.

6

Epilogue

The Fall and Fall of the Roman Empire

"Why did the Roman Empire fall?" Thus Willem Jongman opened his *Economy and Society of Pompeii*, knowing it to be a sure way to fire up the imagination of his readers.[1] The question remains a source of undying fascination. But despite decades and even centuries of debate within the scholarly community, the last word on the matter has still not been said. Novel ways of approaching it continue to be proposed. As noted in chapter 5, Kyle Harper has recently made a forceful case for environmental change as the catalyst for Rome's sociopolitical disintegration. Waves of deadly pathogens and a deteriorating climate joined forces, ultimately to overwhelm the Roman empire.[2] Other scholars in similar fashion have turned to ecological factors to explain the empire's disappearance from the world stage.[3] In the previous chapter I cautioned that the human element should not be discounted in all this, but I am convinced that the thrust of the environmental argument is correct.

But regardless of where we think the balance should lie between endogenous and exogenous explanations, given the empire's agonized and protracted buckling, its "fall" is arguably a misnomer. Governments fall; societies collapse. Speaking of a fall has perhaps become commonplace because it conveys a sense of just desert. Moralizing ways of thinking about Rome's demise are at least as old as Edward Gibbon's *History* (1776–89).[4] In addition, much previous scholarship did in fact take the fall of a government as the end of the Roman world: the quiet deposition of the western emperor Romulus Augustulus by the non-Roman warlord Odoacer in the early days of September, 476 CE.

1. Jongman 1988: 15.

2. Harper 2017.

3. See, e.g., McCormick 2001: 28–41; Koepke and Baten 2005; contributions by McCormick, Cook and Manning to Harris 2013.

4. The most current example is probably Acemoglu and Robinson 2012: 158–75.

Set in the larger political context, that event does not seem to have been of any great consequence. In the west it indeed did not register as particularly significant. That it has come to be seen as pivotal results from its presentation as such by early-sixth-century authors working in Constantinople. But their "manufacture of a turning point," in the words of Brian Croke, reflects the self-serving viewpoint from the east, leaving the eastern emperor as the sole remaining legitimate Roman ruler.[5] This take on western developments by eastern near-contemporaries may well have provided Justinian with an ideological justification for his invasion of Italy in 535 CE, an event I will come to in a moment.

At any rate, beyond Romulus' deposition, much history remains that is recognized as Roman today. But if we focus on collapse instead, a temporal marker separating Roman antiquity from the Middle Ages is much harder to find. No matter where we draw the dividing line, the choice will always be somewhat arbitrary. Still, the termination of government-subsidized grain shipments could, with good justification, be taken as the moment when the Roman world ceased to exist. That in any case seems to be Michael McCormick's view: "In 618, the distribution of public bread ended in Constantinople forever. With it died a political culture founded on ancient ideals; with it too died a substantial part of the maritime culture of the Mediterranean."[6] If a terminus for antiquity had to be chosen, this one seems to me to be entirely defensible.

Of course, the empire had already been on a centuries-long downward glide by the time events arrived at that point. One aspect of that descent has been touched on in the discussion so far but has not been made explicit: the Roman state was weakening. Social order may have been restored after the crisis of the third century, and a monotheistic religion may have been imposed after Constantine, but state power had not reattained previous levels. Most tellingly in this regard, the state was no longer able to hold on to all its territory. The empire that in the second century CE had stretched from the Thames Valley to the Nile Valley and had controlled the Spanish silver mines and the Dacian gold mines split in two and steadily shrank.[7]

The ability to maintain territorial integrity is a key measure of state strength. As discussed in chapter 1, control over a defined area is an all but universal aspect of how states are conceptualized in the social sciences. Douglass North characterized a state as "an organization with a comparative advantage in violence, extending over a geographic area whose boundaries are determined by

5. Croke 1983.

6. McCormick 2001: 110.

7. Third- and fourth-century territorial losses: MacMullen 1988: 177–91.

its power to tax constituents."[8] That part of his definition seems uncontroversial, even if his resulting conclusions about third-party enforcement should be used advisedly, as explained at length throughout this book. But anyway, North's definitional emphasis on territory and taxes gives us a useful yardstick by which to measure the success or failure of the Roman state.

By 271 CE, incursions of Gothic and Carpi tribes had forced the emperor Aurelian to abandon the province of Dacia, a conquest made only in 106 CE and celebrated at the time with a magnificent Roman victory monument, the Forum of Trajan.[9] Apart from territorial loss, the Roman retreat meant the loss of the gold mines at Alburnus Maior, mentioned in chapter 4, which reduced imperial state revenue, although by how much we do not know. During Aurelian's reign other signs of trouble were appearing on the empire's edges. The emperor had to deal with a de facto secession attempt by the Syrian trading city of Palmyra, whose queen Zenobia managed to create a breakaway state and extend its territory as far north as Asia Minor and as far south as Egypt.[10] Zenobia would ultimately be defeated, but doing so would take considerable effort. Palmyra lived on in late antiquity, although its character changed. Diocletian stationed a large military force there, incorporating it into the late-Roman defensive system. The city's greatness as a mercantile center was at any rate behind it by then, and the tax revenue it produced must have diminished appreciably.

Perhaps less consequential than the events in Dacia and Palmyra, but of equal if not greater symbolic significance, in the 270s CE, Rome had to be surrounded by walls again and in haste at that. To reduce cost and speed up construction, the defensive works incorporated many existing buildings, including tombs and sections of an aqueduct. The urgency was due to an imminent threat of attack from roaming bands of Alemanni, who had contrived to breach Roman lines and pour into Italy. The last time city walls had been erected around Rome had been six and a half centuries earlier, and for all imperial history the capital had done without walls.[11] The sudden exposure of its vulnerability must have had a profound psychological impact on the urban citizenry. Around 155 CE, Aelius Aristides in the Roman Oration (26.79–80) had waxed lyrical about how the city did not need defensive structures because it was protected by the imperial frontiers. Appian (praef. 7) around the same time and Herodian (Rom. Hist. 2.11.5) again ca. 240 CE had made

8. North 1981: 21.

9. MacKendrick 1975: 155–62. Forum of Trajan: Packer in Steinby 1995: vol. 2, 348–56.

10. Matthews 1984: 169; Potter 2014: 262–64, 266–68.

11. Aurelian walls: Pisani Sartorio in Steinby 1996: vol. 3, 290–99; "Servian" walls: Andreussi in Steinby 1996: vol. 3, 319–24.

similar congratulatory remarks. But the tide had turned. The Aurelian walls would be necessary for the remainder of Roman history. They would be heightened and reinforced first by Maxentius early in the fourth century and then again by Honorius in 401–03 CE.

Other signs of the empire's growing distress were visible in Egypt. Trade between the east and Alexandria brought in high tax revenue, explaining why the state invested in the infrastructure connecting the Red Sea harbors to the Nile Valley. Public charge of the desert roads included the maintenance of fortified wells and cisterns.[12] But in the course of the third century, the imperial authorities encountered mounting problems securing the overland routes, which were made increasingly unsafe by Bedouin raids. In the fourth century it seems the effort was abandoned altogether. Trade continued in the fifth and sixth centuries, but increasing numbers of merchants seem to have preferred struggling upwind through the Red Sea to Aela and Clysma, a less favorable route than the one going through the Eastern Desert and then downstream on the Nile.[13]

The reign of Diocletian and the organizational reforms he initiated increased the stability of the empire. But chronic problems with migrating and plundering Goths, Alemanni and Vandals continued in the fourth century.[14] Despite the walls that had gone up around Rome, the city was sacked and pillaged in 410 CE by the Visigoths under their leader, Alaric. Sixteen years earlier Alaric and his men had fought on the side of the emperor Theodosius against the usurper Eugenius at the Battle of the Frigidus.[15] They had received little reward for their contribution, and resentment had turned them into a hostile force. After a multi-year rampage through Greece and the southern Balkans, they had besieged Rome with the aim of reaching a settlement deal. When they failed to get one after protracted negotiations, they sacked the city.[16] The event wrought material but most of all ideological damage. The besiegers were Christians, albeit of Arian persuasion. It was bad enough that for the first time in eight centuries Rome had fallen to foreign invaders. But that the now Christian city had been attacked by a Christian force also produced a rhetorical problem for the imperial establishment in its ongoing struggle against pagan traditionalists. Augustine, the bishop of Hippo, attempted to explain away the embarrassment with *The City of God*, but whether

12. Wilson 2015: 20–21.

13. Wilson 2015: 28–31.

14. Williams and Friell 1999: 17–19; Ward-Perkins 2005: 33–38.

15. See Harris 2016: 442–49 on the religious dimension of the conflict.

16. Blockley 1998: 114–15, 125–28; Williams and Friell 1999: 8–9, 21–24.

he managed to convince many people with his learned theological exposition may be open to doubt.[17]

During the first decades of the fifth century, Rome also faced a threat of a less direct but ultimately more serious nature. Bands of Vandals had been on a meandering journey south through the Roman empire, arriving in North Africa from Spain in 429 CE. They were bound by treaty to the Romans, who had granted them African territory in return for military manpower. But in 439 CE the Vandals broke the treaty and attacked Carthage. Western emperors continuously planned to dislodge the invaders but could never gather enough strength to do so. With the provinces of Proconsularis and Byzacena wrested from their control, the African grain ships stopped coming to Rome.

From the early fifth century onward the Alexandrian grain fleet provisioned Constantinople exclusively, and consequently Rome was dependent on its possessions in North Africa for its food distributions. But if any grain still reached the city from Vandal-held territories, it now did so through commercial, not fiscal transactions. Western emperors were seriously squeezed for resources, and whatever purchases they may have made would not have balanced out the loss. The situation became even more dire when in the 460s CE the Vandals took Sardinia, which had been an alternative source of Roman grain supplies. As Rome could not be fed solely from its hinterland, its population size began an inexorable decline.[18]

Meanwhile the Vandals continued to operate the intact Roman institutional infrastructure they had found in North Africa. Under their king, Geiseric, and his successors, the area did well enough to enrich a local ruling elite, in large part because tax revenue now stayed in the area and sustained the local economy.[19] Nevertheless, the severance of North Africa from the Roman empire had a negative impact on Carthage, which declined in size, wealth and splendor, despite becoming the center of the new Vandal kingdom. This decline fits a pattern in which areas that had been net contributors to the Roman state's finances did not experience a rise in prosperity after the disappearance of imperial taxation.[20] That surprising outcome suggests that the regions of the empire had benefited from being part of a political, economic and institutional unit, in turn implying that the Roman empire had been more than the sum of its parts.

17. See Ward-Perkins 2005: 28–29, also discussing the reaction of Jerome and Orosius.

18. Wickham 2005: 87–88, 730.

19. Ward-Perkins 2000b: 355–58; Wickham 2005: 88–92, 711, 730.

20. Ward-Perkins 2000b: 377–81. But cf. De Vos 2013 on the Medjerda Valley under Vandal rule.

Perhaps the most dramatic event affecting the empire as a territorial and fiscal entity was its division into a western and eastern half. In 395 CE the emperor Theodosius I died, leaving as his successors two sons: Arcadius, placed on the throne in the east, and Honorius, who received the west. This arrangement had precedent going back to the tetrarchy of Diocletian and was not intended as a constitutional split. However, events would turn it into one. Both Honorius and Arcadius were incapable of ruling on their own. The men governing in their stead were quickly at loggerheads, and a period of intrigues and deteriorating diplomatic relations followed. The situation was made worse by badly coordinated attempts to deal with Alaric's Visigoths and by the increasing disarray of the Roman military.[21] Ultimately what resulted was a slowly crumbling western empire, and an eastern empire that managed to regain stability and strength.

Good relations with neighboring Persia had helped the eastern empire create conditions favorable to a recovery. On the accession of Theodosius II in 408 CE the court established a friendly alliance with the Persian king, defusing a potential source of trouble on its eastern frontier. Diplomatic relations with the west also improved. In 410 CE the court in Constantinople felt secure enough militarily to send a crack corps of 4,000 men to help Honorius defend Ravenna, by then the seat of government in the west.[22] That the eastern government could spare the troops is telling about its strength, especially in light of the Hunnic threat it faced. Only about a year earlier a large force of Huns under their leader, Uldin, had crossed the Danube and attacked Lower Moesia and Thrace. But the health of the eastern empire had improved enough to ward off the attack and force the Huns into retreat, using a combination of divisive diplomacy and military tactics.

Meanwhile, in the west, the northwestern provinces saw the gradual but steady erosion of governmental infrastructure over the course of the fifth century. Most significantly, the Roman legions were in retreat, often forcing the local population to fend for themselves. A particularly egregious example of that process is provided by developments in Roman Britain. Around 407 CE, Constantine III withdrew the majority of Roman troops from the province. When the Britons ca. 410 CE requested military aid against raids by roaming brigands, the response was a legal change allowing the civilian population to bear arms and organize their own defense.[23] In that case a single imperial decision caused the immediate departure of most military forces, but generally

21. Cameron 1993: 138–39, 148–49; Blockley 1998: 113–25.
22. Blockley 1998: 128–29; Williams and Friell 1999: 25–29.
23. Wood 2000: 504–05.

speaking neither the Roman government nor the Roman army was suddenly absent from the northwestern provinces. Rather, their incremental fading characterized the situation there during the fifth and early sixth century, which has been dubbed a "sub-Roman" period.[24] An increase in the number of rural fortified sites reflects how the instability of the times affected the local population.[25]

With the failure of the Roman military to be a protecting presence, much of the rationale for the Roman state disappeared along with the rationale for imperial tax payments. The effect was a vacuum to be occupied by whoever had the wherewithal to do so. In Spain and Gaul, competing groups of invaders, including the Visigoths, Alans, Franks and Burgundians, began to carve out kingdoms for themselves. Unlike the Roman empire, those kingdoms did not depend on a paid standing army financed through taxation. Instead they relied on a personal following of kings and local aristocrats. What was happening in Britain, Gaul and Spain provides another real-world example from antiquity of Mancur Olson's ideas about state behavior. In Olson's terminology, the western empire became incapable of acting as a stationary bandit, allowing roving bandits to occupy its place.[26]

Following the steady disintegration of the western empire, the center of gravity of the Roman world shifted eastward toward Asia Minor and Constantinople. During the first half of the sixth century it would see the long rule of a remarkable emperor, Justinian (527–65 CE). However, the historical judgment of his reign varies. It has been seen as "a time of triumph, marking the re-establishment of strong imperial rule. . . . Equally, it has been seen as an autocracy, marked by persecution and ending in failure."[27] Undeniably, Justinian's achievements are extraordinary. The church of St. Sophia he constructed in Constantinople (now the Istanbul Ayasofya museum) is one of the most astonishing buildings to survive from antiquity. On an intellectual plane, his codification of imperial law, the *Corpus Iuris Civilis*, stands as a monument to Roman legal thinking. It was to have a lasting influence on the western legal tradition, providing the basis for many continental European law codes.

As for the Roman state's ability to control territory, Justinian's reign was exceptional as well, temporarily reversing the trend of an ever-shrinking empire. Starting in 533 CE the emperor expanded his dominions westward,

24. Wood 2000: 497–99, 502, 504.
25. Ward-Perkins 2000a: 335–36.
26. Olson 1991; 2000.
27. Cameron 2000: 65.

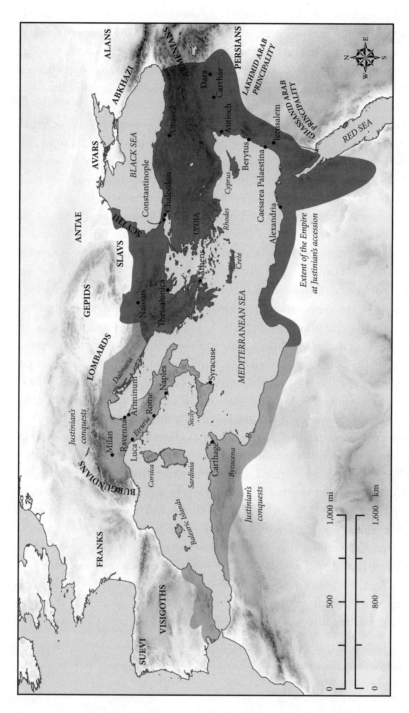

FIG. 6.1. The empire under Justinian in 565 CE.

retaking parts of provinces lost by western emperors and establishing his authority in the old imperial heartland of Italy (fig. 6.1).

Rather than forming a consciously planned reconquest, this westward expansion may have developed in stages, fueled by its own initial success. Either way, the first step in the enterprise consisted of the dispatch of a military force, 15,000 men strong, to Vandal-controlled Africa. The campaign exceeded expectations and the emperor's armies quickly seized Carthage, which by that time had not been under imperial control for almost a century.[28] A triumph ceremony was subsequently held in Constantinople, and the spoils from the African war were carried through the city in a celebratory procession. Procopius, a historian who had personally joined the military expedition, claims that the captured booty included the treasures from the Jewish temple in Jerusalem, taken to Rome by the future emperor Titus in 70 CE and then by the Vandals to Carthage in 455 CE (*Wars* 4.9.1–5).

The victory over the Vandals inspired another campaign two years later, this time in Italy. Sicily was taken fairly easily, but defeating the Goths on the mainland proved to be much more difficult.[29] In 536 CE the Roman general Belisarius entered Rome, only to suffer a year-long siege there in 537. War dragged on in Italy throughout the 540s and the first half of the 550s, draining the imperial treasury and putting a heavy burden on the inhabitants of Italian cities. Meanwhile, it had become evident that holding the conquered territory in Africa was far harder than invading it had been. Establishing effective control required large investments of men and resources, and just like Italy, the area suffered considerably from the ongoing hostilities. Maintaining the simultaneous war effort in Italy and Africa was made more difficult still by an outbreak of bubonic plague in 541 CE, which decreased fiscal revenue by killing many of the empire's taxpayers.[30] Ultimately, by the mid-550s CE, Justinian's western campaigns were successful, but they had come at a heavy price.

The hard-fought position of the empire on the Italian peninsula turned out to be shaky. By the late sixth century the Lombard kingdom had whittled Constantinople's territorial possessions down to the areas around Ravenna, Rome and Naples. Tiberius II (574–82 CE) was keen on restoring Roman authority in Italy, but the situation in the Balkans was deteriorating rapidly and military operations there had to be given priority.[31] Meanwhile in Spain, the conquered areas were lost again to the Visigoths. The Roman influence in North

---

28. Cameron 2000: 73.
29. Cameron 2000: 74–78.
30. Justinianic plague: Harper 2017: 206–45.
31. Cameron 2000: 82–83; Whitby 2000: 91, 96–98.

Africa lasted longer, although the region saw a steady reduction in involvement from Constantinople, as emperors increasingly turned their attention to Asia Minor. Still, the empire continued to be a presence in North Africa. More radical change would not arrive there until the Arab conquests of the mid-seventh century.

If nothing else, this enduring influence in the West Mediterranean shows the remarkable resilience of the Roman empire, which in the late sixth century "was still the mightiest single political institution in the Mediterranean or near eastern world, even if it was not powerful enough to dominate simultaneously on all frontiers."[32] All the same, when in 617 CE the Persians took Egypt and halted the shipments of Alexandrian public grain to Constantinople, the empire was a shadow of what it had been at its height.

Rome's Collapse and the Economy

The early seventh-century CE events in Egypt provide an imperfect yet convenient marker for the end of the Roman world, but the initial moment of decline is harder to establish. It is tempting to take the mid-160s CE as a starting point, the years in which the so-called Antonine plague (more likely an outbreak of smallpox) first struck the empire.[33] However, its demographic effects were uneven. The Antonine plague may have been the start of irreversible contraction in the west, but in parts of the east, population numbers would rebound to be higher in the fourth, fifth and even sixth centuries than they had been in the second.[34] Economically, as well, many eastern cities and regions flourished in late antiquity. But the diverging trajectory of east and west should not distract us from the larger picture. "The overall economic trend of the Roman world from c. 200 to 700 was downward."[35] One obvious aspect of that trend was a drop in total economic output. Lack of statistics makes quantification impossible, but proxy data, including from (but not limited to) shipwrecks and atmospheric lead pollution, suggest a precipitous fall.[36] If some eastern regions did as well in late antiquity as they had done in the second century CE, and others even did better, the overall economy had shrunk dramatically.

But the decline in aggregate output is only part of the story. The disintegration of the empire also led to a pronounced decrease in economic connectiv-

32. Whitby 2000: 108.

33. Harper 2017: 98–118.

34. Ward-Perkins 2000a: 320–27; McCormick 2001: 30–38; Scheidel 2007: 48–49; Erdkamp 2016.

35. McCormick 2001: 30.

36. MacMullen 1988: 1–15; De Callataÿ 2005; Ward-Perkins 2005: 87–168; Jongman 2007a.

ity and complexity, a process going well beyond contraction. As Bryan Ward-Perkins has emphasized, it amounted to nothing short of a structural collapse:

> The phenomenon we are looking at is not a simple shrinkage, as if the economy of the seventh century were essentially similar to that of the fourth, but on a more restricted scale. Rather, there was a remarkable qualitative change in economic life, with whole areas of specialization and exchange disappearing and, in some regions, even very basic technology apparently ceasing to exist.[37]

To assess the impact of these dramatic changes on the population of the empire, what we would most like to know is how they affected individual welfare. As with the question of total economic output, archaeology provides us with the most informative data in that respect.

It seems reasonable to assume that a greater availability of higher-quality goods—especially goods that met basic human needs of clothing, sustenance and shelter—meant that people lived better lives. Much of the physical evidence for such goods is perishable and does not survive well in the archaeological record. But luckily ceramics do. Because of their mundane nature they provide an accurate reflection of everyday living conditions. Large amounts of professionally made and well-fired pottery, brick and roof tile attest to the ready availability throughout the Roman world of excellent cookware and sturdy dwellings. After the collapse of the empire, Roman levels in both quantity and quality would not be seen again for many centuries in the west, including Italy, although much of the east presents a decidedly brighter picture.[38]

Another find that survives well archaeologically and that is highly informative on standards of living is animal bone. In Rome's premodern economy, the real incomes of most people allowed them to eat only a basic diet containing limited amounts of animal protein. Their propensity to improve their food intake by spending any surplus income on meat was high. At the same time, they were forced to scale back on meat almost immediately following an income squeeze. Because of the high income elasticity of demand, changing consumption patterns are good indicators of changing standards of living.

Datasets from Italy and the northwestern provinces seem to suggest that meat consumption rose quickly in the last centuries BCE, stayed at high levels until the late fourth century CE and then dropped off sharply.[39] The picture is still incomplete geographically and, as Andrew Wilson has cautioned,

37. Ward-Perkins 2000b: 361.

38. Ward-Perkins 2005: 104–10, 124.

39. Jongman 2006: 245–46; 2007a: 192; 2016. See also MacKinnon 2015: 251–52 for pork.

uncertainty about volumetric data on excavated soil reduces the strength of the conclusions.[40] All the same, the preliminary results are intriguing and at least suggestive of actual patterns. Supporting the notion that those patterns might be real is the increase in size of Roman livestock during the imperial era. Pigs, cows and sheep on average grew larger than under the republic, falling back to prehistoric sizes in the post-Roman centuries.[41] In the imperial period the Romans seem not only to have kept more animals than before or after but also bigger animals that yielded more meat, milk and wool.

The problem with ceramic and faunal data is, of course, that they are still a step removed from physical human welfare. As Ward-Perkins observed, if "we did want to know more about individual physical well-being and longevity, we would have to put more effort into establishing the study of human bones on a sure footing and on recovering datable and well-preserved groups of skeletons."[42] Since he wrote those words, much effort has in fact gone into the study of Roman skeletal remains. Bone data provide information on people's quality of life in a variety of ways; for instance, showing how much their bodies had been worn by physical labor and to what degree they had suffered from certain diseases. But one indicator is the most straightforward to measure and assess, at least in theory: individual height.

Following the pioneering work of modern economists such as Robert Fogel, Roman economic historians have taken stature as a proxy variable for health.[43] But using bone data to substitute for the military records that Fogel used is tricky. Many Roman skeletons are incomplete, and total body length is often only a reconstruction from measurements of long bones, particularly the femur.[44] Perhaps unsurprisingly given the imperfect data and the still early stage of this research, the results have been ambiguous and present a host of problems.

In a study of some years ago, Geoffrey Kron set out to compare ancient and modern Italian male height based on skeletal remains on the one hand, and military records on the other.[45] To calculate the stature of men living in ancient Italy and Sicily he synthesized the results of long bone measurements from adult male skeletons dated from ca. 500 BCE to ca. 500 CE. The combined measurements led him to estimate a weighted mean height of ancient males of 168.3 centimeters, which appears to compare favorably to the data on

40. Wilson: 2014: 155.

41. Ward-Perkins 2005: 145; MacKinnon 2015; Erdkamp 2016: 8; Jongman 2016.

42. Ward-Perkins 2000b: 366.

43. Stature as a measure of health: Fogel 2004. See also Boix 2015: 171–201.

44. Koepke and Baten 2005: 69–71; Kron 2005: 79–80; Jongman 2007a: 193–95; 2007b: 607–09.

45. Kron 2005.

modern Italian conscripts. The cohort born in 1854 had an average height of only 162.64 centimeters, while the first cohort to reach Kron's estimated average again would be the one born in 1936.

Of course, a comparison between a thousand-year and a one-year average is imperfect, to say the least. In addition, the data are problematic, as Harper has pointed out. By refining the dataset and adding a chronological dimension he was able to conclude that Romans living in Italy in the imperial period were shorter than their Iron-Age and republican ancestors.[46] Moreover, the post-Roman population of central Italy seems to have been growing taller again, as a different study based on more robust data shows.

However, the authors of the latter study caution that their results might not have general validity because of the "significant migratory fluxes, particularly during the Roman and Medieval periods."[47] Invasions and migrations might indeed have influenced the data on late-antique Italian height variation. The obvious way to overcome that problem would be to expand the dataset geographically to see if the observed changes similarly affected populations elsewhere in the Roman world. Migratory flows occurred widely in the later Roman empire, but a dataset capturing larger segments of the population would decrease the distorting effects.

A paper by Nikola Koepke and Joerg Baten aimed to provide such a picture of empire-wide height variation.[48] They studied both male and female stature based on skeletal data from the first to the eighteenth century CE originating from three European regions: Central/Western, Eastern/Northern and the Mediterranean. The data suggest that heights fluctuated somewhat during the first four centuries CE but on balance stagnated. A marked increase in average height then seems to have occurred in the fifth century, continuing halfway into the sixth. The disaggregated data by both gender and region show similar patterns, lending support to the validity of the overall trend. Koepke and Baten also incorporated climatic effects into their study. According to their data the average temperature in Europe during the first six centuries CE declined measurably, a finding confirmed by the much more recent and in-depth analysis by Harper.[49] If so, one could argue that stagnating Roman height during the first four centuries CE was an economic achievement, given the increasingly adverse climatic conditions. However, that argument would not explain why, during the fifth century and the first half of the sixth, stature began to rise while temperatures continued to fall.

46. Harper 2017: 76–77, 299–303 and 325 n. 25.
47. Giannecchini and Moggi-Cecchi 2008: 289.
48. Koepke and Baten 2005.
49. Koepke and Baten 2005: 82, fig. 5; Harper 2017: 39–54.

Jongman in recent research has also focused on Roman body length and nutrition, compiling a large database of measurements of femur bones originating from all over the empire. The preliminary results led him to conclude that human stature rose in Roman imperial times and declined in late antiquity.[50] But in his most current study he reaches the opposite conclusion: average height hit a low point in the first century CE and then continued to rise until the mid-sixth century.[51] Those findings are difficult to interpret in light of the information from other datasets. The increase in body length during the first three centuries CE could conceivably still be attributed to improving living standards, in line with the results from studies of animal bones and other archaeological finds. But the continued rise thereafter presents a problem, as contemporary data generally suggest a decline in living standards and material welfare, certainly in the west.

As things stand currently, it appears that average human stature increased during a period in which the economy of the empire unraveled. On the face of it, Malthusian forces seem to provide a logical explanation for that phenomenon. It could be argued that sometime in the third century CE the Roman empire reached its carrying capacity and that subsequently a positive check occurred. Demographic decline eased the pressure on scarce resources, leading to an increase in living standards comparable to the one that the survivors of the Black Death enjoyed in the Middle Ages.

But that explanation is at odds with the archaeological data on rising real incomes during the first centuries CE. Stable isotope analysis of Roman bone tissue does also not suggest widespread malnutrition, the kind of evidence we would expect to see in a population in the grips of a Malthusian check.[52] In addition, the idea that the empire might have hit a Malthusian ceiling is inconsistent with the pattern of population distribution in the Roman world, as Paul Erdkamp observed. In the third century CE and beyond, demographic decline was severe and sustained in the west, which was always the more thinly populated part of the empire. By contrast, after temporary setbacks following the Antonine plague, population numbers continued to rise in parts of the east including Egypt and Syria, which were already the most densely populated areas in the second century CE.[53] An explanation other than a Malthusian one needs to be found to put the different and sometimes conflicting strands of evidence into a coherent narrative.

50. Jongman 2007a: 194, fig. 7.

51. Jongman 2016. Note that northwestern Europe is overrepresented in the data.

52. Harper 2017: 78.

53. Erdkamp 2016: 4–6. Second-century CE population densities per region: Scheidel 2007: 48 table 3.1.

The hypothesis favored by Jongman, Erdkamp and Harper is that despite high levels of material welfare, the urbanized Roman lifestyle produced deteriorating health during the peak of the empire. Human stature responds to two factors in particular: diet and the disease environment to which the body is exposed.[54] Roman cities, as premodern cities generally, were unhealthy and dangerous places where density-dependent infectious diseases were rampant.[55] Decent nutrition notwithstanding, continuous exposure to such an environment would have stunted the growth of Roman city dwellers, who were numerous by preindustrial standards. A deurbanization process triggered by the collapse of the empire would have relieved the stress of pathogens, leading to improved overall health. Erdkamp further proposes that an increased availability of animal protein following an expansion of herding at the cost of arable farming might have amplified that effect.[56]

Attractive though these explanations might be, one can see how they leave several problems unresolved. For one thing, the data available to us so far suggest that in late antiquity meat consumption did not go up but went down, along with the average size of domesticated animals. They do not, therefore, appear to be in accordance with Erdkamp's idea of a rise in overall protein intake. Meat consumption aside, it would seem that in a crumbling and deurbanizing empire, deteriorating levels of material welfare and a reduced exposure to infectious diseases were counterbalancing forces, more likely to produce stagnating than growing human height. Finally, from the earliest days of the empire, the east was more urbanized and densely populated than the west. Yet rising body length seems to have occurred equally in both regions. If urban pathogenic stress stunted human growth more heavily in the east than in the west, we would expect to see a more pronounced height increase there as a result of deurbanization.

Obviously, more data collection and analysis needs to be done to see if the patterns detected so far hold true and to solve the puzzles they present. But the results will be exciting. In years to come we will gain a much more fine-grained picture of how the collapse of the Roman empire affected the welfare of the population living within its confines.

54. Jongman 2016; Harper 2017: 75.
55. See Zuiderhoek 2017: 71–77 for a discussion with references.
56. Erdkamp 2016: 5. Similarly, Koepke and Baten 2005: 82, 90.

7

Concluding Remarks

IT IS NOT CURRENTLY IN vogue to treat the economic development of the ancient world from the Iron Age to the end of the Roman empire as a unified history. Scholars have moved away from Moses Finley's idea of a single "ancient economy," put forward most famously in his 1973 book by that title.[1] The nature of what Finley saw as "the" ancient economy was determined by the value system of the elite as the social group controlling most of the factors of production. Whether Greek or Roman, elites had an outlook aimed at self-sufficiency and "satisficing," which dissuaded them from investment in industry and trade. Instead, they preferentially invested their available surplus in agricultural land to draw a steady income from rents. As a consequence, markets were limited in importance and local and regional in nature.

Criticism leveled at Finley centered on the role of markets, which many scholars maintained was much larger than he allowed. Equally important, many also countered that a single model did not do justice to the diversity of ancient societies. Size apart, the economy of classical Athens was structurally different from that of the Roman empire, which in turn was structurally different from that of the Hellenistic kingdoms. An emphasis on the specifics of ancient societies became the leading mode of research, and I think that few scholars would now subscribe to the idea of a single ancient economy in the sense of Finley.

The focus on societal dissimilarities has been fruitful and has brought necessary nuance. But it has come at a price: it has led us to abandon an overarching economic view of the ancient world. This loss of a unifying perspective is all the more regrettable as long-term archaeological datasets are increasingly suggesting that we should adopt one. With this book I emphatically advocate a return to a larger, encompassing narrative.

1. Reprinted in 1999 with a foreword by Ian Morris. On Finley's ideas, see also Saller 2002.

I have offered such a narrative in discussing positive and negative ways in which the institutional environment created by the state influenced ancient economic performance. In taking that approach I have followed the dominant paradigm in ancient economic history of Neo-Institutionalism, to which I fundamentally subscribe. But a crucial point I set out to make is that positive performance should not be seen as the result of Greco-Roman states assuming the role of third-party enforcers. Private-order mechanisms were and remained essential to how well the economies of the ancient world performed.

Another crucial point I set out to make is that it would be a mistake to see the private and the public domain as separate spheres of economic activity. The impact of the one on the other has been recognized, for the Roman empire most famously by Keith Hopkins (see chapter 1).[2] Yet even in his monetary-flow model, taxes and trade are conceptualized as counterbalancing and thus ultimately discrete forces. I propose that the public and the private realm in the Roman world, and in the ancient world generally, also interacted in fluid ways, especially in the institutional infrastructure that underpinned trade.

One example of such fluid interaction discussed in this book is local city governments exercising authority over their native trade diasporas, as the Phoenician cities of Tyre and Sidon did. Another example is public institutions increasing the efficacy of private order by setting the rules of social interaction. Roman imperial ideology falls into that category, as do classical Greek institutions of public friendship. Yet another instance where the public and the private were linked all but inextricably is provided by the Ptolemaic kingdom's governance of its overseas possessions. Its highest-ranking officials were incentivized to behave as "stationary bandits," resulting in the creation of public goods including the active support of public order.

I contend that the economic growth visible in our long-term datasets past ca. 700 BCE was chiefly Smithian in nature and supported by public institutions, which emerged in an ongoing process of state formation. But in line with standard Neo-Institutional thinking, I have included negative state influence on economic growth in my discussion. I argued that a major case is presented by the turn toward a compulsory state religion initiated by fourth-century CE emperors. In legislating against cultic diversity, emperors created a religiously intolerant environment, thereby upsetting the equilibrium of economic trust established in diaspora trade. I have set that policy in the context of the empire's increasing weakness, which in essence was a process of state formation in reverse.

2. Hopkins 1980; 2002.

This book is by no means intended to be an exhaustive exploration of institutions with a determining effect on ancient economic performance. The ones singled out for study are in my view particularly significant, but others could be identified and hopefully will be by future scholarship. As for the approach to Mediterranean economic history adopted here, much of the argument has revolved around institutional persistence on the one hand and change on the other. That approach makes practical sense, but has its limits, which deserve to be made explicit.

As John Wallis has cautioned, to look for institutional changes with lasting effects inevitably means introducing sample-selection bias into the analysis. Many changes do not persist and get "winnowed out," in Wallis' words. This is an ever ongoing process, as a "steady stream of continuous institutional change and a lumpy stream of episodic changes feed into society every day, month, and year."[3] The near impossibility to take full account of it means that any presentation of historical institutional developments necessarily remains incomplete. Perhaps more important, the focus on outcomes means that the process of change itself remains imperfectly understood.

To Wallis' thought that some institutional changes get winnowed out, I add that others fail to emerge at all, which we then obviously do not see and cannot study. But understanding their non-emergence might still be possible, although it requires some imagination and counterfactual thinking. As a concluding thought, I tentatively posit here that the establishment of Roman rule over the entire Mediterranean had a dampening effect on innovation.

Once the major wars of conquest had been fought and won, Rome's unification of the Mediterranean Basin undoubtedly created transaction-cost benefits. However, it may also have created imperial inertia. David Hollander recently hinted at that idea in a discussion of economic competition, which in his opinion "has rarely received the attention it deserves among ancient historians."[4] He distinguishes between two basic forms: consumer competition and entrepreneurial rivalry. The first is exemplified by auction sales, which were a typical feature of Roman economic life, well attested in our sources. But competition for buyers among sellers and producers is much less visible in the evidence. Hollander proposes, no doubt rightly, that the literary predilections of elite Roman authors are in large part to blame for that result. But he also speculates that the muted evidence for entrepreneurial rivalry might to some degree reflect a historical reality.

Government regulation and state-run monopolies may have suppressed competition, while private trading associations may have done the same by

3. Wallis 2014: 40.
4. Hollander 2015: 158.

policing the price and supply of manufactured goods. In addition, there may have been "perfect competition" in markets for commodities such as grain, traded in low-barrier markets with many small-scale buyers and sellers who individually were too insignificant to alter the market outcome.[5] The effect would have been a reduced economic rivalry among all market players.

Those are thought-provoking suggestions, but I remain skeptical especially about the last two. Price-setting by trading organizations and "perfect competition" in commodities markets would have equally affected the medieval and Early-Modern world, which nonetheless produced the Commercial Revolution.[6] Yet I also think that Hollander is right in suggesting that reduced economic competition is worth considering in our evaluation of Roman economic performance. Specifically, I suggest that imperial rule may have held back innovation by reinforcing the institutional status quo.

A collective status-quo bias at the institutional level is difficult to prove directly, but can be made credible by the counterexample of a politically fragmented world. As discussed briefly in chapter 1, a political constellation of multiple small, self-governing societies has economic advantages. One of those is an increased potential for efficiency-enhancing innovation. If states form part of a larger system in which they compete directly, they can feel compelled to be creative in a continuous fashion. Europe in the Middle Ages and Early-Modern Period provides the best known example of that forward driving dynamic. Single European states were usually technologically innovative for short bursts, managing to maintain an edge over competitors only temporarily. But as Joel Mokyr has noted, this observation

> holds for individual European societies, of course, but precisely because Europe was fragmented it does not hold for the continent as a whole. It is as if technological creativity was like a torch too hot to hold for long; each individual society carried it for a short time. . . . No society, then, was able to hold on long to leadership, but competition among independent political entities (known as the "states system") ensured that as long [as] there was at least one nation that was truly creative, the others would have to follow suit.[7]

This effect of steady innovation propelled by ongoing competition among small polities was not limited to technological progress. Oscar Gelderblom has shown how, in the thirteenth to seventeenth centuries, a fierce commercial rivalry led largely self-governing cities in the Low Countries to engage in

5. Hollander 2015: 162–66.
6. Ogilvie 2011. But cf. my remarks in chapter 1.
7. Mokyr 2002: 276. See also Mokyr 2016: 165–78.

competitive attempts to lure professional, "footloose" foreign traders. Collectively those traders were involved in a continuous process of innovation in contracting, forcing city governments constantly to improve the institutional infrastructure they had on offer. As Gelderblom explains,

> merchants influenced each other's contracting practices, and as trade expanded in new directions they developed new contracting forms that upset conventional wisdom. In other words, securing contract enforcement at the lowest possible cost required the continuous adaptation of legal institutions, and this was exactly the strength of commercial cities like Bruges, Antwerp, and Amsterdam. Their legal autonomy allowed the town magistrates to adapt the local legal system to the changing demands of the mercantile community, and because they were keen to attract as many international traders as possible, they did so time and again.[8]

As for potential Roman parallels, during the time of the late republic Roman law went through rapid and profound changes in reaction to an expansion of commerce and an increase in elite wealth from imperialism.[9] But under the empire a steady, competitive push toward institutional innovation analogous to the one described by Gelderblom is not detectable. To be sure, Roman law continued to develop, albeit slowly, creating among other things an appeals process.[10] But innovation seems not to have been driven by merchants constantly adjusting their contracting practices and by the Roman state constantly updating its legal institutions in response. Rather, the evidence on witnessing discussed in chapter 4 would suggest that by the time of the empire both the Roman state and its subjects were invested in the institutional status quo. The rules on social standing determined by Rome's civic order were used publicly to embed contracts. No one, it would seem, had any incentive to change that system, which allowed for the maintenance of social order on the one hand and individual status on the other. Moreover, as the practice was inherently useful to contract enforcement it produced satisfactory societal outcomes.

On the level of cities, competition for a slice of long-distance trade was not absent under the empire. The evidence, cited in chapter 2, for urban governments' involvement in their native diasporas suggests that at least some cities were well aware of the benefits of capturing the gains from trade. But even if Roman cities were self-governing to a large degree, they were ultimately beholden to the central administration in the imperial capital. Whatever auton-

8. Gelderblom 2013: 139.
9. Frier 1985.
10. Rüfner 2016.

omy they may have enjoyed, they had far less room to maneuver in setting the institutional parameters of trade than the later mercantile centers in northern Europe.

In addition, we should take into account here that the urbanism of ancient empires, including the Roman, differed from that of later European societies. The economic, demographic and political forces driving imperial urbanization were less conducive to producing an economically influential segment of middling cities comparable to the ones that Gelderblom studied. As Arjan Zuiderhoek observed,

> the urban systems of the empires of Classical Antiquity were dominated by some very large cities the size of which was inflated because they were home to courts and imperial or high provincial elites. These cities attracted a large and continuous stream of migrants because of the economic opportunities they offered and drew in extremely large quantities of agricultural surplus in the form of rents and taxes, ... thus leaving comparatively little room for the development of a layer of middle-range centres with a more regional focus, such as existed in the politically far more fragmented world of early modern Europe.[11]

In my view it is worth entertaining the idea that the politically unified Roman Mediterranean was unlikely to produce the accelerating pace of technological and institutional innovation seen in late-medieval and Early-Modern Europe. That notion would certainly need further study and demonstration. But however preliminary at present, it might help us explain why only the fragmented world that emerged out of the ruins of the Roman empire would eventually achieve the breakthrough progress that would bring us the fruits of the Industrial Revolution.

11. Zuiderhoek 2017: 53.

BIBLIOGRAPHY

Epigraphic and Papyrological Corpora

AE = *L'Année épigraphique.*

CIIP = Hannah M. Cotton et al. *Corpus Inscriptionum Iudaeae/Palaestinae*, 3 vols. Berlin, Boston: De Gruyter. 2010–14.

CIL = *Corpus Inscriptionum Latinarum.*

CIS = *Corpus Inscriptionum Semiticarum.*

EA = Anson F. Rainey Z"L and William M. Schniedewind. *The El-Amarna Correspondence: A New Edition of the Cuneiform Letters from the Site of El-Amarna based on Collations of all Extant Tablets*, 2 vols. Leiden, Boston: Brill. 2015.

FIRA = Salvatore Riccobono, Giovanni Baviera, Contardo Ferrini, Giuseppe Furlani and Vincenzo Arangio-Ruiz. *Fontes Iuris Romani Antejustiniani*, 3 vols. Florence: S.A.G. Barbèra. 1940–43.

I.Cos = Mario Segre. *Iscrizioni di Cos*, 2 vols. (= *Monografie della scuola archeologica di Atene e delle missioni italiane in Oriente*, vol. 6). Rome: L'Erma di Bretschneider. 1993.

ID = André Plassart, Jacques Coupry, Félix Dürrbach, Pierre Roussel and Marcel Launey. *Inscriptions de Délos*, 7 vols. Paris: H. Champion and E. de Boccard. 1926–72.

IG = *Inscriptiones Graecae.*

IGRR = René Cagnat, Jules Toutain, Pierre Jouguet and Georges Lafaye. *Inscriptiones Graecae ad Res Romanas Pertinentes*, 3 vols. Paris: Ernest Leroux. 1911–27.

IGUR = Luigi Moretti. *Inscriptiones Graecae Urbis Romae*, 4 vols. Rome: Istituto Italiano per la Storia Antica. 1968–90.

I.Lindos = Christian S. Blinkenberg. *Lindos* II: *Inscriptions*. Copenhagen, Berlin: De Gruyter. 1941.

ILS = Hermann Dessau. *Inscriptiones Latinae Selectae*, 3 vols. Berlin: Weidmann. 1892–1916.

I.Porto = Giulia Sacco. *Iscrizioni greche d'Italia: Porto*. Rome: Edizioni di storia e letteratura. 1984.

KAI = Herbert Donner and Wolfgang Röllig. *Kanaanäische und Aramäische Inschriften*, 3 vols. Wiesbaden: Harrassowitz. 1962–64.

MF = Marie-Thérèse Couilloud. *Exploration Archéologique de Délos* 30: *Les Monuments Funéraires de Rhénée*. Paris: E. de Boccard. 1974.

NSER = Amedeo Maiuri. *Nuova silloge epigrafica di Rodi e Cos*. Florence: Le Monnier. 1925.

OGIS = Wilhelm Dittenberger. *Orientis Graeci Inscriptiones Selectae: Supplementum Sylloges Inscriptionum Graecarum*, 2 vols. Leipzig: S. Hirzel. 1903–05.

P.Cair.Zen. = Campbell C. Edgar, Octave Guéraud and Pierre Jouguet. *Zenon papyri: Catalogue général des antiquités égyptiennes du Musée du Caire,* 5 vols. Cairo: Institut français d'archéologie orientale. 1925–40.

P.Col.Zen. = William L. Westermann, Elizabeth S. Hasenoehrl, Clinton W. Keyes and Herbert Liebesny. *Zenon Papyri: Business Papers of the Third Century B.C. dealing with Palestine and Egypt,* 2 vols. New York: Columbia University Press. 1934–40.

P.Cornell = William L. Westermann and Casper J. Kraemer jr. *Greek Papyri in the Library of Cornell University.* New York: Columbia University Press. 1926.

P.Edgar = Campbell C. Edgar. *Selected Papyri from the Archives of Zenon,* variously published in *Annales du service des antiquités de l'Égypte,* issues 18–24. 1919–24.

P.Hib. = Bernard P. Grenfell, Arthur S. Hunt and Eric G. Turner. *The Hibeh Papyri,* 2 vols. London: Egypt Exploration Society. 1906–55.

P.L.Bat. = Pieter W. Pestman. *Papyrologica Lugduno-Batava* 20: *Greek and Demotic Texts from the Zenon Archive.* Leiden: Brill. 1980.

P.Lond. = Frederic G. Kenyon, H. Idris Bell, Walter E. Crum and Theodore C. Skeat. *Greek Papyri in the British Museum,* 7 vols. London: British Museum. 1893–1974.

P.Mich.Zen. = Campbell C. Edgar. *Zenon Papyri in the University of Michigan Collection.* Ann Arbor: University of Michigan Press. 1931.

P.Oxy. = *The Oxyrhynchus Papyri.*

PSI = *Papiri greci e latini.*

P.Tebt. = Bernard P. Grenfell, Arthur S. Hunt and J. Gilbart Smyly. *The Tebtunis Papyri,* part 1. London: H. Frowde. 1902.

P.Vindob = *Papyri Vindobonensis.*

RÉS = *Répertoire d'Épigraphie Sémitique.*

SEG = *Supplementum Epigraphicum Graecum.*

TH = *Tabulae Herculanenses.*

TPSulp. = Giuseppe Camodeca. *Tabulae Pompeianae Sulpiciorum: Edizione critica dell'archivio puteolano dei Sulpicii.* Rome: Quasar. 1999.

Series and Periodicals

AC = *L'Antiquité Classique*

ACF = *Annuaire du Collège de France*

AJA = *American Journal of Archaeology*

AJP = *American Journal of Philology*

AJPA = *American Journal of Physical Anthropology*

AKÖG = *Archiv für österreichischer Geschichtsquellen*

ANRW = *Aufstieg und Niedergang der römischen Welt*

ASNSP = *Annali della Scuola Normale Superiore di Pisa: Classe di Lettere e Filosofia,* series 3

BA = *Biblical Archaeologist*

BABesch = *Bulletin Antieke Beschaving*

BASOR = *Bulletin of the American Schools of Oriental Research*

BASP = *Bulletin of the American Society of Papyrologists*

BCH = *Bulletin de Correspondance Hellénique*

BER = *Bulletin of Economic Research*
CAH = *The Cambridge Ancient History*
CB = *Classical Bulletin*
CCSL = *Corpus Christianorum, Series Lanina*
CdÉ = *Chronique d'Égypte*
CQ = *Classical Quarterly*
CRAI = *Comptes-rendus des séances de l'Académie des Inscriptions et Belles-lettres*
EEH = *Explorations in Economic History*
EHR = *Economic History Review*
Environ.Sci.Technol. = *Environmental Science & Technology*
Eph.Nap. = *Ephemeris Napocensis*
EREH = *European Review of Economic History*
ERS = *Ethnic and Racial Studies*
EVO = *Egitto e Vicino Oriente*
FO = *Folia Orientalia*
IJNA = *International Journal of Nautical Archaeology*
IJRR = *Interdisciplinary Journal of Research on Religion*
JAOS = *Journal of the American Oriental Society*
JEA = *Journal of Egyptian Archaeology*
JECH = *Journal of Early Christian History*
JECS = *Journal of Early Christian Studies*
JEH = *Journal of Economic History*
JEL = *Journal of Economic Literature*
JITE = *Journal of Institutional and Theoretical Economics*
JJP = *Journal of Juristic Papyrology*
JLS = *Journal of Legal Studies*
JNES = *Journal of Near Eastern Studies*
JOIE = *Journal of Institutional Economics*
JPE = *Journal of Political Economy*
JRA = *Journal of Roman Archaeology*
JRS = *Journal of Roman Studies*
LCL = *Loeb Classical Library*
MAAR = *Memoirs of the American Academy in Rome*
MEFRA = *Mélanges de l'École Française de Rome: Antiquité*
MHR = *Mediterranean Historical Review*
MUSJ = *Mélanges de l'Université Saint-Joseph*
PCPS = *Proceedings of the Cambridge Philological Society*
PNAS = *Proceedings of the National Academy of Sciences of the United States of America*
Puteoli = *Puteoli, studi di storia antica*
RSF = *Rivista di Studi Fenici*
SAAB = *State Archives of Assyria Bulletin*
SCO = *Studi classici e orientali*
SDHI = *Studia et Documenta Historiae et Iuris*
SPAL = *Revista de prehistoria y arqueología de la Universidad de Sevilla*

WA = *World Archaeology*
ZPE = *Zeitschrift für Papyrologie und Epigraphik*
ZRG rom. = *Zeitschrift der Savigny-Stiftung für Rechtsgeschichte, romanistische Abteilung*

Abbreviations of Ancient Authors and Works

Amm. Marc. = Ammianus Marcellinus
Appian *Mithr.* = Appian, *The Mithridatic Wars*
Appian *praef.* = Appian, *praefatio* to *Roman History*
Appian *Pun.* = Appian, *The Punic Wars*
Arrian *Anab.* = Arrian, *Anabasis of Alexander*
Ath. *Deip.* = Athenaeus, *Deipnosophistae*
Augustine *Ep.* = Augustine, *Epistulae*
Augustine *Serm.* = Augustine, *Sermones*
Aulus Gellius *NA* = Aulus Gellius, *Noctes Atticae*
Chron. = Chronicles
Cicero *Ad Att.* = M. Tullius Cicero, *Epistulae ad Atticum*
Clement *Prot.* = Clement of Alexandria, *Protrepticus*
Cod. Just. = *Codex Justinianus*
Cod. Theod. = *Codex Theodosianus*
Curtius Rufus = Quintus Curtius Rufus, *History of Alexander*
Dig. = The *Digest* of Justinian
Dio = Cassius Dio, *Roman History*
Dion. Hal. *Din.* = Dionysius of Halicarnassus, *On Dinarchus*
Eunap. *VS* = Eunapius, *Vitae Sophistarum*
Eusebius *Vita Const.* = Eusebius, *Vita Constantini*
Exp. Tot. Mundi = *Expositio Totius Mundi et Gentium*
Ez. = Ezekiel
Gaius *Inst.* = Gaius, *Institutes*
Gal. = Galen, *On the Properties of Foodstuffs*
Gregory of Nazianzus *Or.* = Gregory of Nazianzus, *Orations*
Hdt. = Herodotus, *Histories*
Herodian *Rom. Hist.* = Herodian, *Roman History*
Hom. *Od.* = Homer, *Odyssey*
Hp. *Morb.* = Hippocrates, *De Moribus*
Isa. = Isaiah
Isocrates *Trap.* = Isocrates, *Trapeziticus*
Jerome *Comm.Ezech.* = Jerome, *Commentarii in Ezechielem*
Jerome *Comm.Isa.* = Jerome, *Commentarii in Isaiam*
Jerome *Ep.* = Jerome, *Epistulae*
Jerome *Vita Hilar.* = Jerome, *Vita Hilarionis*
John of Ephesus *HE* = John of Ephesus, *Historia Ecclesiastica*
John Malalas *Chron.* = John Malalas, *Chronicle*

Josephus *A.J.* = Flavius Josephus, *Antiquitates Judaicae*
Josephus *C.Ap.* = Flavius Josephus, *Contra Apionem*
Julian *Ep.* = Julian, *Epistulae*
Justinian *Nov.* = Justinian, *Novellae Constitutiones*
Juvenal *Sat.* = Juvenal, *Satires*
Kgs = Kings
Libanius *Or.* = Libanius, *Orations*
Mar. Com. *Chron.* = Marcellinus Comes, *Chronicon*
Marc. Diac. *Vita Porph.* = Marcus Diaconus, *Vita Porphyrii*
Martial *Ep.* = Martial, *Epigrams*
NRSV = Bible, *New Revised Standard Version*
Paul. *Festi* = Paulus Diaconus, *Epitome Festi*
Paul. *Sent.* = Julius Paulus, *Sententiae*
Petr. *Sat.* = Petronius, *Satyricon*
Pliny *Ep.* = Pliny the younger, *Epistulae*
Pliny *NH* = Pliny the elder, *Naturalis Historiae*
Plutarch *Alex.* = Plutarch, *The Life of Alexander*
Plutarch *Sulla* = Plutarch, *The Life of Sulla*
Procopius *Wars* = Procopius, *The Wars of Justinian*
Ptolemy *Geogr.* = Ptolemy, *Geography*
Quintilian *Inst.Or.* = Quintilian, *Institutio Oratoria*
Rufin. *HE* = Rufinus of Aquileia, *Historia Ecclesiastica*
Seneca *De Ben.* = Seneca, *De Beneficiis*
Seneca *Ep.* = Seneca, *Epistulae Morales*
Sil. Ital. *Pun.* = Silius Italicus, *Punica*
Socr. *HE* = Socrates of Constantinople, *Historia Ecclesiastica*
Soz. *HE* = Sozomen, *Historia Ecclesiastica*
Strabo *Geogr.* = Strabo, *Geography*
Suet. *Nero.* = Suetonius, *Nero*
Suet. *Vesp.* = Suetonius, *Vespasianus*
Theod. *HE* = Theodoret of Cyrrhus, *Historia Ecclesiastica*
Vell. Pat. = Velleius Paterculus, *Roman History*
Xenophon *Por.* = Xenophon, *Poroi*
Zacharias *Vita Sev.* = Zacharias Scholasticus, *Vita Severi*

General Bibliography

Acemoglu, Daron, and James A. Robinson. 2012. *Why Nations Fail: The Origins of Power, Prosperity, and Poverty*. London: Profile Books.

Adams, Winthrop L. 2006. "The Hellenistic Kingdoms." In *The Cambridge Companion to the Hellenistic World*, edited by Glenn R. Bugh. Cambridge: Cambridge University Press. 28–51.

Ameling, Walter. 1990. "Κοινὸν τῶν Cιδωνίων." ZPE 81: 189–99.

Ameling, Walter. 2013. "Carthage." In *The Oxford Handbook of the State in the Ancient Near East and Mediterranean*, edited by Peter F. Bang and Walter Scheidel. Oxford: Oxford University Press. 361–82.

Amidon, Philip R. 1997. *The Church History of Rufinus of Aquileia: Books 10 and 11*. Oxford: Oxford University Press.

Anagnostou-Canas, Barbara. 1991. *Juge et sentence dans l'Égypte romaine*. Paris: Éditions L'Harmattan.

Ando, Clifford. 2000. *Imperial Ideology and Provincial Loyalty in the Roman Empire*. Berkeley: University of California Press.

Andreau, Jean. 1974. *Les affaires de monsieur Jucundus*. Rome: École française de Rome.

———. 1983. "À propos de la vie financière à Pouzzoles: Cluvius et Vestorius." In *Les "bourgeoisies" municipales italiennes aux IIe et Ier siècles av. J.-C.*, edited by Mireille Cébeillac-Gervasoni. Naples: Centre Jean Bérard. 9–20.

Arnaud, Pascal. 2014. "Maritime Infrastructure: Between Public and Private Initiative." In *Infrastruktur und Herrschaftsorganisation im Imperium Romanum*, edited by Anne Kolb. Berlin: De Gruyter. 161–79.

Ascough, Richard S., Philip A. Harland, and John S. Kloppenborg. 2012. *Associations in the Greco-Roman World: A Sourcebook*. Waco: Baylor University Press.

Ashton, Sally-Ann. 2004. "Ptolemaic Alexandria and the Egyptian Tradition." In *Alexandria, Real and Imagined*, edited by Anthony Hirst and Michael Silk. Aldershot: Ashgate. 15–40.

Astour, Michael C. 1965. "The Origin of the Terms 'Canaan,' 'Phoenician,' and 'Purple.'" *JNES* 24: 346–50.

Athanassiadi, Polymnia. 2010. *Vers la pensée unique: La montée de l'intolérance dans l'Antiquité tardive*. Paris: Les Belles Lettres.

Aubet, María E. 2001. *The Phoenicians and the West: Politics, Colonies and Trade*, translated from the Spanish by Mary Turton, 2nd edition. Cambridge: Cambridge University Press.

———. 2008. "Political and Economic Implications of the New Phoenician Chronologies." In *Beyond the Homeland: Markers in Phoenician Chronology*, edited by Claudia Sagona. Leuven: Peeters. 247–59.

Bagnall, Roger S. 1976. *The Administration of the Ptolemaic Possessions outside Egypt*. Leiden: Brill.

Bagnall, Roger S., and Peter Derow. 2004. *The Hellenistic Period: Historical Sources in Translation*. Oxford: Blackwell.

Baslez, Marie-Françoise. 1986. "Cultes et dévotions des phéniciens en Grèce: Les divinités marines." In *Religio Phoenicia* (*Studia Phoenicia* 4), edited by Corinne Bonnet, Edward Lipiński, and Patrick Marchetti. Namur: Société des Études Classiques. 289–305.

———. 1987. "Le rôle et la place des Phéniciens dans la vie économique des ports de l'Égée." In *Phoenicia and the East Mediterranean in the First Millennium B.C.* (*Studia Phoenicia* 5), edited by Edward Lipiński. Leuven: Peeters. 267–85.

Bauschatz, John. 2007. "Ptolemaic Prisons Reconsidered." *CB* 83: 3–48.

———. 2013. *Law and Enforcement in Ptolemaic Egypt*. Cambridge: Cambridge University Press.

Beard, Mary, John North, and Simon Price. 1998. *Religions of Rome*, 2 vols. Cambridge: Cambridge University Press.

Bechtold, Babette, and Roald Docter. 2010. "Transport Amphorae from Carthage: An Overview." In *Motya and the Phoenician Ceramic Repertoire between the Levant and the West: 9th–6th Century BC*, edited by Lorenzo Nigro. Rome: Missione archeologica a Mozia. 85–116.

Beitzel, Barry J. 2010. "Was There a Joint Nautical Venture on the Mediterranean Sea by Tyrian Phoenicians and Early Israelites?" *BASOR* 360: 37–66.

Belayche, Nicole. 2009. "Foundation Myths in Roman Palestine: Traditions and Reworkings." In *Ethnic Constructs in Antiquity: The Role of Power and Tradition*, edited by Ton Derks and Nico Roymans. Amsterdam: Amsterdam University Press. 167–88.

Bell, Carol. 2016. "Phoenician Trade: The First 300 Years." In *Dynamics of Production in the Ancient Near East: 1300–500 BC*, edited by Juan Carlos Morena García. Oxford: Oxbow Books. 91–105.

Bénichou-Safar, Hélène. 1982. *Les tombes puniques de Carthage: Topographie, structures, inscriptions et rites funéraires*. Paris: Éditions du Centre National de la Recherche Scientifique.

Berger, M. Philippe. 1903. "Vase de plomb avec inscription bilingue découvert à Carthage." *CRAI* 47: 194–98.

Beu-Dachin, Eugenia. 2003. "Două inscripţii votive inedite de la Alburnus Maior." *Eph.Nap.* 13: 187–93.

Bikerman, Élias. 1939. "Sur une inscription grecque de Sidon." In *Mélanges syriens offerts à monsieur René Dussaud*, vol. 1. Paris: P. Geuthner. 91–99.

Bingen, Jean. 2007. *Hellenistic Egypt: Monarchy, Society, Economy, Culture*, edited with an introduction by Roger S. Bagnall. Berkeley: University of California Press.

Blackman, David J. 1982a. "Ancient Harbours in the Mediterranean: Part 1." *IJNA* 11: 79–104.

———. 1982b. "Ancient Harbours in the Mediterranean: Part 2." *IJNA* 11: 185–211.

Bliquez, Lawrence J. 1975. "Gnaeus Octavius and the Echinaioi." *Hesperia* 44: 431–34.

Blockley, Roger C. 1998. "The Dynasty of Theodosius." In *CAH* vol. 13: *The Late Empire, A.D. 337–425*, edited by Averil Cameron and Peter Garnsey. Cambridge: Cambridge University Press. 111–37.

Bogaert, Raymond. 1981. "Le statut des banques en Égypte ptolémaïque." *AC* 50: 86–99.

———. 1983. "Les modèles des banques ptolémaïques." In *Egypt and the Hellenistic World: Proceedings of the International Colloquium, Leuven, 24–26 May 1982*, edited by Edmond van 't Dack, Peter van Dessel and Willem van Gucht. Leuven: Publications de l'Institut Orientaliste. 13–29.

———. 1991. "Zénon et ses banquiers." *CdÉ* 66: 308–15.

Boix, Carles. 2015. *Political Order and Inequality: Their Foundations and Their Consequences for Human Welfare*. Cambridge: Cambridge University Press.

Bondì, Sandro Filippo. 1978. "Note sull'economia fenicia I: Impresa privata e ruolo dello stato." *EVO* 1: 139–49.

———. 2014. "Phoenicity, Punicities." In *The Punic Mediterranean: Identities and Identification from Phoenician Settlement to Roman Rule*, edited by Josephine Crawley Quinn and Nicholas C. Vella. Cambridge: Cambridge University Press. 58–68.

Bonifay, Michel, and André Tchernia. 2012. "Les réseaux de la céramique africaine (Ier-Ve siècles)." In *Rome, Portus and the Mediterranean*, edited by Simon Keay. Oxford: Oxbow Books. 315–33.

Bonnet, Corinne. 2014. "Phoenician Identities in Hellenistic Times: Strategies and Negotiations." In *The Punic Mediterranean: Identities and Identification from Phoenician Settlement to Roman Rule*, edited by Josephine Crawley Quinn and Nicholas C. Vella. Cambridge: Cambridge University Press. 282–98.

Bordreuil, Pierre, and Ahmed Ferjaoui. 1988. "À propos des 'fils de Tyr' et des 'fils de Carthage.'" In *Carthago* (*Studia Phoenicia 6*), edited by Edward Lipiński. Leuven: Peeters. 137–42.

Bowersock, Glen W. 1982. "The Imperial Cult: Perceptions and Persistence." In *Jewish and Christian Self-Definition*, vol. 3: *Self-Definition in the Graeco-Roman World*, edited by Ben F. Meyer and Edward P. Sanders. Philadelphia: Fortress Press. 171–82.

Brashear, William M., and Francisca A.J. Hoogendijk. 1990. "Corpus Tabularum Lignearum Ceratarumque Aegyptiarum." *Enchoria* 17: 21–54.

Bravo, Benedetto. 1980. "*Sulân* représailles et justice privée contre des étrangers dans les cités grecques (étude du vocabulaire et des institutions)." *ASNSP* 10: 675–987.

Breeze, David J. 2016. *The Roman Army*. London: Bloomsbury.

Bresson, Alain. 2007. "L'entrée dans les ports en Grèce ancienne: Le cadre juridique." In *Gens de passage en Méditerranée de l'Antiquité à l'époque moderne: Procédures de contrôle et d'identification*, edited by Claudia Moatti and Wolfgang Kaiser. Paris: Maisonneuve et Larose. 37–78.

———. 2012. "Wine, Oil, and Delicacies at the Pelousion Customs." In *Das imperiale Rom und der hellenistische Osten: Festschrift für Jürgen Deininger zum 75. Geburtstag*, edited by Linda-Marie Günther and Volker Grieb. Stuttgart: Franz Steiner. 69–88.

———. 2016. *The Making of the Ancient Greek Economy: Institutions, Markets, and Growth in the City-States*, translated by Steven Rendall. Princeton: Princeton University Press.

———. Forthcoming. "Flexible Interfaces of the Ancient Mediterranean World." In *Festschrift for Pierre Rouillard*.

Brock, Sebastian P., and Brian Fitzgerald, trans. 2013. *Two Early Lives of Severos, Patriarch of Antioch*. Liverpool: Liverpool University Press.

Broodbank, Cyprian. 2013. *The Making of the Middle Sea: A History of the Mediterranean from the Beginning to the Emergence of the Classical World*. Oxford: Oxford University Press.

Brown, Peter. 1972. *Religion and Society in the Age of Saint Augustine*. London: Faber and Faber.

Brubaker, Rogers. 2005. "The 'Diaspora' Diaspora." *ERS* 28: 1–19.

Bruneau, Philippe. 1970. *Recherches sur les cultes de Délos à l'époque hellénistique et à l'époque impériale*. Paris: E. de Boccard.

———. 1978. "Les cultes de l'établissement des Poseidoniastes de Bérytus à Délos." *Hommages à Maarten J. Vermaseren*, vol. 1. Leiden: Brill. 160–90.

Bruns, Karl Georg. 1882. *Kleinere Schriften*, vol. 2. Weimar: Böhlau.

Buchanan, James M. 1975. *The Limits of Liberty: Between Anarchy and Leviathan*. Chicago: University of Chicago Press.

Bulbulia, Joseph, and Richard Sosis. 2011. "Signalling Theory and the Evolution of Religious Cooperation." *Religion* 41: 363–88.

Burrell, Barbara. 2004. Neokoroi: *Greek Cities and Roman Emperors*. Leiden: Brill.

Calzini Gysens, Jacqueline. 1982. "Osservazioni sulle fase I e II del santuario con riferimento alle ultime campagne di scavo." In *L'area del 'santuario siriaco del Gianicolo': Problemi archeologici e storico-religiosi*, edited by Mirella Mele and Claudio Mocchegiani Carpano. Rome: Quasar. 59–73.

Cameron, Averil. 1993. *The Later Roman Empire: AD 284–430*. Cambridge, MA: Harvard University Press.

———. 2000. "Justin I and Justinian." In *CAH* vol. 14: *Late Antiquity: Empire and Successors, A.D. 425–600*, edited by Averil Cameron, Bryan Ward-Perkins, and Michael Whitby. Cambridge: Cambridge University Press. 63–85.

Camodeca, Giuseppe. 1977. "L'ordinamento in *regiones* e i *vici* di Puteoli." *Puteoli* 1: 62–98.

———. 1979. "La *gens Annia* puteolana in età giulio-claudio: Potere politico e interessi commerciali." *Puteoli* 3: 17–34.

———. 1982. "Per una riedizione dell'archivio puteolano dei Sulpicii. I. Le TP. 67 e 68; II. Nuovi documenti processuali." *Puteoli* 6: 3–53.

———. 1992. *L'archivio puteolano dei Sulpicii*. Naples: Eugenio Jovene.

———. 1993. "Archivi privati e storia sociale delle città campane: Puteoli ed Herculaneum." In *Prosopographie und Sozialgeschichte: Studien zur Methodik und Erkenntnismöglichkeit der kaiserzeitlichen Prosopographie*, edited by Werner Eck. Cologne: Böhlau. 339–50.

———. 2000. "*Tabulae Herculanenses*: riedizione delle *emptiones* di schiavi (*TH* 59–62)." In *Quaestiones Iuris: Festschrift für Joseph Georg Wolf zum 70. Geburtstag*, edited by Ulrich Manthe and Christoph Krampe. Berlin: Duncker & Humblot. 53–76.

Casson, Lionel. 1971. *Ships and Seamanship in the Ancient World*. Princeton: Princeton University Press.

———. 1990. "New Light on Maritime Loans: P. Vindob. G 40822." *ZPE* 84: 195–206.

Cauuet, Béatrice. 2014. "Gold and Silver Extraction in Alburnus Maior Mines, Roman Dacia (Rosia Montana, Romania): Dynamics of Exploitation and Management of the Mining Space." In *Paisagens mineiras antigas na Europa Ocidental: investigação e valorização cultural*, edited by Luís Fontes. Boticas: Câmara Municipal de Boticas. 83–104.

Chabot, Jean-Baptiste. 1926. "Une inscription funéraire grecque d'époque punique découverte à Carthage par le R. P. Delattre." *CRAI* 70: 41.

Chaniotis, Angelos. 2003. "The Divinity of Hellenistic Rulers." In *A Companion to the Hellenistic World*, edited by Andrew Erskine. Oxford: Blackwell. 431–45.

Checkland, Peter. 1999. "Systems Thinking." In *Rethinking Management Information Systems: An Interdisciplinary Perspective*, edited by Wendy L. Currie and Robert D. Galliers. Oxford: Oxford University Press. 45–56.

Chelbi, Fehti. 1992. *Céramique à vernis noir de Carthage*. Tunis: Institut national d'archéologie et d'art.

Chiusi, Tiziana J. 2013. "'*Fama*' and '*Infamia*' in the Roman Legal System: The Cases of Afrania and Lucretia." In *Judge and Jurist: Essays in Memory of Lord Rodger of Earlsferry*, edited by Andrew Burrows, David A. Johnston, and Reinhard Zimmermann. Oxford: Oxford University Press. 143–65.

Ciongradi, Carmen. 2009. *Die römischen Steindenkmäler aus Alburnus Maior*. Cluj-Napoca: Editura Mega.

Ciulei, Georges. 1983. *Les triptyques de Transylvanie: Études juridiques*. Zutphen: Tesink.

Clarke, Graeme W., trans. 1974. *The Octavius of Marcus Minucius Felix*. New York: Newman Press.

Clarysse, Willy, and Katelijn Vandorpe. 1995. *Zenon, un homme d'affaires grec à l'ombre des pyramides*. Leuven: Leuven University Press.

Cohen, Abner. 1971. "Cultural Strategies in the Organization of Trading Diasporas." In *The Development of Indigenous Trade and Markets in West Africa*, edited by Claude Meillassoux. London: Oxford University Press for the International African Institute. 266–81.

Cohen, Edward E. 1973. *Ancient Athenian Maritime Courts*. Princeton: Princeton University Press.

Cohen, Getzel M. 1983. "Colonization and Population Transfer in the Hellenistic World." In *Egypt and the Hellenistic World: Proceedings of the International Colloquium, Leuven, 24–26 May 1982*, edited by Edmond van 't Dack, Peter van Dessel and Willem van Gucht. Leuven: Publications de l'Institut Orientaliste. 63–74.

Cohen, Rudolph. 1982. "New Light on the Date of the Petra-Gaza Road." *BA* 45: 240–47.

Cooke, George A. 1903. *A Text-Book of North-Semitic Inscriptions: Moabite, Hebrew, Phoenician, Aramaic, Nabataean, Palmyrene, Jewish*. Oxford: Clarendon Press.

Cooter, Robert D., Stephen G. Marks, and Robert H. Mnookin. 1982. "Bargaining in the Shadow of the Law: A Testable Model of Strategic Behavior." *JLS* 11: 225–51.

Cornell, Timothy J. 1995. *The Beginnings of Rome: Italy and Rome from the Bronze Age to the Punic Wars (c. 1000–264 BC)*. London: Routledge.

Cotton, Hannah. 1993. "The Guardianship of Jesus Son of Babatha: Roman and Local Law in the Province of Arabia." *JRS* 83: 94–108.

Croke, Brian. 1983. "A.D. 476: The Manufacture of a Turning Point." *Chiron* 13: 81–119.

Crook, John A. 1967. *Law and Life of Rome*. Ithaca: Cornell University Press.

Culasso Gastaldi, Enrica. 2004. *Le prossenie ateniensi del IV secolo a.C.: Gli onorati asiatici*. Alessandria: Edizione dell'Orso.

Curtin, Philip D. 1984. *Cross-Cultural Trade in World History*. Cambridge: Cambridge University Press.

Dana, Dan. 2003. "Les Daces dans les ostraca du désert oriental de l'Égypte: Morphologie des noms daces." *ZPE* 143: 166–86.

D'Arms, John H. 1974. "Puteoli in the Second Century of the Roman Empire: A Social and Economic Study." *JRS* 64: 104–24.

Davies, John K. 2001. "Hellenistic Economies in the Post-Finley Era." In *Hellenistic Economies*, edited by Zofia H. Archibald, John Davies, Vincent Gabrielsen, and Graham J. Oliver. London, New York: Routledge. 11–62.

———. 2006. "Hellenistic Economies." In *The Cambridge Companion to the Hellenistic World*, edited by Glenn R. Bugh. Cambridge: Cambridge University Press. 73–92.

De Callataÿ, François. 2005. "The Graeco-Roman Economy in the Super Long-Run: Lead, Copper, and Shipwrecks." *JRA* 18: 361–72.

Delattre, Alfred-Louis. 1905. "Lettre à M. Ph. Berger, membre de l'Académie, inscriptions puniques." *CRAI* 49: 168–76.

Demetriou, Denise. 2012. *Negotiating Identity in the Ancient Mediterranean: The Archaic and Classical Greek Multiethnic Emporia*. Cambridge: Cambridge University Press.

Denzau, Arthur T., and Douglass C. North. 1994. "Shared Mental Models: Ideologies and Institutions." *Kyklos* 47: 3–31.

De Romanis, Federico. 2008. "*Cultores huius loci*: Sulle coabitazioni divine del *lucus Furrinae*." In *Culti orientali: Tra scavo e collezionismo*, edited by Beatrice Palma Venetucci. Rome: Artemide. 149–57.

De Vos, Mariette. 2013. "The Rural landscape of Thugga: Farms, Presses, Mills, and Transport." In *The Roman Agricultural Economy: Organization, Investment, and Production*, edited by Alan K. Bowman and Andrew I. Wilson. Oxford: Oxford University Press. 143–218.

Díaz-Bautista Cremades, Adolfo A. 2013. *El embargo ejecutivo en el proceso cognitorio romano (pignus in causa iudicati captum)*. Madrid: Marcial Pons.

Dijkstra, Jitse. 2015. "Religious Violence in Late Antique Egypt Reconsidered." *JECH* 5: 24–48.

Di Segni, Leah, Joseph Patrich, and Kenneth G. Holum. 2003. "A Schedule of Fees (*Sportulae*) for Official Services from Caesarea Maritima, Israel." *ZPE* 145: 273–300.

Docter, Roald F., et al. 2006. "Carthage Bir Massouda: Second Preliminary Report on the Bilateral Excavations of Ghent University and the Institut National du Patrimoine (2003–2004)." *BABesch* 81: 37–89.

Dubois, Charles. 1907. *Pouzzoles antique (histoire et topographie)*. Paris: Fontemoing.

Du Plessis, Paul J. 2015. *Borkowski's Textbook on Roman Law*, 5th edition. Oxford: Oxford University Press.

Durand, Xavier. 1997. *Des Grecs en Palestine au IIIe siècle avant Jésus-Christ: Le dossier syrien des archives de Zénon de Caunos (261–252)*. Paris: J. Gabalda.

Durliat, Jean. 1990. *De la ville antique à la ville byzantine: Le problème des subsistances*. Rome: École française de Rome.

Duthoy, Françoise, and Jiri Frel. 1996. "Observations sur le sanctuaire syrien du Janicule." In *Orientalia Sacra Urbis Romae: Dolichena et Heliopolitana: Recueil d'études archéologiques et historico-religieuses sur les cultes cosmopolites d'origine commagénienne et syrienne*, edited by Gloria M. Bellelli and Ugo Bianchi. Rome: L'Erma di Bretschneider. 289–303.

Earle, Timothy. 1991. "Property Rights and the Evolution of Chiefdoms." In *Chiefdoms: Power, Economy, and Ideology*, edited by Timothy Earle. Cambridge: Cambridge University Press. 71–99.

Edwards, Jeremy, and Sheilagh Ogilvie. 2012. "Contract Enforcement, Institutions and Social Capital: The Maghribi Traders Reappraised." *EHR* 65: 421–44.

Egberts, Arno. 1991. "The Chronology of the 'Report of Wenamun.'" *JEA* 77: 57–67.

Engen, Darel T. 2010. *Honor and Profit: Athenian Trade Policy and the Economy and Society of Greece, 415–307 B.C.E.* Ann Arbor: University of Michigan Press.

Erdkamp, Paul. 2016. "Economic Growth in the Roman Mediterranean World: An Early Goodbye to Malthus?" *EEH* 60: 1–20.

Érdy, János. 1856. *De tabulis ceratis in Transylvania repertis*. Pest: Ferdinánd Eggenberger.

Errington, R. Malcolm. 1988. "Aspects of Roman Acculturation in the East under the Republic." In *Alte Geschichte und Wissenschaftsgeschichte: Festschrift für Karl Christ zum 65. Geburtstag*, edited by Peter Kneissl and Volker Losemann. Darmstadt: Wissenschaftliche Buchgesellschaft. 140–57.

Fales, F. Mario. 2017. "Phoenicia in the Neo-Assyrian Period: An Updated Overview." *SAAB* 23: 181–295.

Ferjaoui, Ahmed. 1992. *Recherches sur les relations entre l'Orient phénicien et Carthage*. Tunis: Fondation Nationale "Beït Al-Hikma."

Finley, Moses I. 1965. "Technical Innovation and Economic Progress in the Ancient World." *EHR* 18: 29–45.

Finley, Moses I. 1999. *The Ancient Economy*, 2nd edition with a foreword by Ian Morris. Berkeley: University of California Press.

Fischer-Bovet, Christelle. 2014. *Army and Society in Ptolemaic Egypt*. Cambridge: Cambridge University Press.

———. Forthcoming. "Ptolemaic Imperialism in Southern Anatolia (Lycia, Pamphylia and Cilicia)." In *Building a New World Order: Hellenistic Monarchies in the Ancient Mediterranean World*, edited by Mark H. Munn. Berlin: De Gruyter.

Fishwick, Duncan. 1991. *The Imperial Cult in the Latin West*, vol. 2.1. Leiden: Brill.

Flohr, Miko. 2017. "Quantifying Pompeii: Population, Inequality, and the Urban Economy." In *The Economy of Pompeii*, edited by Miko Flohr and Andrew I. Wilson. Oxford: Oxford University Press. 53–84.

Floriani Squarciapino, Maria. 1962. *I culti orientali ad Ostia*. Leiden: Brill.

Fogel, Robert W. 2004. *The Escape from Hunger and Premature Death, 1700–2100: Europe, America, and the Third World*. Cambridge: Cambridge University Press.

Frankfurter, David. 1998. *Religion in Roman Egypt: Assimilation and Resistance*. Princeton: Princeton University Press.

Frey-Kupper, Suzanne. 2014. "Coins and their Use in the Punic Mediterranean: Case Studies from Carthage to Italy from the Fourth to the First Century BCE." In *The Punic Mediterranean: Identities and Identification from Phoenician Settlement to Roman Rule*, edited by Josephine Crawley Quinn and Nicholas C. Vella. Cambridge: Cambridge University Press. 76–110.

Friedman, Hannah. Forthcoming. "Atmospheric Pollution Proxies for Roman Metal Production." In *Mining, Metal Supply, and Coinage in the Roman World*, edited by Alan K. Bowman and Andrew I. Wilson. Oxford: Oxford University Press.

Frier, Bruce W. 1985. *The Rise of the Roman Jurists: Studies in Cicero's* Pro Caecina. Princeton: Princeton University Press.

Fuhrmann, Christopher J. 2012. *Policing the Roman Empire: Soldiers, Administration, and Public Order*. Oxford: Oxford University Press.

Gabrielsen, Vincent. 2001. "The Rhodian Associations and Economic Activity." In *Hellenistic Economies*, edited by Zofia H. Archibald, John Davies, Vincent Gabrielsen, and Graham J. Oliver. London, New York: Routledge. 215–44.

———. 2003. "Piracy and the Slave-Trade." In *A Companion to the Hellenistic World*, edited by Andrew Erskine. Oxford: Blackwell. 389–404.

———. 2007. "Brotherhoods of Faith and Provident Planning: The Non-Public Associations of the Greek World." *MHR* 22: 183–210.

———. 2011. "Profitable Partnerships: Monopolies, Traders, Kings, and Cities." In *The Economies of Hellenistic Societies, Third to First Centuries BC*, edited by Zosia H. Archibald, John K. Davies, and Vincent Gabrielsen. Oxford: Oxford University Press. 216–50.

———. 2013. "Rhodes and the Ptolemaic Kingdom: The Commercial Infrastructure." In *The Ptolemies, the Sea and the Nile: Studies in Waterborne Power*, edited by Kostas Buraselis, Mary Stefanou, and Dorothy J. Thompson. Cambridge: Cambridge University Press. 66–81.

———. 2016. "Be Faithful and Prosper: Associations, Trust and the Economy of Security." In *Antike Wirtschaft und ihre kulturelle Prägung*, edited by Kerstin Droß-Krüpe, Sabine Föllinger, and Kai Ruffing. Wiesbaden: Harrassowitz. 87–111.

Gaddis, Michael. 2005. *There Is No Crime for Those Who Have Christ: Religious Violence in the Christian Roman Empire*. Berkeley: University of California Press.

Galsterer, Hartmut. 1986. "Roman Law in the Provinces: Some Problems of Transmission." In *L'impero romano e le strutture economiche e sociali delle province*, edited by Michael H. Crawford. Como: New Press. 13–27.

Garland, Robert. 1987. *The Piraeus from the Fifth to the First Century B.C.* Ithaca, NY: Cornell University Press.

Garnsey, Peter. 1970. *Social Status and Legal Privilege in the Roman Empire*. Oxford: Clarendon Press.

———. 1984. "Religious Toleration in Classical Antiquity." In *Persecution and Toleration*, edited by William J. Sheils. Oxford: Blackwell. 1–27.

———. 1988. *Famine and Food Supply in the Graeco-Roman World: Responses to Risk and Crisis*. Cambridge: Cambridge University Press.

Gauckler, Paul. 1912. *Le sanctuaire syrien du Janicule*. Paris: A. Picard.

Gawlikowski, Michal. 1994. "Palmyra as a Trading Centre." *Iraq* 56: 27–33.

Gelderblom, Oscar. 2013. *Cities of Commerce: The Institutional Foundations of International Trade in the Low Countries, 1250–1650*. Princeton: Princeton University Press.

Giannecchini, Monica, and Jacopo Moggi-Cecchi. 2008. "Stature in Archeological Samples from Central Italy: Methodological Issues and Diachronic Changes." *AJPA* 135: 284–92.

Giardino, Claudio. 1992. "Nuragic Sardinia and the Mediterranean: Metallurgy and Maritime Traffic." In *Sardinia in the Mediterranean: A Footprint in the Sea. Studies in Sardinian Archaeology Presented to Miriam S. Balmuth*, edited by Robert H. Tykot and Tamsey K. Andrews. Sheffield, UK: Sheffield Academic Press. 304–16.

Gibson, John C.L. 1982. *Textbook of Syrian Semitic Inscriptions*, vol. 3: *Phoenician Inscriptions Including in the Mixed Dialect of Arslan Tash*. Oxford: Clarendon Press.

Glucker, Carol A.M. 1987. *The City of Gaza in the Roman and Byzantine Periods* (= BAR International Series 325). Oxford: BAR International Series.

Goddard, Christophe J. 2008. "Nuove osservazioni sul santuario cosiddetto 'siriaco' al Gianicolo." In *Culti orientali: Tra scavo e collezionismo*, edited by Beatrice Palma Venetucci. Rome: Artemide. 165–73.

Goitein, Shelemo D. 1967–88. *A Mediterranean Society: The Jewish Communities of the Arab World as Portrayed in the Documents of the Cairo Geniza*, 5 vols. Berkeley: University of California Press.

———. 1973. *Letters of Medieval Jewish Traders*. Princeton: Princeton University Press.

Goldberg, Jessica L. 2012. *Trade and Institutions in the Medieval Mediterranean: The Geniza Merchants and their Business World*. Cambridge: Cambridge University Press.

Gómez Toscano, Francisco. 2002. "La ocupación protohistórica entre el Guadiana y el Guadalquivir: Del mito a la realidad." *SPAL* 11: 151–59.

Goodhue, Nicholas. 1975. *The Lucus Furrinae and the Syrian Sanctuary on the Janiculum*. Amsterdam: A.M. Hakkert.

Grainger, John D. 1991. *Hellenistic Phoenicia*. Oxford: Clarendon Press.

Greene, Kevin. 2000. "Technological Innovation and Economic Progress in the Ancient World: M.I. Finley Reconsidered." *EHR* 53: 29–59.

Greif, Avner. 1989. "Reputation and Coalitions in Medieval Trade: Evidence on the Maghribi Traders." *JEH* 49: 857–82.

———. 2006. *Institutions and the Path to the Modern Economy: Lessons from Medieval Trade.* Cambridge: Cambridge University Press.

———. 2012. "The Maghribi Traders: A Reappraisal?" *EHR* 65: 445–69.

Greig, Gary G. 1990. "The *sḏm=f* and *sḏm.n=f* in the Story of Sinuhe and the Theory of the Nominal (Emphatic) Verbs." In *Studies in Egyptology Presented to Miriam Lichtheim*, edited by Sarah Israelit-Groll, 2 vols. Jerusalem: Magnes Press. 264–348.

Griffin, Miriam, and Brad Inwood, trans. 2011. *Seneca, On Benefits.* Chicago: University of Chicago Press.

Guzzo Amadasi, Maria Giulia, and Vassos Karageorghis. 1977. *Fouilles de Kition III: Inscriptions Phéniciennes.* Nicosia: Zavallis Press.

Haensch, Rudolf. 1996. "Die Verwendung von Siegeln bei Dokumenten der kaiserzeitlichen Reichsadministration." In *Archives et Sceaux du Monde Hellénistique / Archivi e Sigilli nel Mondo Ellenistico*, edited by Marie-Françoise Boussac and Antonio Invenizzi. Athens: École française d'Athènes. 449–96.

———. 2015. "From Free to Fee? Judicial Fees and Other Litigation Costs during the High Empire and Late Antiquity." In *Law and Transaction Costs in the Ancient Economy*, edited by Dennis P. Kehoe, David M. Ratzan, and Uri Yiftach. Ann Arbor: University of Michigan Press. 253–72.

Hahn, Johannes. 2004. *Gewalt und religiöser Konflikt: Studien zu den Auseinandersetzungen zwischen Christen, Heiden und Juden im Osten des Römischen Reiches (von Konstantin bis Theodosius II.).* Berlin: Akademie.

Hamarneh, Saleh K. 1971. "The Ancient Monuments of Alexandria According to Accounts by Medieval Arab Authors (IX–XV Century)." *FO* 13: 77–110.

Hansen, Mogens H. 2002. "Was the *Polis* a State or a Stateless Society?" In *Even More Studies in the Ancient Greek Polis*, edited by Thomas Heine Nielsen. Stuttgart: Franz Steiner. 17–47.

———. 2013. "Greek City-States." In *The Oxford Handbook of the State in the Ancient Near East and Mediterranean*, edited by Peter F. Bang and Walter Scheidel. Oxford: Oxford University Press. 259–78.

Harland, Philip A. 2009. *Dynamics of Identity in the World of the Early Christians: Associations, Judaeans, and Cultural Minorities.* London: T&T Clark.

Harper, George McLean Jr. 1928. "A Study in the Commercial Relations between Egypt and Syria in the Third Century before Christ." *AJP* 49: 1–35.

Harper, Kyle. 2017. *The Fate of Rome: Climate, Disease, and the End of an Empire.* Princeton: Princeton University Press.

Harré, H. Romano. 1985. *The Philosophies of Science*, 2nd edition. Oxford: Oxford University Press.

Harris, William V. 1979. *War and Imperialism in Republican Rome, 327–70 B.C.* Oxford: Clarendon Press.

———, ed. 2013. *The Ancient Mediterranean Environment between Science and History.* Leiden: Brill.

———. 2016. "Religion on the Battlefield: From the *Saxa Rubra* to the *Frigidus*." In *Miscellanea di studi storico-religiosi in onore di Filippo Coarelli nel suo 80° anniversario*, edited by Valentino Gasparini. Stuttgart: Franz Steiner. 437–50.

————. 2017. "Rome at Sea: The Beginnings of Roman Naval Power." *Greece & Rome* 64: 14–26.

Hauben, Hans. 2006. "Kriton, stolarque au service d'Apollonios le diœcète." *Ancient Society* 36: 175–219.

Hefele, Charles-Joseph. 1907–52. *Histoire des Conciles d'après les documents originaux*, 11 vols. Paris: Letouzey et Ané.

Herman, Gabriel. 2006. *Morality and Behaviour in Democratic Athens: A Social History*. Cambridge: Cambridge University Press.

Hicks, John. 1969. *A Theory of Economic History*. Oxford: Clarendon Press.

Hillman, Aubrey L., et al. 2017. "Lead Pollution Resulting from Roman Gold Extraction in Northwestern Spain." *Holocene* 27: 1465–74.

Hirt, Alfred M. 2010. *Imperial Mines and Quarries in the Roman World: Organizational Aspects 27 BC–AD 235*. Oxford: Oxford University Press.

Hodos, Tamar. 2006. *Local Responses to Colonization in the Iron Age Mediterranean*. London: Routledge.

Hollander, David B. 2007. *Money in the Late Roman Republic*. Leiden: Brill.

————. 2015. "Risky Business: Traders in the Roman World." In *Traders in the Ancient Mediterranean*, edited by Timothy Howe. Chicago: Ares. 141–72.

Holt, Emily M. 2014. "Nuragic Culture and Architecture (Bronze Age to Iron Age)." In *The Encyclopedia of Global Archaeology*, edited by Claire Smith. New York: Springer. 5538–45.

Hong, Sungmin, Jean-Pierre Candelone, Clair C. Patterson, and Claude F. Boutron. 1994. "Greenland Ice Evidence of Hemispheric Lead Pollution Two Millennia Ago by Greek and Roman Civilizations." *Science* 265: 1841–43.

Hopkins, Keith. 1978. *Conquerors and Slaves*. Cambridge: Cambridge University Press.

————. 1980. "Taxes and Trade in the Roman Empire (200 B.C.–A.D. 400)." *JRS* 70: 101–25.

————. 1998. "Christian Number and Its Implications." *JECS* 6: 185–226.

————. 2002. "Rome, Taxes, Rents and Trade." In *The Ancient Economy*, edited by Walter Scheidel and Sitta von Reden. New York: Routledge. 190–230.

Horden, Peregrine, and Nicholas Purcell. 2000. *The Corrupting Sea: A Study of Mediterranean History*. Oxford: Blackwell.

Humbert, Jean-Baptiste, ed. 2000. *Gaza Méditerranéenne: Histoire et archéologie en Palestine*. Paris: Éditions Errance.

Hunt, David. 1993. "Christianizing the Roman Empire: The Evidence of the Code." In *The Theodosian Code: Studies in the Imperial Law of Late Antiquity*, edited by Jill Harries and Ian N. Wood. Ithaca, NY: Cornell University Press. 143–58.

Hurst, Henry, and Lawrence E. Stager. 1978. "A Metropolitan Landscape: The Late Punic Port of Carthage." *WA* 9: 334–46.

Iara, Kristine. 2015. "Senatorial Aristocracy: How Individual Is Individual Religiosity?" In *Group Identity and Religious Individuality in Late Antiquity*, edited by Éric Rebillard and Jörg Rüpke. Washington, DC: Catholic University of America Press. 165–214.

Irwin, Douglas A. 1991. "Mercantilism as Strategic Trade Policy: The Anglo-Dutch Rivalry for the East India Trade." *JPE* 99: 1296–314.

Jakab, Éva. 2015. "Sale and Community from the Roman World." In *Sale and Community. Documents from the Ancient World: Individuals' Autonomy and State Interference in the Ancient World*, edited by Éva Jakab. Budapest: Edizioni Università di Trieste. 213–31.

Jigoulov, Vadim S. 2010. *The Social History of Achaemenid Phoenicia: Being a Phoenician, Negotiating Empires.* London: Routledge.

Jones, Arnold H.M. 1970. *A History of Rome through the Fifth Century*, vol. 2. *The Empire.* London: Palgrave Macmillan.

Jones, Arnold H.M., John R. Martindale, and John Morris. 1971–92. *The Prosopography of the Later Roman Empire*, 3 vols. Cambridge: Cambridge University Press.

Jones, Geoffrey. 2007. "Globalization." In *The Oxford Handbook of Business History*, edited by Geoffrey Jones and Jonathan Zeitlin. Oxford: Oxford University Press. 141–68.

Jongman, Willem M. 1988. *The Economy and Society of Pompeii.* Amsterdam: J.C. Gieben.

———. 2006. "The Rise and Fall of the Roman Economy: Population, Rents and Entitlement." In *Ancient Economies, Modern Methodologies: Archaeology, Comparative History, Models and Institutions*, edited by Peter F. Bang, Mamoru Ikeguchi, and Hartmut G. Ziche. Bari: Edipuglia. 237–54.

———. 2007a. "Gibbon Was Right: The Decline and Fall of the Roman Economy." In *Crises and the Roman Empire*, edited by Olivier Hekster, Gerda de Kleijn, and Daniëlle Slootjes. Leiden: Brill. 183–99.

———. 2007b. "The Early Roman Empire: Consumption." In *The Cambridge Economic History of the Greco-Roman World*, edited by Walter Scheidel, Ian Morris, and Richard P. Saller. Cambridge: Cambridge University Press. 592–618.

———. 2014. "Re-constructing the Roman Economy." In *The Cambridge History of Capitalism*, vol. 1: *The Rise of Capitalism: From Ancient Origins to 1848*, edited by Larry Neal and Jeffrey G. Williamson. Cambridge: Cambridge University Press. 75–100.

———. 2016. "Rome: Standard of Living." Paper read at Collège de France, Paris, November 16. https://www.college-de-france.fr/site/jean-pierre-brun/guestlecturer-2016-11-16-17h00.htm.

Kaizer, Ted. 2015. "On the Origins of Palmyra and Its Trade." (Review of *Palmyra's Reichtum durch Weltweiten Handel*, edited by Andreas Schmidt-Colinet and Waleed al-As'ad). *JRA* 28: 881–88.

Kajanto, Iiro. 1965. *The Latin Cognomina.* Helsinki: Keskuskirjapaino.

Kaser, Max, and Karl Hackl. 1996. *Das römische Zivilprozessrecht*, 2nd edition. Munich: C.H. Beck.

Katzenstein, H. Jacob. 1982. "Gaza in the Egyptian Texts of the New Kingdom." *JAOS* 102: 111–13.

———. 1983. "The Phoenician Term Ḥubūr in the Report of Wen-Amon." In *Atti del I congresso internazionale di studi fenici e punici*, vol. 2. Rome: Consiglio Nazionale delle Ricerche. 599–602.

———. 1997. *The History of Tyre from the Beginning of the Second Millenium B.C.E. until the Fall of the Neo-Babylonian Empire in 539 B.C.E.*, 2nd edition. Jerusalem: Ben-Gurion University of the Negev Press.

Kay, Philip. 2014. *Rome's Economic Revolution.* Oxford: Oxford University Press.

Kehoe, Dennis P. 2007. "The Early Roman Empire: Production." In *The Cambridge Economic History of the Greco-Roman World*, edited by Walter Scheidel, Ian Morris, and Richard P. Saller. Cambridge: Cambridge University Press. 543–69.

———. 2015. "Contracts, Agency, and Transaction Costs in the Roman Economy." In *Law and Transaction Costs in the Ancient Economy*, edited by Dennis P. Kehoe, David M. Ratzan, and Uri Yiftach. Ann Arbor: University of Michigan Press. 231–52.

Kent, John H. 1948. "The Temple Estates of Delos, Rheneia, and Mykonos." *Hesperia* 17: 243–338.

Keynes, John Maynard. 1920. *The Economic Consequences of the Peace*. London: Macmillan.

———. 1930. *A Treatise on Money*, 2 vols. London: Macmillan.

Kitchen, Kenneth. 2001. "Economies in Ancient Arabia: From Alexander to the Augustans." In *Hellenistic Economies*, edited by Zofia H. Archibald, John Davies, Vincent Gabrielsen, and Graham J. Oliver. London: Routledge. 157–73.

Kloppenborg, John S. 2006. *The Tenants in the Vineyard: Ideology, Economics, and Agrarian Conflict in Jewish Palestine*. Tübingen: Mohr Siebeck.

Koepke, Nikola, and Joerg Baten. 2005. "The Biological Standard of Living in Europe during the Last Two Millennia." *EREH* 9: 61–95.

Kourou, Nota. 2003. "Rhodes: The Phoenician Issue Revisited: Phoenicians at Vroulia?" In Πλόες. *Sea Routes: Interconnections in the Mediterranean 16th–6th c. BC*, edited by Nicholas C. Stampolidis and Vassos Karageorghis. Athens: University of Crete and the A.G. Leventis Foundation. 249–62.

Krahmalkov, Charles R. 2000. *Phoenician-Punic Dictionary* (*Studia Phoenicia* 15). Leuven: Peeters and Departement Oosterse Studies.

Kron, J. Geoffrey. 2005. "Anthropometry, Physical Anthropology, and the Reconstruction of Ancient Health, Nutrition, and Living Standards." *Historia* 54: 68–83.

Lambert, Stephen D. 2006. "Athenian State Laws and Decrees, 352/1–322/1: III Decrees Honouring Foreigners. A. Citizenship, Proxeny and Euergesy." *ZPE* 158: 115–58.

———. 2012. *Inscribed Athenian Laws and Decrees 352/1–322/1 BC: Epigraphical Essays*. Leiden: Brill.

Lancel, Serge. 1992. *Carthage*. Paris: Librairie Arthème Fayard.

Landa, Janet Tai. 1994. *Trust, Ethnicity, and Identity: Beyond the New Institutional Economics of Ethnic Trading Networks, Contract Law, and Gift-Exchange*. Ann Arbor: University of Michigan Press.

Lapeyre, Gabriel-Guillaume. 1939. "Les fouilles du Musée Lavigerie à Carthage de 1935 à 1939." *CRAI* 83: 294–304.

Lazer, Estelle. 2009. *Resurrecting Pompeii*. London: Routledge.

Leeson, Peter T. 2014. *Anarchy Unbound: Why Self-Governance Works Better Than You Think*. Cambridge: Cambridge University Press.

Liebeschuetz, J.H. Wolf G. 2015. *East and West in Late Antiquity: Invasion, Settlement, Ethnogenesis and Conflicts of Religion*. Leiden: Brill.

Liebesny, Herbert. 1936. "Ein Erlass des Königs Ptolemaios II Philadelphos über die Deklaration von Vieh und Sklaven in Syrien und Phönikien (PER Inv. Nr. 24.552 gr.)." *Aegyptus* 16: 257–88.

Lightfoot, Jane L., ed and trans. 2003. *Lucian: On the Syrian Goddess*. Oxford: Oxford University Press.

Lipiński, Edward. 2004. *Itineraria Phoenicia* (*Studia Phoenicia* 18). Leuven: Peeters and Departement Oosterse Studies.

Litewski, Wiesław. 1974. "*Pignus in causa iudicati captum*." *SDHI* 40: 205–302.

Lo Cascio, Elio. 2006. "The Role of the State in the Roman Economy: Making Use of the New Institutional Economics." In *Ancient Economies, Modern Methodologies: Archaeology, Comparative History, Models and Institutions*, edited by Peter F. Bang, Mamoru Ikeguchi, and Hartmut G. Ziche. Bari: Edipuglia. 215–34.

Ma, John. 2013. "Hellenistic Empires." In *The Oxford Handbook of the State in the Ancient Near East and Mediterranean*, edited by Peter F. Bang and Walter Scheidel. Oxford: Oxford University Press. 324–57.

Mack, William. 2015. *Proxeny and Polis: Institutional Networks in the Ancient Greek World*. Oxford: Oxford University Press.

MacKendrick, Paul. 1975. *The Dacian Stones Speak*. Chapel Hill: University of North Carolina Press.

Mackil, Emily. 2015. "The Greek *Polis* and *Koinon*." In *Fiscal Regimes and the Political Economy of Premodern States*, edited by Andrew Monson and Walter Scheidel. Cambridge: Cambridge University Press. 469–91.

MacKinnon, Michael. 2015. "Changes in Animal Husbandry as a Consequence of Developing Social and Economic Patterns from the Roman Mediterranean Context." In *Ownership and Exploitation of Land and Natural Resources in the Roman World*, edited by Paul Erdkamp, Koenraad Verboven, and Arjan Zuiderhoek. Oxford: Oxford University Press. 249–73.

MacMullen, Ramsay. 1982. "The Epigraphic Habit in the Roman Empire." *AJP* 103: 233–46.

———. 1984. *Christianizing the Roman Empire (A.D. 100–400)*. New Haven, CT: Yale University Press.

———. 1988. *Corruption and the Decline of Rome*. New Haven, CT: Yale University Press.

Maehler, Herwig. 2004. "Alexandria, the Mouseion, and Cultural Identity." In *Alexandria, Real and Imagined*, edited by Anthony Hirst and Michael Silk. Aldershot, UK: Ashgate. 1–14.

Malaise, Michel. 1972. *Les conditions de pénétration et de diffusion des cultes égyptiens en Italie*. Leiden: Brill.

———. 1984. "La diffusion des cultes égyptiens dans les provinces européennes de l'Empire romain." *ANRW* 2.17.3: 1615–91.

Manders, Erika. 2012. *Coining Images of Power Patterns in the Representation of Roman Emperors on Imperial Coinage, A.D. 193–284*. Leiden: Brill.

Manfredi, Lorenza-Ilia. 2003. *La politica amministrativa di Cartagine in Africa*. Rome: Accademia nazionale dei Lincei.

Manning, Joseph G. 2003. *Land and Power in Ptolemaic Egypt: The Structure of Land Tenure*. Cambridge: Cambridge University Press.

———. 2004. "Property Rights and Contracting in Ptolemaic Egypt." *JITE* 160: 758–64.

———. 2005. "The Relationship of Evidence to Models in the Ptolemaic Economy (332 BC–30 BC)." In *The Ancient Economy: Evidence and Models*, edited by Joseph G. Manning and Ian Morris. Stanford, CA: Stanford University Press. 163–86.

———. 2008. "Coinage as 'Code' in Ptolemaic Egypt." In *The Monetary Systems of the Greeks and Romans*, edited by William V. Harris. Oxford: Oxford University Press. 84–111.

———. 2015a. "Hellenistic Trade(rs)." In *Traders in the Ancient Mediterranean*, edited by Timothy Howe. Chicago: Ares. 101–39.

———. 2015b. "Ptolemaic Governance and Transaction Costs." In *Law and Transaction Costs in the Ancient Economy*, edited by Dennis P. Kehoe, David M. Ratzan, and Uri Yiftach. Ann Arbor: University of Michigan Press. 99–117.

———. 2018. *The Open Sea: The Economic Life of the Ancient Mediterranean World from the Iron Age to the Rise of Rome*. Princeton: Princeton University Press.

———. Forthcoming. "Courts, Justice and Culture in Ptolemaic Law, or the Rise of the Egyptian Jurists." In *Administration, Law and Administrative Law*, edited by Heather D. Baker, Michael Jursa, and Hans Taeuber. Vienna: Austrian Academy of Sciences.

Marfoe, Leon. 1979. "The Integrative Transformation: Patterns of Sociopolitical Organization in Southern Syria." *BASOR* 234: 1–42.

Markoe, Glenn E. 2000. *Phoenicians*. Avon: Bath Press.

Masson, Olivier. 1969. "Recherches sur les Phéniciens dans le monde hellénistique." *BCH* 93: 679–700.

Masson, Olivier, and Maurice Sznycer. 1972. *Recherches sur les Phéniciens à Chypre*. Geneva: Librairie Droz.

Matthews, John F. 1984. "The Tax Law of Palmyra: Evidence for Economic History in a City of the Roman East." *JRS* 74: 157–80.

Mazza, Federico. 1988. "The Phoenicians as Seen by the Ancient World." In *The Phoenicians*, edited by Sabatino Moscati. New York: Abbeville Press. 548–67.

McCloskey, Deirdre N. 2016. "Max U *versus* Humanomics: A Critique of Neo-Institutionalism." *JOIE* 12: 1–27.

McConnell, Joseph R., et al. 2018. "Lead Pollution Recorded in Greenland Ice Indicates European Emissions Tracked Plagues, Wars, and Imperial Expansion during Antiquity." *PNAS* 115: 5726–31.

McCormick, Michael. 2001. *Origins of the European Economy: Communications and Commerce, A.D. 300–900*. Cambridge: Cambridge University Press.

———. 2012. "Movements and Markets in the First Millennium: Information, Containers, and Shipwrecks." In *Trade and Markets in Byzantium*, edited by Cécile Morrisson. Washington, DC: Dumbarton Oaks Research Library and Collection. 51–98.

McGuire, Martin C., and Mancur Olson. 1996. "The Economics of Autocracy and Majority Rule: The Invisible Hand and the Use of Force." *JEL* 34: 72–96.

McKenzie, Judith S., Sheila Gibson, and Andres T. Reyes. 2004. "Reconstructing the Serapeum in Alexandria from the Archaeological Evidence." *JRS* 94: 73–121.

McKenzie, Judith S., et al. 2013. Manar al-Athar Photo-Archive, Oxford. Available at http://www.manar-al-athar.ox.ac.uk.

Meiggs, Russell. 1973. *Roman Ostia*. Oxford: Clarendon Press.

Meyer, Elizabeth A. 2004. *Legitimacy and Law in the Roman World*. Cambridge: Cambridge University Press.

———. 2016. "Evidence and Argument: The Truth of Prestige and Its Performance." In *The*

Oxford Handbook of Roman Law and Society, edited by Paul J. du Plessis, Clifford Ando, and Kaius Tuori. Oxford: Oxford University Press. 270–82.

Meyer, Jørgen Christian. 2006. "Trade in Bronze Age and Iron Age Empires, a Comparison." In *Ancient Economies, Modern Methodologies: Archaeology, Comparative History, Models and Institutions*, edited by Peter F. Bang, Mamoru Ikeguchi, and Hartmut G. Ziche. Bari: Edipuglia. 89–106.

Migeotte, Léopold. 1984. *L'emprunt public dans les cités grecques: Recueil des documents et analyse critique*. Paris: Les Belles Lettres.

Mihailescu-Bîrliba, Lucrețiu. 2011. Ex toto orbe Romano: *Immigration into Roman Dacia*. Leuven: Peeters.

Millar, Fergus. 2006. "The Phoenician Cities: A Case-Study of Hellenisation." *Rome, the Greek World, and the East*, vol. 3: *The Greek World, the Jews, and the East*, edited by Hannah M. Cotton and Guy M. Rogers. Chapel Hill: University of North Carolina Press. 32–50.

Mishra, Pankaj. 2017. *Age of Anger: A History of the Present*. New York: Farrar, Straus and Giroux.

Mokyr, Joel. 2002. *The Gifts of Athena: Historical Origins of the Knowledge Economy*. Princeton: Princeton University Press.

———. 2009. *The Enlightened Economy: An Economic History of Britain 1700–1850*. New Haven, CT: Yale University Press.

———. 2016. *A Culture of Growth: The Origins of the Modern Economy*. Princeton: Princeton University Press.

Monson, Andrew. 2015. "Hellenistic Empires." In *Fiscal Regimes and the Political Economy of Premodern States*, edited by Andrew Monson and Walter Scheidel. Cambridge: Cambridge University Press. 169–207.

Mooren, Leon. 1983. "The Nature of the Hellenistic Monarchy." In *Egypt and the Hellenistic World: Proceedings of the International Colloquium, Leuven, 24–26 May 1982*, edited by Edmond van 't Dack, Peter van Dessel, and Willem van Gucht. Leuven: Publications de l'Institut Orientaliste. 205–40.

Morel, Jean-Paul. 1969. "Kerkouane, ville punique du cap Bon: Remarques archéologiques et historiques." *MEFRA* 81: 473–518.

Morelli, Donato. 1956. "Gli stranieri in Rodi." *SCO* 5: 126–90.

Moretti, Luigi. 1953. *Iscrizioni agonistiche greche*. Rome: Angelo Signorelli.

Morris, Ian. 2004. "Economic Growth in Ancient Greece." *JITE* 160: 709–42.

———. 2013. "Greek Multicity States." In *The Oxford Handbook of the State in the Ancient Near East and Mediterranean*, edited by Peter F. Bang and Walter Scheidel. Oxford: Oxford University Press. 279–303.

Mouritsen, Henrik. 2013. "The Roman Empire I: The Republic." In *The Oxford Handbook of the State in the Ancient Near East and Mediterranean*, edited by Peter F. Bang and Walter Scheidel. Oxford: Oxford University Press. 383–411.

Mrozek, Stanisław. 1977. "Die Goldbergwerke im römischen Dazien." *ANRW* 2.6: 95–109.

Mussies, Gerard. 1990. "Marnas, God of Gaza." *ANRW* 2.18.4: 2413–57.

Musurillo, Herbert A. 1954. *The Acts of the Pagan Martyrs: Acta Alexandrinorum*. Oxford: Clarendon Press.

Nachtergael, Georges. 1998. "Un alabastre ptolémaïque inscrit." *ZPE* 123: 145–48.

Negbi, Ora. 1992. "Early Phoenician Presence in the Mediterranean Islands: A Reappraisal." *AJA* 96: 599–615.

Neigebaur, J.D. Ferdinand. 1851. *Dacien. Aus den Ueberresten des klassischen Alterthums, mit besonderer Rücksicht auf Siebenbürgen*. Kronstadt: Johann Gött.

Neville, Ann. 2007. *Mountains of Silver and Rivers of Gold: The Phoenicians in Iberia*. Oxford: Oxbow Books.

Niemeyer, Hans Georg. 1990. "The Phoenicians in the Mediterranean: A Non-Greek Model for Expansion and Settlement in Antiquity." In *Greek Colonists and Native Populations: Proceedings of the First Australian Congress of Classical Archaeology Held in Honour of Emeritus Professor A. D. Trendall*, edited by Jean-Paul Descoeudres. Oxford: Clarendon Press. 469–89.

Noethlichs, Karl L. 2015. "The Legal Framework of Religious Identity in the Roman Empire." In *Group Identity and Religious Individuality in Late Antiquity*, edited by Éric Rebillard and Jörg Rüpke. Washington, DC: Catholic University of America Press. 13–27.

North, Douglass C. 1981. *Structure and Change in Economic History*. New York: W.W. Norton and Company.

———. 1990. *Institutions, Institutional Change and Economic Performance*. Cambridge: Cambridge University Press.

———. 2005. *Understanding the Process of Economic Change*. Princeton: Princeton University Press.

North, Douglass C., and Robert P. Thomas. 1973. *The Rise of the Western World: A New Economic History*. Cambridge: Cambridge University Press.

North, Douglass C., John J. Wallis, and Barry R. Weingast. 2009. *Violence and Social Orders: A Conceptual Framework for Interpreting Recorded Human History*. Cambridge: Cambridge University Press.

Noy, David. 2000. *Foreigners at Rome: Citizens and Strangers*. London: Duckworth/Classical Press of Wales.

Ober, Josiah. 2015. *The Rise and Fall of Classical Greece*. Princeton: Princeton University Press.

Ogilvie, Sheilagh C. 2011. *Institutions and European Trade: Merchant Guilds, 1000–1800*. Cambridge: Cambridge University Press.

Olson, Mancur. 1991. "Autocracy, Democracy, and Prosperity." In *Strategy and Choice*, edited by Richard J. Zeckhauser. Cambridge, MA: MIT Press. 131–57.

———. 2000. *Power and Prosperity: Outgrowing Communist and Capitalist Dictatorships*. New York: Basic Books.

Orrieux, Claude. 1983. *Les papyrus de Zénon: L'horizon d'un grec en Égypte au IIIe siècle avant J.C.* Paris: Éditions MACULA.

———. 1985. *Zénon de Caunos*, parépidèmos, *et le destin grec*. Paris: Les Belles Lettres.

Osborne, Robin G. 2009. *Greece in the Making 1200–479 BC*, 2nd edition. London: Routledge.

Panagopoulou, Katerina. 2016. "Gold in Ptolemaic Egypt: Exchange Practices in Light of P.Cair. Zen I 59021." *ZPE* 197: 179–90.

Pappa, Eleftheria. 2013. *Early Iron Age Exchanges in the West: Phoenicians in the Mediterranean and the Atlantic*. Leuven: Peeters.

Parker, Anthony J. 1992. *Ancient Shipwrecks of the Mediterranean and the Roman Provinces*. London: Tempus Reparatum.

Parpola, Simo, and Kazuko Watanabe. 1988. *State Archives of Assyria*, vol. 2: *Neo-Assyrian Treaties and Loyalty Oaths*. Helsinki: Helsinki University Press.

Pérez Macías, Juan Aurelio. 1996–97. "Pico del Oro (Tharsis, Huelva): Contraargumentos sobre la crisis metalúrgica tartésica." *Arx* 2–3: 93–106.

Pestman, Pieter W. 1981. *A Guide to the Zenon Archive*. Leiden: Brill.

Pharr, Clyde, trans. 1952. *The Theodosian Code and Novels and the Sirmondian Constitutions*. Princeton: Princeton University Press.

Pilkington, Nathan L. 2013. "An Archaeological History of Carthaginian Imperialism." Diss. Columbia University.

Piso, Ioan. 2004. "Gli Illiri ad Alburnus Maior." In *Dall'Adriatico al Danubio: L'Illirico nell'età greca e romana*, edited by Gianpaolo Urso. Pisa: Edizioni ETS. 271–307.

Pólay, Elemér. 1971. "Der *status civitatis*, der Ursprung und die Berufe der in den siebenbürgischen Wachstafeln vorkommenden Personen." *JJP* 16–17: 71–83.

———. 1982. "Verträge auf Wachstafeln aus dem römischen Dakien." *ANRW* 2.14: 509–23.

Posner, Eric A. 2000. *Law and Social Norms*. Cambridge, MA: Harvard University Press.

Potter, David S. 2014. *The Roman Empire at Bay: AD 180–395*, 2nd edition. London, New York: Routledge.

Prag, Jonathan R.W. 2014. "*Phoinix* and *Poenus*: Usage in Antiquity." In *The Punic Mediterranean: Identities and Identification from Phoenician Settlement to Roman Rule*, edited by Josephine Crawley Quinn and Nicholas C. Vella. Cambridge: Cambridge University Press. 11–23.

Rapp, Claudia. 2000. "The Elite Status of Bishops in Late Antiquity in Ecclesiastical, Spiritual, and Social Contexts." *Arethusa* 33: 379–99.

———. 2001. "Mark the Deacon, *Life of St. Porphyry of Gaza*." In *Medieval Hagiography, an Anthology*, edited by Thomas Head. London: Routledge. 53–75.

Ratzan, David M. 2015. "Transaction Costs and Contract in Roman Egypt: A Case Study in Negotiating the Right of Repossession." In *Law and Transaction Costs in the Ancient Economy*, edited by Dennis P. Kehoe, David M. Ratzan, and Uri Yiftach. Ann Arbor: University of Michigan Press. 185–230.

Rauh, Nicholas K. 1993. *The Sacred Bonds of Commerce: Religion, Economy, and Trade Society at Hellenistic Roman Delos, 166–87 B.C.* Amsterdam: J.C. Gieben.

Reekmans, Tony. 1996. *La consommation dans les archives de Zénon*. Brussels: Fondation Égyptologique Reine Élisabeth.

Rees, Ray. 1985a. "The Theory of Principal and Agent, Part 1." *BER* 73: 3–26.

———. 1985b. "The Theory of Principal and Agent, Part 2." *BER* 73: 75–95.

Reger, Gary. 1994. *Regionalism and Change in the Economy of Independent Delos*. Berkeley: University of California Press.

———. 2003. "The Economy." In *A Companion to the Hellenistic World*, edited by Andrew Erskine. Oxford: Blackwell. 331–53.

———. 2013. "Networks in the Hellenistic Economy." In *Belonging and Isolation in the Hellenistic World*, edited by Sheila L. Ager and Riemer A. Faber. Toronto: University of Toronto Press. 143–54.

Reinach, Théodore. 1908. "ΠΑΡΘΕΝΩΝ." *BCH* 32: 499–513.

Renberg, Gil H., and William S. Bubelis. 2011. "The Epistolary Rhetoric of Zoilos of Aspendos and the Early Cult of Sarapis: Re-reading *P. Cair.Zen.* I 59034." *ZPE* 177: 169–200.

Renberg, Ingemar, Richard Bindler, and Maja-Lena Brännvall. 2001. "Using the Historical Atmospheric Lead-Deposition Record as a Chronological Marker in Sediment Deposits in
Europe." *Holocene* 11: 511–16.

Rey-Coquais, Jean-Paul. 1961. "Une prétendue 'dynastie' syrienne dans la Délos hellénistique."
MUSJ 37: 249–54.

Ribichini, Sergio. 1995. "Les phéniciens à Rhodes face à la mythologie classique: Ruses, calem-
bours et prééminence culturelle." In *Actes du IIIe congrès international des études phéniciennes
et puniques*, edited by Mohamed Hassine Fantar and Mansour Ghaki, vol. 2. Tunis: Institut
National du Patrimoine. 341–47.

Richardson, Lawrence. 1992. *A New Topographical Dictionary of Ancient Rome*. Baltimore: Johns
Hopkins University Press.

Rigsby, Kent J. 2010. "Two Texts of the *Dioiketes* Apollonios." *BASP* 47: 131–39.

Rives, James B. 1999. "The Decree of Decius and the Religion of Empire." *JRS* 89: 135–54.

Robert, Jeanne, and Louis Robert. 1983. *Les fouilles d'Amyzon en Carie*, vol. 1: *Exploration, histoire, monnaies et inscriptions*. Paris: Éditions de Boccard.

Robert, Louis. 1973a. "Sur le Décret des Poseidoniastes de Bérytos." In *Études Déliennes*, BCH
Suppl. 1. Paris: Éditions de Boccard. 486–89.

———. 1973b. "Épigraphie et antiquités grecques." *ACF* 73: 473–92.

Rosman, Kevin J.R., Warrick Chisholm, Sungmin Hong, Jean-Pierre Candelone, and Claude F.
Boutron. 1997. "Lead from Carthaginian and Roman Spanish Mines Isotopically Identified
in Greenland Ice Dated from 600 B.C. to 300 A.D." *Environ.Sci.Technol.* 31: 3413–16.

Rostovtzeff, Michael I. 1922. *A Large Estate in Egypt in the Third Century B. C.: A Study in Economic History*. Madison: University of Wisconsin Press.

Rotroff, Susan I. 2006. "Material Culture." In *The Cambridge Companion to the Hellenistic World*,
edited by Glenn R. Bugh. Cambridge: Cambridge University Press. 136–57.

Rowlandson, Jane, ed. 1998. *Women and Society in Greek and Roman Egypt: A Sourcebook*. Cambridge: Cambridge University Press.

Rowlandson, Jane, and Andrew Harker. 2004. "Roman Alexandria from the Perspective of the
Papyri." In *Alexandria, Real and Imagined*, edited by Anthony Hirst and Michael Silk. Aldershot, UK: Ashgate. 79–111.

Rüfner, Thomas. 2016. "Imperial *Cognitio* Process." In *The Oxford Handbook of Roman Law and
Society*, edited by Paul J. du Plessis, Clifford Ando, and Kaius Tuori. Oxford: Oxford University Press. 257–69.

Saller, Richard P. 2002. "Framing the Debate over Growth in the Ancient Economy." In *The
Ancient Economy*, edited by Walter Scheidel and Sitta von Reden. New York: Routledge
251–69.

Salzman, Michele R. 2011. "The End of Public Sacrifice: Changing Definitions of Sacrifice in
Post-Constantinian Rome and Italy." In *Ancient Mediterranean Sacrifice*, edited by Jennifer
W. Knust and Zsuzsanna Várhelyi. Oxford: Oxford University Press. 167–83.

Sartre, Maurice. 2005. *The Middle East under Rome*, translated by Catherine Porter and Elizabeth
Rawlings with Jeannine Routier-Pucci. Cambridge, MA: Harvard University Press.

Savage, Susan M. 1940. "The Cults of Ancient Trastevere." *MAAR* 17: 26–56.

Scheck, Thomas P., trans. 2017. *St. Jerome: Commentary on Ezekiel*. New York: Newman Press.

Scheidel, Walter. 2007. "Demography." In *The Cambridge Economic History of the Greco-Roman*

World, edited by Walter Scheidel, Ian Morris, and Richard P. Saller. Cambridge: Cambridge University Press. 38–86.

———. 2011. "A Comparative Perspective on the Determinants of the Scale and Productivity of Roman Maritime Trade in the Mediterranean." In *Maritime Technology in the Ancient Economy: Ship-Design and Navigation,* edited by William V. Harris and Kristine Iara. Portsmouth, RI: *JRA* Suppl. 84: 21–37.

———. 2015. "The Early Roman Monarchy." In *Fiscal Regimes and the Political Economy of Premodern States,* edited by Andrew Monson and Walter Scheidel. Cambridge: Cambridge University Press. 229–57.

Scholl, Reinhold. 1983. *Sklaverei in den Zenonpapyri: Eine Untersuchung zu den Sklaventermini, zum Sklavenerwerb und zur Sklavenflucht.* Trier: Trierer Historische Forschungen.

Schürer, Emil. 1986. *The History of the Jewish People in the Age of Jesus Christ (175 B.C.–A.D. 135),* vol. 3, part 1, revised and edited by Geza Vermes, Fergus Millar, and Martin Goodman. Edinburgh: T.&T. Clark.

Seidl, Johann G. 1856. "Beiträge zu einer Chronik der archäologischen Funde in der österreichischen Monarchie." *AKÖG* 15: 239–336.

Serrati, John. 2006. "Neptune's Altars: The Treaties between Rome and Carthage (509–226 B.C.)." *CQ* 56: 113–34.

Seyrig, Henri. 1951. "Antiquités syriennes." *Syria* 28: 191–228.

Sirago, Vito A. 1979. "La personalità di C. Vestorio." *Puteoli* 3: 3–16.

Smith, Joanna S. 2008. "Cyprus, the Phoenicians and Kition." In *Beyond the Homeland: Markers in Phoenician Chronology,* edited by Claudia Sagona. Leuven: Peeters. 261–303.

Sommer, Michael. 2007. "Networks of Commerce and Knowledge in the Iron Age: The Case of the Phoenicians." *MHR* 22: 97–111.

Sosis, Richard. 2005. "Does Religion Promote Trust? The Role of Signaling, Reputation, and Punishment." *IJRR* 1: 2–30.

Stager, Lawrence E. 2003. "Phoenician Shipwrecks in the Deep Sea." In Πλόες. *Sea Routes: Interconnections in the Mediterranean 16th–6th c. BC,* edited by Nicholas C. Stampolidis and Vassos Karageorghis. Athens: University of Crete and the A.G. Leventis Foundation. 233–47.

Stambaugh, John E. 1972. *Sarapis under the Early Ptolemies.* Leiden: Brill.

Stasavage, David. 2011. *States of Credit: Size, Power, and the Development of European Polities.* Princeton: Princeton University Press.

Stein, Gil J. 1999. *Rethinking World-Systems: Diasporas, Colonies, and Interaction in Uruk Mesopotamia.* Tucson: University of Arizona Press.

Steinby, Eva M., ed. 1993–2000. *Lexicon Topographicum Urbis Romae,* 6 vols. Rome: Quasar.

Stemberger, Günter. 2000. *Jews and Christians in the Holy Land: Palestine in the Fourth Century,* translated by Ruth Tuschling. Edinburgh: T&T Clark.

Straus, Jean A. Forthcoming. "Papyrological Evidence." In *The Oxford Handbook of Greek and Roman Slaveries,* edited by Stephen Hodkinson, Marc Kleijwegt, and Kostas Vlassopoulos. Oxford: Oxford University Press.

Strootman, Rolf. 2011. "Kings and Cities in the Hellenistic Age." In *Political Culture in the Greek City after the Classical Age,* edited by Onno M. van Nijf and Richard Alston with the assistance of Christina G. Williamson. Leuven: Peeters. 141–53.

Tan, James K. 2015. "The Roman Republic." In *Fiscal Regimes and the Political Economy of Premodern States*, edited by Andrew Monson and Walter Scheidel. Cambridge: Cambridge University Press. 208–28.

Taubenschlag, Raphael. 1972. *The Law of Greco-Roman Egypt in the Light of the Papyri, 332 B.C.–640 A.D.*, 2nd edition. Warsaw: Państwowe Wydawnictwo Naukowe.

Taylor, Lily Ross. 1912. *The Cults of Ostia*. Bryn Mawr: Bryn Mawr College/J.H. Furst.

Tcherikover, Victor A. 1937. "Palestine under the Ptolemies: A Contribution to the Study of the Zenon Papyri." *Mizraim* 4–5: 9–90.

Tchernia, André. 1969. "Les fouilles sous-marines de Planier (Bouches-du-Rhône)." *CRAI* 113: 292–309.

Teixidor, Javier. 1979. "Les fonctions de *rab* et de suffète en Phénicie." *Semitica* 29: 7–19.

———. 1980. "L'assemblée législative en Phénicie d'après les inscriptions." *Syria* 57: 453–64.

Terpstra, Taco T. 2008. "Roman Law, Transaction Costs and the Roman Economy: Evidence from the Sulpicii Archive." In *Pistoi dia tèn technèn: Bankers, Loans and Archives in the Ancient World: Studies in Honour of Raymond Bogaert*, edited by Koenraad Verboven, Katelijn Vandorpe, and Véronique Chankowski. Leuven: Peeters. 345–69.

———. 2013. *Trading Communities in the Roman World: A Micro-Economic and Institutional Perspective*. Leiden: Brill.

———. 2014a. "The Materiality of Writing in Karanis: Excavating Everyday Writing in a Town in Roman Egypt." *Aegyptus* 94: 89–119.

———. 2014b. "The 'Piazzale delle Corporazioni' Reconsidered: The Architectural Context of Its Change in Use." *MEFRA* 126: 119–30.

———. 2015. "Roman Trade with the Far East: Evidence for Nabataean Middlemen in Puteoli." In *Across the Ocean: Nine Essays on Indo-Mediterranean Trade*, edited by Federico de Romanis and Marco Maiuro. Leiden: Brill. 73–94.

———. 2016. "The Palmyrene Temple in Rome and Palmyra's Trade with the West." In *Palmyra: City, Hinterland and Caravan Trade between Occident and Orient*, edited by Jørgen Christian Meyer, Eivind H. Seland, and Nils Anfinset. Oxford: Archaeopress. 39–48.

———. 2017. "Communication and Roman Long-Distance Trade." In *Mercury's Wings: Exploring Modes of Communication in the Ancient World*, edited by Richard J.A. Talbert and Fred S. Naiden. Oxford: Oxford University Press. 45–61.

———. Forthcoming. "The Imperial Cult and the Sacred Bonds of Roman Overseas Commerce." In *The Epigraphy of Port Societies*, edited by Simon Keay and Pascal Arnaud. Cambridge: Cambridge University Press.

Terrenato, Nicola, and Donald C. Haggis, eds. 2011. *State Formation in Italy and Greece: Questioning the Neoevolutionist Paradigm*. Oxford: Oxbow Books.

Thelamon, Françoise. 1981. *Païens et chrétiens au IVe siècle: L'apport de l' "Histoire ecclésiastique" de Rufin d'Aquilée*. Paris: Études augustiniennes.

Thonemann, Peter. 2015. *The Hellenistic World: Using Coins as Sources*. Cambridge: Cambridge University Press.

Thür, Gerhard. 2015. "Transaction Costs in Athenian Law." In *Law and Transaction Costs in the Ancient Economy*, edited by Dennis P. Kehoe, David M. Ratzan, and Uri Yiftach. Ann Arbor: University of Michigan Press. 36–50.

Tilly, Charles. 1990. *Coercion, Capital, and European States, AD 990–1990*. Cambridge, MA: Blackwell.

———. 2005. *Trust and Rule*. Cambridge: Cambridge University Press.

Tran tam Tinh, Victor. 1972. *Le culte des divinités orientales en Campanie en dehors de Pompéi, de Stabies et d'Herculanum*. Leiden: Brill.

Trapp, Michael B. 2004. "Alexandria in the Second Sophistic." In *Alexandria, Real and Imagined*, edited by Anthony Hirst and Michael Silk. Aldershot, UK: Ashgate. 113–32.

Trombley, Frank R. 1993–94. *Hellenic Religion and Christianization c. 370–529*, 2 vols. Leiden: Brill.

Trümper, Monika. 2011. "Where the Non-Delians Met in Delos. The Meeting-Places of Foreign Associations and Ethnic Communities in Late Hellenistic Delos." In *Political Culture in the Greek City after the Classical Age*, edited by Onno M. van Nijf and Richard Alston with the assistance of Christina G. Williamson. Leuven: Peeters. 49–100.

Varga, Rada. 2014. *The Peregrini of Roman Dacia*, translated by Cosmin Gabriel Coatu. Cluj-Napoca: Editura Mega.

Verboven, Koenraad. 2015. "The Knights who Say NIE: Can Neo-Institutional Economics Live up to Its Expectation in Ancient History Research?" In *Structure and Performance in the Roman Economy: Models, Methods and Case Studies*, edited by Paul Erdkamp and Koenraad Verboven. Brussels: Latomus. 33–57.

Von der Fecht, Wolf-Rüdiger. 1999. *Die Forderungspfändung im römischen Recht: Der Vollstreckungszugriff auf Forderungen im Rahmen des pignus in causa iudicati captum und des Fiskalrechts der römischen Kaiserzeit*. Cologne: Böhlau.

Von Reden, Sitta. 2007. *Money in Ptolemaic Egypt from the Macedonian Conquest to the End of the Third Century BC*. Cambridge: Cambridge University Press.

———. 2010. *Money in Classical Antiquity*. Cambridge: Cambridge University Press.

———. 2011. "Demand Creation, Consumption, and Power in Ptolemaic Egypt." In *The Economies of Hellenistic Societies, Third to First Centuries BC*, edited by Zosia H. Archibald, John K. Davies, and Vincent Gabrielsen. Oxford: Oxford University Press. 421–40.

Wagner, Carlos G., and Jaime Alvar. 1989. "Fenicios en occidente: La colonización agrícola." *RSF* 17: 61–102.

Walbank, Michael B. 1985. "Athens, Carthage and Tyre (IG ii² 342+)." *ZPE* 59: 107–11.

Wallace, Malcolm B. 1970. "Early Greek 'Proxenoi.'" *Phoenix* 24: 189–208.

Wallis, John J. 2014. "Persistence and Change in Institutions: The Evolution of Douglass C. North." In *Institutions, Property Rights, and Economic Growth: The Legacy of Douglass North*, edited by Sebastian Galiani and Itai Sened. Cambridge: Cambridge University Press. 30–49.

Ward-Perkins, Bryan. 2000a. "Land, Labour and Settlement." In *CAH* vol. 14: *Late Antiquity: Empire and Successors, A.D. 425–600*, edited by Averil Cameron, Bryan Ward-Perkins, and Michael Whitby. Cambridge: Cambridge University Press. 315–45.

———. 2000b. "Specialized Production and Exchange." In *CAH* vol. 14: *Late Antiquity: Empire and Successors, A.D. 425–600*, edited by Averil Cameron, Bryan Ward-Perkins, and Michael Whitby. Cambridge: Cambridge University Press. 346–91.

———. 2005. *The Fall of Rome and the End of Civilization*. Oxford: Oxford University Press.

Watson, Alan. 1998. *The Digest of Justinian: English-Language Translation Edited by Alan Watson*, 4 vols. Philadelphia: University of Pennsylvania Press.

Watts, Edward J. 2010. *Riot in Alexandria: Tradition and Group Dynamics in Late Antique Pagan and Christian Communities*. Berkeley: University of California Press.

———. 2015a. "Christianization." In *Late Ancient Knowing: Explorations in Intellectual History*, edited by Catherine M. Chin and Moulie Vidas. Oakland: University of California Press. 197–217.

———. 2015b. *The Final Pagan Generation*. Oakland: University of California Press.

Weber, Max. 1965. *Politics as a Vocation*, translated by Hans H. Gerth and C. Wright Mills. Philadelphia: Fortress Press.

Whitby, Michael. 2000. "The Successors of Justinian." In *CAH* vol. 14: *Late Antiquity: Empire and Successors, A.D. 425–600*, edited by Averil Cameron, Bryan Ward-Perkins, and Michael Whitby. Cambridge: Cambridge University Press. 86–111.

White, John L. 1986. *Light from Ancient Letters*. Philadelphia: Fortress Press.

Whittaker, Charles R. 1974. "The Western Phoenicians: Colonisation and Assimilation." *PCPS* n.s. 20: 58–79.

Wickham, Christopher. 2005. *Framing the Early Middle Ages: Europe and the Mediterranean, 400–800*. Oxford: Oxford University Press.

Wiesehöfer, Josef. 2013. "Iranian Empires." In *The Oxford Handbook of the State in the Ancient Near East and Mediterranean*, edited by Peter F. Bang and Walter Scheidel. Oxford: Oxford University Press. 199–231.

Wilke, Thomas. 2002. "The Investment Theory of Wars: Belligerent Dictators in the McGuire/North-Model of Autocracy." *Public Choice* 112: 319–33.

Wilkes, John J. 1969. *Dalmatia*. Cambridge, MA: Harvard University Press.

———. 1992. *The Illyrians*. Oxford: Blackwell.

Williams, Stephen, and Gerard Friell. 1999. *The Rome That Did Not Fall: The Survival of the East in the Fifth Century*. London: Routledge.

Williams, Wynne. 1975. "Formal and Historical Aspects of Two New Documents of Marcus Aurelius." *ZPE* 17: 37–78.

Wilson, Andrew I. 2002. "Machines, Power and the Ancient Economy." *JRS* 92: 1–32.

———. 2011. "Developments in Mediterranean Shipping and Maritime Trade from the Hellenistic Period to AD 1000." In *Maritime Archaeology and Ancient Trade in the Mediterranean*, edited by Damian Robinson and Andrew I. Wilson. Oxford: Oxford Centre for Maritime Archaeology. 33–59.

———. 2013. "Trading across the Syrtes: Euesperides and the Punic World." In *The Hellenistic West: Rethinking the Ancient Mediterranean*, edited by Jonathan R.W. Prag and Josephine Crawley Quinn. Cambridge: Cambridge University Press. 120–56.

———. 2014. "Quantifying Roman Economic Performance by Means of Proxies: Pitfalls and Potential." In *Quantifying the Greco-Roman Economy and Beyond*, edited by François de Callataÿ. Bari: Edipuglia. 147–67.

———. 2015. "Red Sea Trade and the State." In *Across the Ocean: Nine Essays on Indo-Mediterranean Trade*, edited by Federico de Romanis and Marco Maiuro. Leiden: Brill. 13–32.

Wilson, Andrew I., Katia Schörle, and Candace Rice. 2012. "Roman Ports and Mediterranean Connectivity." In *Rome, Portus and the Mediterranean*, edited by Simon Keay. Oxford: Oxbow Books. 367–91.

Wolf, Joseph G. 2001. "Der neue pompejanische Urkundenfund, zu Camodecas 'Edizione critica dell'archivio puteolano dei Sulpicii.'" *ZRG rom.* 118: 73–132.

Wood, Ian N. 2000. "The North-Western Provinces." In *CAH* vol. 14: *Late Antiquity: Empire and Successors, A.D. 425–600*, edited by Averil Cameron, Bryan Ward-Perkins, and Michael Whitby. Cambridge: Cambridge University Press. 497–524.

Xella, Paolo. 2014. "'Origini' e 'identità': Riflessioni sul caso dei Fenici." *MEFRA* 126: 381–91.

Yarbrough, Beth V., and Robert M. Yarbrough. 1997. "Dispute Settlement in International Trade: Regionalism and Procedural Coordination." In *The Political Economy of Regionalism*, edited by Edward D. Mansfield and Helen V. Milner. New York: Columbia University Press. 134–63.

Yon, Marguerite. 1997. "Kition in the Tenth to Fourth Centuries B.C." *BASOR* 308: 9–17.

Young, Gary K. 2001. *Rome's Eastern Trade: International Commerce and Imperial Policy, 31 BC–AD 305*. London: Routledge.

Zirra, Vlad V., et al. 2003. "The Sacred Space of 'Dalea' Site." In *Alburnus Maior* I, edited by Paul Damian. Cluj-Napoca: Editura Mega. 335–80.

Zuiderhoek, Arjan. 2009. *The Politics of Munificence in the Roman Empire: Citizens, Elites and Benefactors*. Cambridge: Cambridge University Press.

———. 2017. *The Ancient City*. Cambridge: Cambridge University Press.

INDEX

Page numbers in *italics* refer to illustrations.

THE PRINCETON ECONOMIC HISTORY
OF THE WESTERN WORLD

Joel Mokyr, Series Editor

Growth in a Traditional Society: The French Countryside, 1450–1815 by Philip T. Hoffman

The Vanishing Irish: Households, Migration, and the Rural Economy in Ireland, 1850–1914 by Timothy W. Guinnane

Black '47 and Beyond: The Great Irish Famine in History, Economy, and Memory by Cormac Ó Gráda

The Great Divergence: China, Europe, and the Making of the Modern World Economy by Kenneth Pomeranz

The Big Problem of Small Change by Thomas J. Sargent and François R. Velde

Farm to Factory: A Reinterpretation of the Soviet Industrial Revolution by Robert C. Allen

Quarter Notes and Bank Notes: The Economics of Music Composition in the Eighteenth and Nineteenth Centuries by F. M. Scherer

The Strictures of Inheritance: The Dutch Economy in the Nineteenth Century by Jan Luiten van Zanden and Arthur van Riel

Understanding the Process of Economic Change by Douglass C. North

Feeding the World: An Economic History of Agriculture, 1800–2000 by Giovanni Federico

Cultures Merging: A Historical and Economic Critique of Culture by Eric L. Jones

The European Economy since 1945: Coordinated Capitalism and Beyond by Barry Eichengreen

War, Wine, and Taxes: The Political Economy of Anglo-French Trade, 1689–1900 by John V. C. Nye

A Farewell to Alms: A Brief Economic History of the World by Gregory Clark

Power and Plenty: Trade, War, and the World Economy in the Second Millennium by Ronald Findlay and Kevin H. O'Rourke

Power over Peoples: Technology, Environments, and Western Imperialism, 1400 to the Present by Daniel R. Headrick

Dark Matter Credit: The Development of Peer-to-Peer Lending and Banking in France by Philip T. Hoffman, Gilles Postel-Vinay, and Jean-Laurent Rosenthal

The European Guilds: An Economic Analysis by Sheilagh Ogilvie

Trade in the Ancient Mediterranean: Private Order and Public Institutions by Taco Terpstra

A NOTE ON THE TYPE

This book has been composed in Arno, an Old-style serif typeface in the
classic Venetian tradition, designed by Robert Slimbach at Adobe.